T0329120

Ethical and Social Marketing in Asia

ELSEVIER
ASIAN STUDIES SERIES

Series Editor: Professor Chris Rowley,
Centre for Research on Asian Management,
Cass Business School,
City University, UK; HEAD Foundation, Singapore
(email: c.rowley@city.ac.uk)

Elsevier is pleased to publish this major series of books entitled *Asian Studies: Contemporary Issues and Trends*. The Series Editor is Professor Chris Rowley, Director, Centre for Research on Asian Management, City University, UK and Director, Research and Publications, HEAD Foundation, Singapore.

Asia has clearly undergone some major transformations in recent years and books in the series examine this transformation from a number of perspectives: economic, management, social, political and cultural. We seek authors from a broad range of areas and disciplinary interests covering, for example, business/management, political science, social science, history, sociology, gender studies, ethnography, economics and international relations, etc.

Importantly, the series examines both current developments and possible future trends. The series is aimed at an international market of academics and professionals working in the area. The books have been specially commissioned from leading authors. The objective is to provide the reader with an authoritative view of current thinking.

New authors: we would be delighted to hear from you if you have an idea for a book. We are interested in both shorter, practically orientated publications (45,000+ words) and longer, theoretical monographs (75,000—100,000 words). Our books can be single, joint or multi-author volumes. If you have an idea for a book, please contact the publishers or Professor Chris Rowley, the Series Editor.

Dr Glyn Jones
Elsevier Publishing
Email: g.jones.2@elsevier.com

Professor Chris Rowley
Cass Business School, City University
Email: c.rowley@city.ac.uk
www.cass.city.ac.uk/faculty/c.rowley

Elsevier Asian Studies Series

Ethical and Social Marketing in Asia

Incorporating Fairness Management

Edited By

Bang Nguyen
Chris Rowley

ELSEVIER

AMSTERDAM • BOSTON • HEIDELBERG • LONDON • NEW YORK • OXFORD
PARIS • SAN DIEGO • SAN FRANCISCO • SINGAPORE • SYDNEY • TOKYO

Elsevier
Radarweg 29, PO Box 211, 1000 AE Amsterdam, Netherlands
The Boulevard, Langford Lane, Kidlington, Oxford OX5 1GB, UK
225 Wyman Street, Waltham, MA 02451, USA

Notices
Knowledge and best practice in this field are constantly changing. As new research and experience
broaden our understanding, changes in research methods, professional practices, or medical treatment
may become necessary.

Practitioners and researchers must always rely on their own experience and knowledge in evaluating and
using any information, methods, compounds, or experiments described herein. In using such information
or methods they should be mindful of their own safety and the safety of others, including parties for
whom they have a professional responsibility.

To the fullest extent of the law, neither the Publisher nor the authors, contributors, or editors, assume any
liability for any injury and/or damage to persons or property as a matter of products liability, negligence
or otherwise, or from any use or operation of any methods, products, instructions, or ideas contained in
the material herein.

ISBN: 978-0-08-100097-7
The Library of Congress Control Number: 2014952990.

British Library Cataloguing-in-Publication Data
A catalogue record for this book is available from the British Library

Library of Congress Cataloging-in-Publication Data
A catalog record for this book is available from the Library of Congress

For information on all Elsevier publications
visit our website at http://store.elsevier.com/

Typeset by MPS Limited, Chennai, India
www.adi-mps.com

Printed and bound in the US and UK.

Working together
to grow libraries in
developing countries

www.elsevier.com • www.bookaid.org

Dedication

To Mr S. Huang in recognition of our friendship and his support for human capital development in Asia.

To Harry

Contents

List of figures

List of tables

About the editors

Bang Nguyen, PhD, is Associate Professor of Marketing at East China University of Science and Technology (ECUST), School of Business in Shanghai, China. Previously, he held faculty positions at Oxford Brookes University and RMIT International University Vietnam and was a Visiting Scholar at CEIBS. His research interests include customer relationship management, services marketing, consumer behavior, branding, social marketing and fairness management. Bang has extensive knowledge in service organizations (consumer products/services) and has published widely in journals such as the *Journal of Marketing Management, Journal of Services Marketing, Journal of Strategic Marketing, Journal of Consumer Marketing, The Service Industries Journal, Harvard Business Review (Chinese), Int. Journal of Technology Management, Journal of General Management, Information Technology & Management, Systems Research & Behavioral Science*, etc. He has published in more than 70 peer reviewed scientific articles, books, conference papers, and book chapters, and presented at both national and top international conferences including EMAC and Academy of Marketing. Bang is an experienced consultant and advises on marketing and brand development for SMEs and start-ups. He has lived and worked professionally in Denmark, the USA, the UK, Vietnam, China and Taiwan.

Professor Chris Rowley is Director of Research and Publications, HEAD Foundation, Singapore and Professor of Human Resource Management at Cass Business School, City University, London, UK. He is Editor of the leading journal *Asia Pacific Business Review*, and Series Editor of the Working in Asia and Asian Studies book series. He has given a range of talks and lectures to universities and companies internationally with research and consultancy experience with unions, business and government. Professor Rowley has published widely in the area of HRM and Asian business, with over 500 articles, books and chapters and practitioner pieces.

About the contributors

Chapter 2

Ruizhi Yuan is a doctoral student in the Marketing Department at the Nottingham University Business School China. She received an MSc Distinction degree in Marketing at University of Nottingham. Her research interest centres around the determinants of green consumption, particularly with regard to perceived green value and utilities of consumption. Ruizhi has presented several papers at the International Conference of the Association for Consumer Research (ACR) and European Marketing Academy (EMAC). Her dissertation research has been placed as the finalist in the EMAC 2014 Best Paper Award.

Martin J. Liu, PhD is an assistant professor in Marketing and Innovation at the Nottingham University Business School China and associate fellow at the University of Warwick. Martin's primary research interests lie in the areas of branding, marketing innovation and e-marketing. He publishes in leading refereed journals including Journal of Business Research, Journal of Marketing Management and Expert System with Applications. He also has extensive consultancy experience in the UK, USA and China.

Jianchang Liu is the Associate Dean and Associate Professor at Business School of Zhejiang Fashion Institute of Technology, P.R. China. He received his MBA from Zhejiang University in 2004. He worked as a Visiting Scholar supported by China Scholarship Council at MBA Centre of Springfield College, Massachusetts, USA from July 2012 to January 2013. He attended a small business conference in New York City and his paper was well received and published in the Eastern Small Business Institute's Conference Proceedings for 2012. He was awarded a 2012 University of Chinese Academy of Sciences Case Competition Certificate for the case study entitled 'Feixiang to Fotile: growth of a family business'. The case study and teaching notes written by him and Dr Kathryn Carlson Heler were published in *Emerald Emerging Markets Case Studies* in 2012. He does research in the areas of strategic management, marketing and strategy for the fashion industry. He had a series of books and papers published in China. He is one of the expert consultants of the Ningbo Private Entrepreneurs' Association. Since April 2014, he has been one of the expert reviewers of *Emerald Emerging Markets Case Studies*.

Chapter 3

Steve Chen is a senior lecturer in marketing at Oxford Brookes University, UK. He is also MSc Marketing Subject Coordinator there. His research interests include consumer behaviour, trust and information technology-related studies. Steve has extensive knowledge in consumer behaviour in luxury consumption, in-game advertising and trust establishment in online marketplace. His work appears in *Service Industries Journal*, *Journal of Targeting, Measuring and Analysis for Marketing*, *Journal of Internet Commerce* and *Review of Business Research*. Steve has presented at national/international conferences, including the Academy of Marketing and European Marketing Academy.

Sharon Wu is a Teaching Fellow in Fashion Management and Fashion Marketing Branding at Winchester School of Art, University of Southampton. She is also a PhD candidate at Royal Holloway, University of London. She earned her MBA (Marketing and International Business) and BA (Economics) from Willamette University and the University of Oregon, USA. She came from an international businesses background and obtained a Certificate of Educator qualification in Taiwan before pursuing her PhD. Her PhD research focuses on luxury consumer behaviour, e-luxury consumption in the digital era, self-concept and conspicuous consumption. She has been involved in several research projects in the past three years. Previously, she has been lecturing various subjects in marketing management, consumer behaviour, advertising and promotion at Royal Holloway, University of London and Fooying University (Taiwan). Her works have appeared in *Qualitative Market Research: An International Journal*, *The Academy of Marketing*, and *Collougue Luxe et Contrefacon, Monaco Symposium on Luxury*.

Dr T.C. Melewar (BSc, MBA, PhD) is Professor of Marketing and Strategy at Middlesex University Business School, London, UK. He has previous experience at Brunel, ZHAW School of Management and Law, Switzerland, Warwick Business School, MARA Institute of Technology in Malaysia, Loughborough University and De Montfort University. Dr Melewar teaches Brand and Marketing Management, and International Marketing on a range of undergraduate, MSc, MBA and executive courses with companies such as Nestlé, Safeway, Tata and Sony. He is a Visiting Professor at the University of Lincoln. His research interests include branding, corporate identity and international marketing strategy. He has published in the *Journal of Marketing Management*, *Management Decision*, *Journal of Brand Management* and *International Journal of Management Reviews*, among others.

Chapter 4

Professor Mithileshwar Jha received his engineering degree from the G.B. Pant University of Agriculture and Technology, Pantnagar, Uttarakhand, India (1977) and master's (1979) and doctoral (1985) degrees in management from the Indian Institute of Management Ahmedabad. He is a member of the American Marketing Association, and life member of the Rural Marketing Association of India. Professor Jha has been a Professor of Marketing at Indian Institute of Management Bangalore since 1993. He held the Escotel-CRM Chair of Marketing at the Indian Institute of Management Lucknow (IIML) and also served as the Dean (Academic) during 2003−05. He was a Visiting Professor at ESCP-EAP, Paris, France in 2006 and Gothenburg University, Sweden in 2009. In an academic career of 25 years, Professor Jha has contributed to the national policy making in the areas of public distribution system, handlooms and bio-gas. In 1988−89, he advised the **Planning Commission, Government of India, New Delhi** on the setting up of the Public Distribution System. He has been a consultant to the international agencies such as the **Swiss Agency for Development and Cooperation** (SDC), **NORAD** and the **Canadian Hunger Foundation**. He has trained senior managers of most of the important companies in India (e.g. **Grasim Industries, HMT Ltd., Indian Telephone Industries Ltd., BPL, Siemens India, Reliance Industries, Ranbaxy Laboratories, Berger Paints**). He was a member on the Boards of Governors of the IIM Bangalore (2001−03), the IIM Lucknow (2003−05), and the Gandhi Peace Center (1998−00). Professor Jha has written 12 cases in marketing that are widely used in graduate modules across the globe. Further, his textbook entitled *Marketing Management − A South Asian Perspective*, co-authored with Philip Kotler, Kevin L. Keller and Abraham Koshy, has gone through three successful editions (12th in 2005, 13th in 2009, and 14th in 2012; Pearson Education, New Delhi). This marketing textbook is used in most of the management schools of South Asia.

Chapter 5

Jeremy Pearce is a senior lecturer in strategic management at the University of Lincoln. He has extensive senior management experience in both the public and private sectors, and has worked as a consultant in corporate governance and corporate responsibility with the World Bank in Vietnam and board advisory at KPMG in Australia. He has been instrumental in running MBA programmes in Asia in both the graduate and executive streams. Jeremy has been published in international law, corporate governance and ethics, including as sole author of the book *Directors' Powers and Duties in Vietnam*. He is a member of the Australian Sustainability Leaders Forum, the World Council for Corporate Governance and an Associate of the Bond Centre for Commercial Law. Jeremy holds master's degrees in international law (Sydney University) and law and management (AGSM) and a doctorate of legal science (SJD) from Bond University. During his time at Bond, Jeremy received the law school research candidate of the year award. He is currently completing further studies in international human rights law at new college, Oxford University.

Mattia Miani is a manager of enterprise and executive education at RMIT Vietnam where he also teaches into the EMBA. From 2003 to 2010 he worked in Italy as a lecturer at the business school of the University of Bologna, and as a marketing consultant and entrepreneur advising cooperative enterprises, advertising agencies and government organisations on their communication strategies. From 2008 to 2011, Mr Miani served as a director in the board of the Centre for Training and Initiative on Cooperative Enterprise and Business Ethics, a joint venture between the University of Bologna and the Italian cooperative movement. Before coming to Asia, Mr Miani spent time on international assignments in the United States, Canada, Austria, Croatia and Bosnia-Herzegovina. Mr Miani is the author of four books on marketing communication, with a special focus on new media. His research interests include ethics, social enterprise, consumer behaviour and creativity.

Michael Segon is a Senior Lecturer at the Graduate School of Business & Law at RMIT University in Australia. He achieved his PhD from Queensland University of Technology. His teaching interests are in the areas of business ethics, governance, organisational structure and design, and management.

Chapter 6

Stephan Dahl is senior lecturer in marketing at Hull University Business School in the UK and adjunct associate professor at James Cook University in Australia. His research interests include health and social marketing, social media and cross-cultural marketing, and consumer behaviour. He has published in a range of academic journals, and is the author of several books, including *Social Media Marketing* (Sage) and co-author of *Marketing Communications* (Routledge) and *Social Marketing* (Pearson).

Chapter 7

Professor Sharyn Rundle-Thiele leads Social Marketing @ Griffith (http://www. griffith.edu.au/social-marketing) and is Editor of the *Journal of Social Marketing*. Sharyn's research focuses on behaviour change and she has published and presented over 160 papers and books. She currently serves as an advisor on a diverse range of social marketing projects. Her current projects include changing adolescent attitudes towards drinking alcohol (see http://gameon.rcs.griffith.edu.au) and increasing healthy eating and physical activity to combat obesity. Research partners include VicHealth, SA Health, Department of Health and Aging, Siggins Miller Consulting, the Defence Science and Technology Organisation, Queensland Catholic Education Commission and Mater Health Services.

Chapter 8

Dilip S. Mutum is a lecturer in Marketing and Advertising at Coventry Business School, Coventry University. He has previously taught at Universiti Utara Malaysia and the University of Warwick. Before joining academia, Dilip worked with various organisations in different capacities. An avid blogger, he has also advised various organisations on their search engine optimisation and social media marketing campaigns. His research interests include digital consumption, customer relationship management and social marketing. His research work has been published within a range of publications. He co-edited the book *Marketing Cases from Emerging Markets*. Further information can be found at http://www.dilipmutum.com.

Ezlika Ghazali is Senior Lecturer at the Department of Marketing, University of Malaya. Ezlika completed her PhD at the Warwick Business School, University of Warwick. Her research interests include switching barriers, online retailing and online consumer behaviour. She has published in a number of reputed journals and presented at several international conferences.

Anvita Kumar is Lecturer in Marketing and Advertising with Coventry Business School. Her teaching areas are international marketing, contemporary issues in marketing and consumer behaviour. She has taught on various management programmes: the University of Bournemouth Masters programme and the Herriot-Watt MBA programme. Her research interests are marketing communication strategies, brand placement strategies, emotions and consumer behaviour. She acts as consultant for internet-based marketing strategies for companies in India and the UK. In 2007, her team won the Proof of Concept Award (2007) at Leeds University for their start-up company and were shortlisted for the NatWest Start up Business Plan of the Year and UK Student Education Consultancy (UKSEC) National Business Plan Competition. She received her PhD from the Cass Business School, City University.

Chapter 9

Lukas Parker is currently Assistant Professor in Marketing in the Centre of Commerce and Management at RMIT University Vietnam. Prior to joining RMIT University Vietnam in 2007, he worked as an information, education and communications advisor for a rural water supply and sanitation project in the Mekong Delta. Lukas holds a PhD from Swinburne University of Technology, Australia and also holds a Bachelor of Business (Honours). His research focus is currently on social marketing and the environment in Vietnam, road safety and family decision making. He has conducted significant research into consumer trust and banking, and consumer privacy issues related to Internet websites. Lukas has authored and co-authored a number of peer-reviewed publications as well as being the co-editor of the recent book *Growing Sustainable Communities: A Development Guide for Southeast Asia* (Tilde University Press, 2013).

Linda Brennan is the Inaugural Professor of Advertising at RMIT University. In the lead-up to becoming a full time academic, Professor Brennan had an active consulting practice in marketing and strategic research, working with a variety of markets, projects and industries. Her industry projects have included government, not-for-profit and educational marketers. Her research interests are social and government marketing, and especially the influence of marketing communications and advertising on behaviour, particularly among older people and within linguistically and culturally diverse contexts. She has published widely in the area of social marketing, with a focus on family communication and public health. Her most recent books include *Social Marketing and Behaviour Change: Models, Theory, Applications* (Edward Elgar, 2014) and *Growing Sustainable Communities: A Development Guide for Southeast Asia* (Tilde University Press, 2013). She is a Fellow of the Australian Institute of Marketing (Certified Practising Marketer), and a full member of the Australian Social and Marketing Research Society (Qualified Practising Market Researcher). Her qualifications include a PhD in Consumer Psychology from the University of Melbourne, a Bachelor of Business Marketing (Honours) from Monash University, a Diploma of Training and Assessment, a Diploma of Frontline Management and a Diploma in Market Research.

Dang Nguyen is an early career researcher in the Centre of Commerce & Management at RMIT University Vietnam, with a degree in Communication. She has published in scholarly journals and academic conferences in the areas of social marketing and social change communication, and has co-authored a book on behaviour change. She is expecting to finish her graduate degree in Social Science of the Internet at Oxford Internet Institute, University of Oxford in 2015. Her research interests include social change communication, digitally enabled social change and public policy communication. She has received a number of honours, including the RMIT Vietnam President's Commendation 2012, RMIT Vice-Chancellor's List for Academic Excellence Award 2012 and the prestigious Chevening Scholarship in 2014.

Chapter 10

Sooyeon Nikki Lee-Wingate teaches marketing at Ernest C. Trefz School of Business, University of Bridgeport. She received her doctorate in Marketing from Stern School of Business, New York University, and has previously taught at New York University, Rutgers Business School and Fairfield University. Prior to academic appointments, she worked as a management consultant at McKinsey &

Company in Seoul, Korea. Her research focuses on managing the influence of negative affect on consumer behaviour, especially in domains involving consumer fairness perceptions and in pharmaceutical advertising. She has published in *Marketing Letters, Psychology & Marketing, Journal of Marketing Theory and Practice, International Journal of Pharmaceutical and Healthcare Marketing*, and proceedings of American Marketing Association, Association for Consumer Research and Society for Consumer Psychology.

Chapter 11

Dr Syed Alwi is a lecturer of Corporate Brand Marketing at Brunel Business School, Brunel University London. She has a PhD from Manchester Business School, UK and was formerly a senior lecturer of Marketing at the University of Malaya. She has more than 15 years' experience in teaching and research. Her taught subjects include corporate brand management courses such as applied corporate brand management, strategic corporate brand consulting and strategic corporate marketing. Her research works have appeared in the *Journal of Business Research, European Journal of Marketing, Journal of Product and Brand Management, Marketing Intelligence and Planning, Corporate Reputation Review* and *Journal of Brand Management*. She is also a Principal Investigator of three major projects, including: (1) A Collaboration of University of Malaya/Malaysia and Oxford Said Business School on Islamic Branding and Marketing For Malaysia, funded by the Malaysian Ministry of Higher Education; (2) Socioeconomic Impact of the National Broadband Initiative, funded by Multimedia Development Corporation; and (3) Malaysia and Customer Satisfaction Index, funded by Asian Institute of Finance in Malaysia. She has also co-authored a book (with Professor T.C. Melewar) entitled *Corporate Brand: Area, Arena and Approaches* (Routledge, forthcoming 2015).

Lyndon Simkin joined Henley Business School from Oxford Brookes, where he was Professor of Strategic Marketing and Research Lead. Before that, Lyndon was at Warwick Business School for over 20 years, helping to launch and develop Warwick's MBA programme, becoming its Academic Director. He also created and launched Warwick's MSc in Marketing and Strategy. Lyndon is an acknowledged expert in strategy creation, planning processes and implementation management, guiding practitioners with their execution and mentoring CEOs and leadership teams. He is part of the Academy of Marketing's Research Committee, Associate Editor of the *Journal of Marketing Management* and co-chair of the Academy's special interest groups in CRM and Market Segmentation and Strategy. Lyndon is author of many books, including the market-leading *Marketing: Concepts & Strategies, Marketing Essentials, Marketing Planning, Marketing Briefs, The Marketing Casebook* and *Market Segmentation Success: Making It Happen!*

Chapter 12

Sanjit Kumar Roy is Assistant Professor of Marketing at the University of Western Australia. His research interests include services marketing and consumer-brand relationships. He has guest edited a special issue on India for *International Journal of Bank Marketing*. He also co-edited *Marketing Cases for Emerging Markets*. He has published in a wide range of journals, including *European Journal of Marketing, Journal of Strategic Marketing, Journal of Services Marketing* and *Journal of Brand Management*. He was a Visiting Research Scholar at Bentley University, USA.

Chapter 13

Xiaoyu Yu is an associate professor in the Department of Business Administration of School of Management at Shanghai University, China. He has degrees from Jilin University and Shanghai Jiao Tong University, and has many years' experience in high-technology industry, including establishing a new venture in the satellite communication industry in Shanghai. He worked as a Visiting Scholar at Jonkoping International Business School, Jonkoping University, in 2011 and as Associate Researcher at Neeley School of Business of Texas Christian University from 2013 to 2014. He is the Deputy Secretary-General of Shanghai Behavioral Science Society, Member of the Expert Committee for Shanghai MBA Case Development & Sharing Platform, and Corresponding Reviewer Expert of *One Hundred National Excellent Management Cases Selection in China*. He is the Principal Investigator for several projects funded by the National Natural Science Foundation of China, Shanghai Municipal Education Commission and Shanghai University, leading a team in the research of 'impact of learning from entrepreneurial failure to subsequent entrepreneurial intention'. He has co-authored more than 50 journal and conference papers and books on entrepreneurship and technology management and marketing. His current research interests include informal entrepreneurship, effectuation behaviour, and interdisciplinary research of entrepreneurship and marketing.

Foreword by Dr Bradley R. Barnes

This newly edited book touches on a highly topical issue of importance not only in the marketing discipline, but for management *per se*. In recent times we have experienced significant interest in both social and ethical issues, particularly in the West, with a growing number of firms claiming to be environmentally friendly, green and sustainable. This area is having major implications for the study of management, with the subject at large being incorporated into specific modules and even taught outright. This book is timely, particularly with its focus on Asia, a region which has often been criticised unfairly for its social, environmental policies and work practices. I am intrigued by the scope of the book, covering 14 different economies in Asia. It provides great potential for us to learn more about this region, and I hope you will enjoy the comprehensive read.

Dr Bradley R. Barnes
Associate Dean and Professor of International Management & Marketing
Sheffield University Management School

Foreword by Sally Dibb

The relevance of social marketing has never been greater. Recent meltdown of global financial markets has had far-reaching societal consequences which have impacted the lives of many. The effect of these changes has been immense, precipitating fundamental questions about the sustainability of how we live, consume and do business. As the corporate world is called to account for its role in the crisis, in the shifting political landscape governments have reacted to the recessionary pressures by cutting public spending and placing greater responsibility for delivering services in the hands of voluntary and charitable organisations. Marketers have also come under pressure to address the ethical consequences of their practices. For social marketing, these changes have triggered a dramatic broadening of potential applications. These encompass health and lifestyle issues, problems associated with financial literacy and debt, and challenges linked to promoting environmental and social sustainability. Now is the time for marketing to respond to these social and ethical pressures.

Sally Dibb (PhD MSc BSc FCIM)
Professor of Marketing and Director of the Institute
for Social Marketing (ISM-Open)
The Open University

Acknowledgements

The authors would like to thank Professor Gordon Redding and the HEAD Foundation for their support and Dr Glyn Jones and his colleagues for all their publishing efforts.

Introduction to ethical and social marketing in Asia: incorporating fairness management

1

Bang Nguyen and Chris Rowley

Introduction

There is a growing interest in ethical and social marketing adoption by companies among academics and practitioners alike. Ethical marketing is the application of ethics to the marketing process. Social marketing seeks to influence a target audience, not just for the organisations' or marketers' benefit, but for the greater social good, such as the general society. Fairness management is concerned with justice and morality. Fairness is the quality of being honest and just, and is associated with morality, impartiality and uprightness.

However, the study of ethical and social marketing topics in Asia and their links to fairness management is limited. We found only a few books exploring similar topics as ours (Arnold, 2009; French et al., 2011; Gilliland et al., 2005). Also, our book is particularly unique both in linking the three topics of ethical marketing, social marketing and fairness management and in doing so comprehensively across 14 diverse economies.

While some parts of Asia are often known for copyright infringements, labour exploitation, environmental pollution and other unethical business practices, other parts are known for fair trade, consumer welfare and strict government regulation to mitigate unethical issues. Thus the sheer diversity of Asian countries provides a perplexing environment for the development and management of ethical and social marketing. Varying cultures, economic development stages, resources, politics and consumption behaviours all require correspondingly varied emphasis in different markets.

The belief that bottom-line profit is enough for a company is often not favourably viewed by Asian countries emphasising collective, social and long-term benefits for the people and country. Indeed, in many ways, social marketing should be particularly well received by Asian firms and consumers because of its emphasis on the greater societal good, which is often promoted by countries. Due to these interesting characteristics and inherent complexities, we view the study of ethical and social marketing and fairness management in Asia to be timely topics for further investigation. Our book therefore addresses the following three areas.

1. **Ethics:** Readers will gain insights into research on ethical marketing issues in Asia. Our book will enable readers to compare, contrast and comprehend how firms organise and

manage ethics in different parts of Asia. For example, we observe how issues such as corruption, labour exploitation, bribery and copyright infringements are viewed differently across countries. Furthermore, our book presents important aspects of decision-making processes, influencing consumer perceptions towards ethical marketing and general management.

2. **Social:** Readers will be exposed to differing perspectives of social marketing in Asia and its effects on consumption behaviour. We present a wide-ranging collection of cases. This covers business-to-business and business-to-consumers, encompassing different industries and sectors, including non-profit organisations. Readers will be exposed to differing management approaches that, once applied to their organisation, could increase the likelihood of successful implementation of social marketing, as well as being of relevance for managing more generally.

3. **Fairness:** An innovative aspect of our book is the inclusion of fairness in the ethical and social marketing processes. Our book explores fairness from extant consumer behavioural and psychological theories and research. Important aspects of cultural and social indicators that influence consumers' fairness perceptions in the Asian context are provided. This enables readers to understand the role of fairness and subsequent application towards both managing their own marketing approaches and managing more broadly.

Overview

We include original and recent works in ethical marketing, social marketing and fairness management in Asia, creating a unique book in marketing and management. The organisation of our sections has been structured for the individual seeking to grasp the realities and peculiarities of particular marketplaces, methodologies and sectors. Each chapter, written by internationally renowned experts in the field from around the world, includes an interesting mix of reviews of the literature, theory, research findings, competing perspectives and practices that will provide knowledge, information, examples and cases for students, academics and practitioners of both marketing and management. As such, our book is also useful for management in a more general sense, especially for practitioners with an interest in the Asian economies that we cover.

Our book provides key reviews and analyses of ethical and social marketing theory, practice and fairness management across Asia. We treat the nature of ethical and social marketing in the Asian context comprehensively. By drawing from varying perspectives, our book explores research and practices in different areas, industries, and commercial and non-commercial sectors and organisations. In terms of sectors and industries, the coverage of our book is wide. It includes: services, retail, advertising, media, hospitality, real estate, e-commerce, legal, online finance, banking, tourism, health, non-profit, government, aviation, pharmaceuticals, manufacturing, electronics, technology production and beverages.

Throughout our book we have included features such as 'Stop and reflect' and 'In practice' boxes where appropriate; these highlight interesting points and managerial implications arising from the text. For example, we ask questions such as: 'How are marketers making (or how should they make) ethical decisions across countries?' These questions encourage readers to reflect and contemplate issues in more depth.

The text can be used on a variety of courses, including: marketing management; international marketing; consumer behaviour; contemporary issues in marketing; and ethical marketing/social marketing. These courses are widely taught. Often all undergraduate students undertaking degrees in marketing are required to select at least two of these courses. Moreover, often all undergraduate students in business or management have the option to take contemporary issues in marketing, international marketing or ethical marketing options – and many do. Marketing management is a required course for MBA programmes worldwide and for many MSc programmes in business. Thus this book will have worldwide appeal.

Our book provides those interested in marketing, management and business with a comprehensive treatment of the nature of ethical and social marketing and fairness management in the Asian context. We hope it will become a key and handy resource for students, academics and practitioners, from a range of areas in management, who require more than anecdotal evidence of different ethical and social marketing application and fairness management, as well as Asian economies and contexts more generally.

Coverage

An overview of our book's coverage by structure and content is provided in Table 1.1. It would have been difficult to cover all Asian countries with the limited resources and space available, so we selected a mixture of developing and developed economies with varied social, economic and political backgrounds, context and histories of colonialism and wars, communism and capitalism. We follow the same sequence of regions and economies across Asia in each of our three theme-based parts. The sequence is geographically based on 'clusters':

- North East (China, Taiwan, Japan and South Korea);
- South East (in two groups: Singapore, Malaysia and Thailand; and Vietnam, Cambodia, the Philippines and Indonesia); and
- South Asia (India, Pakistan and Bangladesh).

Appendix A, at the end of this chapter, provides an overview of these countries in terms of size, economy and demographics. These are interesting and useful snapshots in their own right, but they are also key factors in helping to ground and contextualise our work and ethical and social marketing and fairness management.

Table 1.2 summarises all the chapters by content in terms of highlights, countries, cases and sectors. This not only provides readers with a useful quick and handy overview of our book, but also allows them to dip in more easily and quickly to sections that especially interest them, and to see the sectors and cases provided for their use and teaching, and gain an overview of content and the similarities and differences across chapters.

Table 1.1 Outline: structure, content and titles

Chapters	Titles
1	Introduction to ethical and social marketing in Asia: incorporating fairness management
Part One: Ethical Marketing	
Revolves around research studies on ethical marketing issues in Asia. Enables readers to compare, contrast and comprehend how firms organise and manage ethics. Presents aspects of decision-making processes influencing perceptions towards ethical marketing.	
2	Ethical marketing: China, Taiwan, Japan, South Korea
3	Ethical marketing: Singapore, Malaysia, Thailand
4	Ethical marketing: India, Pakistan, Bangladesh
5	Ethical marketing: Vietnam, Cambodia, the Philippines, Indonesia
Part Two: Social Marketing	
Examines differing perspectives of social marketing and its effects on consumption behaviour. Wide-ranging presentation of social marketing cases across different sectors.	
6	Social marketing: China, Taiwan, Japan, South Korea
7	Social marketing: Singapore, Malaysia, Thailand
8	Social marketing: India, Pakistan, Bangladesh
9	Social marketing: Vietnam, Cambodia, the Philippines, Indonesia
Part Three: Fairness Management	
Covers fairness from extant consumer behavioural and psychological theories and research. Important cultural and social indicators, influencing consumers' fairness perceptions included. Enables readers to understand role of fairness and subsequent application.	
10	Fairness management: China, Taiwan, Japan, South Korea
11	Fairness management: Singapore, Malaysia, Thailand
12	Fairness management: India, Pakistan, Bangladesh
13	Fairness management: Vietnam, Cambodia, the Philippines, Indonesia
Part Four: Conclusion	
14	Conclusion to ethical and social marketing in Asia: incorporating fairness management

Table 1.2 Content highlights and definitions

Chapter	Highlights	Countries	Case	Sectors	Definition
2	• Discusses key elements and antecedents of ethical marketing decision-making. • Compares ethical marketing issues and facts. • Framework elements include: economic environment, legal, management culture, consumer perspectives, ethical products, ethical advertising, green issues, organisational issues, etc.	China, Taiwan, Japan, South Korea.	Da Vinci's furniture scandal – failure to label country of origin of products properly.	Service, retail, manufacturing, advertising, electronics.	Ethical marketing can be defined as 'an inquiry into the nature and grounds of moral judgments, standards, and rules of conduct relating to marketing decisions and marketing situations' (Hunt & Vitell, 1986, p. 4).
3	• Uses country-branding framework to comprehend how firms organise and manage ethical marketing. • Incorporates ethical dimension in overall framework, which includes: physical, human capital, export, foreign investments,	Singapore, Malaysia, Thailand.	Ethical beliefs and intentions of young Malaysian consumers – explores the case of piracy.	Tourism, government, manufacturing, retail, NGOs.	Defines ethical marketing as 'the application of marketing ethics into the marketing process, referring to the philosophical examination, from a moral standpoint, of particular marketing issues that are matters of moral judgment and

(Continued)

Table 1.2 (Continued)

Chapter	Highlights	Countries	Case	Sectors	Definition
	culture and heritage, social and political. • Other topics include face, status, collectivism/ individualism and country-of-origin perceptions.				may result in a more socially responsible and culturally sensitive business community' (Nguyen et al., 2015).
4	• Discusses ethics, reflecting on views of the dominant religions of Hinduism and Islam. • Examines ethical marketing in specific context of population, poverty, literacy, income inequality, etc. • Dharma, bribery, corruption, poverty, inequality, values and codes of conduct. • Implications relate to marketing: internal, integrated, relationship and performance.	India, Pakistan, Bangladesh.	Employee ethics: two experiences: (1) Ethics of unethical (2) Ethics of poor: May the tribe of Ramjee Gurung thrive.	Government, banking.	'The vedanta law of morality does not ask us to act without motives, but asks us to serve humanity, without any selfish desires or petty interests, without envy or jealousy, regardless of party or personality… An action is good, not because of its external consequences, but on account of its inner will. Virtue is a mode of being and not of doing' (Radhakrishnan, 1914, p. 168).

5	• Identifies several marketing associations and examines these and their marketing code of ethics. • Reviews ethics dimensions and ethical decision-making. • Other themes include: consequentialism, ethics by process, rights, justice, fairness, due process, virtue and character.	Vietnam, Cambodia, the Philippines, Indonesia.	Mini-cases of ethical decision-making in Vietnam.	Legal, government, non-profit organisation, pharmaceutical, advertising.	'Ethics is concerned with what is right, fair, just or good; about what we ought to do, not just what is the case or what is most acceptable or expedient' (Preston, 1996, p. 16).
6	• Examines how cultural factors influence social marketing practice and research, using the Framework for Cross-cultural Social Marketing Research. • Investigates differences in issues addressed by social marketing campaigns and message framing based on examples of social marketing campaigns and research.	China, Taiwan, Japan, South Korea.	Illustrative case study about waste management in the densely populated city of Hong Kong.	Advertising, communication, media, health.	Social marketing defined as 'seeking to develop and integrate marketing concepts with other approaches to influence behaviour that benefits individuals and communities for the greater social good' (AMA, 2007).

(Continued)

Table 1.2 (Continued)

Chapter	Highlights	Countries	Case	Sectors	Definition
	• Framework dimensions include: cultural, psycho-social, social, economic and historical contexts.				
7	Introduces concept of social marketing as means to change voluntary behaviour in individuals and influence policy. • Explains varying definitions and how social marketers adopt them in practice. • Framework of benchmark criteria include: behaviour change, audience research, segmentation, exchange, marketing mix and competition.	Singapore, Malaysia, Thailand.	Outlines factors deemed to be essential or important by social marketing experts from across the globe.	Retail, health, public policy, media, beverages.	'The design, implementation and control of programs calculated to influence the acceptability of social ideas and involving considerations of product planning, pricing, communication, distribution, and marketing research' (Kotler & Zaltman, 1971, p. 5).
8	• Explores diversities and issues with special reference to	India, Pakistan, Bangladesh.	The Blue Star Programme (BSP), one of the most	Government, retail, health, NGOs.	Social marketing – using marketing theories, tools and techniques to

9	• Provides overview of social marketing practice and theory. • Contends that downstream, mid-stream and upstream social marketing needs to be tailored to unique cultural and social contexts of countries studied.	Vietnam, Cambodia, the Philippines, Indonesia.	Helmets and Beyond: the Asian Injury Prevention Foundation in Vietnam.	NGOs, government, health.	Social marketing is a complex enterprise that often aims to rectify the perceived wrongs of global society by creating positive social change (Kotler, 2013; Spotswood et al., 2012; Wood, 2012).
	• contraceptive social marketing programmes. • Presents important aspects of decision-making processes, influencing consumers' perceptions towards social marketing. • Focuses on contraception and family planning social marketing programmes, including history, major issues and challenges of campaigns. • Challenges include effects of coercive policies and selling focused approaches.		successful programmes launched by the Social Marketing Company in Bangladesh.		address social issues (Mutum et al., 2015).

(Continued)

Table 1.2 (Continued)

Chapter	Highlights	Countries	Case	Sectors	Definition
	• Explores campaigns at four levels: socio-cultural, community, local and individual. • Provides recommendations for using social marketing to initiate social change.				
10	• Discusses crucial theoretical underpinnings and critical contextual issues to be considered by managers to manage fairness effectively. • Relevant theories from social psychology, marketing and organisational behaviour introduced to help understand: current status of fairness management and how fairness must be managed in the future.	China, Taiwan, Japan, South Korea.	Case study of a Chinese customer's complaint against Mercedes-Benz illustrates the lessons learned.	Service, retail.	Fairness judgments are based on a comparison process, whereby the outcomes of the judge are contrasted with the outcomes received by a comparative referent (Martin & Murray, 1983).

| 11 | • Concepts include: comparison of standards of fairness, fairness principles and moderators, facets of fairness, self-serving bias of fairness perceptions and fairness-related emotions.
• Explores fairness of different customer management practices and favouritism.
• Develops conceptual framework, considering how to overcome CRM paradox and provide managers with a framework for fairer marketing practices.
• Other topics include: nepotism, discrimination, corrupt hiring practices, meritocracy, contracts, consumer protection act and dual pricing. | Singapore, Malaysia, Thailand. | Examples given of favouritism, the CRM paradox, expert favouritism and a short case study on SAS. | Retail, online, finance, legal, tourism, aviation. | Fairness is defined as 'a judgment of whether an outcome and/or the process to reach an outcome are reasonable, acceptable, or just' (Bolton et al., 2003, p. 474). |

(Continued)

Table 1.2 (Continued)

Chapter	Highlights	Countries	Case	Sectors	Definition
12	• Provides an understanding of brand (un)fairness and brand fairness management. • Adopting enlightened approach to fairness management, identifies critical success factors of brand fairness management and conceptualises issues for further investigation. • Links fairness to 'enlightened market orientation' as a strong response to the current marketing paradigm.	India, Pakistan, Bangladesh.	The Indian Food Place, a special foods retail store in Mumbai, gave away food for free when cash registers broke down.	Retail, advertising, government, technology, production.	Fairness 'emphasises marketers' responsibility toward all stakeholders e.g. customers, employees, investors, channel members, regulators, and the community, highlighting that their actions and decisions should be of value to all' (AMA, 2014).
13	• Links fairness management with CRM and explores important aspects of cultural and social indicators, influencing consumers' fairness perceptions. • Explores fairness in several streams, each within their separate	Vietnam, Cambodia, the Philippines, Indonesia.	Case study of a broken CRM system at a hotel leading to unfairness perceptions by a loyal customer.	Service, retail, e-commerce, real estate, manufacturing, government, hospitality.	Different cultures influence perceived fairness in different ways: (1) through comparisons of own interaction with another person's, or comparing current with previous interactions; (2) the attributions (or blame)

contexts: general fairness, price fairness, service fairness and retail fairness. • Presents examples of unfairness, including: land conflicts, exploitation and unfair treatment of workers, negative word of mouth, and unfair and discriminatory laws, which stereotype women.			for an unfair purchase situation; and (3) general social norms and beliefs (Xia et al., 2004).

Content

In the first part of the book, ethical marketing issues in Asia are explored. Chapter 2 discusses key elements and antecedents of ethical marketing decision-making by comparing ethical marketing issues and facts in China, Taiwan, Japan and South Korea. As an illustrative example, it includes a case study of a Chinese furniture company scandal – Da Vinci's failure to label the country of origin of products properly. Hunt and Vitell (1986, p. 4) define ethical marketing as 'an inquiry into the nature and grounds of moral judgments, standards, and rules of conduct relating to marketing decisions and marketing situations'. It is suggested that ethical marketing is the extension of marketing knowledge, techniques and concepts into influencing the acceptability of ethical ideas. This chapter focuses on transparent, trustworthy and responsible personal and organisational marketing policies and activities that indicate integrity as well as fairness to consumers and other stakeholders (Murphy, Laczniak, Bowie, & Klein, 2005). To set the initial impression of differences between the countries, it is noted that contemporary studies on marketing ethics differ with respect to emphasis on the role of individual differences, cultural values and ethical climates in forming ethical decision-makers' reasoning and subsequent decisions. However, current understanding of the multi-country dynamics underlying marketing ethics is limited. Furthermore, while research suggests that business ethics practices are relatively similar between these countries, since they are heavily influenced by Confucian ethics (Ardichvili, Jondle, & Kowske, 2009), there is evidence to show that each country developed a unique subset of Confucianism, and so ethical marketing practices in these nations are not all the same (Chung, Eichenseher, & Taniguchi, 2008).

In China, to a large extent, the discipline of Chinese marketing today does not address ethical issues arising out of the transition from a planned economy towards a more market economy. Marketing ethics issues increasingly arise from this. However, marketing scandals have put China at the forefront of growing concern, not only about its products, but also relating to its marketing decision-making ethics. For the Chinese, Confucianism has a preference for management by ethics rather than by law (Ramasamy, Yeung, & Chen, 2013). One of the central virtues of Confucianism is ren (human). Ren is often described as incorporating the case and concern for consumers, and for society as a whole. Abiding by these principles encourages managers to behave more ethically. Despite the positive effect of Chinese traditional culture on management ethical decision-making, the literature also suggests that certain cultural values may lead to negative ethical beliefs among organisations. In particular, business and political corruption are by no means uncommon in China.

In Taiwan, the government established a consumer protection mechanism specifically to improve the quality of products and maintain a fair consumption environment (Consumer Protection Committee, Executive Yuan, 2011). Furthermore, it has engaged in various aspects of consumer education practices, leading to an increased level of consumer consciousness and self-awareness among consumers. In addition, the mechanism also involves an effective dispute-handling system. When consumer disputes arise, consumers can quickly and accurately obtain appropriate compensation (Consumer Protection Committee, Executive Yuan, 2011). Nowadays, more Taiwanese companies are turning their attention towards environmental sustainability. As a result, 'green marketing' has become a more common feature of advertising messages, using phrases such as 'environment friendly', 'green', 'eco' and 'sustainability'. Although the government discourages so-called 'greenwash' activities (where companies claim unsubstantiated environmental functionality of products), these are still popular in the market. Consumers have learned about the drawbacks of greenwash and they perceive that the environmental claims of green products are neither true nor transparent (Chen & Chang, 2013). Consequently, consumer confusion and perceived risk are found to be a barrier to green marketing product consumption in the marketplace.

In Japan, Japanese managers consider unethical practices relating to marketing activities as the most unacceptable. Choi and Nakano's (2008) research found that the top three unethical practices that Japanese managers would most like to eliminate were price collusion, price discrimination, and giving of gifts, gratuities and bribes. Furthermore, several empirical studies suggest that company policy is the primary factor influencing managers' ethical decisions in Japan. For example, Nakano (1997) found that among the factors influencing Japanese managers' ethical or unethical decisions, company policy is one of the most important. This study also reveals that Japanese managers tend to choose what is in the interest of the company over their own ethical beliefs when these conflict with each other.

In South Korea, advertising to children has been the subject of considerable concern for the public. For example, it is argued that TV food advertisements have had a noticeable impact on the incidence of obesity. Childhood obesity rates have been doubling every year since 1998 and in 2008 reached 13.7 per cent for boys and 7.5 per cent for girls (Moon, 2013). Several studies on TV food advertising showed that such advertisements aired during children's prime-time viewing hours are dominated by energy-dense and nutrient-poor (EDNP) foods, thus leading to increased consumption of such foods (Kim, 2012). In recent years, public demand for regulations targeting food advertisements has increased dramatically. Therefore, the Special Act finally went into effect in 2010, restricting marketing activities for food products containing high levels of fat, sugar, salt and calories. This Act targets 4−18-year-olds and it restricted TV advertising of EDNP foods between 5pm and 7pm.

Chapter 3 considers ethical marketing in Singapore, Malaysia and Thailand. Using a country-branding framework, a new framework is developed by adding an ethical dimension to the application and analyses. With this ethical dimension permeating other aspects of country branding and a strong focus on ethics itself, countries may reinforce the positive values of the country's brand, creating a strong citizen brand. The challenges are many, the most prevalent being to ensure that the development of products can add long-term benefits without reducing the products' desirable qualities. Research shows that consumers are less trusting of ethical claims in advertisements. Media attention on ethics has resulted in many top brands suffering from consumer boycotts. Therefore, country-branding focusing on ethics may also require care. Again, the countries vary.

In Singapore, the key to success lies in the emphasis on human capital dimensions (Szondi, 2006). This is the economy's most competitive asset and Singapore has consequently attracted well-developed and highly qualified workers, giving the country a competitive edge (Wanjiru, 2005). These human capital qualities also influence visitors (Idris & Arai, 2006) by making a lasting impression (Wanjiru, 2005) and contributing to a country brand's performance in global markets. To win over the public, it is suggested that Singapore needs to continue its focus on businesses and investment, but also highlight more of their good causes and global ethical and social responsibility issues, which are beneficial for investors and citizens alike.

In Malaysia, emphasis should be on human capital dimensions due to the country's diversified and multicultural population. To this end, Malaysia could incorporate and differentiate itself among its competitors by highlighting the country's openness towards different religious and moral beliefs, thus creating associations with increased ethical concerns and trust in their human capital and other areas. To win over the public, it is suggested that Malaysia needs to be more involved with good causes and global issues. Social and ethical factors are key elements in a country's competitive advantage, and Malaysia should mainly brand internally towards its own citizens.

In Thailand, places like Bangkok city centre and beach resort holidays are world-class holiday destinations. However, frequent natural disasters, such as flooding and tsunamis, risk reducing tourism and inward investment, diminishing competitiveness (Wanjiru, 2005), as do political and civil tension, conflicts and unrest. The country has vast raw material resources, such as rice production, in which they enjoy core competencies that others cannot replicate (Gilmore, 2002). To win over the public, it is suggested that Thailand must expand their ethical management to areas that involve human capital, to overcome images of stereotyping. In addition, it is vital that ethics are strongly embedded in all aspects of their country-branding, namely their politics and government.

Chapter 4 presents contemporary issues in ethical marketing in India, Pakistan and Bangladesh. Ethical marketing here has to be examined and understood in the specific context (population, poverty, literacy, income inequality, etc.) of these countries. All are perceived as high on corruption scales, with India having a slightly better rank (the lower the rank, less corrupt the country) of 94 (out of 180 countries), and Pakistan and Bangladesh are at 127 and 136, respectively. Corruption scandals are rife; corruption, unemployment and development have dominated elections. The growth of certain new political parties, like the Aam Admi Party (AAP) in India and Tahree-e-Insaaf in Pakistan, is mainly attributed to the increasing concerns of citizens about corruption and the inability of traditional political parties to deal with it. Whatever may be the reasons for corruption, it affects the ethical behaviour of all the stakeholders involved in a transaction. It also deeply impacts on ethical marketing.

Chapter 5 reviews the current state of ethical marketing in Vietnam, Cambodia, the Philippines and Indonesia. In Vietnam, marketers still lack active professional associations enforcing strict codes of ethics. As of 2013, Vietnam ranked 112 of 182 countries in the Transparency International's Corruption Perception Index, well behind countries like Thailand and China. The Government Inspectorate of Vietnam in 2013 detected 45 corruption cases involving 99 people and 354 billion Vietnamese dong ($16.7 million) embezzled (Global Times, 2014). The Government Inspectorate found that corruption and waste occurred mainly in the areas of land use, credit, banking, asset management and capital, causing huge economic losses and public discontent. The presence of such unethical practices is damaging Vietnam's reputation as a place for conducting business. From a marketing perspective, support from both the government and international community may assist Vietnamese businesses and in particular marketers to improve their procedures, outcomes and (not least) their virtue and morality. Awareness and training are needed, however, on many levels. Ethics by virtue and character are also warranted in order to further improve the reputation of Vietnam. With time and proper institutional frameworks, marketers in Vietnam may join various associations and adhere to their code of ethics. In this way, companies and customers alike will be better off.

In Cambodia, there is little written on the topic of ethical marketing. However, there is evidence that it is practised to a great extent. According to StartSomeGood. com, a crowd-funding platform for non-profit organisations and social entrepreneurs, campaigns using ethical marketing approaches are in evidence. For example, a project by the Cambodian Children's Trust (CCT), proposes to teach children not what to think, but *how* to think. The focus in the CCT's approach involves studying ethics and philosophy at an early age, as they believe that such knowledge will give children the necessary skills to use good thinking as a guide by which to live. For marketers, early education in ethics, fairness and morality may foster greater awareness and improved ethical marketing skills. The future of Cambodia depends on it.

In the Philippines, business ethics are greatly influenced by geographic fragmentation, plurality of languages and ethnicities, and the predominant Roman Catholic religion, together with the still relatively short experience of nationhood. Among the countries in this chapter, the Philippines is probably the most advanced in terms of different professional bodies related to codes of ethics, including the marketing society MORES (Marketing and Opinion Research Society). Such a code of ethics provides integrity and trust to the marketing profession, which is an excellent starting point to improve the reputation of marketing. However, problems are also apparent. Recently, Philippines-based pharmaceutical companies have been urged by a coalition of health professionals and health advocates to follow a voluntary international code of business ethics in the bio-pharmaceutical industry that seeks to ensure the best interest of patients. Overall, it seems that the Philippines is on the right track towards marketing ethics, and its influences are fruitful for their international reputation as a place to conduct business and for foreign investors, tourists and other stakeholders.

In Indonesia, issues with corruption and other unethical concerns are highlighted. In the wake of revelations, many government officials were found to have suspiciously large bank accounts, for suggesting that ethics had not taken hold among public servants. Many call for the development of a code of ethics to prevent corruption, and note how important codes of ethics and standards for behaviour are as instruments for enforcing discipline in state institutions. Marketers are not exempt from this either.

The second part of the book covers differing perspectives of social marketing in Asia. Chapter 6 presents key reviews, and analyses leading thinking on social marketing in China, Taiwan, Japan and South Korea. Social marketing is seen as 'seeking to develop and integrate marketing concepts with other approaches to influence behaviour that benefits individuals and communities for the greater social good' (International Social Marketing Association, 2013, p. 1). The chapter expands this definition by examining how cultural factors influence social marketing practice and research, using the Framework for Cross-cultural Social Marketing Research (Dahl, 2009). This framework introduces a number of different points to consider and, therefore, contextualises social marketing interventions in the wider cultural and social context in which they occur, providing an important perspective.

In developed and Western countries, much emphasis is placed on issues such as energy consumption, safer driving, anti-smoking, and prevention of alcohol and drug abuse, while in developing countries, much of the social marketing focus centres on basic health issues, such as sanitation, family planning, and maternal and child health (Saini & Mukul, 2012). The countries here are a mixture of developing and developed countries, as per the IMF classification (International Monetary Fund, 2012). Taiwan, South Korea and Japan are classified as highly developed countries with advanced economies, while China is categorised as a developing country. Despite the controversial nature of such a classification system, it may nevertheless give some insights into the likely impact of using the framework classification of economic contexts on issues likely to arise in the different countries.

In China, wide-ranging reform plans were launched in 2009 with the aim of achieving universal health coverage by 2020. However, despite this progress, wide inequalities remain, including a health care system that has been described as 'hindered by waste, inefficiencies, poor quality of services, and scarcity and maldistribution of the qualified workforce' (Yip, 2012, p. 833). Social issues, such as urban migration on a massive scale, have resulted in significant problems related to environmental quality, including air and water pollution in urban centres. Furthermore, increases in road traffic and vehicle ownership have increased road-safety issues in urban and rural areas, which are both pressing and potentially addressable by social marketing interventions. In South Korea, sustainable behaviours, such as purchasing of organic food, responsible use of transportation and donating to charity, have been found to be significantly more common than in the USA and Germany. In Japan, the increase in obesity rates has not mirrored those of China.

Chapter 7 introduces the concept of social marketing as a means to change voluntary behaviour in individuals and to influence policy. Covering Singapore, Malaysia and Thailand, the chapter explores the formal definition of social marketing: this seeks to develop and integrate marketing concepts with other approaches, to influence behaviour that benefits individuals and communities for the greater social good, and explains how this definition is adopted in practice by social marketers today. Examples from the three diversified countries are used to demonstrate how social marketing is being implemented in practice.

For example, research findings from Singapore found obesity was not caused by a lack of knowledge among individuals. Research indicates that 66 per cent of Singaporeans would like to lose weight and 62 per cent acknowledged the importance of regular exercise. Yet knowing that one should eat a balanced diet and exercise regularly is not the same as actually doing it. Many individuals who vowed to lose weight found it challenging to modify their lifestyles.

In Malaysia, a study by Sajahan et al. (2012) evaluated the Anti Drug Campaign carried out by the National Drug Agency. Results of the survey indicated that only 2.5 per cent of respondents were not aware of the campaign and 25.5 per cent also agreed that the anti-drug campaign helped them to turn away from drugs. The study concluded that while anti-drug campaigns obtained a positive response from the community, campaigns alone did not change drug-taking behaviour. Insights from the evaluation would be useful to develop campaigns further to ensure that drug-taking behaviour is minimised.

In Thailand, Population Development Associates (PDA) is a private organisation that markets a range of products and services through community development centres. A water tank project run by PDA builds water tanks in villages to help improve the quality of life for villagers. It was not designed to provide revenue, although it covers some overheads for PDA (Andreasen, 1988). Many commercial marketing concepts do not translate easily to social marketing, and these are areas being examined by social marketing researchers.

Chapter 8 looks at social marketing in India, Pakistan and Bangladesh. Issues are explored with special reference to contraceptive social marketing programmes. In India, despite impressive economic growth and wealth creation, there are huge disparities in human development. Some 37 per cent of India's population (about 410 million people) fall below the poverty line, which translates to roughly one-third of the world's poor (World Bank, 2014a). Other social challenges facing the country include gender inequality (UNDP, 2014). Among all the challenges faced, unsustainable population growth remains one of the biggest areas of concern. It affects and is related to a number of other social issues. Soon after its independence in 1947, the government recognised the country's 'population problem', which then was seen as an impediment to development. Consequently, the government launched a family planning programme supported by various international organisations. In fact, social marketing was first introduced in India in the 1960s to tackle this problem. However, experts are divided about the success rates of social marketing campaigns targeted at tackling this problem. Thus this chapter focuses on contraception and family planning social marketing programmes, which used social marketing, by giving a brief history and then examining some of the major issues and challenges faced by various social marketing campaigns.

In Pakistan, human development has also become a critical concern for sustainable economic growth, especially in the light of the high mortality rates of infants and under-5s. Of interest, perhaps, for the current discussion, is that the country is currently ranked as one of the lowest spenders on education and health in the region (at about 2 per cent of GDP) (World Bank, 2014b). However, Pakistan has made impressive reductions in its poverty rate; this currently stands at an estimated 17.2 per cent in 2007−8 as compared to around 34.5 per cent in 2001−2.

Bangladesh has been more successful in improving the social conditions compared to its two neighbours. A lot of the credit can be attributed to running social marketing campaigns effectively. Schellstefe and Ciszewski (1984) analysed the success of the Social Marketing Project, which was managed by Population Services International. This contraceptive and family planning programme was launched on a national scale in 1975.

Chapter 9 gives an overview of the current state of play of social marketing practice and theory in the context of Vietnam, Cambodia, the Philippines and Indonesia. The case examples include health and sanitation programmes in Vietnam and Indonesia, oral health in the Philippines, road safety campaigns in Cambodia and Vietnam, and reproductive health campaigns throughout the region. The 'Behavioural Ecological Model' (Hovell, Wahlgren, & Gehrman, 2002), consisting of four levels (social/cultural, community, local, individual), is adopted and applied.

In Vietnam, the case study examines where UNICEF has been working on providing equitable education and health care to the children of ethnic minority groups. They have done this through providing bilingual programmes and free immunisation. Another campaign is that of promoting breastfeeding for new mothers by working, with Vietnam's National Assembly on legislative frameworks that enable women to work and continue to breastfeed.

In Cambodia, the organisation '17 Triggers' created a viral campaign to raise awareness about orphanage tourism and protection of children's right to privacy and from possible sexual abuse. The organisation provided information on its web page, prompting the online global community to share the message. In another case, by taking into account the significance of Buddhism as the national religion, UNICEF sought cooperation with numerous pagodas throughout Cambodia to form a health support programme through building a sense of community.

In Indonesia, the International Labour Office and its office in Jakarta launched a social marketing campaign with an educational angle to promote responsible workplace practice. They targeted both workers' rights and sustainable economic development. In another campaign, the Bill and Melinda Gates Foundation funded DKT Indonesia to establish clinics for Indonesian midwives, in order to improve capacity to insert and remove intrauterine devices safely, and to create an environment whereby women gain increased access to family planning.

In the Philippines, disaster resilience is a critical issue, especially in coastal areas. When the country was severely devastated by Typhoon Haiyan in 2013, the United Nations vowed to provide assistance, especially for children, by supporting back-to-learning efforts, developing a child protection system, rebuilding water systems for sanitation, supplying safe vaccines for prevention of diseases and providing services to children threatened by malnutrition. In a different social marketing campaign, the government took a leading role in initiating and supporting numerous health programmes, including one that cut across all ages by improving oral health in the country for children, adolescents, pregnant women and elderly people, with a mixture of oral service provision, product provision, health education and development of relevant policies and protocols.

The third part of our book covers studies exploring fairness in extant consumer behavioural and psychological theories and research. Important aspects of cultural and social indicators influencing consumers' fairness perceptions in the Asian context are included. This enables readers to understand the role of fairness and its subsequent application in managing their marketing approaches and beyond, into areas of general management.

Chapter 10 considers the current state of fairness management in China, Taiwan, Japan and South Korea. In China, consumers are known to be more sensitive to 'in-group' versus 'out-group' differences than American consumers because of concerns for 'face' − that is, status earned in a social network (Bolton, Keh, & Alba, 2010). This is where in-group versus out-group memberships may play a role, especially in Asian countries with strong membership ties from various life-stage-related organisations (e.g. hometowns, schools, clubs, companies, etc.). Comparison within the relevant reference groups (in-groups) becomes more important and significant in determining fairness perceptions in countries with high collectivistic tendencies. In China and Taiwan, *guanxi* denotes the informal, socio-emotional and obligational nature of the relationship imposed on all involved parties within any business contexts. It is more than give and take. It emphasises social obligations that each participant must execute in a tight-knit in-group, in order for the group's success against other out-groups. Inherently implied in this concept is the notion of individual sacrifice for the greater good of the in-group.

In Taiwan, unequal pay among same-level co-workers is acceptable in business settings, but equal payoffs are expected in personal settings (Loewenstein, Thompson, & Bazerman, 1989). This reasoning supports how Hong Kong and Taiwan differ. Although they are both of Chinese culture, the overriding goal of society in Hong Kong has always been more economic, thus changing the fairness perceptions and resulting quality-of-life perceptions (Liao, Fu, & Yi, 2005). Deutsch (1975) argued that the collective goal of a group or society influenced the selection of a dominant fairness principle. When economic productivity is a primary goal, equity will be the dominant principle; when fostering or maintenance of enjoyable social relations is the primary emphasis, equality is the typically selected principle.

In Japan, when the other party is perceived as powerless, many feel that it is inappropriate to take advantage of the powerless party − hence they divide according to the equality principle. It is considered fair that the party with greater power earns a smaller portion of the surplus, sharing more with the weaker partner. This contrasts with the USA, where it is believed that it is fair for the party with greater power to take a larger share of the surplus (Buchan, Croson, & Johnson, 2004). Interestingly, the Japanese who strongly believe in a 'just world' display larger self-serving bias than those who weakly believe in it (Tanaka, 1999). Like *guanxi*, there is the importance of *giri* and *con* in networks and relationships (Rowley & Harry, 2011).

In South Korea, equality rather than equity may be preferred. Support is found from studies investigating consumer reactions to variable pricing or price increases.

In one study involving hotel pricing tactics, Korean consumers perceived the variable-pricing practices as less fair than American consumers did (Choi & Mattila, 1993). If using the equity principle, considerations should be given to defining what constitutes a valid input. For example, Koreans are more sensitive to differences in seniority, education and family size in determining fairness of pay, whereas Americans are more sensitive to variations in individual job performance and work effort (Hundley & Kim, 1997). In terms of networks and relationships, like *guanxi*, there is the importance of *inmaek* (Rowley & Harry, 2011).

Chapter 11 presents issues in fairness management in Singapore, Malaysia and Thailand. In Singapore, cases of unfairness, discrimination and public outcry are often found in several areas, such as nepotism, school admission for the wealthy, fast-track promotions, preferential hiring according to nationality, etc. While these issues are not entirely unique to Singapore, they tend to be more prevalent in a country that greatly supports meritocracy (Singapore Armchair Critic, 2013). Influential bloggers such as the Singapore Armchair Critic (SAC) have published numerous articles on the topic, observing how meritocracy has caused great unfairness among its citizens. For example, American regulators recently opened a probe on the hiring practice of JPMorgan Chase in China. The ongoing investigation has sought to establish if the bank's recruitment practices have been favourable towards the offspring of high-ranking and influential Chinese officials ('princelings') as a quid pro quo for coveted business deals. Such practices are prohibited under the Foreign Corrupt Practices Act (SAC, 2013). One case involves the son of a former banking regulator and the other the daughter of a now-disgraced railway official. This has led to speculation about similar practices in Singapore.

In Malaysia, Amin (2013) notes that in their everyday lives, consumers enter into various types of contracts for the supply of goods or services. However, in most cases, these contracts contain terms that are more favourable to traders and unfair to consumers. Unfair terms typically occur in the form of exemption clauses, which are seen or printed on receipts, invoices and other sale documents. These standard form contracts are often designed by traders, thus they are commonly created out of self-interest, and are therefore biased and lead to unfair terms for consumers. These terms may be extremely harsh against consumers, restricting their rights or denying them all together.

In Thailand, examples of price discrimination between local residents and foreigners are not uncommon. As noted by Daoruang (2014), a 'Dual Price System' operates, in which shopkeepers trick foreign tourists into paying more. Thailand has its own numbering system, which is unique to the Thai language. When tourists shop, they will often see the price written using Arabic numbers. While this is convenient for tourists, especially at some attractions, many do not know that there is a two-tier system by which they charge foreign visitors more than local people. Daoruang (2014, p. 1) comments:

> *Usually the entrance fee is always written using Arabic numbers. If you spot the prices written in Thai numbers and Arabic numbers then for sure there are two prices. I think they do it this way because they are ashamed to let you know they are charging you double. I can't think of any other reason to hide the prices like this.*

Chapter 12 discusses issues relating to brand fairness management in India, Pakistan and Bangladesh. It is noted that the marketing landscape today is dominated by suspicion and distrust as a result of practices that include hidden fees, deception, manipulation and information mishandling. In such a pessimistic situation, marketers are re-conceptualising the notion of brand fairness in marketing and customer management, so that progress and advancement in marketing can flourish, avoiding further control and imposed regulation.

In India, the study of 'conscious capitalism' is drawn from Roy and Modi's (2014) concept of 'enlightened market orientation' in response to extensive criticism of marketing. Conscious capitalism has two key elements: firstly, companies should articulate a higher purpose that transcends profit maximisation; and secondly, they should be managed for the benefit of all stakeholders in their 'ecosystem', not just shareholders. The chapter discusses the rise of conscious capitalism (Aburdene, 2005; Mackey, 2007), which reflects people's higher levels of consciousness about themselves and the world around them. In India, this is due to natural evolution and the rapid aging of society, which has resulted in a higher proportion of people in mid-life and beyond. As consciousness is raised, people place great demands for transparency on companies, using the internet to accelerate this trend.

In Pakistan, tactical concerns towards brand fairness are covered and guidelines suggested for managers to consider – to ask what should be done to avoid the potential for such unfairness effect and to be perceived as a fairer and more trustworthy organisation in customers' minds. These guidelines are presented along with the Pakistan context. These dimensions include: awareness and problem diagnosis; managing both targeted and non-targeted customers; and emphasis on positive associations and goodwill.

In Bangladesh, the focus is on the educational sector and the education of marketing, emphasising morality in marketing. The chapter notes that re-education in fairer ways for marketing and Customer Relationship Management (CRM) managers must be implemented early on. Fairness issues should be taught in books and classes early on, in order to achieve the true concept of relationship building and to obtain quality relationships between the involved parties (Zeithaml, Berry, & Parasuraman, 1996). Students must learn what the determinants of a good relationship are (Britton & Rose, 2004). The idea is not to eliminate these technologically advanced CRM applications, philosophies and approaches, but rather to find the causes of misbehaviour and work against them. If managers do not understand where unfairness in CRM comes from, it will continue to grow. This is why it is imperative to find and understand the causes, and counteract them. This message is more relevant in today's environment than ever.

Chapter 13 explores fairness from extant consumer behavioural and psychological theories and research applied to Vietnam, Cambodia, the Philippines and Indonesia. The chapter analyses the fairness concept as part of CRM, suggesting that to achieve successful CRM implementation and long-lasting relationships, it is important to highlight four fundamental factors pertaining to a strong relationship: trust; satisfaction; symmetry and dependence; and fairness. An extended discussion of future research directions for fairness management is also provided.

In Vietnam, many local companies can offer goods that are the same quality as foreign products, but general belief and social norms hold that the local companies' products are inferior. So, if the local company sets their prices at the same level as their foreign counterparts, consumers may believe that the local company is cheating their customers with sub-standard products and services, or overly inflated prices. Many consumers will find this unfair and not buy their goods. In another case, near the capital Hanoi, thousands of police overwhelmed villagers who were trying to protect a 70-hectare (170-acre) plot of land, slated for use in a satellite city development (Win, 2012). The examples of conflicts over land are a major source of friction between the public and officials, where rising land prices have led officials to move farmers off their land for more lucrative projects, often with little compensation.

In Cambodia, the actor Minnie Driver highlighted issues of exploitation and unfairness, by urging multinational companies to change their buying practices so poor workers could have better lives. She took the opportunity to say that she visited Cambodia not as a global economist or an expert on Cambodia, but as a Western consumer. She further made a passionate plea to the heads of large corporations to consider their buying and outsourcing practices. In particular, she emphasised how every time corporations squeeze their employees to get lower production costs or faster production, the working women and their families back home suffer from such unfair treatment.

In the Philippines, there were strong reactions towards a pension provider when consumers felt unfairly treated. The case quickly spread across the internet, gathering the support of many other consumers, who together spread their complaints and negative word of mouth via social media and the *Philippine Star*, a national news outlet. The case started when Ocampo (2013), a popular online blogger, detailed how Pryce Plans, Inc. tried to induce him into accepting only 40 per cent of the cash value of his P300,000 (approximately £4,088) pension plan that had matured five years previously, or taking 80 per cent equivalent in liquefied petroleum gas or memorial plots (Ocampo, 2013). It was seen as a clear violation of social norms and an unfair deal by the company.

In Indonesia, many women and girls face unchallenged social attitudes, unfair laws and stereotyped gender roles in their struggle for fair and equal treatment (Jakarta Post, 2010). Salil Shetty, of Amnesty International, comments that some of the barriers women face are a direct result of laws and policies that discriminate against them. The latest report by Amnesty International states that these discriminatory laws and bylaws in Indonesia have altered the personal lives of poor and marginalised women by denying them full control of their reproductive systems. Shetty observes, 'Other barriers are a result of discriminatory attitudes and practices among health workers and members of the community' (Jakarta Post, 2010, p. 1).

Finally, in chapter 14, Nguyen and Rowley summarise all the key practical elements from the chapters. They also present guidelines for managing ethical, social and fairness issues in Asia.

Conclusion

We hope this book will become a key resource for students, academics and practitioners interested in ethical and social marketing and fairness management issues and in the countries discussed more generally. We cover a range of diverse perspectives on ethical marketing, social marketing and fairness management, providing essential knowledge in these three interlinked subjects as well as information and insight on 14 diverse economies across Asia. We also provide a plethora of 'real life' examples and case studies to reflect on and use.

Our book also has wider usage beyond just marketing. It provides interesting and useful insights into context and operations on the ground and doing business in Asia. Therefore, all students and managers, from all areas and functions, can gain important knowledge on doing business in this fascinating region of the world known as Asia.

We hope you will enjoy the book.

References

Aburdene, P. (2005). *Megatrends 2010: The rise of conscious capitalism.* Charlottesville, VA: Hampton Roads.

AMA. (2007). American marketing association < https://www.ama.org/Pages/default.aspx >.

Amin, N. (2013). Protecting consumers against unfair contract terms in Malaysia: The consumer protection (amendment) act 2010. *Malayan Law Journal Articles, 1,* 1−11.

Andreasen, A. R. (1988). Alternative growth opportunities for contraceptive social marketing programs. *Journal of Health Care Marketing, 8,* 38−46.

Ardichvili, A., Jondle, D., & Kowske, B. (2009). Dimensions of ethical business cultures: Comparing data from 13 countries of Europe, Asia, and the Americas. *Proceedings of the tenth international conference on human resource development research and practice across Europe.* Newcastle, 10−12 June.

Arnold, C. (2009). *Ethical Marketing and the New Consumer: Marketing in the New Ethical Economy.* West Sussex, UK: John Wiley & Sons.

Bolton, L. E., Keh, H. T., & Alba, J. W. (2010). How do price fairness perceptions differ across culture? *Journal of Marketing Research, 47,* 564−576.

Bolton, L. E., Warlop, L., & Alba, J. W. (2003). Explorations in price (un)fairness. *Journal of Consumer Research,* 474−491 (March).

Britton, J. E., & Rose, J. (2004). Thinking about relationship theory. In D. Peppers & M. Rogers (Eds.), *Managing customer relationships − a strategic framework* (pp. 38−50). New Jersey: John Wiley and Sons.

Buchan, N. R., Croson, R. T. A., & Johnson, E. (2004). When do fair beliefs influence bargaining behavior? Experimental bargaining in Japan and the United States. *Journal of Consumer Research, 31,* 181−190.

Chen, Y., & Chang, C. (2013). Greenwash and Green Trust: The mediation effects of green consumer confusion and green perceived risk. *Journal of Business Ethics, 114,* 489−500.

Choi, S., & Mattila, A. S. (1993). The role of disclosure in variable hotel pricing. *Cornell Hotel and Restaurant Administration Quarterly, 47,* 27−35.

Choi, T. H., & Nakano, C. (2008). The evolution of business ethics in Japan and Korea over the last decade. *Human Systems Management, 27,* 183−199.

Chung, K., Eichenseher, J., & Taniguchi, T. (2008). Ethical perceptions of business students: Differences between East Asia and the USA and among 'Confucian' cultures. *Journal of Business Ethics, 79,* 121−132.

Consumer Protection Committee, Executive Yuan. (2011). *Annual report of the policy evaluation 2010.* Available from <http://www.cpc.ey.gov.tw> Accessed 02.01.14.

Dahl, S. (2009). *Cross-cultural advertising research: What do we know about the influence of culture on advertising?* Available from <http://ssrn.com/paper=658221>.

Daoruang, P. (2014). *Dual pricing system in Thailand — giving tourists the right to choose.* Available from <http://www.2pricethailand.com/how-they-trick-foreign-tourists-into-paying-more>.

Deutsch, M. (1975). Equity, equality, and need: What determines which value will be used as the basis of distributive justice? *Journal of Social Issues, 31,* 137—149.

French, J., Merritt, R., & Reynolds, L. (2011). *Social marketing casebook,* London: Sage.

Gilliland, S. W., Steiner, D. D., Skarlicki, D. P., & van den Bos, K. (2005). *What motivates fairness in organizations?* USA: Information Age Publishing.

Gilmore, F. (2002). A country — can it be repositioned? Spain — the success story of country branding. *Journal of Brand Management, 9,* 281—293.

Global Times. (2014). 55 corruption cases detected in Vietnam in 2013. Available from <http://www.globaltimes.cn/content/836540.shtml#.U0oOhRZx2ZY> Accessed 13.04.14.

Hovell, M. F., Wahlgren, D. R., & Gehrman, C. (2002). The behavioral ecological model: Integrating public health and behavioral science. In R. J. DiClemente, R. Crosby, & M. Kegler (Eds.), *New and emerging theories in health promotion practice and research* (pp. 347—385). San Francisco, CA: Jossey-Bass Inc.

Hundley, G., & Kim, J. (1997). National culture and the factors affecting perceptions of pay fairness in Korea and the United States. *The International Journal of Organizational Analysis, 4,* 325—341.

Hunt, S. D., & Vitell, S. (1986). A general theory of marketing ethics. *Journal of Macromarketing, 6,* 5—15.

Idris, K., & Arai, H. (2006). The intellectual property-conscious nation: Mapping the path from developing to developed, World Intellectual Property Organization: <http://www.wipo.int/export/sites/www/freepublications/en/intproperty/988/wipo_pub_988.pdf>.

International Monetary Fund. (2012). *World economic outlook, April 2012: Growth resuming, dangers remain.* Washington, DC: International Monetary Fund.

International Social Marketing Association. (2013). Consensus definition of social marketing (04.10.13).

Jakarta Post. (2010). Amnesty: RI women continue to face unfair laws, prejudice. *The Jakarta Post,* 05.11.10 <http://www.thejakartapost.com/news/2010/11/05/amnesty-ri-women-continue-face-unfair-laws-prejudice.html> Accessed 12.04.14.

Kim, S. (2012). Restriction of television food advertising in South Korea: Impact on advertising of food companies. *Health Promotion International, 28,* 17—25.

Kotler P. (2013). The larger context for social marketing. Paper presented at the World Social Marketing Conference, Toronto, Canada.

Kotler, P., & Zaltman, G. (1971). Social marketing: An approach to planned social change. *Journal of Marketing, 35,* 3—12.

Liao, P., Fu, Y., & Yi, C. (2005). Perceived quality of life in Taiwan and Hong Kong: An intra-culture comparison. *Journal of Happiness Studies, 5,* 43—67.

Loewenstein, G. F., Thompson, L., & Bazerman, M. H. (1989). Social utility and decision making in interpersonal contexts. *Journal of Personality and Social Psychology, 57,* 426—441.

Mackey, J. (2007). *Conscious capitalism: Creating a new paradigm for business.* <http://www.flowidealism.org/Downloads/JM-CC-1.pdf>.

Martin, J., & Murray, A. (1983). Distributive injustice and unfair exchange. In David M. Messick, & Karen S. Cook (Eds.), *Equity theory: Psychological and sociological perspectives* (pp. 169—205). New York: Praeger.

Moon, Y. S. (2013). Examination of health messages in food advertising: A case of South Korea. *Journal of Food Products Marketing, 19,* 387—405.

Murphy, P. E., Laczniak, G. R., Bowie, N. E., & Klein, T. A. (2005). *Ethical marketing.* Upper Saddle River, NJ: Pearson Prentice-Hall.

Mutum, D. S., Ghazali, E., & Kumar, A. (2015). Social marketing in India, Pakistan, and Bangladesh. In B. Nguyen, & C. Rowley (Eds.), *Ethical and social marketing in Asia.* Oxford: Chandos Publishing.

Nakano, C. (1997). A survey study on Japanese managers' views of business ethics. *Journal of Business Ethics, 16,* 1737−1751.

Nguyen, B., Chen, C. H. S., Wu, S., & Melewar, T. C. (2015). Ethical marketing in Singapore, Malaysia, and Thailand. In B. Nguyen, & C. Rowley (Eds.), *Ethical and social marketing in Asia.* Oxford: Chandos Publishing.

Ocampo, S. C. (2013). Other victims outraged by Pryce Plans unfairness. *The Philippine Star,* 27.04.13 < http://www.philstar.com/opinion/2013/04/27/935449/other-victims-outraged-pryce-plans-unfairness > Accessed 11.04.14.

Preston, N. (1996). *Understanding ethics.* Annadale: Federation Press.

Radhakrishnan, S. (1914). The ethics of the Vedanta. *International Journal of Ethics, 24,* 168−183.

Ramasamy, B., Yeung, M. C. H., & Chen, J. (2013). Selling to the urban Chinese in East Asia: Do CSR and value orientation matter? *Journal of Business Research, 66,* 2485−2491.

Rowley, C., & Harry, W. (2011). *Managing people globally: An Asian perspective.* Oxford: Chandos Publishing.

Roy, S. K., & Modi, P. (2014). Enlightened market orientation and consumer well-being. Working paper.

Saini, G. K., & Mukul, K. (2012). What do social marketing programmes reveal about social marketing? Evidence from South Asia. *International Journal of Nonprofit and Voluntary Sector Marketing, 17,* 303−324.

Sajahan, M. S., Khir, M. R. M., Johari, N. R., & Jaafar, E. (2012). Social marketing practice in 'anti drug campaign' as an alternative of continuous improvement in public awareness. *Interdisciplinary Journal of Contemporary Research in Business, 3,* 58−70.

Schellstede, W. P., & Ciszewski, R. L. (1984). Social marketing of contraceptives in Bangladesh. *Studies in Family Planning,* 30−39.

Singapore Armchair Critic. (2013). *How meritocracy entrenches inequality.* 9 September, <http://singaporearmchaircritic.wordpress.com/2013/09/09/how-meritocracy-entrenches-inequality>.

Spotswood, F., French, J., Tapp, A., & Stead, M. (2012). Some reasonable but uncomfortable questions about social marketing. *Journal of Social Marketing, 2,* 163−175.

Szondi, G. (2006). The role and challenges of country branding in transition countries: The Central and Eastern European experience. *Place Branding and Public Diplomacy, 3,* 8−20.

Tanaka, K. (1999). Judgments of fairness by just world believers. *The Journal of Social Psychology, 139,* 631−638.

United Nations Development Programme. (UNDP). (2014). *About India: Challenges.* Available from <http://www.in.undp.org/content/india/en/home/countryinfo/challenges.html> Accessed 13.03.14.

Wanjiru, E. (2005). Branding African countries: A prospect for the future. *Place Branding, 2,* 84−95.

Win, T. L. (2012). Vietnam Land Law revision should improve fairness transparency − analysis. < http://www.so.undp.org/content/dam/vietnam/docs/UNDP-in-the-News/31294_Vietnam_Land_Law_revision_should_improve_fairness.pdf > Accessed 11.04.14.

World Bank. (2014a). *India: Country results profile.* Available from <http://web.worldbank.org/WBSITE/EXTERNAL/NEWS/0,,contentMDK:22888405~menuPK:141310~pagePK:34370~piPK:34424~theSitePK:4607,00.html> Accessed 13.03.14.

World Bank. (2014b). Pakistan overview. Available at <http://www.worldbank.org/en/coun-
try/pakistan/overview> Accessed 18.03.14.
Wood, M. (2012). Marketing social marketing. *Journal of Social Marketing*, 2, 94–102.
Xia, L., Monroe, K. B., & Cox, J. L. (2004). The price is unfair! A conceptual framework of
price fairness perceptions. *Journal of Marketing*, 68, 1–15.
Yip, W. C. M. (2012). Early appraisal of China's huge and complex health-care reforms. *The
Lancet*, 379, 833–842.
Zeithaml, V. A., Berry, L. L., & Parasuraman, A. (1996). The behavioral consequences of
service quality. *Journal of Marketing*, 60, 31–46.

Appendix A: Brief overview of the 14 countries

China	Area: 9,596,961 km^2 Economy: GDP: $13.39 trillion (2013 est.) GDP by sector: agriculture: 10% industry: 43.9% services: 46.1% (2013 est.) Demographics: Population: 1,355,692,576 (July 2014 est.) Age: 0–14 years: 17.1% (male 124,340,516/female 107,287,324) 15–24 years: 14.7% (male 105,763,058/female 93,903,845) 25–54 years: 47.2% (male 327,130,324/female 313,029,536) 55–64 years: 9.6% (male 77,751,100/female 75,737,968) 65 years and over: 9.4% (male 62,646,075/female 68,102,830) (2014 est.)
Taiwan	Area: 35,980 km^2 Economy: GDP: $926.4 billion (2013 est.) GDP by sector: agriculture: 2% industry: 29.4% services: 68.6% (2013 est.) Demographics: Population: 23,359,928 (July 2014 est.) Age: 0–14 years: 14% (male 1,683,381/female 1,575,789) 15–24 years: 13.4% (male 1,613,197/female 1,526,344) 25–54 years: 47.4% (male 5,539,606/female 5,539,654) 55–64 years: 12% (male 1,506,657/female 1,571,208) 65 years and over: 11.6% (male 1,301,420/female 1,502,672) (2014 est.)

Japan   Area: 377,915 km^2
                   Economy:
                   GDP: $4.729 trillion (2013 est.)
                   GDP by sector:
                   agriculture: 1.1%
                   industry: 25.6%
                   services: 73.2% (2013 est.)
                   Demographics:
                   Population: 127,103,388 (July 2014 est.)
                   Age:
                   0−14 years: 13.2% (male 8,681,728/female 8,132,809)
                   15−24 years: 9.7% (male 6,429,429/female 5,890,991)
                   25−54 years: 38.1% (male 23,953,643/female 24,449,655)
                   55−64 years: 25.8% (male 8,413,872/female 8,400,953)
                   65 years and over: 24.8% (male 14,218,655/female 18,531,653) (2014 est.)

South Korea   Area: 99,720 km^2
                   Economy:
                   GDP: $1.666 trillion (2013 est.)
                   GDP by sector:
                   agriculture: 2.6%
                   industry: 39.2%
                   services: 58.2% (2013 est.)
                   Demographics:
                   Population: 49,039,986 (July 2014 est.)
                   Age:
                   0−14 years: 14.1% (male 3,603,943/female 3,328,634)
                   15−24 years: 13.5% (male 3,515,271/female 3,113,257)
                   25−54 years: 47.3% (male 11,814,872/female 11,360,962)
                   55−64 years: 12.7% (male 3,012,051/female 3,081,480)
                   65 years and over: 12.3% (male 2,570,433/female 3,639,083) (2014 est.)

Singapore   Area: 697 km^2
                   Economy:
                   GDP: $339 billion (2013 est.)
                   GDP by sector:
                   agriculture: 0%
                   industry: 29.4%
                   services: 70.6% (2013 est.)
                   Demographics:
                   Population: 5,567,301 (July 2014 est.)
                   Age:
                   0−14 years: 13.4% (male 381,452/female 364,050)
                   15−24 years: 17.8% (male 487,593/female 502,637)
                   25−54 years: 50.3% (male 1,365,872/female 1,434,495)
                   55−64 years: 8.5% (male 279,243/female 278,852)
                   65 years and over: 8.1% (male 214,665/female 258,442) (2014 est.)

Malaysia	Area: 329,847 km^2
	Economy:
	GDP: $525 billion (2013 est.)
	GDP by sector:
	agriculture: 11.2%
	industry: 40.6%
	services: 48.1% (2013 est.)
	Demographics:
	Population: 30,073,353 (July 2014 est.)
	Age:
	0−14 years: 28.8% (male 4,456,033/female 4,206,727)
	15−24 years: 16.9% (male 2,580,486/female 2,511,579)
	25−54 years: 41.2% (male 6,277,694/female 6,114,312)
	55−64 years: 5.5% (male 1,163,861/female 1,122,746)
	65 years and over: 5.3% (male 777,338/female 862,577) (2014 est.)
Thailand	Area: 513,120 km^2
	Economy:
	GDP: $673 billion (2013 est.)
	GDP by sector:
	agriculture: 12.1%
	industry: 43.6%
	services: 44.2% (2013 est.)
	Demographics:
	Population: 67,741,401 (July 2014 est.)
	Age:
	0−14 years: 17.6% (male 6,117,993/female 5,827,981)
	15−24 years: 15% (male 5,194,332/female 4,999,669)
	25−54 years: 46.9% (male 15,685,882/female 16,097,245)
	55−64 years: 9.5% (male 3,468,620/female 3,893,925)
	65 years and over: 9.8% (male 2,830,418/female 3,625,336) (2014 est.)
India	Area: 3,287,263 km^2
	Economy:
	GDP: $4.962 trillion (2013 est.)
	GDP by sector:
	agriculture: 16.9%
	industry: 17%
	services: 66.1% (2013 est.)
	Demographics:
	Population: 1,236,344,631 (July 2014 est.)
	Age:
	0−14 years: 28.5% (male 187,016,401/female 165,048,695)
	15−24 years: 18.1% (male 118,696,540/female 105,342,764)
	25−54 years: 40.6% (male 258,202,535/female 243,293,143)
	55−64 years: 5.8% (male 43,625,668/female 43,175,111)
	65 years and over: 5.7% (male 34,133,175/female 37,810,599) (2014 est.)

Pakistan	Area: 796,095 km^2
	Economy:
	GDP: $574.1 billion (2013 est.)
	GDP by sector:
	agriculture: 25.3%
	industry: 21.6%
	services: 53.1% (2013 est.)
	Demographics:
	Population: 196,174,380 (July 2014 est.)
	Age:
	0−14 years: 33.3% (male 33,595,949/female 31,797,766)
	15−24 years: 21.5% (male 21,803,617/female 20,463,184)
	25−54 years: 35.7% (male 36,390,119/female 33,632,395)
	55−64 years: 4.3% (male 5,008,681/female 5,041,434)
	65 years and over: 4.3% (male 3,951,190/female 4,490,045) (2014 est.)
Bangladesh	Area: 143,998 km^2
	Economy:
	GDP: $324.6 billion (2013 est.)
	GDP by sector:
	agriculture: 17.2%
	industry: 28.9%
	services: 53.9% (2013 est.)
	Demographics:
	Population: 166,280,712 (July 2014 est.)
	Age:
	0−14 years: 32.3% (male 27,268,560/female 26,468,883)
	15−24 years: 18.8% (male 14,637,526/female 16,630,766)
	25−54 years: 38% (male 29,853,531/female 33,266,733)
	55−64 years: 5% (male 4,964,130/female 4,870,447)
	65 years and over: 4.9% (male 4,082,544/female 4,237,592) (2014 est.)
Vietnam	Area: 331,210 km^2
	Economy:
	GDP: $358.9 billion (2013 est.)
	GDP by sector:
	agriculture: 19.3%
	industry: 38.5%
	services: 42.2% (2013 est.)
	Demographics:
	Population: 93,421,835 (July 2014 est.)
	Age:
	0−14 years: 24.3% (male 11,946,656/female 10,800,602)
	15−24 years: 17.8% (male 8,598,360/female 8,023,377)
	25−54 years: 44.8% (male 20,983,638/female 20,861,243)
	55−64 years: 5.7% (male 3,149,494/female 3,763,309)
	65 years and over: 5.6% (male 2,034,721/female 3,260,435) (2014 est.)

Cambodia   Area: 181,035 km^2
                  Economy:
                  GDP: $39.64 billion (2013 est.)
                  GDP by sector:
                  agriculture: 34.8%
                  industry: 24.5%
                  services: 40.7% (2013 est.)
                  Demographics:
                  Population: 15,458,332 (July 2014 est.)
                  Age:
                  0−14 years: 31.6% (male 2,460,659/female 2,423,619)
                  15−24 years: 20.5% (male 1,565,135/female 1,596,099)
                  25−54 years: 38.9% (male 2,938,366/female 3,082,496)
                  55−64 years: 4% (male 298,733/female 482,588)
                  65 years and over: 3.9% (male 229,684/female 380,953) (2014 est.)

Philippines   Area: 300,000 km^2
                  Economy:
                  GDP: $454.3 billion (2013 est.)
                  GDP by sector:
                  agriculture: 11.2%
                  industry: 31.6%
                  services: 57.2% (2013 est.)
                  Demographics:
                  Population: 107,668,231 (July 2014 est.)
                  Age:
                  0−14 years: 33.7% (male 18,493,668/female 17,753,359)
                  15−24 years: 19% (male 10,416,358/female 10,044,724)
                  25−54 years: 37% (male 20,031,638/female 19,796,545)
                  55−64 years: 4.5% (male 2,882,719/female 3,372,485)
                  65 years and over: 4.4% (male 2,103,596/female 2,773,139) (2014 est.)

Indonesia   Area: 1,904,569 km^2
                  Economy:
                  GDP: $1.285 trillion (2013 est.)
                  GDP by sector:
                  agriculture: 14.3%
                  industry: 46.6%
                  services: 39.1% (2013 est.)
                  Demographics:
                  Population: 253,609,643 (July 2014 est.)
                  Age:
                  0−14 years: 26.2% (male 33,854,520/female 32,648,568)
                  15−24 years: 17.1% (male 22,067,716/female 21,291,548)
                  25−54 years: 42.3% (male 54,500,650/female 52,723,359)
                  55−64 years: 6.5% (male 9,257,637/female 10,780,724)
                  65 years and over: 6.4% (male 7,176,865/female 9,308,056) (2014 est.)

Source: TheWorld Factbook (https://www.cia.gov/library/publications/the-world-factbook/geos/id.html).

Part One

Ethical Marketing

Ethical marketing: China, Taiwan, Japan and South Korea

2

Ruizhi Yuan, Martin J. Liu and Jianchang Liu

Introduction

Marketing is an extraordinary rich field in which to study ethics, because the marketing function provides an interface between the organisation and its environment. In recent years it has been far more common for marketing scholars to comment on ethics in relation to specific marketing activities.

> *Marketing activities have a formidable influence on the ethical and social values of society. Although it may be reasonably argues that such institutions as education, religion and government have a significant influence on shaping this country's values, only marketing commends the tremendous resources that are used to convey a single message, 'consume'.*
>
> *(Kangun, 1972, xiv)*

Ethical marketing can be defined as 'an inquiry into the nature and grounds of moral judgments, standards, and rules of conduct relating to marketing decisions and marketing situations' (Hunt & Vitell, 1986, p. 4). The idea of ethical marketing is simply the extension of marketing knowledge, techniques and concepts into influencing the acceptability of ethical ideas and causes, rather than just economic goods and services. From a normative perspective, ethical marketing means focusing on transparent, trustworthy and responsible personal and organisational marketing policies and activities that indicate integrity as well as fairness to consumers and other stakeholders (Murphy, Laczniak, Bowie, & Klein, 2005). Two broad domains can be evaluated in the extant marketing literature. First, ethics are introduced and considered during, and as a result of, marketing decision-making processes. Second, marketing ethics are evaluated as part of a product and service augmentation.

Concern for ethical issues in marketing and organisations has dramatically emerged over the last 20 years. Both academics and practitioners have shown an intense interest in understanding the implications of ethical issues for marketing practices. For example, both the *Journal of Business Ethics* and the *Business Ethics Quarterly* came into existence in the 1980s. The interest in marketing ethics has been steadily increasing in many Asian countries, particularly in the twenty-first century. This is mainly due to the rise in consumer activism, producing sophisticated customers who are scrutinising marketing practices more than ever before. Yet Asia cannot be considered a homogeneous entity. Different nation cultures and environments have a strong influence on marketing managers' ethical attitudes.

The main purpose of this chapter is to study the differences in ethical marketing in China, Taiwan, Japan and South Korea, and consider whether these differences offer clues for marketing managers who want to be ethical in their marketing practices in these countries.

Learning objectives

After reading this chapter, you should be able to:

- understand the definition of ethical marketing;
- outline the scope of ethical issues which confront marketing decision-makers;
- compare and contrast the ethical marketing practices in China, Taiwan, Japan and South Korea; and
- demonstrate the importance of ethical marketing both at an academic level and in terms of marketing practices in organisations.

Route map: ethical marketing: China, Taiwan, Japan and South Korea

This chapter begins with a discussion of ethical marketing in the decision-making processes. We look at the models of ethical marketing decision-making in the previous literature. We also explore the factors affecting these marketing processes. Using a case-by-case evaluation, we will differentiate between the ethical marketing practices in China, Taiwan, Japan and South Korea. The economic, legal and cultural environment among these four countries will be examined. The analysis of ethical marketing issues in these nations will also be considered, along with examples.

Considerations of ethics in relation to the marketing decision-making process are certainly nothing new. Even before the concept of marketing became known and used, questions of ethics were associated with the way that buyers and sellers conduct exchanges, particularly in terms of fairness — fair prices, fair information, fair competition and fair production (Levy & Zaltman, 1975). The question now of dealing ethically with consumers crosses a wide range of issues and problems (see Figure 2.1).

- Product: *product safety, product quality, design, packaging and labelling. Nowadays products are becoming more ethical in terms of whether they are fair trade certified, organic or animal-friendly.*
- Pricing: *price unfairness, price discrimination and misleading price. For example, a price war is a result of selling a product or service at a very low price, intending to drive competitors out of the market or to create an entry barrier to the market.*
- Place: *as the emerging marketing channels, online marketing and telemarketing push the borders of ethical and legal issues more significantly for marketers.*
- Advertising: *the use of untruthful or deceptive claims, containing offensive images such as sexual appeal, stereotyping of particular groups, advertising*

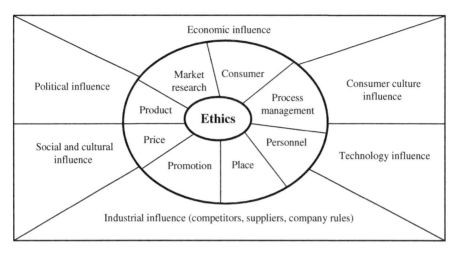

Figure 2.1 The marketing ethics in the marketing literature.

> that targets children, and generally encouraging materialism and buying of
> things that people don't need. For example, Pizza Hut and Calvin Klein
> have used controversy as a strategy in their marketing communications.
> Controversial advertisements may cause negative responses and boycotts of
> product.

- Illegal/immoral activities: *polluting the environment, maintaining unsafe working conditions; product/technology copying where protection of patents, trade-
  marks or copyrights has not been enforced.*
- Marketing research: *privacy issues. Mostly these relate to dangers posed by
  developments in information and communication technology, especially the
  issue of online privacy.*
- Green marketing: *misleading green marketing claims, greenwash (where companies claim environmental functionality of their products that cannot be
  substantiated).*
- Global marketing: *difference standards of consumer protection, expansion of
  cultural homogenisation, targeting low-income consumers in developing
  countries.*

> *(Schlegelmilch & Oberseder, 2010)*

In ethical marketing literature, a remarkable number of theoretical models can
be found that examine unethical situations. Some of these models have been widely
spread, but none of them has been pronounced as definitive (Malhotra & Miller,
1998). There are three main models:

1. 'The General Theory of Marketing Ethics' focused on ethical inference (i.e. deontology
   and teleology) in decision-making (Hunt & Vitell, 1986);
2. 'A Contingency Framework for Understanding Ethical Decision Making in Marketing' is
   developed by Ferrell and Gresham (1985); and
3. 'A Synthesis of Ethical Decision Models for Marketing' is introduced by Ferrell,
   Gresham, and Fraedrich (1989).

The state of art in ethical marketing: China, Taiwan, Japan and South Korea

The significant effect of marketing-related decisions on a wide range of stakeholders is a main driving force behind the increased interest in ethical marketing. Various professional academies are engaged in debate and in research including scholars, marketing managers and lawmakers. A principle purpose of the research field has become the evaluation of factors influencing moral sensitivity and contributing to the formulation and quality of ethical decisions (see Table 2.1). The growing body of literature has investigated the role of inter-individual differences (e.g. culture, beliefs, religion), organisation-level differences (e.g. organisational culture, interpersonal interaction) and external environment impacts (e.g. legal system, business norms) on the ethical decision-making process (Ferrell & Gresham, 1985; Fritzsche, 1997; Knouse & Giacalone, 1992; Kuntz, Kuntz, Elenkov, & Nabirukhina, 2013; Trevino, 1986). Contemporary studies on marketing ethics differ with respect to emphasis on the role of individual differences, cultural values and ethical climate in forming ethical decision-makers' reasoning and subsequent decisions. However, our understanding of the multi-country dynamics underlying marketing ethics is limited.

Previous research has investigated similarities in business ethics practices between the East Asian countries of Japan, China and South Korea, since they are heavily influenced by Confucian ethics (Ardichvili, Jondle, & Kowske, 2009). However, there is evidence to show that these countries have each developed a unique subset of Confucianism, and thus, ethical marketing practices in these nations are not the same (Chung, Eichenseher, & Taniguchi, 2008). Hence, in the remainder of this section, we will discuss some of the differences and similarities between ethical marketing practices identified in the following four countries: China, Taiwan, Japan and South Korea. To be clear, this section does not aim to examine individual stage of ethical attitudes and behaviours; rather, we will focus on contextual, organisational and cultural factors that account for ethical marketing issues, as well as several ethical marketing issues in these countries.

China

There are two stages of the development of marketing ethics in China (Lu, 2009). The first stage is from domestic economic reforms in 1978 to 2001 when China entered the World Trade Organization (WTO). Domestic economic reform moved China away from a planned economy to a market economy. This reform altered not only people's economic interests, but also their ethical values towards business. Chinese traditional ethics, for example, Marxist ethics, focus on the value 'yi', which refers to the principle or norms of obtaining and distributing benefits or profits, rather than 'li', which refers to material benefits or profits. In this stage, the

Table 2.1 **Categorization for ethical marketing literature**

	Normative (examination of what ought to be)	Descriptive (examination of what is)
Macro	• What should be the role of marketing ethics in a free enterprise, private-property system? • What should be the role of marketing ethics in nondemocratic societies and transitional societies? • What should be the relationship between law and ethics? • What should be marketers' role in helping to solve societal problems? • What should be marketers' ethical responsibility towards society? • Which ethical position should marketers take when acting in foreign cultures with different value systems? • What should be the role of consumer sovereignty? • What should be marketers' responsibility towards vulnerable consumers?	• What is the role of marketing ethics in a free enterprise, private-property system? • What is the role of marketing ethics in nondemocratic societies and transitional societies? • What is the impact of laws on marketing ethics? • What are marketers doing to help solve societal problems? • What is the ethical decision-making process of aggregated groups of marketers? • What is the relationship between ethics and profits? • What are marketers' differing value systems across cultures? • What are (if any) universally accepted ethical norms? • What is the role of consumer sovereignty in marketing decisions?
Micro	• How should firms define their ethical responsibility? • How should firms make ethical decisions in marketing? • How should firms deal with specific ethical challenges? • How should firms implement marketing ethics? • How should a code of conduct be designed? • How should firms train marketing ethics? • How should marketers cope with intrapersonal value conflicts?	• What are common ethical dilemmas? • How do firms define their ethical responsibility? • How do firms implement marketing ethics? • How do firms train their people in marketing ethics? • What is the role of codes of conduct? • How are marketers coping with intrapersonal value conflicts? • What are conflicts between personal values and the marketer's occupational role? • What is the ethical decision-making process in firms?

(Continued)

Table 2.1 **(Continued)**

Topics	*Function areas – issues related to:*
	• product
	• price
	• placement
	• promotion.
	Sub-disciplines of marketing – issues related to:
	• sales
	• consumers
	• international matters
	• marketing ethics education
	• marketing research
	• social marketing
	• the internet
	• law and ethics.
	Specific ethics-related topics – issues related to:
	• ethics and society
	• ethical decision-making models
	• ethical responsibility toward marketers' stakeholders
	• ethical values
	• norm generation and definition
	• marketing ethics implementation
	• relationship between ethics and religion
	• discrimination- and harassment
	• green marketing
	• vulnerable consumer
	• cross-culture.

Adapted from Nill & Schibrowsky (2007).

ethics in marketing were mostly emphasised by academia (e.g. conducting research, establishing courses of ethics in universities, publishing relevant articles and books).

In the second stage, which covers the period from when China entered the WTO in 2001 until the time of writing, the Chinese government changed legal business environment to comply with WTO rules. Chinese companies now focus not just on economic interests but also on ethical requirements, and consumers are increasingly aware of their own rights and interests. To a large extent, the discipline of Chinese marketing today does not address ethical issues arising out of the transition from a planned economy to a market economy. Marketing ethics issues increasingly arise from the market economy, which is now the basic model of China's economic operations. However, the nation's marketing scandals have put China at the forefront of growing concern, not only about its products, but also relating to its marketing decision-making ethics.

Economic environment – In 10 November 2001, China entered the World Trade Organization (WTO) and subsequently experienced a rapid economic rise. China's GDP increased to 40 trillion yuan (US $6.29 trillion) in 2010, almost four times that of 2001, making China the world's second largest economy (Enderle & Niu,

2012). Each year, China's GDP has grown at an average rate of 9 per cent (World Bank, 2014).

Legal environment – The legal system in China is in fact a major contributor to the Chinese ethical dilemma, because of the lack of sufficient regulatory environments. Prior to 1980, most business transactions in China were determined by the central government. Thus the Chinese people had a high degree of uncertainty about what constitutes acceptable/ethical business behaviour (Tsalikis, Seaton, & Li, 2008). Until 2001, in China, the overall business environment was not conducive to ethical behaviour, in part because companies – even large multinational companies – did not develop clear ethical standards for their marketing practices.

China's entry into the WTO in 2001 resulted in the requirements for Chinese government laws to become more transparent and consistent with international practices. Companies made even more effort to increase their enforcement of intellectual property rights. The effectiveness of this is debatable. On the one hand, public awareness is increased. China has witnessed a 22 per cent increase in patent filings from 2002, as well as a new rise in local Chinese companies resolving intellectual property disputes (Gabriel, 2008). On the other hand, the concern about intellectual property rights among Chinese managers and the enforcement of these laws are still vague and unimposing. In 2003, China reported 12,900,000 pirated products seized, as a result of which almost 2,000 illegal businesses were shut down.

Management culture – The power and influence of culture in ethical business decision-making is greater than ever before. A significant body of literature has explored key characteristics of Chinese culture (e.g. Wright, Szeto, & Cheng, 2002; Yang, 2002). Although these studies provide valuable insights into national cultural features specific to the Chinese context, there is a limited amount of research that explicitly examines the management side of cultural values. For Chinese people, Confucianism has a preference for management by ethics rather than by law (Ramasamy, Yeung, & Chen, 2013). One of the central virtues of Confucianism is *ren* (i.e. human). *Ren* is often described as incorporating the case and concern for consumers, and for society as a whole. Abiding by these principles will encourage managers to behave more ethically. Despite the positive effect of Chinese traditional culture on management ethical decision-making, the literature also suggests that certain cultural values may lead to negative ethical beliefs among organisations. In particular, business and political corruption are by no means uncommon in China. Harvey (1999) stated that the development of business ethics and morality had not matched the progress of Chinese market reform.

Consumer perspective – The demands placed by Chinese consumers on marketing practices to be ethical are constantly becoming more complex. The primary difference between Western and Eastern culture is the 'relative focus on the good-of-the-group' (collectivism) in the East compared to the 'good-of-the-individual' (individualism) in the West. According to the 2012 Goodpurpose Survey, 50 per cent of Chinese consumers considered that business needed to place at least equal weight on ethical interests as on business interests (Goodpurpose, 2012). Moreover, nearly 67 per cent of Chinese consumers preferred to purchase products from a company with a strong reputation for fair trade. However, another impact of Confucianism is the power distances among the classes. Society is divided into the classes of scholar/administrator, farmer, artisan and merchant (Tsalikis et al., 2008). As a result, consumers perceive businesspeople as being at the bottom of the society, which in turn affects their perceptions of ethical behaviour in business. In general, Chinese consumers perceive the companies as powered by self-interest, and consequently not trustworthy.

Product ethical dilemma in China – Perhaps the most common ethical problem in the Chinese marketing domain relates to product quality safety. Food scandals, fraudulent financial statements and rumours of charity money embezzlement have exploded in recent years in China. For example, Da Vinci recently faked its production location as being in Italy, while at the same time selling counterfeit products in China. In 2008, China's Ministry of Health reported that more than 300,000 children were affected by San Lu milk and infant formula products containing traces of melamine (Watson, 2013), a chemical that can cause renal failure. Food safety scandals have increased consumers' risk perceptions of foods and decreased their trust in food safety. Moreover, the company solutions to food safety scandals (i.e. recall) are certain to be costly and could have killed the brand. It seems that there are two roots of this food safety issue in China. First, Chinese management of industry standards lagged behind both international and domestic practices. Second, Chinese companies lack technical capacity and materials, resorted to deception and lowered their standards rather than investing to improve their technology. A more recent report shows that 29 per cent of Chinese people believed that the current food safety issues in China are due to 'illegal food processing companies and individual greed', 30 per cent perceived that the 'punishment of dishonest enterprises and individuals has not been enough', while 35 per cent said that 'law enforcement supervision has not been adequate' (Lu, 2009). The results indicate that the business sector is perceived as greedy and dishonest, while the government's regulations and punishments have not been effective.

Advertising ethical issue in China – Chinese advertising has gone through a late start, but phenomenal growth during the last two decades, and it is now the second biggest advertising marketing in Asia, ranking behind Japan (Gao, 2005). According to Chinese regulations, an advertisement would be considered deceptive when it misleads the customer about the advertised product or service, and leads the customer to have an understanding of the product or service that is different from the real thing (Liu, 1999). The regulations also regard unfair competition in advertising in the same way as deceptive advertising, because misleading advertisement may harm the interest of competitors. Although none of China's advertising rules provides a clear definition of deceptive advertising, Chinese government, compared to other countries, has strict legislation on advertising. Advertisers of products such as medicine, medical equipment and agricultural chemicals are required to obtain advertising certification from the government and to go through official censorship before going to the media. However, based on Pollay, Tse, and Wang (1990) research, Chinese consumers are less than satisfied with the honesty of information in advertising. According to the official report, 37,707 cases of illegal advertising were prosecuted in 1998, an increase of 18.7 per cent from 1997, while the figure increased to 51,494 in 1999, and to 66,824 in 2000 (Gao, 2005).

Taiwan

Economic environment – Taiwan, an island located in East Asia, has evolved over the past 50 years as both a democracy and a capitalist economy. It is well known as one of Asia's four economic tigers (along with South Korea, Hong Kong and Singapore). *The Economist* has forecast that Taiwan's GDP would grow at an average of 4.2 per cent annually during the period 2011 to 2015 (Liu & Chen, 2012). According to the report of 'Countries Forecast – Taiwan' by the UK Economist Information Unit (EIU) 2004, from 2004 to 2008, the Business Environment Forecast for Taiwan ranked 18th among 60 countries, third in the Asian region, which is higher than the rankings of mainland China, Japan and South Korea (Hsu, Zhang, & Lok, 2007).

Legal environment – The government of Taiwan, Republic of China, enacted its first national Consumer Protection Law (CPL) on 13 January 1994 (Juang, 1997). This law protects consumers who are injured by dangerous products or services, by accusing the companies responsible. However, the CPL has been criticised, as 'although many agree that the intent of the CPL is fair, the CPL's various problems, such as ambiguous terminology, favoritism towards consumer protection groups, and the compensation liability defense, must be addressed before the CPL becomes a truly effective piece of legislation that will protect consumers' (Juang, 1997).

Being aware of this problem, the Legislative Yuan decided to amend some portions of the CPL, ensuring consumer safety and providing accurate and full information to consumers. For example, in 2010 the government established a consumer protection mechanism specifically to improve the quality of products, and maintain a fair consumption environment (Consumer Protection Committee, Executive Yuan, 2011). Furthermore, it has engaged in various aspects of consumer education practices, leading to an increased level of consumer consciousness and self-awareness. In addition, the mechanism also involves an effective dispute handling system. When consumer disputes arise, they can quickly and accurately obtain appropriate compensation (Consumer Protection Committee, Executive Yuan, 2011).

Advertising ethical issue in Taiwan – The Fair Trade Commission of Taiwan define false advertisement as 'any information or communication which misrepresents the truth, becomes unacceptable to an adequate number of general public, and which is sufficient to cause the general public to reach erroneous perception or decision'. Any television stations are required to send specific categories of advertisements to the News Bureau for government censorship (Gao, 2005). In comparison, deceptive and unfair advertisements in Taiwan are fewer than China's. According to the Department of Health, in 2001 a total of 1,015 cases of false advertisements for cosmetics, foods and medicine were brought to court by customers.

Green marketing issues in Taiwan – Nowadays, more Taiwanese companies are turning their attention towards environmental sustainability. As a result, green marketing has become a common feature of advertising messages, using phrases such as 'environment friendly', 'green', 'eco' and 'sustainability'. Although local Taiwan government discourages greenwash activities, they are still popular in the market. Taiwanese consumers have learned about the drawbacks of greenwash, and they perceive that the environmental claims of green products are often neither true nor transparent (Chen & Chang, 2013). Consequently, consumer confusion and perceived risk are found to be a barrier to the consumption of green marketing products in the marketplace.

Japan

Economic environment – The industrialised, free market economy in Japan is the world's second largest economy. Japan's industrial leadership, advanced techniques, well-educated and industrious labour force, high saving rates and intensive foreign trade all contribute to its mature industrial economy. Before the 1990s, Japan had achieved one of the highest economic growth rates in the world, but in the early 1990s, when the 'bubble economy' collapsed, Japan's economy slowed dramatically. Japan has eventually recovered from the post-bubble period and gone through sustained economic growth. However, the economic downturn in 2008, the lack of consumer confidence and increased competition from other countries forced Japanese managers to reconsider their business system and management practices (Warner, 2013).

Organisational characteristic – Japan has a unique organisational form known as *Keiretsu*, referring to business groups of diverse companies that have close relationships with one another (McGuire & Dow, 2008). *Keiretsu* is deeply embedded in Japanese industrial business systems. Toyota is, for example, part of such *Mitsui Keiretsu*. The key benefits for *Keiretsu* members are access to stable bank financing, insulation from marketing competition, reduction of risk, monitoring of benefits, reduction of information asymmetries and mutual assistance (ibid.). As a result, product or service quality is ensured by companies building trusted relationships with each other.

Management culture – Japanese managers consider unethical practices relating to marketing activities as most unacceptable. Choi and Nakano's (2008) research found that the top three unethical practices that Japanese managers would most like to eliminate are price collusion, price discrimination and giving of gifts, gratuities and bribes. Furthermore, several empirical studies suggest that company policy is the primary factor influencing managers' ethical decisions in Japan. For example, Nakano (1997) found that among the factors influencing Japanese managers' ethical or unethical decisions, company policy is the one of the most important one. Nakano's study also revealed that Japanese managers tend to choose the interests of the company over their own ethical beliefs when these conflict with each other. Among 45 managers, 42.2 per cent responded that they chose company interests, only 15.6 per cent replied that they chose personal ethics, and the other 42.2 per cent answered, 'It depends on the situation' (Nakano, 1997, p. 7). These findings imply that, for Japanese managers, the company provides their primary framework for their ethical decision-making. It follows that Japanese corporations can help managers to make ethical decisions and can reduce their unethical decisions by incorporating ethical values into their organisation.

Consumer perspective — The Japanese consumer marketing is undergoing a significant change, which has a strong impact on the ethical product and consumption process in Japan. The economic boom or the bubble economy in the 1980s led to a movement from 'active' consumption (i.e. materialism) towards 'steady' consumption (Erffmeyer, Keillor, & LeClair, 1999). 'Steady' modern Japanese consumers see themselves as constructive members of society and as having an improved quality of life, rather than focusing on materialistic things. The Japanese culture — including Confucianism, Shintoism and Buddhism — is transcendental in nature. This transcendentalism affects Japanese working ethics, with an emphasis on groups. In the group environment, a group is regarded as superior to its individuals. Kyosei, which is related to Confucianism, emerged as a significant impact on organisational conduct in Japan (Boardman & Kato, 2003). Kyosei supports the right of businesses to make a profit as long as this is obtained by just and fair means. Japanese consumers, unlike those of other developed nations, are almost exclusively identified with one single ethnic group. This Shinto-based culture emphasises the individual's responsibility to the group, including family, employer and society at large. This culture movement in Japan suggests that the Japanese are moving back to a more traditional role of individual responsibility within society, tending to possess a set of relatively rigid ethical standards. The second impact of the economic recession in the early 1990s was that Japanese consumers are also becoming more price sensitive. Thus, consumers tend to be more reluctant to accept unfair prices.

Fair trade issue in Japan — The fair trade market in Japan is at a turning point for growth and development. According to the Institute for International Trade and Investment's (ITI) survey on Japan, the Japanese fair trade market size grew steadily from 7.3 billion yen in 2007 to 8.1 billion yen in 2008. Licence fees paid to Fairtrade Labeled (FLJ) have kept increasing by more than 40 per cent annually since 2004 (ITI, 2009). These positive trends indicate the potential spreading of fair trade in Japan. However, compared to other developed nations, the market size for Japan is still too small. Organisations also show limited interest in fair trade compared to the worldwide attention it receives. Only around 40 companies in Japan have entered the fair trade market with the licensees of FLJ. Moreover, in the USA and other most European countries, more than 80 per cent of consumers are aware of fair trade (GMO Japan Market Intelligence, 2011), while in Japan only a limited number of consumers are aware of it. A report by GMO Research, an online market research firm, shows that compared with Korea and Taiwan, Japan's awareness level remained lowest. Specifically, over 50 per cent of respondents said, 'I have not heard of fair trade.' Regarding to the question of 'What fair trade products in the lists do you know?', nearly 60 per cent of the respondents said, 'No idea about specific fair trade products' (GMO Japan Market Intelligence, 2011). This low awareness among consumers is mainly due to poor media coverage and the lack of support from central authorities.

South Korea

Economic environment — Known as one of the four big dragons in Southeast Asia since the 1980s, South Korea has undergone dramatic economic growth. South

Korea's GDP in 2005 was the third largest economy in Asia. In 1996, South Korea joined the Organisation for Economic Co-operation and Development (OECD), well known as the 'rich man's club'. However, the economic crisis one year later in 1997 plunged South Korea into economic recession, and it sought a record of US$58 billion emergency rescue fund from the International Monetary Fund (IMF) and the World Bank (Alfaro & Kim, 2007). South Korea has been one of the fastest-growing OECD-member countries. The nation made successful reforms to the financial market, labour market and intellectual property rights.

Management culture — Kibun is one of the most important key aspects of Korean culture that significantly influences business practices in South Korea. *Kibun* refers to a mood or feeling of balance and good behaviour (Chaney & Martin, 2011). Another key aspect of South Korea business culture is *Inhwa*, defined as harmony. As a collectivist society, South Korea put an important weight on *Inhwa* from Confucian beliefs, emphasising harmony between people, and in society as a whole. The impact of this culture on South Korean business manifests especially in decision-making and negotiations. Specifically, South Koreans take longer to make a final decision, because all of the members need to consider others' opinions and values. The decision is based on the careful consideration of the interests of the whole team, while at the same time maintaining the stable *Kibun* environment.

Furthermore, integral to Korean economic development is a particular management system, the *Chaebol*. This is the family-founded, owned and controlled large business grouping with a range of diverse subsidiaries. For example, Samsung is the oldest *Chaebol*; it started as a trading company in 1938, and developed from fruit and sundry goods exporting into the electronics industry. The organisational culture of Korean companies is perceived as more collectivist than Western ones but more individualistic than Japanese ones (Warner, 2013). South Korean organisations are generally much more aware of ethical issues than they were years ago. The number of companies producing ethical reports increased from 11 per cent in 2005 to 42 per cent in 2008.

Consumer perspective — Today's South Korean consumer, who is interested in new and different experiences, is a sophisticated mixture of traditional culture and values with global influences. This characteristic has the potential to provide a major contribution to the improvement of marketing ethics in South Korea. With higher education rates, increases in income and improved living standards, South Korean consumers are also increasingly searching for high-quality products. But although economic development and globalisation have led to an increase in consumer expectation of business ethics, Korean consumers are still not aware of ethical issues in regard to consumption and marketing activities (Wesley, Lee, & Kim, 2012).

Advertising issue in South Korea — Advertising to children has been the subject of considerable concern for public in South Korea. For example, TV food advertisements have a noticeable impact on the incidence of obesity. In South Korea, childhood obesity rates have doubled every year since 1998 (up to 2008). In 2008, the number increased to 13.7 per cent for boys and 7.5 per cent for girls (Moon, 2013). Several studies on TV food advertising in South Korea showed that TV food advertisements aired during children's prime time are dominated by energy-dense and nutrient-poor (EDNP) foods, thus leading to consumption of such foods (Kim et al., 2012). In recent years, public demand for regulations targeting food advertisements has increased dramatically in South Korea. Therefore, the Special Act finally went into effect in 2010, restricting marketing activities for food products containing high levels of fat, sugar, salt and calories. The regulations are intended to target children aged 4–18 years, and restrict the TV advertising of EDNP foods to between 5pm and 7pm.

E-commerce consumer protection in South Korea – In 2007, the total number of Internet users in South Korea was nearly 30 million, accounting for 65 per cent of the population (ITU, 2013). According to the KRNIC 2001 report, which surveyed a total of 125 companies, 107 companies (86 per cent) were identified as having privacy policies (Ministry of Commerce, Industry and Energy Republic of Korea, 2012). Among them, 106 companies (98 per cent) have stated their policies on their websites, with many claiming their commitment of keeping confidential all private information collected. However, when asked whether they had announced changes in their policies regarding protection of privacy, only 33 companies (35 per cent) answered affirmatively. As a result, consumers would find it difficult to keep track of changes in their rights and responsibilities as regards private information in the possession of companies. Thus there are still significant shortcomings in privacy protection and associated rights.

In recent years, the Korean government has observed this shortcoming and started to establish and enforce various acts and regulations, covering issues such as consumer protection and electronic payments. The specific rules include requirements to:

- use order forms that enable consumers to change or confirm their order before validation;
- provide consumers with information about the seller (which should also be available on the seller's website) and about available dispute resolution mechanisms;
- protect consumers' personal information disclosed within the context of the payment process (ITU, 2013).

These rules aim to protect consumers' basic rights and interests relating to e-commerce, and clarify the legal effect of transactions by means of electronic messages to ensure online security and reliability. As a result, in 2011, Korea recorded a trade surplus in e-commerce of US$75 billion, occupying 8 per cent of its domestic GDP for that year (Korea Association for ICT Promotion, 2012).

New research directions

Since the 1990s, a series of studies have paid much attention to corporate managers' perception of business ethics in various countries (e.g. Ford & Richardson, 1994). The field of marketing ethics also experienced a dramatic rise of knowledge during these years (e.g. Gaski, 1999; Smith, 2001). Much progress has been made in achieving a better understanding of marketers' major issues, their personal values, their ethical decision-making process and cross-cultural issues. However, both the ethics of marketing itself and ethical theorising about marketing need further investigation in a number of different directions. The call for more work on ethical marketing is required not only from an academic point of view but also from a practitioner's perspective.

1. In terms of specific ethical topics, there is a lack of research concerning marketing ethics under the influences of new technology innovations. With the various technological innovations in marketing practices, consumers' ethical issues over purchasing (such as privacy, theft, online auctions or hacking) would increase. So, the first question for both marketing academia and practitioners is: what ethical restrictions should marketers adopt in response to the ways in which they should reach customers and how much should they know about the customers they seek to reach? There is also a void of ethics research in pricing, including price gouging, price discrimination and prestige pricing. Perhaps more research in this area is warranted.

2. Further development of the literature should involve continued studies to develop normative ethics that are realistic to apply to practical situations. In particular, the theories of marketing ethics should be expanded to be relevant to questions about marketing ethics.

3. Although there are a number of cross-culture studies investigating the influences of culture values on marketing activities, there is a lack of interest in the examination of other factors among different nations, as well as a lack of interest in evaluating the differences of marketing strategies among these nations. With the increasing impact of globalisation, companies' product development, pricing strategies and advertising programmes will increase intensively. Thus a new direction for future research is to compare and contrast the beliefs and practices of a wide spectrum of culturally diverse managers and companies, and to investigate the factors that influence the ethical propriety of products made, the prices charged, and the ways in which these products are advertised and promoted.

4. Marketing ethicists have tended to focus on the ethical decision-making of individual managers in marketing. However, there is a limited amount of macro-research in marketing ethics. Marketing is also an important aspect of society, and future research should pay more attention to the ethical issues of marketing as an institution in society.

Practising ethical marketing: China, Taiwan, Japan and South Korea

Existing studies have made significant progress in conceptualising ethical marketing, and these findings have elevated the understanding of the ethical implications of marketing practices. First, marketers should learn how to integrate ethics into planning and strategy formulation processes. Ethics should be coordinated throughout the whole marketing process, from product development (e.g. avoiding potentially dangerous, malfunctioning and/or environmentally harmful products, and using quality assurance), setting price schemes (e.g. not engaging in price fixing, predatory pricing or price gouging), developing advertising and promotion strategies (ensuring that marketing communications about products are not intentionally deceptive and misleading) and choosing places to launch products (e.g. protect consumers' personal information online).

Second, understanding consumer culture and their perceptions of marketing ethics motivates marketing managers to establish codes of ethics based on consumer evaluations. Marketing strategies should be aligned with consumer culture values and variations in consumers' ethical evaluations of marketing practices for different marketing segments (e.g. children, the elderly, women). For example, Victoria's Secret's campaign, which featured underwear printed with flirty terms such as 'call me' and 'feeling lucky', was perceived by parents of teenage girls as sexualising young girls (Pan, 2013).

Third, the increasing diversity of the international marketplace has significant and complex implications for marketing practices. In the past, multinational corporations experienced ethical dilemmas with their marketing strategies in other countries. For example, the French retailer Carrefour entered China in 1995, and in 2011 it was accused by China's National Development and Reform Commission of overcharging customers in 11 of its stores (Enderle & Niu, 2012). Specifically, Carrefour used normal prices as sales prices, misleading customers with price figures. As a result, the stores were fined up to US$79,365, the highest ever fine of its sort imposed in China. Thus, how the local communities of the global marketplace evaluate the marketing practices of multinational companies has become an important subject of marketers.

Practice case study

Da Vinci furniture scandal in China

As China has become the world's manufacturing house, there are 'made in China' products all around the world. However, in recent years Chinese consumers have been increasingly interested in buying products from developed countries, or from global brands. This trend was witnessed by Da Vinci, a Singapore-founded and Shanghai-based high-end luxury furniture company in China. Among other luxury brands, it sells Versace Home, Fendi Casa, Kenzo Maison and Cerruti products to wealthy Chinese consumers. A silk-covered couch, for instance, is priced at nearly 110,000 yuan (or US$16,975, as of 2014). The company claimed that its products were all made in Italy and manufactured of rare wood. However, in 2011 the CCTV's Weekly Quality Report programme claimed that, after six months of underground investigation, CCTV reporters found counterfeit furniture in Da Vinci sold as 'made in Italy', but in fact made in China (Rein, 2011). The reporters discovered that a brand of Da Vinci furniture labelled 'made in Italy' was actually made in a factory in Dongguan, Guangdong Province in China. These products were then transported to the Waigaoqiao Bonded Zone before being stored in the company's Shanghai warehouse. Shanghai Customs announced that about 3.5 per cent of Da Vinci's claimed imported products in 2011 were originally made in China. Moreover, some furniture claimed to be made of rare wood was actually made from polymer and other chemicals. The situation caused uproar among

Chinese consumers and became a media circus after the CCTV report. The scandal led to a significant decline in the company's product sales.

Lack of corporate governance, transparency and ethical decision-making were the main issues underlying the Da Vinci scandal. Instead of working towards producing good-quality and honestly labelled products, Da Vinci ignored truthfulness in its product labelling and did not take steps to highlight the situation to consumers. After the media exposure, Doris Phua, founder and CEO of Da Vinci, made a speech giving weak excuses of her misconduct. This stirred up heated discussion among the public about blaming Da Vinci for bribery and counterfeiting.

As consumers become hypersensitive about company's unethical behaviours, managers should build trust with consumers. Deception (e.g. in labelling) can only work as long as people believe what they are being told. As 'ethical and honest communication' is required of both the message and messenger, a misleading message can shed negative light on the messenger and potentially disqualify them as a future supplier.

Further investigation

- *Ethics*: What is (or should be) the role of marketing ethics in marketing systems in China, Taiwan, Japan and South Korea? What are (or should be) the ethical implications for marketers' abilities to solve ethical problems?
- *Ethical issues*: What are the important issues that marketers face now in China, Taiwan, Japan and South Korea? Why have these issues developed?
- *Cross-cultural ethical dilemmas*: How are marketers making (or how should they make) ethical decisions across countries? What drives the decision-making process?
- *Ethical solutions*: What should marketers do when they face ethical issues? How should they change their strategies in order to regain consumer confidence?
- *Consumer-related ethical issues*: What are the ethical decision-making styles of consumers? What are the effects of consumers' ethical perceptions on marketers?
- *Practical ethical issues*: How does marketing ethics theory apply to marketing practices?

References

Alfaro, L., & Kim, R. (2007). *Transforming Korea Inc: Financial crisis and institutional reform*. Harvard, MA: Harvard Business Publishing.
Ardichvili, A., Jondle, D., & Kowske, B. (2009). *Dimensions of Ethical Business Cultures: Comparing Data from 13 Countries of Europe, Asia, and the Americas*. 10th International Conference on Human Resource Development Research and Practice across Europe. Newcastle, 10–12 June.
Boardman, C. M., & Kato, H. K. (2003). The confucian roots of business Kyosei. *Journal of Business Ethics, 48*, 317–325.
Chaney, L. H., & Martin, J. S. (2011). *Intercultural business communication* (4th ed.). Upper Saddle River, NJ: Pearson Prentice Hall.
Chen, Y., & Chang, C. (2013). Greenwash and green trust: The mediation effects of green consumer confusion and green perceived risk. *Journal of Business Ethics, 114*(3), 489–500.

Choi, T. H., & Nakano, C. (2008). The evolution of business ethics in Japan and Korea over the last decade. *Human Systems Management, 27,* 183–199.

Chung, K., Eichenseher, J., & Taniguchi, T. (2008). Ethical perceptions of business students: Differences between East Asia and the USA and among 'Confucian' cultures. *Journal of Business Ethics, 79,* 121–132.

Consumer Protection Committee, Executive Yuan. (2011). Annual Report of the Policy Evaluation 2010. Available from <http://www.cpc.ey.gov.tw> Accessed 02.01.14.

Enderle, G., & Niu, Q. (2012). Discerning ethical challenges for marketing in China. *Asian Journal of Business Ethics, 1,* 143–162.

Erffmeyer, R. C., Keillor, B. D., & LeClair, D. T. (1999). An empirical investigation of Japanese consumer ethics. *Journal of Business Ethics, 18,* 35–50.

Ferrell, O. C., & Gresham, L. G. (1985). A contingency framework for understanding ethical decision making in marketing. *Journal of Business Research, 49,* 87–96.

Ferrell, O. C., Gresham, L. G., & Fraedrich, J. (1989). A synthesis of ethical decision models for marketing. *Journal of Macromarketing, 9,* 55–64.

Ford, R. C., & Richardson, W. D. (1994). Ethical decision making: A review of the empirical literature. *Journal of Business Ethics, 13,* 205–221.

Fritzsche, D. J. (1997). *Business ethics: A global and managerial perspective.* Pennsylvania, USA: McGraw-Hill Companies, Inc.

Gabriel, R. M. (2008). The patent revolution: Proposed reforms in Chinese intellectual property law, policy, and practice are the latest step to bolster patent protection in China. *Asian-Pacific Law & Policy Journal, 9,* 323–355.

Gao, Z. (2005). Harmonious regional advertising regulation? A comparative examination of government advertising regulation in China, Hong Kong, and Taiwan. *Journal of Advertising, 34,* 75–87.

Gaski, J. (1999). Does marketing ethics really have anything to say? A critical inventory of the literature. *Journal of Business Ethics, 18,* 315–334.

GMO Japan Market Intelligence. (2011). A survey of fairtrade: A overview of multinational survey in leading. Three East Asian Countries (regions). Available from <http://www.gmo-jmi.jp> Accessed 12.01.14.

Goodpurpose. (2012). Introducing: Goodpurpose 2012. Available from <http://purpose.edelman.com/slides/introducing-goodpurpose-2012> Accessed 20.12.13.

Harvey, B. (1999). ' Graceful merchants': A contemporary view of Chinese business ethics. *Journal of Business Ethics, 20,* 85–92.

Hsu, C., Zhang, W., & Lok, L. (2007). *Business and investment environment in Taiwan and Mainland China: A focus on the IT and high-tech electronic industries.* River Edge, NJ: World Scientific Publishing Co.

Hunt, S. D., & Vitell, S. (1986). A general theory of marketing ethics. *Journal of Macromarketing, 6,* 5–15.

Institute for International trade and Investment (ITI). (2009). Fair Trade Market Survey Report 2008. Available from <http://www.european-fair-trade-association.org/efta/Doc/FT-in-Japan2008.pdf> Accessed 02.01.14.

ITU. (2013). Regulation and consumer protection in a converging environment. Available from <https://www.itu.int/ITU-D/finance/Studies/consumer_protection.pdf> Accessed 20.01.14.

Juang, C. T. (1997). The Taiwan consumer protection law: Attempt to protect consumers proves ineffective. *Pacific Rim Law & Policy Journal, 6,* 219–243.

Kangun, N. (1972). Introduction. In N. Kangun (Ed.), *Society and marketing: An unconventional view, 2–4.* New York: Harper & Row.

Kim, S., Lee, Y., Yoon, J., Chung, S. J., Lee, S. K., & Kim, H. (2012). Restriction of television food advertising in South Korea: Impact on advertising of food companies. *Health Promotion International*, *28*, 17−25.

Knouse, S. B., & Giacalone, R. A. (1992). Ethical decision-making in business: Behavioral issues and concern. *Journal of Business Ethics*, *11*, 369.

Korea Association for ICT Promotion. (2012). *E-Commerce in Korea*. 10th World Telecommunication/ICT Indicators Meeting, Bangkok, Thailand, 25−27 September.

Kuntz, J. R. C., Kuntz, J. R., Elenkov, D., & Nabirukhina, A. (2013). Characterizing ethical cases: A cross-cultural investigation of individual differences, organizational climate, and leadership on ethical decision-making. *Journal of Business Ethics*, *113*, 317−331.

Levy, S. J., & Zaltman, G. (1975). *Marketing, society and conflict*. Englewood Cliffs, NJ: Prentice Hall.

Liu, H., & Chen, S. (2012). *The Wowprime Corp.: The owner of multiple restaurant brands in Taiwan*. London, Ontario: Richard Ivey School of Business.

Liu, M. (1999). The interpretation and regulation of false promotion activities. (In Chinese.). *Administration of Industry and Commerce*, *99*, 30−31.

Lu, X. (2009). A Chinese perspective: Business ethics in China now and in the future. *Journal of Business Ethics*, *86*, 451−461.

Malhotra, N. K., & Miller, G. L. (1998). An integrated model for ethical decisions in marketing research. *Journal of Business Ethics*, *17*, 263−280.

McGuire, J., & Dow, S. (2008). Japanese Keiretsu: Past, present, future. . *Asia Pacific Journal of Management*, *26*, 333.

Ministry of Commerce, Industry and Energy Republic of Korea. (2012). E-commerce in South Korea. Available from <http://unpan1.un.org/intradoc/groups/public/documents/apcity/unpan007638.pdf> Accessed 10.01.14.

Moon, Y. S. (2013). Examination of health messages in food advertising: A case of South Korea. *Journal of Food Products Marketing*, *19*, 387−405.

Murphy, P. E., Laczniak, G. R., Bowie, N. E., & Klein, T. A. (2005). *Ethical marketing*. Upper Saddle River, NJ: Pearson Prentice-Hall.

Nakano, C. (1997). A survey study on Japanese managers' views of business ethics. *Journal of Business Ethics*, *16*, 1737−1751.

Nill, A., & Schibrowsky, J. A. (2007). Research on marketing ethics: A systematic review of the literature. *Journal of Macromarketing*, *27*, 256−273.

Pan, A. (2013). Victoria's Secret PINK and its Ethics Challenge. Available from <http://buytheway.uscannenberg.org/victorias-secret-pink-and-its-ethics-challenge> Accessed 10.01.14.

Pollay, R. W., Tse, D. K., & Wang, Z. Y. (1990). Advertising, propaganda, and value change in economic development: The new cultural revolution in China and attitudes toward advertising. *Journal of Business Research*, *20*, 83−95.

Ramasamy, B., Yeung, M. C. H., & Chen, J. (2013). Selling to the urban Chinese in East Asia: Do CSR and value orientation matter? *Journal of Business Research*, *66*, 2485−2491.

Rein, S. (2011). China furniture scandal has important lessons for foreign brands. Available from <http://www.cnbc.com/id/43803551> Accessed 09.01.14.

Schlegelmilch, B. B., & Oberseder, M. (2010). Half a century of marketing ethics: Shifting perspectives and emerging trends. *Journal of Business Ethics*, *93*, 1−19.

Smith, C. (2001). Ethical guidelines for marketing practice: A reply to Gaski and some observations on the role of normative ethics. *Journal of Business Ethics*, *32*, 3−18.

Trevino, L. K. (1986). Ethical decision making in organizations: A person-situation interactionist model. *Academy of Management Review, 11*, 601–617.

Tsalikis, J., Seaton, B., & Li, T. (2008). The international business ethics index: Asian emerging economies. *Journal of Business Ethics, 80*, 643–651.

Warner, M. (2013). *Managing across diverse cultures in East Asia*. London: Routledge.

Watson, V.M. (2013). Food Safety and China: Scandal and Consequence. Available from <http://www.worldpolicy.org/blog/2013/08/07/food-safety-and-china-scandal-and-consequence> Accessed 29.12.13.

Wesley, S., Lee, M., & Kim, E. (2012). The role of perceived consumer effectiveness and motivational attitude in socially responsible purchasing behavior in South Korea. *Journal of Global Marketing, 25*, 29–44.

World Bank. (2014) China [ONLINE] Available at <http://search.worldbank.org/all? qterm=china&op=> Accessed 31.07.14.

Wright, P. C., Szeto, W. F., & Cheng, L. T. W. (2002). Guanxi and professional conduct in China: A management development perspective. *International Journal of Human Resource Management, 13*, 156–182.

Yang, M. M. (2002). Rebuttal: The resilience of guanxi and its new deployments: A critique of some new guanxi scholarship. *The China Quarterly, 170*, 459–476.

Further reading

Lund, D. (2000). An empirical examination of marketing professionals' ethical behaviour in differing situations. *Journal of Business Ethics, 24*, 331–342.

Murphy, P., Laczniak, G. R., Bowie, N. E., & Klein, T. A. (2005). *Ethical marketing*. Upper Saddle River, NJ: Prentice Hall.

Nill, A. (2003). Global marketing ethics: a communicative approach. *Journal of Macromarketing, 23*, 90–105.

Ethical marketing: Singapore, Malaysia and Thailand

Bang Nguyen, Cheng-Hao Steve Chen, Meng-Shan Sharon Wu and T.C. Melewar

Introduction

This chapter considers ethical marketing in Singapore, Malaysia and Thailand. The three countries are greatly diversified in many aspects, and have separate ethical concerns, which are explored. For example, current examples of how ethical marketing has influenced consumers' perceptions in this region include issues such as bribery, the mass influx of global brands and how luxury fashion goods may polarise social classes. By integrating a country-branding framework into our chapter, the aim is to enable readers to comprehend how firms organise and manage ethical marketing in different parts of this region. Specifically, the chapter examines the difference in issues addressed by ethical marketing campaigns, and presents examples of both branding and ethical marketing cases and research in relation to Singapore, Malaysia and Thailand. Furthermore, the chapter presents important aspects of both consumers' and firms' decision-making processes, influencing ethical marketing. Theories on ethical marketing are reviewed and extant research is presented.

The chapter incorporates the definition of ethical marketing as the application of marketing ethics in the marketing process. It refers to the philosophical examination, from a moral standpoint, of particular marketing issues that are matters of moral judgment and may result in a more socially responsible and culturally sensitive business community. The establishment of marketing ethics has great benefits for society as a whole, both in the short and long term. Ethical marketing should be part of business ethics in the sense that ethical marketing forms a significant part of any business model, involving the examination of whether or not an honest and factual representation of a company, product or service has been delivered in a framework of cultural and social values.

Learning objectives

After reading this chapter, you should be able to:

- understand the importance of country-branding;
- outline the way in which ethics permeate the country-branding framework, specifically for Singapore, Malaysia and Thailand;
- demonstrate how to organise and manage ethical marketing in different parts of this region; and
- apply the concepts of country-branding and ethical marketing in a case study.

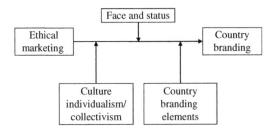

Figure 3.1 A conceptual model of country branding with an ethical perspective.

Route map

Figure 3.1 shows our framework for the present chapter. This framework, which illustrates the key role of ethical marketing in country branding, introduces a number of different points to consider, including face and status, collectivism and individualism, and other branding elements, as detailed in the subsequent sections. Therefore, the framework explains the role of ethical marketing interventions in the wider country-branding context, and their inter-relationships.

The state of the art in ethical marketing: Singapore, Malaysia and Thailand

Taking a branding perspective, the present chapter focuses on country branding and incorporates ethical issues into the overall framework. This adds a new perspective to both brand management and ethical marketing management. Country branding is gaining popularity among academicians and practitioners alike (e.g. Anholt, 2006; Dinnie, 2004). Many countries engage in branding and rebranding (Gudjonsson, 2005), as they recognise that a favourable country brand attracts tourists, investors, media and potential citizens to their country (Gertner & Kotler, 2004). Scholars regard country branding as a strategic positioning tool to enhance a country's economic, political and social conditions (Domeisen, 2003; Papadopoulos, 2004), and a critical element towards achieving a competitive advantage in today's marketplace (Kubacki & Skinner, 2006). Existing literature, however, emphasises country branding from varying macro-economic views, with little attention given to country branding from an ethical marketing perspective among its own citizens and firms. Even less research takes an ethical marketing perspective in the country-branding frameworks of Singapore, Malaysia and Thailand. To form successful country brands, these countries must be both competitive in retaining and enhancing resources, and viewed by their stakeholders as places with opportunities to exercise their skills and interests (Kotler, 2004). It is crucial for a country to have high standards of ethics and morality, which create supportive and proud citizens, companies and consumers. These stakeholders are a reflection of the country brand (Blichfeldt, 2005), and their views towards ethical issues may be the foundation to achieve such a well-regarded country brand.

While extensive research has shown the influence of ethics on marketing, relatively few studies exist in relation to the areas of ethical and brand management specifically, and very few studies are published on ethical marketing from the perspectives of Singapore, Malaysia and Thailand. Most known materials are published case studies, which are not systematically researched using academic frameworks from the theoretical literature. In the present chapter, we therefore lay out our presentation as follows:

- First, we review the most important country branding constructs and add an ethical marketing perspective, before examining ethical marketing cases as part of the wider country-branding framework.
- Next, we systematically focus on cultural and local issues, which permeate each of the three countries, and address how these issues can be influenced by the use of ethical marketing.
- Finally, we conclude with a framework for managing brands and ethical marketing in this diversified region.

Country-branding framework: an ethical perspective

Researchers define 'country branding' as the use of a country's image, products and attractiveness to promote different aspects related to a country's identity, in order to appeal to tourists and foreign direct investors (e.g. Anholt, 2005a, 2005b). Country branding concerns attitudes and perceptions towards its goods and services (Idris & Arai, 2006). It is an effective platform that influences its country's brands' ability to compete in global marketplaces (Gudjonsson, 2005). For example, the country of origin, design or manufacture is known to give rise to certain country-of-origin (COO) associations in consumers' minds (Aaker, 1991; Gurhan-Canli & Maheswaran, 2000), and a common theme among country-branding definitions rests on image building (Keller, 1993). Country-of-origin refers to the economic status of the country (macro effect) or products produced in the country (micro effect). Keller (1993) proposes that country image is similar to brand image, which carries a set of country-of-origin connections, categorised into groups. In addition, many scholars note that a country's image consists of composite elements such as history, geography, industry, culture, media, tourism, art and music, famous citizens and commercial products (Kotler & Gertner, 2002; Kubacki & Skinner, 2006).

There are many definitions of the COO effect. According to Gurhan-Canli and Maheswaran (2000, p. 309): 'COO effects refer to the extent to which the place of manufacture influences product evaluation.' In other words, COO can be translated as 'made in' (Johansson, 1989; Peterson & Joilbert, 1995). From a marketing point of view, Martin, Wailee, and Lacey (2011) perceive COO as embedding this phenomenon into the brand name or slogan, or using specific pictures that could immediately be associated with a company's image. Moreover, Lee and Lee (2009) agree that COO is highly influenced by national ethnocentrism, which may lead to a negative judgment of imported goods based on customers' subjective knowledge of the product. Arguably, Hamzaoui and Merunka (2006) pinpoint the importance of country of design (COD) and country of manufacture (COM) as the main indicators in purchasing behaviour. According to these researchers, multinational products cause several problems, such as consumer confusion during purchase, as these products are associated not only with COD (where the product was established) but also with varying COM connotations (the 'made in' effect) about where they have been manufactured. However, despite this issue being of such great importance, very little material exists on countries' branding links with ethical marketing.

Researchers identify multiple dimensions of country branding through indexes and models (e.g. Gudjonsson, 2005). For instance, the Nation Brands Index captures six dimensions of national competence, including: export, governance, investment and immigration, cultural and heritage, people, and tourism (Anholt, 2005a). The Fombrun-RI Country Reputation Index (CRI) measures six dimensions of country branding, which are: emotional, physical, financial, leadership, cultural and social (Passow, Fehlmann, & Grahlow, 2005). The National Brand Pentagon is a model used by Taiwan for their advertisement campaigns focusing on tourism, exports brands, foreign policy, investment and culture (Amine & Chao, 2005). In similar campaigns, Sweden's National Brand Hexagons emphasises tourism, exports brands, foreign and domestic policies, investment, culture and heritage, and people. Che, Yahya, Nguyen, Melewar, and Chen (2014) assert four core dimensions to explain country branding: tourism branding, public diplomacy, export promotion and investment promotion activities. These include a blend of theory and practice. Finally, Johansson (2005) stresses that a country brand is at least a mixture of six components, which include a country's export, government policy, citizen, investment and talent, cultural exports and tourist experience. Table 3.1 presents the differences between country branding and commercial branding, categorised under five features: offer attributes, benefit image association, purpose, dimension and ownership audience.

Based on the above indexes and models, and following previous studies (Anholt, 2005a; Che Ha et al., 2014; Kotler & Gertner, 2002; Kubacki & Skinner, 2006; Passow et al., 2005), we include eight elements to best describe the country branding of Singapore, Malaysia and Thailand. Our framework comprises:

- physical
- human capital;
- export
- investment
- FDI (foreign direct investment);
- culture and heritage;
- social;
- political; and
- ethical.

We integrate these variables in a multidimensional country-branding framework and view them as significant constructs for branding a country. We believe that ethical issues permeate all the dimensions, but at the same time, the role of ethics is so important that we included it as a separate dimension. Our framework has important implications for tourism marketers, policymakers, brand managers and ethical stakeholders due to our

Table 3.1 Comparison between country branding and commercial branding

	Nation brand	Product brand	Corporate brand
Offer attributes	• Nothing on offer • Too complicated to define in simple terms	• A product or service on offer • Clearly defined	• Related to the product or sector • Well defined
Benefits of image association	• Purely emotional • Complicated, diverse, vague • Secondary, numerous and diverse	• Functional and emotional • Simple, clear • Primary and secondary, relatively fewer and more specific	• Mainly emotional • Simple, visible or hidden • Mainly secondary, fewer and specific
Purpose	• To enhance a nation's reputation	• To help sales and develop relationship	• To enhance reputation and develop relationships
Dimension	• Political, economic, social and cultural	• Mainly economic	• Economic and social
Ownership audience	• Multiple stakeholders, unclear • International, diverse, 'significant others'	• Sole owner • Targeted segment	• Sole owner • General public or target

analysis of consumers' underlying perceptions and preferences. In the next section, we briefly present each of the country branding elements in relation to ethical marketing.

1. *Physical* refers to a country's geography. Attributes include nature, climate, position, cities, residents, infrastructures, disasters and richness in natural beauty. The role of ethics in the physical realm may come in various forms, including ethical concerns about environmental sustainability, and the preservation of forests and nature.
2. *Human capital* is (if properly utilised and capitalised) the most powerful communication tool in branding a country. People act as ambassadors and create positive images for their country. Citizens' ethical concerns about a country and their high level of awareness regarding ethical issues are often favourably viewed by stakeholders, such as investors and tourists. Where citizens are concerned about ethics and moral responsibilities, it may be suggested that a better country brand and image are evident. These citizens may foster more and more fair trade, ethical consumption, social responsibility towards child labour, working conditions and sustainability, to name a few issues.
3. *Exporting* brands is a powerful approach to building a country image, as they generate positive associations among consumers, representing exceptionality and appealing features for the country of origin. Export brands thus say something about 'what the country is famous for' (Papadopoulos, 2004). For countries like Singapore, Malaysia and Thailand, which are known for (among other things) food, tourism and diversified citizens/consumers, adding a new perspective of ethical shoppers and morality towards their exporting may greatly enhance their countries' brands.

4. *Foreign direct investment (FDI)* creates a multitude of advantages by bringing technology, employment, increased quality standards, a flow of skilled and knowledgeable employees, increased interactions between countries, and other advances and innovations. With more focus on ethical business and marketing that leads to ethical shoppers and citizens, ethics (if used more systematically) may provide a source of differentiation for any country's branding efforts. By focusing on ethics, countries will convey the messages of reliability, honesty, trust and fairness — elements that investors may strongly consider when settling and investing in a country.

5. *Culture and heritage* exist in all aspects of economics, management, politics and psychology, among others. They are uniquely connected to the country's past and present, and the spiritual and intellectual qualities of its people and institutions. A country with a heritage and culture of unethical business practices, such as bribery and corruption, or child labour, is often at a disadvantage when it comes to attracting investors and tourists. Corruption is a particular problem in many Asian countries, creating inequalities among citizens. The research on cultural influence on ethics is extensive, and encompasses diverse issues such as the setting of ethical or unethical prices, social concerns, the use of sex in advertising, and moral judgment. Later in the chapter we shall focus on several aspects including the roles of collectivism, status and face in Singapore, Malaysia and Thailand.

6. *Social* refers to support and attention concerning social or environmental issues. By using environmental causes and social marketing to promote their social responsibility, countries are able to gain goodwill and win public attention and global support. Indeed, the relationship between social and ethical concerns is close and somewhat interrelated. The greater the focus on socially and ethically responsible marketing, the more goodwill and better reputation the country may enjoy. Consequently, both social and ethical marketing must be used together in order to form a significant business model for any country's branding efforts.

7. *Politics* are important for understanding a country's culture, government and social system. Politics affect all levels across a country's image, and political issues deeply affect citizens' daily lives. The role of ethics in politics is crucial, inasmuch as that without ethics, the political system would not gain citizens' trust, and thus would not work. Ethical concerns in politics cover issues of bribery, corruption and lack of morality. The establishment of ethical marketing in politics has the potential to benefit society as a whole, in both the short and the long term — for example, by increasing fair legal systems and supporting causes that include the reduction of energy consumption and waste. As a result, the country's brand may be improved.

8. *Ethical* (new dimension) — Taken together with the above issues, we offer a new dimension of country branding: the ethical dimension. This dimension refers to the application of ethics into the country branding and marketing processes. It promotes a socially responsible and culturally sensitive business community, so that a product or service can be trusted and delivered through a framework of cultural and social values. There are many qualitative benefits to customers, which companies providing products or services may not have previously recognised. The concerns with ethical issues — such as child labour, work environment, relationships with third-world countries and environmental problems — have encouraged Western attitudes into a more socially responsible way of thinking. This has influenced companies, and their response is often to market their products in a more socially responsible way. For example, in Western countries, the increasing trend of fair trade is an example of the impact of ethical marketing. In the 'Ethical Shoppers Price Index Survey' (2014), fair trade was the most popular ethical badge that products could have. However, the survey also revealed that many consumers distrusted claims of green behaviour and fairness.

With the ethical dimension permeating other aspects of country branding and a strong focus on ethics itself, countries may reinforce the positive values of the country brand, creating a strong citizen brand. The challenges are many, the most prevalent being to ensure that the development of products can add long-term benefits without reducing the products' desirable qualities. Research shows that consumers are less trusting of ethical claims in advertisements. Media focus on ethics has resulted in many top brands suffering consumer boycotts. Thus, country branding that centres on ethics may also need careful attention. Although many brands have tried to use green issues, it has been noted in research that two-thirds of consumers responded more to ethical claims that relate to people than to the environment. A government should adopt ethical branding in their regulations as a legal remedy intended to mitigate or correct an ethical issue, such as air pollution. This, in turn, may lead to an 'enlightened ethical marketing' approach, which encourages stakeholders to recognise further improvements for humankind unrelated to those enforced by governments or public opinion. By way of example, the Co-operative Group refuses to invest money in tobacco, fur or any countries with oppressive regimes.

Cross-cultural marketing: the role of face, status and collectivism

In the next section, we further develop our framework by presenting the underlying cultural issues, which permeate the way country branding and ethical marketing are perceived and managed in Singapore, Malaysia and Thailand. The focus is on collectivism (and individualism), the role of face, and status.

The key to successful international marketing lies in the localisation of marketing strategies to fit cultural characteristics of their customers, even for selling the same products (Aaker & Williams, 1998). For example, Coca-Cola adapted more happiness-arousal adverts to Singaporean customers but more sex-arousal adverts to their Thai customers. Marketers who know their customers' cultures and norms gain greater advantage, because they are viewed as sensitive and supportive of the local culture and customs. To achieve such an advantage in Singapore, Malaysia and Thailand, it is imperative that marketers understand consumers' underlying cultural behaviour, including their collectivistic behaviour, concerns with face and status.

From the consumers' point of view, culture-specific values are more likely to affect their social reinforcement and different communication channels (e.g. families, friends and society). These cultural values may modify consumers' thoughts and behaviours, namely their consumer purchasing procedures, decision-making styles and psychology. In an international marketplace, the key challenge for retailers or organisations is to identify and fulfil consumers' interests and demands. This requires an understanding of consumer research and cultural models (Hofstede, Jan-Benedict, Steenkamp, & Wedel, 1999), due to two reasons: (1) consumer behaviour does not change rapidly when national borders are crossed (Farley & Lehmann, 1994); and (2) consumers who have crossed national borders might be more similar to each other than those within the same country (Hassan & Katsanis, 1994).

Scholars suggest that consumers' ethical concerns, as a function of culture, can be explained by the common assumption that differences in social relationships and self-definition guide their reactions and perceptions (Bolton, Keh, & Alba, 2010). In our country-branding framework, such differences are investigated based on the distinction between individualism/collectivism. These two variables reflect a basic cultural element in human nature, i.e. an individual's differences (independent versus interdependent), and are usually studied in anthropology, cultural psychology and international business cultures (Hofstede, 1980). Individualism suggests that everyone is expected to look after themselves and their immediate family only. It emphasises personal achievement at the expense of group goals, resulting in a strong sense of competition. This is the opposite of collectivism, which suggests that people are integrated into strong cohesive in-groups, emphasising family and work group goals above individual needs or desires. Individualism and collectivism deeply permeate cultures and, consequently, consumers' and citizens' ethical and moral judgments. The United States and Western Europe are often considered to be examples of individualist cultures, whereas China, Korea and Japan have collectivist cultures.

Between Singaporean, Malaysian and Thai populations, different levels of interpersonal connectedness exist. Singelis, Triandis, Bhawuk, and Gelfand (1995) measured the interdependent and independent self-construal through the Self-Construal Scale (SCS). The 'separateness-connectedness' dimension reflects the degree to which an individual perceives others as an extension of the self, or the self as distinct from others (Wang & Mowen, 1997). In addition, researchers explain that Singapore demonstrates more characteristics of independence (more individualism-based), whereas Malaysians and Thai people prefer more interdependent and mutually reliant characteristics (more collectivism-based) (Ang, 2000; Chang & Lu, 2007). This is supported by Hofstede's (1980) classic cross-cultural study.

Despite some criticism (Brewer & Chen, 2007), it is commonly held that the distinction attributes collectivism to Asian and individualism to Western cultures. Our chapter adopts this view to explain the behaviours of the three groups of consumers. The differences between Eastern and Western cultures are well supported. According to Markus and Kitayama (1991), Western cultures tend to define the self in terms of individual autonomy, suggesting that individuals are independent of one another. This is a contrast to Eastern cultures, which tend to define the self in terms of social connectedness, signifying a greater sensitivity to relationship context. For example, in Western culture, friends, co-workers, managers, business owners and so on are treated on an equal basis, compared to the East (here: Singapore, Thailand and Malaysia), which is more prone to a hierarchical structure (Hofstede, 1980) and more sensitive to group membership (Hui, Triandis, & Yee, 1991).

Researchers propose that the cultural distinction between individualism versus collectivism also differ in the sensitivity to the concept of 'face'. The concept of face was first introduced and discussed academically by Goffman (1955). Brown and Levinson (1987, 1978) proposed a distinction between positive and negative face, whereby a positive face value represents others' consideration and approval of an individual's demands. Face values reflect individuals' social self-esteem and the desire to be respected in social contexts (Ting-Toomey & Kurogi, 1998). Such concerns indicate that many people pay more attention to their social needs rather than their personal needs (Wong & Ahuvia, 1998). Consumers who have stronger face consciousness are more likely to attach importance to the extrinsic attributes (e.g. brand and logo) than intrinsic attributes (e.g. service and quality) of products in order to demonstrate their status, esteem and self-image (Belk, 1988; Belk & Pollay, 1985). Other scholars have indicated that in order to obtain and preserve face, consumers are willing to pay more for brand names (Li & Su, 2007). These consumers believe that a name-brand product, or a brand name with high social recognition and a high price tag, will enhance their social status and position (Tse, 1996). Some studies have examined the influence of face in Chinese consumer behaviour: *Mianzi* is a principal characteristic of the Chinese persona (Lu, 1934), which directly links with social status and the demonstration of one's wealth (Yang, 1994). These consumers are often concerned with gaining and saving face, or avoiding losing face, when they make contact with others (Hwang, 1987). More importantly, face can represent the esteemed status of self (Yang, 1994; Zhai, 2005), the importance of face value between individuals and societies (Li & Su, 2007; Zhou & Belk, 2004; Zhou & Nakamoto, 2000), the association with relatives, friends and even colleagues (Kashima et al., 1995), and the concept of social self (Hwang, 1987). These facts can be identified and described in most Chinese-oriented countries like China, Malaysia and Singapore. Ho (1976) suggests that a loss of face is associated with a loss in status, and similarly, a gain of face is a gain in status. Indeed, the concept of face is inextricably linked to status earned in a social network (Chang & Holt, 1994). Previous studies suggest that collectivist cultures are more concerned with face (e.g. Oetzel & Ting-Toomey, 2003). This is evidenced in all three countries of Singapore, Malaysia and Thailand, which are heavily influenced by Chinese ancestry and language. Collectivist cultures typically score higher on measures of face concern (Zane & Yeh, 2002) and face consciousness (Bao, Zhou, & Su, 2003). This is especially evident in interpersonal conflict settings where the Chinese have greater concern for face than those in the West (Oetzel & Ting-Toomey, 2003).

Although face is receiving greater attention in consumer behavioural research (Li & Su, 2007), research is limited in understanding the role of face with regard to ethical marketing and country branding. Our study proposes that citizens and consumers differ in their responses to ethical marketing, as a result of different concerns to face. For example, as noted by Bolton et al. (2010), Chinese consumers experience greater loss of face when paying a higher price to a vendor with whom they have a long-term relationship than to a new vendor. In an individualist culture, there is less variance in this relationship. This shows the varying differences in response to the concept of face, and should thus be considered in any country-branding strategy focusing on ethics.

Issues in ethical marketing in Singapore, Malaysia and Thailand

The importance of ethical issues in marketing heavily depends on the country and external factors. For example, in developed and Western countries, much emphasis is placed on issues such as ethical pricing, advertising, research and competitive strategies, while in developing countries, much of the ethical marketing focus centres on bribery, piracy (fake products), corruption, sweatshop working conditions and environmental damage. The countries this chapter is particularly concerned with are a mixture of developing and developed countries. Singapore may be classified as a highly developed country with an advanced economy, while Malaysia and Thailand are classified as developing countries. Each of the three countries will now be presented in detail.

Singapore

Singapore has branded itself as a financial hub, in line with New York, London and Tokyo. To compete effectively with the neighbouring countries and mega cities it is critical for those in Singapore to understand the underlying key factors for success of its country.

Physical: Singapore has many attractions and attributes, such as climate, location and entertainment venues, including Universal Studios, that affect people's perceptions, and subsequently their emotions, towards the country (Anholt, 2006; Gudjonsson, 2005). Singapore is famous for many things, such as its skyscrapers and beautiful city with surrounding waters (Brymer, 2003). However, it is commonly known that Singapore has few natural resources, which makes it a very expensive country. While this may increase the risks of losing tourism and inward investment, Singapore has managed to overcome these and successfully branded itself as a highly attractive destination (Wanjiru, 2005). Using ethical marketing, Singapore may improve its goodwill even further by focusing on efforts to sustain the environment and nature.

Human capital: The key to Singapore's success lies in its emphasis on the human capital dimensions (Szondi, 2006). It is the most competitive asset for the country, and has enabled it to attract well-developed and highly qualified workers, thus giving the country a competitive edge (Wanjiru, 2005). These qualities of human capital influence visitors (Idris & Arai, 2006) by making a lasting impression (Wanjiru, 2005) and contributing to Singapore's brand performance in global markets. As people are the most important element in country branding (Gudjonsson, 2005) Singapore must continuously focus on attracting qualified workers, and by developing its image around ethical concerns.

Export: Singapore is often associated with its exported financial services, which contributes to the countrry's reputation for success and high achievers (Papadopoulos, 2004). Countries like Singapore with well-branded exports thus contribute to sustaining the country's image (Anholt, 2003). It is not, however, evidenced how 'Made in Singapore' might assist in the country's branding, and perhaps Singapore should develop this concept further with the perspective of ethical associations.

Investment and FDI: Singapore is a country with very few natural resources, so it has gained competitive advantage with enormous investment opportunities and business. The Singaporean government offers strong financial incentives, including tax exemption and infrastructure investment, to lure prospective investors (Kotler & Gertner, 2002). While capitalism and money have comprised the superior branding strategy for Singapore, in the long term, the country may need to focus on the softer sides such as ethics and social responsibility, which are already evident in many industries. For example, the Singaporean government is supporting the local economy by allowing foreign investment from Genting Group Malaysian in financing the establishment of Resorts World Sentosa. The US$4.93 billion resort, developed by Genting Singapore, is one of the world's most expensive casino properties, and employs more than 10,000 people.

Culture and heritage: The Singaporean culture is the national identity of the country. Singapore has used its culture and heritage of multiculturalism to great effect, as 'tools' of competitive advantage. These are elements that are considered by investors or buyers (Gudjonsson, 2005; Schulz & Soontiens, 2004). Since culture and heritage are critical for Singapore, it must continuously influence people's perceptions of these in order to sustain a desirable and ethically responsible population.

Social: Singapore's social issues include economic polarisation between the super-rich and the poor. People there may consider optimising the country's social benefits to develop its country brand (Robinson, 2003). Further, the emphasis on capitalism and shareholder wealth maximisation may not be a sustainable long-term strategy, and instead a different focus may be needed on a 'conscious' and more enlightened approach to business that includes ethical marketing (Mehta & Kau, 1984).

Political: Singapore has a parliamentary representative democratic republic whereby the President of Singapore is the head of state, and the Prime Minister of Singapore is the head of government of a multi-party system. Singapore is known for its favourability towards FDI and businesses in general. Elements like tax exemption and benefits play a major role in developing the Singaporean country brand. Singapore is considered to have a stable political environment.

Ethical: To win over the public, Singapore needs to continue its focus on businesses and investment, but also highlight more about its good causes and global ethical and social responsible issues, which are beneficial for investors and citizens alike. By increasing fair trade and reducing environmentally damaging energy consumption and waste, Singapore may continue to be a desirable place for investors, tourists and other stakeholders.

Malaysia

Malaysia has branded itself as 'Truly Asia'. To compete effectively with neighbouring countries, including Singapore and Thailand, and others in the world, it is critical for Malaysia to understand the underlying spirit of its country. We posit that a framework is needed to assist the Malaysian tourism marketers and policymakers in gauging Malaysians' views about branding their country.

Physical: Malaysia's attractions and attributes, such as geography, nature, climate, position and cities, create images that affect people's perceptions, and subsequently their emotions, towards the country (Anholt, 2006; Gudjonsson, 2005). Malaysia desires to create impressions at various places like ports of entry and city centres (Brymer, 2003). Kuala Lumpur, the capital, is a vibrant and dynamic city with its famous Petronas Twin Towers, as a physical landmark. Such a landmark is a useful starting point for country branding, to show Malaysia's ambition to become a world-class industrial city.

Human capital: Instead of relying on natural and physical characteristics, Malaysia emphasises the human capital dimensions due to its diversified and multicultural population (Szondi, 2006). When branding a country, human capital is regarded as the most competitive asset for a country (Shurchuluu, 2002). If human capital is not well developed and managed, a country often lags behind (Wanjiru, 2005). Moreover, since the qualities of human capital influence visitors (Idris & Arai, 2006), Malaysia should aim to make a lasting impression (Wanjiru, 2005) by enhancing its human capital, thus contributing to its country brand's performance in global markets. Malaysia may, in this vein, incorporate and differentiate itself from its competitors by highlighting its openness towards varying religious and moral beliefs, creating associations with increased ethical concerns and trust toward the country's human capital and other areas.

Export: The image of a country is associated with its exported goods and services, which in turn, influence a country's reputation, self-confidence and success (Papadopoulos, 2004). Malaysian consumers must try to avoid purchasing products from countries with a bad image, including those that engage in malicious military, political or economic acts. By setting an example, they show a high level of awareness towards ethical issues, promoting their softer sides. Thus, when stakeholders from around the world learn that something is 'Made in Malaysia', even when they have no prior experience or knowledge on the product, this country-of-origin label may be evaluated positively. Countries with such well-branded exports thus contribute to sustaining the country's image (Anholt, 2003). If Malaysia is able to associate its country branding with an ethical nature − for example, by increasing their products' reputation with sustainability − it may have an edge in building a better reputation than its competing neighbours.

Investment and FDI: Wanjiru (2005) asserts that a country does not gain competitive advantage if it lacks investment opportunities. He notes that a country must offer strong financial incentives, including tax exemption and infrastructure investment, to lure prospective investors (Kotler & Gertner, 2002). Another issue for investors' consideration is whether the country has high ethical concerns for the welfare of the workers, their moral judgments, and whether such issues may lead to problems such as demonstrations and public anger. Therefore, the inclusion of ethical concerns in this aspect is very valid to attract more FDI to Malaysia.

Culture and heritage: In country branding, culture is a starting point for connecting people's interest in a country and vice versa (Anholt, 2005a). Culture is regarded as the social glue that attracts and holds people together (Warner & Joynt, 2002). Countries like Malaysia can, from their culture and history, compete over customers' hearts and minds (Wanjiru, 2005) and assist in branding their desired visions. Malaysia, a country rich in culture and heritage, has much to utilise in its country branding. In response to the theme of the chapter, ethical concerns remain the key element in achieving a greater future for the country, both short and long term. For example, by ensuring equality, fair working conditions and rights for all minorities, Malaysia may promote itself as an attractive destination for potential multinational organisations.

Social: In Malaysia, other issues affecting people's decisions relating to holiday destinations, exports and places for investment (Wanjiru, 2005) include social issues such as economic and political instability, war and malnourished children. While these issues may not be of concern to Malaysia, it must continuously optimise its social benefits in order to attract visitors and investors (Robinson, 2003), and create opportunities for increasing exports and competitiveness. These, in turn, will develop into more long-lasting ethical sustainability. For example, Malaysia must focus on preserving its landscape, develop a stable social model, preserve its deep culture and heritage, and broaden people's worldviews. These components will assist Malaysia to develop its competitive advantage.

Political: A country's top leaders are associated with the country brand, and affect people's impressions − good, bad or indifferent − of that particular country (Quelch & Jocz, 2005). In this case, Malaysia's public diplomacy and politics play a major role in developing a country brand. The country's ethical concerns means that it must avoid corruption, bribery and political deception, which have been rife in neighbouring Thailand. Gilmore (2002) suggests that a country uses political events as a barrier to competitive threat. Quelch and Jocz (2005) claim that those in politics and business must formulate a common policy in order to constitute the country's competitive advantage. Malaysia must be careful to retain political stability, as certain political events have the ability to wreak havoc, damaging the country brand.

Ethical: Taken together, the above elements have all demonstrated ethical elements, which are important for the country branding of Malaysia. This separate ethical dimension encapsulates a broader and more holistic ethical concept, which refers to the management of ethics and ethical marketing. To win over the public, Malaysia needs to be more involved with good causes and global issues. Social and ethical factors are a key relationship to country's competitive advantage; thus Malaysia must consider ethical branding for its own citizens as well as global stakeholders.

Thailand

Thailand has branded itself as one of the best tourist destinations anywhere in the world. To compete effectively with neighbouring countries, it is critical for Thailand to develop and enhance the spirit of its diversified country further. As before, we use our framework to explain their country branding elements in detail.

Physical: Thailand has a great number of attractions and attributes, such as world-class beaches, climate, nature and cities, to mention a few, which affect stakeholders' emotional responses towards the country. Thailand continues to desire to create impressions about various places like Bangkok city centre and the beaches. However, as it suffers frequent natural disasters, such as flooding and tsunamis, Thailand faces risks of losing tourism and inward investment, diminishing its competitiveness. However, the country has vast raw material deposits, such as rice fields and production, considered as their core competencies that cannot be easily replicated by others (Gilmore, 2002).

Human capital: The qualities of human capital in Thailand remain key to their competitive country branding. By making a lasting impression, the tourism industry not only attracts new people but also creates loyal visitors, who keep returning, thus contributing to Thailand's brand performance in global markets. While people are the most important element in country branding (Gudjonsson, 2005), stereotypes still exist. These stereotypes are sometimes negative and difficult to change (Szondi, 2006), such as those of transsexuals and prostitutes, which may be damaging to Thailand's country brand.

Export: The image of Thailand exports and 'Made in Thailand' include associations with white rice. These products are bought all over the world and contribute greatly to Thailand's GDP. When consumers have no prior experience of a rice product, but know that the country of origin is Thailand, this label is often used to evaluate a product's quality and reliability. Such well-branded exports thus contribute to sustaining Thailand's image.

Investment and FDI: Thailand currently lacks investment opportunities. To develop these, it should consider offering strong financial incentives, including tax exemption and infrastructure investment, to lure investors (Kotler & Gertner, 2002). Another approach is to develop its country branding around its culture and strong ethical heritage, as explained next.

Culture and heritage: Thailand has a deep heritage based on Buddhist ethnicities and religious rituals. Such strong heritage may form a competitive advantage, due to the focus on morality, honesty and trustworthiness. Such concepts of peacefulness and enlightenment link well with the notion of social and ethical responsibility towards others and nature. Thus, Thailand can effectively develop its country branding to focus on its rich cultural life as an attractive destination.

Social: Social issues such as economic and political instability, war and poverty are high on Thailand's agenda. In the past, these issues have been troubling in the country and thus must be resolved effectively if the country is to optimise its social benefits to attract visitors and investors. In addition, Thailand must preserve its landscape, a stable social model, and deep culture and heritage, so that outsiders' views of Thailand become components of the country's competitive advantage.

Political: In recent years, the citizens of Thailand have been involved in many major demonstrations against the government, demanding more transparency and democratisation. While such chaos may be devastating in the short term, in the long run, Thailand may use political events as a competitive differentiation strategy to lure more support from the international community. By showing the world that its citizens do not tolerate corruption, a reputation for high concern about ethics has been achieved. Thailand must use this to its advantage and claim that those in politics and business must formulate a common policy in order to constitute the country's competitive advantage. If not, its politics and political events have the ability to wreak havoc, damaging the country.

Ethical: Thailand has many good causes that are built around ethics and moral judgments. To win over the public, we suggest that Thailand must expand its ethical management into areas that involve human capital, to overcome images of stereo-typing. In addition, it is vital that ethics are strongly embedded in all aspects of country branding, namely Thailand's politics and government.

Conclusion

As mentioned earlier, countries need to compete for investors, tourists, consumers, donors, immigrants, the media and also the governments of different nations. Countries need not only to gain the attention, respect and trust of their stakeholders, but also to compete with other countries. This requires actively management of their reputation in order to gain and sustain competitive advantage (Passow et al., 2005). To achieve sustainable competitive advantage, countries require a robust, positive brand identity (Kotler & Gertner, 2002). Porter (1989, p. 71) highlights four factors that determine national advantage or competence:

1. factor conditions: the nation position itself in factors of production, such as skilled labour or infrastructure;
2. demand conditions: the nature of home demand for the industry's product or services;
3. related and supporting industries: the presence or absence of internationally competitive supplier industries and related industries; and
4. form strategy, structure and rivalry: the condition governing how companies are created, organised and managed, and the nature of domestic rivalry.

Gudjonsson (2005) asserts that even though the economy is often seen as the driving force behind measuring country competitiveness, other factors such as people, culture, politics and geography are fundamental to a country's competitive advantage. The framework presented in this chapter has utilised these elements to form a more comprehensive country branding approach, and may be used for future studies.

The chapter offers insights into how Singapore, Malaysia and Thailand are branding themselves. Specifically, we reveal that Malaysia can be branded through its culture and heritage, and more efforts are needed to enhance Malaysia's involve-ment in social responsibility. Singapore, as successful as it is, may continue to brand itself as Asia's top financial investment destination, but also should focus more on the softer sides. Finally, Thailand, with its political instability and great tourism destinations, may need to refocus its branding on its heritage and overcome the stereotyping of prostitution, for example. Across all three countries, there is a need for a deeper focus on ethics and morality.

Successful country branding assists these countries in gaining popularity from external audiences. We suggest that the process of country branding needs to start with citizens' ethical and social concerns. If the public believe and support factors that contribute to a country's branding, this will assist the country in embedding a sense of loyalty and retention among its citizens. Consequently, it is essential for a country to ensure that country branding is nurtured strongly inside the minds and hearts of its citizens.

New research directions

Despite many issues affecting ethical marketing campaigns in South East Asia, few studies have examined ethical marketing in Singapore, Malaysia and Thailand systematically. Drawing from a country-branding perspective, the chapter examines several issues pertaining to physical, human capital, export, investment and FDI, culture and heritage, political, and social dimensions, and the new one, ethical. Each of the elements in the framework offer an exploratory basis, which are useful for future research that aims to examine the elements influencing country branding. We call for more empirical evidence in future studies in this interesting region.

The Corruption Perceptions Index report reveals how countries fare on corruption (Transparency International, 2014). Broadly speaking, there is a common perception that countries in South East Asia tend be more corrupt and less ethical than Western countries. Some scholars suggest that *guanxi* (networks) plays an important role in the differing views towards corruption. For example, with political *guanxi*, internal social networks are created among friends and family, with abundant examples of nepotism and favours. Thus, citizens often lack trust in people engaging in *guanxi* in terms of ethics and moral principles. Singaporeans are said to associate *guanxi* with what money can do for them, implying that such relationships are of importance to get ahead. These same notions of unethical practices may apply to other developing countries like Thailand, Malaysia and Taiwan. Such notions further affect a country's brand and image simultaneously. We call for more research into understanding the role of *guanxi* and ethical perceptions among various stakeholders, from Asia and Western countries alike.

Practising ethical marketing in Singapore, Malaysia and Thailand

For tourism marketers and policymakers, a useful finding from this study is the adaption of ethical marketing in country branding. The identification of ethical concerns and the broad and holistic view of ethics allow organisations to detect public opinions about important elements within a country's state of affairs. This enables marketers to develop regional/national systems that are localised, and adjust campaigns based on both the characteristics of the population and their corresponding views towards the country's branding elements.

The chapter investigates elements of country branding perceptions from Singaporeans, Malaysians and Thai citizens. We subsequently explore elements that we believe are critical for gaining a competitive edge, as the countries are competing with neighbours such as Vietnam and other South East Asian countries, which are well-known brands and tourist destinations in the world. Our study indicates that the best way to portray Singapore, Malaysia and Thailand is through physical, human capital, export, culture and heritage, politics, social, and ethical dimensions. These elements are important to foster positive emotions among citizens, and are therefore key tools to build a competitive advantage with specific focus on ethical considerations. They have important implications for tourism marketers and policy-makers, by highlighting the importance of branding with an ethical perspective towards a country's citizens and investors, revealing elements that are relevant for country branding and competitive advantage.

The key agenda in this study has been to recognise the uncertainties related to ethical marketing from a branding perspective, and to identify the factors that can help to manage these uncertainties that are associated with the perceptual differences among the countries. The chapter may equip managers with a better understanding of ethical issues, so that they can deploy a more morals-based approach to ethical marketing. This minimises costly mistakes and helps managers to manage their resources more fairly.

The identification of the cross-cultural differences in the countries is key to understanding a successful marketing strategy. The feelings associated with status, face and each of the country elements allow managers to develop a better grouping of their stakeholders to identify the group which needs more attention, and to take actions in order to keep their customers loyal. This identification and awareness of cultural differences in the three counties will assist marketers to develop more tailored approaches for targeting customers who are sensitive to perceptions concerning face, status and other country brand elements. A firm operating in these countries, and with this information, will be able to take action and improve their reputation and goodwill regarding any ethical issues.

In conclusion, there is actionable managerial guidance regarding ethical marketing and country-branding tactics, and how to manage the stakeholders in Singapore, Malaysia and Thailand. Specifically, the findings indicate that physical, human capital, export, investment and FDI, political, social and ethical dimensions are the key offerings to enhance relationships with visitors, investors and others. The chapter provides managers with the capability to identify and utilise an appropriate tactic in order to enhance relationships. In order to create a successful country-branding strategy, firms need to manage these elements and understand the level of impact they have in a globalised marketplace.

Practice case study

A country or nation brand combines all perceptions of a nation in the minds of international stakeholders, which include: people, place, culture, language, history, food, fashion, celebrities, public icons, global brands and so on. Fan (2006) states

that 'a nation's brand exists, with or without any conscious effects in nation branding, as each country has a certain image to its international audience, be it strong or
weak, current or outdated, clear or vague' (p. 12). Based on the concept of nation
branding (Fan, 2006), successful nation branding campaigns will assist in establishing a more favourable image among international consumers/audiences, thus further
enhancing a country's image (Fan, 2008). Pappu, Quester, and Cooksey (2007) note
that 'consumers' macro and micro country images can influence the equity they
associate with a brand from that country. Furthermore, country image can influence
the key dimensions of brand equity such as brand associations, perceived quality
and brand loyalty' (p. 728). A country brand's shared image or association are
referred to as country equity (Shimp et al., 2005). In the following sections, examples of young Malaysians' ethical consumption will be discussed in a case study.

Ethical beliefs and intention of young Malaysian consumers

China, India, Malaysia and Thailand are known as the home of piracy (Haque,
Khatibi, & Rahman, 2009). A report by the Organisation for Economic Cooperation and Development (OECD) identified that nearly 60 per cent of seizures
by US customs authorities originated from China, Thailand, Hong Kong, Korea and
Malaysia (Barraclough, 2007). The report shows that China is the largest sole
source of counterfeit products in the world's markets (International Chamber of
Commerce, 2007). Countries like Thailand, Hong Kong, Korea and Malaysia are
the leading sources of counterfeit products to US and major European markets.
The report further reveals that Malaysian counterfeit products include software
(e.g. CDs, VCDs, DVDs), apparel (e.g. clothing, shoes, handbags) and medicine
(Havoscope Global Market Indexes, 2011). In another report on the Eradication of
Counterfeit Products published by Ministry of Domestic Trade, Co-operatives and
Consumerism, Malaysia was found to have increased their seizure cases from
409 cases in 2009 to 870 cases in 2010, with a total seizure value equal to
Malaysia Ringgit $9,425,568.17 (approximately £1.74 million) (Ministry of
Domestic Trade, Co-operatives and Consumerism, 2011).

In order to stop the development of piracy trading, the Malaysian government
has been actively involved and has played its role to eradicate this issue through
many campaigns and actions. These included briefings, seminars and workshops,
with the aim of creating awareness among Malaysians about how to stop unethical
consumption and behaviour. In 2011, the Malaysian government introduced an
advertising campaign called 'Original Sales Carnival' to provide knowledge to consumers and educate them about the differences between authentic and pirated products (Ministry of Domestic Trade, Co-operatives and Consumerism, 2011).
Although the government has been trying to stop unethical trading via seizures, its
laws and enforcements thereof are facing many challenges and problems (Stumpf,
Peggy, & Leeann, 2011).

In Malaysia, vibrant population growth and purchasing power signify the vast
potential of the consumer market. Due to socio-economic changes, rising affluence
and education status, consumers' lifestyle are evolving and improving. Based on

current market conditions, it appears that Malaysian consumers have become more Westernised and cosmopolitan. More high-profile international retailers are gradually accessing the Malaysian market (Lau & Choe, 2009). In 2003, it was estimated that 43 per cent of Malaysia's 25 million people were less than 20 years old (PricewaterhouseCoopers, 2004). As the country aims to become one of the high-income countries by the year 2020, the growing affluence and potentially declining moral and religious standards might affect consumers' ethical responsibility, especially among young Malaysian consumers. As market conditions change, young consumers must deal with ethical issues of consumerism, which are different from those of their elder generation in terms of the moral thinking required. As Vittell and Muncy (2005) described, a group of people's and individuals' behaviour can be altered by the influence of moral principles.

In consumer behaviour studies, Cowe and Williams (2000) discovered that many young consumers have yet to settle in their purchase behavioural patterns. The main issue is the ethical stance of young Malaysian consumers on their acceptance of ethical and potentially unethical situations (e.g. the consumption of counterfeit products). Will these young Malaysian consumers accept unethical consumption, or are they less tolerant of this? Many scholars are investigating the effects of young Malaysian consumers' personalities and their attitudes regarding unwillingness to participate in unethical consumptions (Amran, Nurul Adzwina, Norazah, & Zyhal, 2012; Lambkin & Tyndall, 2009; Lau, 2012). These studies have mainly focused on the factors that influence young Malaysian consumers' purchase intentions and attitudes towards unethical consumption, but not on the factors of why young Malaysian consumers value these pirated products. Owing to this limitation, these studies have provided deeper knowledge regarding the underlying reason why young Malaysian consumers show higher moral and ethical values, which in turn reflects on their unwillingness to put up with unethical consumption.

While pursuing pirated products might provide immediate benefits to individuals, it is damaging to brand owners and workforces. Research demonstrates that the intention not to participate in unethical consumption is influenced by attitudes and ethical values regarding pirated goods. More importantly, those attitudes and purchase intentions towards pirated goods are influenced by individual values towards consciousness, ethical perceptions, novelty seeking and integrity. This highlights that young Malaysian consumers, who are often novelty seekers, will not have any intention of participating in unethical consumption, due to their moral principles. From a marketing perspective, young individuals are recognised as a specialised market segment that forms a powerful consumer purchasing segment (Grant & Waite, 2003; Moschis, 1987). It is important that more consumer ethics research are conducted among young consumers, as the ethical orientation of this group gives researchers and policymakers the possibility to address ethical issues early, while consumers are still receptive and impressionable. This is beneficial to retailers and designers, who can then manufacture products that are more challenging to counterfeit. In addition, manufacturers and retailers can advertise their products' unique selling points and increase their brand prestige while opposing the purchase of pirated goods (Roslin & Melewar, 2008). For retailers, it is key to cooperate with the government to educate consumers, and to develop schemes that enhance young Malaysian consumers' ethical values and moral principles.

In conclusion, the case study notes that inappropriate perception of corruption has crept into the minds of young consumers. In a period of transition from adolescence to early adulthood, young individuals are seeking to establish their own personas and form behavioural attitudes and values, including those relating to their own consumption interests and purchase intentions. Young individuals make purchases to express themselves and to construct an individual identity (Holbrook & Schindler, 1989). These behavioural routines are likely to be carried on through the individual's lifetime (Moschis, 1987). Therefore, marketers and retailers often target these young individuals and make them loyal consumers, in order to increase their lifetime value (Feldman, 1999; Speer, 1998). Furthermore, young individuals are more receptive towards the negative effects of consuming pirated products that may harm society, the industry and country branding. If marketers are able to stimulate their purchases and decision-making (Grant & Waite, 2003), they may act as a change agent by influencing society and culture, and the younger generations (Leslie, Sparling, & Owen, 2001). Indeed, more education will strengthen the moral principle of young Malaysian at an early age, and is critical for long-term success.

Further investigation

Key areas to focus on:

- The design of ethical marketing campaigns in multicultural markets.
- Relationships between government-induced, political and organisational ethical marketing.
- The role of social media in ethical marketing.
- Short- and long-term motivators for ethical marketing.
- Cross-cultural studies of ethical marketing with a particular focus on Singapore, Malaysia and Thailand.

References

Aaker, D. A. (1991). *Managing brand equity*. New York: The Free Press.

Aaker, J. L., & Williams, P. (1998). Empathy versus pride: The influence of emotional appeals across culture. *Journal of Consumer Research, 25*(4), 241–261.

Amine, L. S., & Chao, M. C. H. (2005). Managing country image to long-term advantage: The case of Taiwan and Acer. *Place Branding, 1*(2), 187–204.

Amran, H., Nurul Adzwina, A. R. B., Norazah, M. S., & Zyhal, H. (2012). Why customers do not buy counterfeit luxury brands? Understanding the effects of personality, perceived quality and attitude on unwillingness to purchase. *Labuan e-Journal of Muamalat and Society, 6*, 14–29.

Ang, S. H. (2000). The power of money: A cross-cultural analysis of business-related beliefs. *Journal of World Business, 35*(1), 43–60.

Anholt, S. (2003). *Brand new justice: The upside of global branding.* Oxford: Butterworth-Heinemann.

Anholt, S. (2005a). Anholt nation brands index: How does the world see America? *Journal of Advertising Research, 45*(3), 296–304.

Anholt, S. (2005b). Some important distinctions in place branding. *Place Branding, 1*(2), 116–121.

Anholt, S. (2006). Why brand? Some practical considerations for nation branding. *Place Branding, 2*(2), 97–107.

Bao, Y., Zhou, K. Z., & Su, C. (2003). Face consciousness and risk aversion: Do they affect consumer decision-making? *Psychology & Marketing, 20*(8), 733–755.

Barraclough, E. (2007). OECD reveals cost of fakes. *Managing Intellectual Property,* Geneva, 27 January.

Belk, R. W. (1988). Possessions and the extended self. *Journal of Consumer Research, 15*(2), 139–167.

Belk, R. W., & Pollay, R. W. (1985). Images of ourselves: The good life in twentieth-century advertising. *Journal of Consumer Research, 11*(March), 887–897.

Blichfeldt, B. S. (2005). Unmanageable place brands? *Place Branding, 1*(4), 388–401.

Bolton, L. E., Keh, H. T., & Alba, J. W. (2010). How do price fairness perceptions differ across culture? *Journal of Marketing Research, 47*(3), 56–76.

Brewer, M. B., & Chen, Y. R. (2007). Where (who) are collectives in collectivism? Toward conceptual clarification of individualism and collectivism. *Psychological Review, 114*(1), 133–151.

Brown, P., & Levinson, S. (1978). Universals in language usage: Politeness phenomena. In E. Goody (Ed.), *Questions and politeness* (pp. 56–311). Cambridge: Cambridge University Press.

Brown, P., & Levinson, S. (1987). *Politeness. Some universals in language usage.* Cambridge: Cambridge University Press.

Brymer, C. (2003). Branding a country: Creating and managing brand value. Interbrand <http://www.brandchannel.com>.

Chang, H. C., & Holt, R. G. (1994). A Chinese perspective on face as inter-relational concern. In S. Ting-Toomey (Ed.), *The challenge of facework* (pp. 95–132). Albany, NY: State University of New York Press.

Chang, K., & Lu, L. (2007). Characteristics of organizational culture, stressors, and well-being – the case of Taiwanese organizations. *Journal of Managerial Psychology, 22*(6), 549–568.

Che Ha, N., Yahya, W.K., Nguyen, B., Melewar, T.C., & Chen, Y.P. (2014). Country branding emerging from citizen emotions and perceptions of competitive advantage: The case of Malaysia, working paper.

Cowe, R., & Williams, S. (2000). *Who are the ethical consumers?* London: The Cooperative Bank.

Dinnie, K. (2004). Place branding: Overview of an emerging literature. *Place Branding, 1*(1), 106–110.

Domeisen, N. (2003). Is there a case for national branding? *International Trade Forum, 1*, 14–16.

Ethical Shoppers Price Index Survey. (2014). <http://makewealthhistory.org/2008/03/24/ethical-shopping-an-index-of-consumer-labels>.

Fan, Y. (2006). Branding the nation: What is being branded? *Journal of Vacation Marketing*, *12*(1), 5–14.

Fan, Y. (2008). Soft power: The power of attraction or confusion. *Place Branding and Public Diplomacy*, *4*(2), 147–158.

Farley, J. U., & Lehmann, D. R. (1994). Cross-national laws and differences in market response. *Management Science*, *40*(1), 111–122.

Feldman, J. (1999). Back-to-school buying guide. *Money*, *28*(9), 165–168.

Gertner, D., & Kotler, P. (2004). How can a place correct a negative image? *Place Branding*, *1*(1), 50–57.

Gilmore, F. (2002). A country – can it be repositioned? Spain – the success story of country branding. *Journal of Brand Management*, *9*(4/5), 281–293.

Goffman, E. (1955). On face-work: An analysis of ritual elements of social interaction. *Psychiatry: Journal for the Study of Interpersonal Processes*, *18*(3), 213–231.

Grant, I. C., & Waite, K. (2003). Following the yellow brick road – young adults' experiences of the information super-highway. *Qualitative Market Research: An International Journal*, *6*(1), 48–57.

Gudjonsson, H. (2005). Nation branding. *Place Branding*, *1*(3), 283–298.

Gurhan-Canli, Z., & Maheswaran, D. (2000). Cultural variations in country of origin effects. *Journal of Marketing Research*, *37*, 309–317.

Hamzaoui, L., & Merunka, D. (2006). The impact of country of design and country of manufacture on consumer perceptions of bi-national products' quality: An empirical model based on the concept of fit. *Journal of Consumer Marketing*, *23*(3), 145–155.

Haque, A., Khatibi, A., & Rahman, S. (2009). Factors influencing buying behavior of piracy products and its impact to Malaysian Market. *International Review of Business Research Papers*, *5*, 383–401, Havocscope Global Market Indexes, 2011.

Hassan, S. S., & Katsanis, L. P. (1994). Global market segmentation strategies and trends. In E. Kaynak, & S. S. Hassan (Eds.), *Globalization of consumer markets: Structures and strategies* (pp. 47–63). New York: International Business Press.

Havoscope Global Market Indexes. (2011). <http://www.havocscope.com>.

Ho, D. Y. F. (1976). On the concept of face. *American Journal of Sociology*, *81*(1), 867–884.

Hofstede, F. T., Jan-Benedict, E., Steenkamp, M., & Wedel, M. (1999). International market segmentation based on consumer-product relations. *Journal of Marketing Research*, *36*, 1–17.

Hofstede, G. (1980). *Culture's consequences: International differences in work-related values*. Newbury Park, CA: Sage.

Holbrook, M. B., & Schindler, R. M. (1989). Some explanatory findings on the development of musical tastes. *Journal of Consumer Research*, *16*(1), 119–124.

Hui, C. H., Triandis, H. C., & Yee, C. (1991). Cultural differences in reward allocation: Is collectivism the explanation?'. *British Journal of Social Psychology*, *30*(3), 145–157.

Hwang, K. K. (1987). Face and favor: The Chinese power game. *American Journal of Sociology*, *92*, 944–974.

Idris, K., & Arai, H. (2006). The Intellectual Property-Conscious Nation: Mapping the Path from Developing to Developed. *World Intellectual Property Organization* <http://www.wipo.int/export/sites/www/freepublications/en/intproperty/988/wipo_pub_988.pdf>.

International Chamber of Commerce. (2007). *Global survey on counterfeiting and piracy*. Paris, January.

Johansson, J. K. (1989). Determinants and effects of the use of 'made-in' labels. *International Marketing Review*, *6*, 27–41.

Johansson, J. K. (2005). The new brand America. *Place Branding*, *1*(2), 153–163.

Kashima, Y., Yamaguchi, S., Kim, U., Choi, S. C., Gelfand, J. H., & Yuki, M. (1995). Culture, gender, and self: A perspective from individualism-collectivism research. *Journal of Personality and Social Psychology, 69*, 925–937.

Keller, K. L. (1993).) 'Conceptualizing, measuring and managing consumer-based brand equity. *Journal of Marketing, 57*(1), 1–22.

Kotler, P. (2004). Opinion pieces – where is place branding heading?' *Place Branding, 1*(1), 12–35.

Kotler, P., & Gertner, D. (2002). Country as brand, product, and beyond: A place marketing and brand management perspective. *Journal of Brand Management, 9*(4/5), 249–262.

Kubacki, K., & Skinner, H. (2006). Poland: Exploring the relationships between national brand and national culture. *Brand Management, 13*(4/5), 284–299.

Lambkin, M., & Tyndall, Y. (2009). Brand counterfeiting: A marketing problem that won't go away. *Irish Marketing Review, 20*(1), 35–46.

Lau, T. C. (2012). *Consumer ethical beliefs and intention: Investigation of young Malaysian consumers*. Lismore, NSW: ePublications by Southern Cross University.

Lau, T. C., & Choe, K. L. (2009). Consumers' acceptance of unethical consumption activities: Implications for the youth market. *International Journal of Marketing Studies, 11* (2), 56–61.

Lee, J. K., & Lee, W. N. (2009). Country-of-origin effects on consumer product evaluation and purchase intention: The role of objective versus subjective knowledge. *Journal of International Consumer Marketing, 21*, 137–151.

Leslie, E., Sparling, P. B., & Owen, N. (2001). University campus settings and the promotion of physical activity in young adults: Lessons from research in Australia and the USA. *Health and Education, 101*(3), 116–125.

Li, J. J., & Su, C. (2007). How face influences consumption: A comparative study of American and Chinese consumers. *International Journal of Market Research, 49*(2), 237–256.

Lu, H. (1934). On face. *Selected works of Lu Hsun* (H.-Y. Yang & G. Yang, Trans.). Peking: Foreign Language Press, 129–32.

Markus, H. R., & Kitayama, S. (1991). Culture and the self: Implications for cognition, emotion, and motivation. *Psychological Review, 98*(4), 224–253.

Martin, B. A. S., Wailee, M. S., & Lacey, C. (2011). Countering negative country of origin effects using imagery processing. *Journal of Consumer Behaviour, 10*, 80–92.

Mehta, S. C., & Kau, A. K. (1984). Marketing executives' perceptions of unethical practice: An empirical investigation of Singapore managers. *Singapore Management Review, 6* (2), 25–35.

Ministry of Domestic Trade, Co-operatives and Consumerism. (2011). <http://www.kpdnkk. gov.my/en/kpdnkk/profil/latarbelakang>.

Moschis, G. P. (1987). *Consumer socialization: A life cycle perspective*. Lexington, MA: Lexington Books.

Oetzel, J. G., & Ting-Toomey, S. (2003). Face concerns in interpersonal conflict. *Communication Research, 30*(6), 599–624.

Papadopoulos, N. (2004). Place branding: Evolution, meaning and implications. *Place Branding, 1*(1), 36–49.

Pappu, R., Quester, P. G., & Cooksey, R. W. (2007). Country image and consumer-based brand equity: Relationship and implications for international marketing. *Journal of International Business Studies, 38*, 726–745.

Passow, T., Fehlmann, R., & Grahlow, H. (2005). Country reputation — from measurement to management: The case of Liechtenstein. *Corporate Reputation Review*, *7*(4), 309—326.

Peterson, R. A., & Joilbert, A. J. P. (1995). A meta-analysis of country of origin effects. *Journal of International Business Studies*, *26*, 883—900.

Porter, M. (1989). *The competitive advantage of nations*. New York: Simon & Schuster Trade.

PricewaterhouseCoopers. (2004). <http://www.pwc.com>.

Quelch, J., & Jocz, K. (2005). Positioning the nation-state. *Place Branding*, *1*(3), 229—237.

Robinson, K. (2003). Tourism: It's about managing competitiveness, too. *International Trade Forum* <http://www.tradeforum.org/Tourism-Its-About-Managing-Competitiveness-Too> Accessed 15.05.14.

Roslin, R. M., & Melewar, T. C. (2008). Hypermarket and the small retailers in Malaysia: Exploring retailers' competitive abilities. *Journal of Asia Pacific Business*, *9*(4), 329—343.

Schulz, P., & Soontiens, W. (2004). *Internationalization and country image — being German in Western Australia*. Working Paper Series 2004. Curtin University of Technology.

Shimp, T. A., Samiee, S., & Sharma, S. (2005). Brand origin recognition accuracy: its antecedents and consumers' cognitive limitations. *Journal of International Business Studies*, *36*, 379—397.

Shurchuluu, P. (2002). National productivity and competitive strategies for the new millennium. *Integrated Manufacturing Systems*, *12*(6), 408—414.

Singelis, T. M., Triandis, H. C., Bhawuk, D. P. S., & Gelfand, M. J. (1995). Horizontal and vertical aspects of individualism. *Personality and Social Psychology Bulletin*, *24*, 1177—1189.

Speer, T. (1998). College come-ons. *American Demographics*, *20*(3), 41—45.

Stumpf, S. A., Peggy, E. C., & Leeann, P. (2011). Fake: Can business stanch the flow of counterfeit products? *Journal of Business Strategy*, *32*(2), 4—12.

Szondi, G. (2006). The role and challenges of country branding in transition countries: The Central and Eastern European experience. *Place Branding and Public Diplomacy*, *3*(1), 8—20.

Ting-Toomey, S., & Kurogi, A. (1998). Facework competence in intercultural conflict: An updated face-negotiation theory. *International Journal of Intercultural Relations*, *22*, 187—225.

Transparency International. (2014). Corruption Perceptions Index. <http://www.transparency.org/country> Accessed 15.03.14.

Tse, D. K. (1996). Understanding Chinese people as consumers: Past findings and future propositions. In M. H. Bond (Ed.), *The handbook of Chinese psychology*. Hong Kong: Oxford University Press.

Vittell, S. J., & Muncy, J. (2005). The Muncy-Vittell consumer ethics scale: A modification and application. *Journal of Business Ethics*, *62*(3), 267—275.

Wang, C. L., & Mowen, J. C. (1997). The separateness-connectedness self-schema: Scale development and application to message construction. *Psychology and Marketing*, *14*, 185—207.

Wanjiru, E. (2005). Branding African countries: A prospect for the future. *Place Branding*, *2*(1), 84—95.

Warner, M., & Joynt, P. (2002). *Managing across cultures: Issues and perspectives* (2nd ed.). London: Thompson Learning.

Wong, N. Y., & Ahuvia, A. C. (1998). Personal taste and family face: Luxury consumption in Confucian and Western societies. *Psychology and Marketing, 15,* 423—432.

Yang, M. M. (1994). *Gifts, favors, and banquets: The art of social relationships in China.* Ithaca. NY: Cornell University Press.

Zane, N., & Yeh, M. (2002). The use of culturally-based variables in assessment: Studies on loss of face. In K. S. Kurasaki, S. Okazaki, & S. Sue (Eds.), *Asian American mental health: Assessment theories and methods* (pp. 123—138). New York, NY: Kluwer Academic/Plenum Publishers.

Zhai, X. (2005). *The reproduction of Renqing, Mianzi and power.* Beijing: Peking University Press.

Zhou, N., & Belk, B. W. (2004). Chinese consumer readings of global and local advertising appeals. *Journal of Advertising, 33*(3), 63—76.

Zhou, N., & Nakamoto, K. (2000). Price perceptions: A cross-national study between American and Chinese young consumers. *Advances in Consumer Research, 28,* 161—168, Provo, UT: Association for Consumer Research.

Ethical marketing: India, Pakistan and Bangladesh

Mithileshwar Jha

Introduction

Ethics and values have been the subject of both scholarly and practitioner interest for centuries across the globe. Periodically, serious concerns have been raised about rapidly changing (mostly implied as declining) ethical standards in society and business. Several definitions of ethics are available in the extant literature. Major concerns captured in the literature focus on the following questions:

- What are ethics?
- Are ethics different from morality?
- How do ethics differ from values?
- How are ethical standards set in societal and business contexts?
- Do these standards have bases in dominant religions?
- Are these standards absolute or relative?
- In the business context, how do ethics differ at organisational versus individual level?
- As marketing interfaces with both internal and external customers, how do organisational culture and top management orientation, leadership style and processes influence the outcome (in this context, marketing decisions and their impact on various stakeholders)?
- Do marketers in countries like India, Pakistan and Bangladesh – with a significant proportion of the population being poor, illiterate, and steeped in traditional values with huge wealth and income disparities, and weak social security measures and regulatory mechanisms – carry a higher degree of ethical responsibility compared to their Western counterparts?
- Do they perceive this responsibility and deliver on it?

This chapter attempts to answer some of the above questions, based on the extant literature and personal observations, experiences and insights of the author.

Learning objectives

After reading this chapter, you should be able to:

- understand ethics in the context of these countries;
- understand ethics in this region from the perspective of two major religions: Hinduism and Islam;
- appreciate the key dilemmas and current status of ethical marketing in the region; and
- get acquainted with new research directions and implications for marketing and management practice.

The state of the art in ethical marketing: India, Pakistan and Bangladesh (IPB)

Ethical marketing can be discussed in the context of understanding ethics and business ethics first.

Ethics and business ethics defined

Gandhi (1999), quoting a 'fair friend' as a source in a *Young India* article published on 20 October 1925, identified seven social sins:

1. politics without principles;
2. commerce without morality;
3. wealth without work;
4. education without character;
5. science without humanity;
6. pleasure without conscience; and
7. worship without sacrifice.

So ethics is not just about what is good (Manikutty, 2011) or morality. It goes much beyond these. Noted Indian philosopher Radhakrishnan (1914), discussing the ethics of the Vedanta, says:

> *The Vedanta law of morality does not ask us to act without motives, but asks us to serve humanity, without any selfish desires or petty interests, without envy or jealousy, regardless of party or personality... An action is good, not because of its external consequences, but on account of its inner will. Virtue is a mode of being and not of doing.*

Tagore (1988) provides an interesting perspective on ethics: 'He (man) can amply afford to say that goodness is for the sake of goodness, and upon this wealth of goodness — where honesty is not valued for being the best policy, but because it can afford to go against policies — man's ethics are founded.'

Haksar (1998) identifies five basic principles of ethical conduct across religions: *Satya* (truth), *Dharma* (righteousness), *Shanti* (peace), *Prema* (love) and *Ahimsa* (non-violence). Vittal (1998) equates ethics with a framework of values, which lead to behaviour. From ethics, we move on to business ethics.

Gupta (2004) provides an interesting insight about what business ethics are and are not. He argues very lucidly that they are:

- not about morality, but about establishment of transparent norms of interrelationships;
- not about philanthropy, but about socially aware entrepreneurship;
- respectful of the stakeholder and not just the shareholder;
- not just about compliance, but help establish employee morale; and
- committed to quality out of a desire for work satisfaction, not just for profit.

He identifies the two most critical features of ethical business as knowing one's company/organisation (in terms of what it stands for) and having explicit rules that apply to all.

So, is this a comprehensive perspective on ethics and business ethics in this region? No, as discussion on this topic cannot be complete without reflecting on the views of the two dominant religions, Hinduism and Islam, which combined are practised by more than 90 per cent of the population in the region.

Ethics from the perspective of Hinduism and Islam

Ethics in Hindu religion

The essence of ethics in Hinduism is based on the concept of *Dharma*. This is defined as 'that which supports, religion in general, code of conduct, set of duties. *Dharma* is the means to attain the ultimate good that is liberation' (Swami, 1996, p. 755). Radhakrishnan (1914, p. 178) also emphasises that 'the ideal of unselfish service of humanity is the only absolute moral rule which ought never to be broken'. Hindu religion identifies four aims of a person's life (*Purusarthas*): *Dharma*, *Artha* (wealth, possessions), *Kama* (desires) and *Moksha* (a state of supreme bliss). *Dharma* is supposed to lead to *Artha* and *Kama*. But the goal of life is to achieve *Moksha*. Thus, Hindu religion is not against possessions and desires (the whole basis of business and marketing), but places emphasis on attaining these through right thoughts, words and deeds. It emphasises the regulation of desires and the aim to attain supreme consciousness, or *Moksha*.

Ethics in Islam

Engineer (2014) explains the emphasis in Islam on establishing a just and fair society, free of all oppression. The religion regulates accumulation of wealth and exhorts individuals to use their wealth for charity. The focus of Islam is on reforming both the individual and society. Engineer articulates three important ethical concepts of Islam:

1. *'amal salih* (simple translation being 'good deeds', but it has a deeper meaning, including to be righteous, to improve, to be suitable and so on);
2. to be truthful; and
3. to observe patience.

Azmi (2014) highlights the basic tenets of Islamic ethic as 'truthfulness, trustworthiness, generosity, and leniency, adherence to fair treatment of workers, avoidance of evil practices (such as fraud, cheating, deceit, hoarding of foodstuff, exploitations, giving short measures etc.)'. He contrasts Western secular ethical values with those of Islam. According to Azmi, Western secular values are mostly utilitarian, relative, situational and without any spiritual sanctioning power. In contrast, Islamic ethics are humane, universal and absolute, and they create a sense of responsibility and accountability in the minds of the believers, whether they are buyers or sellers.

Thus, both the religions emphasise virtuous, truthful conduct and a sense of duties and accountability, supported by religious/spiritual sanction. The above forms the basis for developing a framework for understanding ethical marketing in IPB.

Framework for understanding ethical marketing in India, Pakistan and Bangladesh

Jamnik (2011) provides an interesting framework for understanding ethical marketing. He prefers to call it 'marketing ethics', covering three broad aspects:

1. descriptive studies (what is…);
2. analytical studies (of the nature of ethically relevant marketing concepts and justifications for the development of ethical normative claims); and
3. normative studies (of the values, principles and ideals to which marketers should be held).

Chakraborty (2004) provides another interesting framework in terms of two dimensions of an organisation's ethics (high or low) and a member's ethics (high or low). We propose to combine these two frameworks to classify and discuss literature on ethical marketing in India, Pakistan and Bangladesh, as shown in Figure 4.1.

Most of the studies in the region fall in cells 1 and 5. Few studies fall in cells 2 and 6. Only scholars like Chakraborty (2001); Gupta (2004); Manikutty (2011) and Sekhar (2003) have covered cells 3 and 4, all in their respective books, in the larger context of business ethics.

Ethical marketing in India, Pakistan and Bangladesh

Ethical marketing in this region has to be examined and understood in the specific context (population, poverty, literacy rate, income inequality, etc.) of these three countries.

Serial No.	Nature of study	Study focus	
		Organisation	Individual member
1	Descriptive	1	2
2	Analytical	3	4
3	Normative	5	6

Figure 4.1 Framework for understanding ethical marketing in India, Pakistan and Bangladesh.

The context

Table 4.1 provides data on the corruption perception index of the three countries. All three nations are perceived as high on corruption, with India having a slightly superior rank of 94 (out of 177 countries) and Pakistan and Bangladesh rank at 127 and 136, respectively. (The lower the rank, the less corrupt the country.)

Corruption scandals have dominated all three countries in the recent past. Corruption, unemployment and development have dominated elections in this region. The growth of certain new political parties such as the Aam Admi Party (AAP) in India and Tahree-e-Insaaf in Pakistan is mainly attributed to growing concerns in the citizens of these countries about the menace of corruption and the inability of traditional political parties to deal with it.

Any bribery involves, at a minimum, two parties: the giver and the receiver. It is never voluntary. It can be a rent for a privilege, speed money (i.e. money/bribe paid to speed-up the process of decision-making), extortion by a person with discretionary powers for granting a favour, the cost of doing business in a highly regulated economy plagued by shortages, ambiguous rules — subject to different interpretations and indecisiveness among decision-makers. Bribery can also be seen as a return on investment made for obtaining a coveted job in a government or a private enterprise (Dutta, 1998; Haksar, 1998; Sreedharan & Wakhlu, 2010). Whatever the reason for corruption may be, it deeply impacts the ethical behaviour of all the stakeholders involved in a transaction. It thus impacts ethical marketing. The implications of this menace and some antidotes for it will be discussed in subsequent paragraphs.

Population, income and competitiveness

Population, GDP per capita, global competitiveness and perceived corruption figures for the three countries are shown in Table 4.2. Large population, low GDP per capita, high incidence of corruption and low global competitiveness because of inadequate infrastructure and poor governance are the dominant features of the region.

Impact of poverty and inequality

The IPB region is inhabited by a large number of people living below the poverty line, with high levels of illiteracy, particularly among women, and a lack of

Table 4.1 **Corruption perceptions index, 2013+**

Serial No.	Country	Rank*	Score**
1	Bangladesh	136	27
2	India	94	36
3	Pakistan	127	28

Notes:
*Out of 177 countries (top three ranks/scores: Denmark (1/91), NZ (1/91), Finland (2/89)).
**0−9: highly corrupt; 90−100: very ethical.
Source: www.transparency.org/cpi.

Table 4.2 **Some facts about BIP (Bangladesh, India, Pakistan) 2012+**

Serial No.	Country	Population (millions)	GDP per capita (US$)	GCI 2012–3		Corruption* (%)	Rank**
				Rank (out of 144)	Scores (1–7)		
1	Bangladesh	150.5	818	110	3.7	22.2	(1)
2	India	1250.2	1389	59	4.3	15.8	(2)
3	Pakistan	177.8	1201	124	3.5	17.0	(1)

Notes:
*% of responses as the most problematic factors for doing business.
**The Global Competitiveness Index.
Source: The Global Competitiveness Report 2013–2014, World Economic Forum, pp. 118–9, 198–9, 284–5.

Table 4.3 **Poverty levels and income and consumption disparities in India, Pakistan and Bangladesh**

Serial No.	Country	Poverty % of population living on <$2/day	Gini index +	% share of income or consumption	
				Highest 10%	Bottom 10%
1	India (2010)	68.72	34	29	4
2	Pakistan (2008)	60.19	30	26	4
3	Bangladesh (2010)	76.54	32	27	4

Note: +0 = perfect equality; 100 = perfect inequality.
Source: The World Bank (2014), World Development Indicators: Distribution of income or consumption, available from http://wdi.worldbank.org/table/2.8-2.9.

transparency and poor governance (see Table 4.2). These, together with high wealth/income disparities (see Table 4.3), make a large section of the population — whether they be manufacturers, marketers, intermediaries or customers — vulnerable to greed, exploitation, the seeking of short cuts and sometimes oppression and cruelty (French & Martin, 2013).

Critical issues in ethics in marketing in India, Pakistan and Bangladesh

Critical issues in ethics in marketing in the IPB region are being discussed in the context of the broadened concept of marketing, including commercial, quasi-commercial (not-for-profit, government monopolies and utilities) and non-commercial (politics, governance, developmental organisations, religion, etc.)

entities and activities. These encompass products, services, persons, places, ideas and so on. The commercial organisations/entities can be further classified into: multinationals; large domestic companies (both private and public, including professionally managed, family managed or a combination of both); small and medium enterprises; co-operatives; tiny enterprises; and individual or small groups of farmers, craftsmen, traders and other intermediaries operating in the unorganised sector.

Formal values, codes of conduct and their enforcement

Multinationals and most large domestic companies across the region have formal value statements and written or implicit codes of conduct. However, the evidence of values and codes being practised are mixed (Adnan, Saher, Naureen, Qureshi, & Khan, 2013; Akhtar, Abassi, & Umar, 2011; Anand, Cherian, Gautam, Majmudar, & Raimawala, 2013; BBCMA, 2012; Chakraborty, 2001, 2004; Das, 2009; D'Mello, 2002; French & Martin, 2013; Gupta, 2004; Kanagabasapathi, 2007; Labbai, 2007; Manikutty, 2011; Naeem & Welford, 2009; Paul, Roy, & Mukhopadhyay, 2006; Pervin, Wilman, MacDonald, & Ranchhod, 2011; Rakesh, 2012; RGICS, 1998; Sachan, 2013; Sorab & Sharukh, 2012; Sreedharan & Wakhlu, 2010; Sultana & Khosru, 2011; TERI, 2013; Wise, Ali, & Wise, 2010). As it is not possible to discuss or summarise each of these papers/books in a chapter, some major issues covered in them are summarised below, using a holistic marketing framework (Kotler, Keleer, Koshy, & Jha, 2013), which consists of four pillars: internal marketing, integrated marketing, relationship marketing and performance marketing. Holistic marketing needs to be practised using strategic marketing (segmentation, targeting and positioning) and tactical marketing (marketing-mix elements). So, some critical issues covered in the cited literature are briefly highlighted here using the framework described above.

Internal marketing

Major ethical issues involving employees are their competency, attitude, awareness levels of company policy and motivation to follow it, and a certain degree of identification with the organisation. High customer-contact sectors such as retail, pharmaceuticals, insurance and banking appear to be more prone to unethical practices.

As the literature mostly covers large enterprises, except retail (which is predominantly in the unorganised sector in all three countries), mostly anecdotal evidence is available for the others. Two personal experiences of the author with employees of two different organisations are described in the following box:

Employee ethics: two experiences

1   Ethics of unethical (as shared by a friend)

In the mid-1970s, government office in India, given the authority to issue some critical certificates to citizens, was known for delays and corruption. An informal norm had developed that one had to pay 50 Indian rupees (INR) (equivalent to about US$7 at that time) for a certificate, if it was urgent. The citizen concerned paid the required amount, but could not collect the certificate the same day. Next day, when he came to collect it, he was asked to make payment again, as on the previous day's collection there was a shortfall of INR 50. The citizen loudly protested against this 'injustice'. Immediately, other employees of the organisation rallied behind this citizen, saying, 'One has to suffer for one's counting error, but demanding a bribe twice for the same work is unfair and unethical.' The certificate was handed over without a second payment.

2   Ethics of the poor: may the tribe of Ramjee Gurung thrive

The author was visiting Sikkim, a hill state in North East India, in summer 2013. While travelling during the day to several tourist places, he lost his wallet; he realised this only after reaching his hotel room late in the evening. He had no clue where he could have dropped it. The wallet contained a substantial amount of money, credit cards and, most importantly, identity cards, without which entry to airports would be impossible. On checking about the taxi he had used, he was told that the driver usually stayed on the outskirts of the city and was not accessible by phone. However, he was assured by the hotel staff that taxi drivers in Sikkim were extremely honest and had returned much more valuable items left by tourists in their taxis. This was not much comfort, as the author had no clue whether his wallet had fallen in the taxi or on the road. He spent a sleepless night.

At 6.30am the next morning, he received a call from the hotel reception, asking him to come down to meet a visitor. There he found Mr Ramjee Gurung, the taxi driver, with his wallet — everything intact inside it. On being warmly complimented, the driver's simple reaction was: 'You tourists help me feed my family — how can I even think of cheating you?'

There are several other examples of honesty of poor people in this country. This could leave us with the question: Does greed come with wealth and education?

Both ethical and unethical marketing practices indulged in by employees can be traced to organisational ethics and its enforcement. There are organisations like Unilever subsidiaries, P&G subsidiaries, Nestlé and IBM, and large well-known domestic groups/companies such as Tatas, Infosys, Wipro, Mahindra and Mahindra, Thermax, Narayan Health, MindTree, Aravind Eyecare and Grameen Bank, just to name some examples, known for articulating and enforcing ethical conduct. There are several others with perceived poor ethical conduct, but these are legally problematic to name until or unless they are caught.

The general finding seems to be that even in organisations of good repute, rules are occasionally breached; however, these are mostly individual indiscretions, and are dealt with severely when discovered. In many other organisations, employees indulge in unethical conduct vis-à-vis customers, under the pressure of targets, ambiguous rules, poor personal values and, in some cases, with full organisational backing.

Some other critical ethical issues in internal marketing are:

- fair and inclusive recruitment;
- fair treatment of employees;
- gender equity and treatment;
- providing fair wages or just meeting legal requirements;
- dealing with whistle blowers;
- dealing with contract employees; and
- dealing with restructuring and involuntary retirement.

Integrated marketing

This deals with both integration inside (e.g. brand management, market research, sales, post-sales-service) and outside (e.g. marketing, finance, production, systems) but within an organisation.

Major ethical issues arising in this domain are:

- promises made but not fulfilled, due to lack of coordination, power struggles, personal reasons and so on;
- poor response to customer grievances and complaints due to turf issues, red tape or simply poor processes and culture of ownership; and
- blatant unethical practices such as making false promises, making unsubstantiated claims, using the fine print in warranties to short-change customers, or bribing associates or partners in the organised sector while meeting the legal requirements expected of the corporate entity.

This is just an illustrative list.

Relationship marketing

Relationship marketing is mainly about the long term. It involves mutuality and trust. As most companies survive on a short-term basis in a highly competitive, uncertain environment − aided by poor governance and unorganised and somewhat less demanding customers − this aspect of marketing is the greatest casualty in this region. Spurious medicines, physicians' samples sold in retail, pharmaceutical companies spending huge amounts on gifts to the doctors to generate prescriptions (resulting in tightening of codes more recently in India), vehicle recalls, insurance policies mis-sold, exorbitant pricing of essential drugs, promoting junk food and beverages to children... These are all just illustrative of the menace (i.e. negative practices in the name of relationship marketing).

Even multinationals and large companies are guilty of these behaviours − one only has to analyse the large number of consumer complaints and reviews on the internet to fathom what is happening in this domain.

Some of the most unethical practices on targeting and positioning fall in this domain. These are:

- political parties targeting voters based on religion, caste, sect, etc., with divisive and consolidation agendas;
- seeking votes in the name of religion;
- neglect of the poor and vulnerable by health and education providers through premium pricing; and
- targeting children when selling junk food and beverages.

However, there are ethical marketers who target vulnerable segments with appropriate offerings (e.g. Grameen Bank in Bangladesh), promote unity and consumer awareness (e.g. Ambuja cement and Tata coffee in India), and promote hygiene among the masses (e.g. Hindustan Unilever).

Performance marketing

This consists of three major aspects:

1. performance with regard to customers (including intermediaries and the regulators) in terms of satisfaction and delight;
2. performance with regard to the company in terms of sales, profit, growth, brand equity, and customer acquisition and retention; and
3. performance with regard to society and environment in terms of equity, justice and sustainability.

Major ethical marketing issues with regard to customers seem to be of sporadic interest of a large number of even professionally managed companies that pay lip service only to customer satisfaction, let alone exceeding their expectations. Managing satisfaction indices, in many cases, takes precedence over managing customer relationships.

Major ethical marketing issues with regard to the company seem to be internal frauds, fudging of data, leaking company plans and, in some cases, major frauds. Significant unethical marketing practices impacting companies, which often go unnoticed, is taking short cuts, short-term orientation and short-changing the company of its long-term potential while showing results and reaping rewards.

Summary of major issues

Major issues with regard to ethical marketing in the region are identified using a holistic marketing framework. These mainly refer to dealings with employees, customers, other intermediaries and regulators with a short-term, selfish and (in some cases) dubious perspective.

There are subtle issues of promoting greed, materialistic culture, objectification of women and unsustainable consumption priorities. The critical issue in these cases is: who decides, and on whose behalf? Can strict norms be imposed and enforced in democratic societies?

New research directions

It was observed earlier in this chapter that the major weakness of extant research in this region is a lack of rigorous analytical studies. Ethics, in general, is not an easy subject to research. Ethics in marketing is more complex. There are lots of uncontrolled and uncontrollable variables and entities. There are always possibilities of desirable responses, hidden agendas, reluctance to share data and so on. Arvidson (2013) offers an interesting perspective on cross-cultural sensitivities in qualitative research in this domain.

We attempt to present a thorough framework, which can be used for seeking new directions in researching ethics in marketing (see Figure 4.2). The framework is holistic and self-explanatory. Future research in marketing ethics can aim at positioning itself in one or more of the blocks in the framework, focusing more on the analytical part.

Serial No.	Nature of study	Organisation								Individual member		
		Internal marketing		Integrated marketing		Relationship marketing		Performance marketing		Ability	Willingness	Perceived organisational norm
		S*	T*	S	T	S	T	S	T			
1	Descriptive											
2	Analytical											
3	Normative											

Figure 4.2 A framework for new directions in marketing ethics – a holistic approach.
Notes: * S = strategic (segmentation, targeting, positioning).
T = tactical (marketing – mix elements).

Implications for practising marketing in India, Pakistan and Bangladesh

At the time of writing (April 2014), national elections are taking place in India. Bangladesh and Pakistan have gone through this process in the recent past. Manifestos of the political parties appear to be most deceptive communications and promise a service for which citizens pay with their most precious possession: the right to vote. How can those who win elections with deceit legislate on fair trade practices? 'Fair and lovely' is a very successful Hindustan Unilever innovation – a cosmetic brand of a company which promotes the fair colour of skin as a desirable outcome – but how fair is it? Beverages companies draw huge amount of water in arid areas – they deplete groundwater, making it difficult for citizens to access it affordably, and effluents from these factories pollute other groundwater sources and percolate underground. Such companies may be meeting legal requirements, but are they ethical?

The concept of *matsyanyay* ('big fish eating the small fish') prevails in most supply chains – is it ethical? Paid-for news in media is common knowledge – again, is it ethical? The free market is not so free, and the regulated market is just not enough. So, what are the implications?

There cannot be simple answers to complex problems. But simple steps can be taken. Ex-Prime Minister Mr Atal Behari Vajpayee famously said, 'Corruption has become a low risk–high reward phenomenon in these countries.' So, to contain corruption, can one substantially enhance the risk? This needs to be done.

Can organisations be expected to run ethically just because they have value statements and codes of conduct? Is enforcing compliance good enough? Will these rules and strict enforcement of rules result in more ethical behaviour? Is ethical leadership the answer? Past experience seems to suggest the answer is no.

So, where is the remedy? We need rules. We need enforcement. We need visionary and inspiring leadership. But more than this, we need *conscious* corporates run
by *conscious* individuals at all levels.

The Western and Eastern philosophies have to come together to moderate corporate, societal and individual consciousness to move towards 'regulated desires', a
higher level of consciousness, and sustainable consumption and marketing. Both
corporate bodies and individuals have to move from compliance, to identification,
to the internalisation of the idea of ethical, sustainable behaviour as a superior (and
maybe the only) option.

References

Adnan, A., Saher, N., Naureen, H., Qureshi, S., & Khan, N. Y. (2013). What shapes ethical
    behaviour of sales team? A case study of banking sector of Pakistan. *Interdisciplinary
    Journal of Contemporary Research in Business, 5*(1), 424−442.
Akhtar, W., Abassi, A. S., & Umar, S. (2011). Ethical issues in advertising in Pakistan: An
    Islamic perspective. *World Applied Sciences Journal, 13*(3), 444−452.
Anand, A., Cherian, K., Gautam, A., Majmudar, R., & Raimawala, A. (2013). Business vs.
    ethics: The Indian tradeoff, *Knowledge@ Wharton*, 1−5. Available from <http://knowl-
    edge.wharton.upenn.edu/article/business-vs-ethics-the-india-tradeoff>.
Arvidson, M. (2013). Ethics, intimacy and distance in longitudinal, qualitative research:
    Experiences from reality check Bangladesh. *Progress in Development Studies, 13*(4),
    279−293.
Azmi, S. (2014). An Islamic approach to business ethics, 1−12. Available from <http://
    renaissance.com.pk/myviewpoint2y5.htm>.
BBCMA (2012). *Country Case Study: Bangladesh*. BBC Media Action.
Chakraborty, S. K. (2001). *The management of ethics omnibus*. New Delhi: Oxford
    University Press.
Chakraborty, S. K. (2004). Ethics for business: Drawing on Indian values. *IIMB Management
    Review, 14*(4), 50−53.
Das, G. (2009). *The difficulty of being good*. New Delhi, India: Penguin Books.
D'Mello, B. (2002). Transnational pharmaceutical corporations and neo-liberal business
    ethics in India. *Journal of Business Ethics, 36*, 165−185.
Dutta, S.M. (1998). The context for values and ethics. In RGICS, Project 22, (pp. 36−43).
Engineer, A. A. (2014). Islamic ethic. Available from <http://andromeda.rutgers.edu/
    ~rtavakol/engineer/ethics.htm>.
French, J. J., & Martin, M. (2013). The roof is on fire: The ethical minefield of the textile
    industry in Bangladesh. *Journal of International Academy of Case Studies, 19*, 7.
Gandhi, M. K. (1999). *The collected works of Mahatma Gandhi (electronic book)*.
    New Delhi: Publications Division, Government of India. 33, 135.
Gupta, D. (2004). *Ethics incorporated: Top priority and bottom line*. New Delhi: KPMG in
    arrangement with Harper Collins Publishers.
Haksar, A. (1998). Ethics and governance in the private sector. In RGICS, Project 22, (pp.
    44−49).
Jamnik, A. (2011). The questions of ethical decision in marketing and ethics. *Revista Cultura
    Economica, 29*(80), 41−53.

Kanagasabapathi, P. (2007). Ethics and values in Indian economy and business. *International Journal of Social Economics*, *34*(9), 577–585.

Kotler, P., Keleer, K. L., Koshy, A., & Jha, M. (2013). *Marketing management: A South Asian perspective* (14th ed.). New Delhi: Pearson Education.

Labbai, M. M. (2007). Social responsibility and ethics in marketing. Paper Presented at International Marketing Conference on Marketing and Society proceedings (8–10 April), (pp. 17–27).

Manikutty, S. (2011). Being Ethical: Ethics as the Foundation of Business. Delhi, NOIDA: Random House.

Naeem, M. A., & Welford, R. (2009). A comparative study of corporate social responsibility in Bangladesh and Pakistan. *Corporate Social Responsibility and Environmental Management*, *16*, 108–122.

Paul, P., Roy, A., & Mukhopadhyay, K. (2006). The impact of cultural values on marketing ethical norms: A study in India and the United States. *Journal of International Marketing*, *14*(4), 28–56.

Pervin, S., Wilman, M., MacDonald, L., & Ranchhod, A. (2011). Consumer attitudes towards key ethical retailing issues: A comparison of Bangladesh and the UK. Academy of Marketing Conference, July.

Radhakrishnan, S. (1914). The ethics of the Vedanta. *International Journal of Ethics*, *24*(2), 168–183.

Rajiv Gandhi Institute of Contemporary Studies (RGICS). (1998). Corporate Governance and Ethics – Conference Papers and Proceedings: Report No. 22 of Rajiv Gandhi Institute of Contemporary Studies, New Delhi.

Rakesh, R. (2012). Ethics in marketing – Indian spirituality. *Journal of Emerging Trends in Economics and Management Sciences*, *3*(1), 72–76.

Sachan, D. (2013). Tackling corruption in Indian medicine. *The Lancet*, *382*(9905), e23–e24.

Sekhar, R. C. (2003). *Ethical choices in business* (2nd ed.). New Delhi: Sage.

Sorab, S., & Sharukh, N. T. (2012). Ethical issues in insurance marketing – the case of Western India. *Economica–Acta–univarsitatis*, *8*(5), 140–151.

Sreedharan, E., & Wakhlu, B. (2010). *Restoring values – keys to integrity, ethical behaviour and good governance*. New Delhi: Sage.

Sultana, S., & Khosru, K. H. (2011). Practice of using gifts as promotional materials for marketing of pharmaceutical products in Bangladesh: A study conducted on general physicians and representatives from pharmaceutical companies. *Stamford Journal of Pharmaceutical Science*, *4*(2), 13–18.

Swami, C. S. (1996). Hindu dharma: The universal way of life. Mumbai: Bhartiya Vidya Bhawan.

Tagore, R. (1988). *Lectures and addresses*. Delhi: Macmillan. 81.

TERI. (2013). Developing ethical practices and promoting sustainability reporting in corporate India. Report of the Energy and Research Institute, Prepared for the National Foundation for Corporate Governance, (pp. 1–63).

Vittal, N. (1998). *Ethics and governance for the public sector*. In RGICS, Project 22, (pp. 62–70).

Wise, V., Ali, M. M., & Wise, T. D. (2010). Ethical conduct in business: A case study analysis using Bangladesh experiences. *Problems and Perspectives in Management*, *8*(4), 184–192.

Ethical marketing in Vietnam, Cambodia, the Philippines and Indonesia

Jeremy Pearce, Mattia Miani, Michael Segon and Bang Nguyen

Introduction

The goal of this chapter is to look at the mounting interest in marketing ethics by government regulators, marketing and communication professionals, and the general public in Vietnam, Cambodia, the Philippines and Indonesia. Theories on ethics, examples and cases will be drawn from these interesting and diverse South East Asian countries in order to develop a conceptual framework linking both theory and practice.

Since the enactment of *Doi Moi* ('Renovation') economic policy in 1989, Vietnam has successfully moved from a centrally planned collectivist state economy to a market structure open to private enterprise and individual initiative (Grinter, 2006). Now private entrepreneurs in all sectors, including speculative areas such as real estate development, are respected figures: in some cases, just two decades ago the same people would have been considered criminals (Kim, 2008). Until 1990, advertising was outright illegal in Vietnam (International Business Publications, 2009, p. 71). The marketing profession and practice is thus very new and has been advancing in parallel to this economic development. By the early 2000s, most multinational advertising agency brands had their own affiliates in Vietnam, with head offices generally in Ho Chi Minh City and branches in Hanoi. They serve other multinational and foreign investment companies operating in Vietnam, while a myriad of freelances and small agencies serve the large market of small and medium enterprises (SMEs). Within this context, the general public and the government have quickly become sensitive to the topics of consumer protection and advertising regulation. Due to these interesting developments, the study of ethical marketing in Vietnam, Cambodia, the Philippines and Indonesia are timely topics for further investigation.

Learning objectives

After reading this chapter, you should be able to:

- understand marketing as a profession and its code of ethics;
- comprehend and define ethics, ethical decision-making, outcomes and issues;
- outline the scope of ethical issues in Vietnam, Cambodia, the Philippines and Indonesia;
- acknowledge the duties of ethical marketing and responsible decision-making; and
- demonstrate the importance of ethical marketing in several case studies across the South East Asian region.

Route map: ethical marketing — Vietnam, Cambodia, the Philippines and Indonesia

The aims of the chapter are twofold. First, we review extant literatures on ethics with topics such as the marketing profession, ethical decision-making, ethics by outcome (egoism, altruism and utilitarianism), ethics by process (right, justice, fairness and due process), and ethics by virtue and character. We develop a conceptual framework linking both theory and practice, combining the above topics with responsible decision-making, duties of the marketing professional, regulation and public discourse on marketing ethics (see Figure 5.1). The framework thus allows us to capture a range of potential topics likely to influence marketing practitioners, policymakers and customers.

Second, we incorporate and evaluate the theoretical bases in order to provide further insights into the nature of the marketing ethics in mini-cases across Vietnam, Cambodia, the Philippines and Indonesia, previously suggested as areas for future research. Thus, our chapter fills an important gap in the knowledge dissemination of marketing ethics in the South East Asian region.

The rest of our chapter is structured as follows: first, we present our theoretical framing founded in the ethics literature. Based upon this literature, we discuss the state of the art in ethical marketing, predominantly in Vietnam, but with cases and illustrations in Cambodia, the Philippines and Indonesia. The conceptual model shows the relationships at varying levels of ethics — that is, by outcome, process, and virtue and character. Following this, we present a practice case study of ethical marketing in Vietnam. Finally, we discuss our chapter's implications for theory and practice, with suggestions for future research.

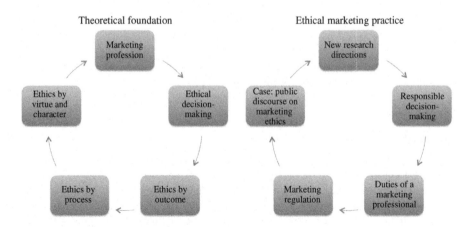

Figure 5.1 Overview of the chapter.

The state of art in ethical marketing: Vietnam, Cambodia, the Philippines and Indonesia

Marketing as a profession

Most occupations consider themselves to be professions; however, as Wilensky (1964) noted, the label of being a professional is loosely applied to increasing specialisation and transferability of skill, the proliferation of objective standards of work, the spread of tenure arrangements, licensing or certification, and the growth of service occupations. Wilensky (1964) advances the view that, in effect, occupations can be placed on a continuum of professionalisation. This suggests that at one end, we find what are often referred as the true professions, being highly specialised, and at the other, we find occupations that are simple and relatively easy to undertake. What is unclear is whether an occupation becomes a profession at a particular point or whether it needs to satisfy a number of critical criteria. Koehn (1994) states that the notion of a professional is essentially a normative one, because who qualifies as a professional varies according to the norms or standards of behaviour that the professional is bound to obey. Reader (1966) states that an occupation's move to professional standing can be linked to the existence and influence of a relevant professional organisation.

Koehn (1994) summarises the basic characteristics of a professional to be clients' trustworthy agent either because (a) they are experts, or (b) they are service providers, who will obey a client's instructions for a fee.

Khurana, Nohria, and Penrice (2005) suggest four criteria for calling an occupation a bona fide profession, including:

1. a common body of knowledge resting on a well-developed, widely accepted theoretical base;
2. a system for certifying that individuals possess such knowledge before being licensed or otherwise allowed to practise;
3. a commitment to use specialised knowledge for the public good, and a renunciation of the goal of profit-maximisation, in return for professional autonomy and monopoly power; and
4. a code of ethics, with provisions for monitoring individual compliance with the code and a system of sanctions for enforcing it.

The professional is also reliant on effective communication skills that enable them to build a climate of trust and legitimacy with potential clients. This includes the highlighting of technical expertise and theoretical knowledge, independence and autonomy in decision-making, and the willingness to abide by a set of standards that include professional ethics (Middlehurst & Kennie, 1997). The importance of professions having a social duty is advanced by numerous authors, including Raelin (1991) and Lennertz (1991), who identify intellectual tradition and a fiduciary relationship to society as prime characteristics. The idea of a social duty is also supported by Camenisch (1983), who describes a profession as a 'moral community'.

Middlehurst and Kennie (1997) state that professionalism is a constructed phenomenon that is maintained due to the fact that professionals can address the needs of clients when facing complex problems. According to Gold, Rodgers, and Smith (2002), a major aspect of professionalism is the power that is derived from expert knowledge and skill, and the ignorance or absence of such knowledge and skill on the part of the client. They further add that the client accessing this information cannot bridge the deficiency in knowledge; rather it has to be transformed into knowledge through considered application within a given context. Eraut (1994) provides a similar position on the nature of the expertise, suggesting that the client is dependent on the professional because they are unable to address their problem by procedural knowledge alone or by following a manual.

This chapter identifies marketing as a discipline, underpinned by a wealth of knowledge that must be understood and able to be transformed according to the type of product or service and the context in which it is being offered. Furthermore, most marketing positions in organisations have undergraduate and postgraduate qualifications as mandatory. This indicates that a substantive body of expert knowledge is required to perform the marketing function. This is consistent with Lusch and O'Brien's (1997) assertion that a profession 'is an occupation that requires extensive formal education and often formal requirements'. Cogan (1953, p. 33) defines it as 'a vocation whose practice is founded upon an understanding of the theoretical structure of some department of learning or science, and upon the abilities accompanying such understanding'. A related issue is the length of time required to obtain mastery, which is often significant and again distinguishes the profession from other occupations and crafts (Wall, 1998; Winch, 2004). Clearly this body of specific marketing knowledge is consistent with that described by Khurana et al. (2005) as a strong theoretical base. Moreover, the importance of understanding consumer behaviour in the Asian region and the differences that exist between Vietnam, Cambodia, the Philippines and Indonesia is also a key factor for the marketing professional. It is this knowledge that organisations value, because it is specialised in nature and cannot be easily acquired.

The emergence of the marketing profession in Vietnam

According to Morgan (1998), the existence of an association or professional body is a key feature that distinguishes the profession from other occupations. He suggests that the association has numerous functions, including restricting membership to the association only to those who satisfy the high standards of practice, thus maintaining the status of the organisation. Morgan (1998) suggests that the association needs to: (1) develop a set of rules or standards to which members must adhere, (2) continue the development of the expert knowledge required and (3) regulate the behaviour of its members, including the expulsion of members who fail to meet the standards or demonstrate required levels of mastery. This is consistent with Beauchamp and Bowie's (1997) position that professional practice standards hold obligations and other standards of moral conduct that are determined by the professional community. Similarly, De George (1999) and Ardagh (2010) describe the role of a professional association as managing the field or discipline and establishing restriction of entry to the field of practice. Flexner (1910) also notes the criteria of admission, legitimate practice and proper conduct as one of the key characteristics of a profession.

Khurana et al. (2005) state that codes are a requirement for any occupation that aspires to be a profession. They distinguish between codes that exist in many occupational groups such as librarians, plumbers, etc. Khurana et al. (2005) also mentions 'true professions', whose approach is far more sophisticated. They argue that true professions teach the meaning and significance of the code as part of the formal education of their members. Furthermore they examine this understanding, as a formal process upon which accreditation or licensing is dependent. Once the professional has been granted the licence to practise, they must abide by the code in order to maintain the right to practise.

While other countries in the region do have established professional bodies representing the marketing profession (such as the Marketing Association of Thailand, The Institute of Marketing Malaysia or the Marketing Institute of Singapore), Vietnam still lacks active professional associations enforcing strict codes of ethics. One partial exception is represented by multinational companies based in Vietnam, which adhere to the international code of practice (for example, the major market research firms in Vietnam belong to their international association, ESOMAR, and claim to act according to its code of conduct). Cambodia is not known to have any marketing association, while both the Philippines and Indonesia also have memberships with recognisable associations such as ESOMAR, which is regionally affiliated with the Philippine Marketing Association and Indonesia Marketing Association (Asosiasi Pemasaran Indonesia), respectively. The ICC (International Chamber of Commerce)/ESOMAR Code on Market and Social Research sets out professional and ethical rules which market researchers follow and has been adopted by more than 4,900 ESOMAR members and 60 national market research associations worldwide (ESOMAR, 2014).

If we look back at the four principles laid down by Khurana et al. (2005), we can conclude that across the South East Asian region, in Vietnam, Cambodia, the Philippines and Indonesia, at the moment, only the first criterion is met (the existence of a body of knowledge, largely drawing on international literature, that is spread through formal education in the higher education system). By all means, in these countries, marketing is still a profession in its infancy. This makes the study of the development of ethical marketing practice even more interesting.

What are ethics?

The fact that marketing is still a profession in its infancy in South East Asia does not mean that professionals, legislators and the general public are not sensitive to ethical considerations in marketing communication.

To address this point, we need to clarify what we mean by ethics. According to Preston (1996, p. 16), ethics is concerned with what is right, fair, just or good; they are about what we ought to do, not just what the case is, or what is most acceptable or expedient. This definition has clear implications for marketing professionals because, like other managers in organisations, they are sometimes pressured into making decisions quickly without critical information or the consideration of the impact of the decision on a range of stakeholders. As Professor Henry Mintzberg of

McGill University found in his landmark studies, decision-making is the essence of a manager; however, he identified that managerial work is characterised by brevity, variety and fragmentation of work. He also noted that managers are not reflective thinkers, but tend to be reactive and make decisions with insufficient information (Mintzberg, 1979). Child (1984, 2005) similarly identified that when confronted with the need to reach a decision, managers tend to look to the first solution that appears that satisfies the minimum decision criteria, rather than taking a considered approach and searching for an optimal solution. Child termed this phenomenon 'satisficing'.

As an employee of an organisation, a marketing professional has the duty to advance the interests of the organisation as its agent. He or she also has a professional duty to act within the limits of professional knowledge and expertise. This may result in dilemmas for which there is no clear resolution when marketers are called upon to diversify a strategy that may increase sales of a product or service, but in a way that is inconsistent with the duties of the profession, for example, developing long-term customer relations. It is these ethical challenges that we as professionals must resolve in the right way, and not necessarily the most expedient way. But what are ethics and how do we make ethical decisions?

Ferrell, Fraedrich, and Ferrell (2011) cite the *American Heritage Dictionary* definition as: the study of the general nature of morals and of specific moral choices; moral philosophy; the study of rules or standards governing conduct of the members of a profession. De George (2010) suggests that ethics are concerned with the goods worth seeking in life, and with the rules that ought to govern human behaviour and social interaction. Similar themes emerge in other definitions, including Velasquez (1998), identifying it as the study of what is good or right for human beings, what goals people ought to pursue and what actions they ought to perform; and Buchholz (1989), who describes it as the actions and practices directed towards improving the welfare of people and attaining a good life.

The concept of 'ought' is critical in an understanding of ethics, because the study of ethics is multifaceted, including as it does the study of morality, the legitimacy of moral claims and basis of justification of decisions. Ferrell et al. (2011) suggest that the study of business ethics does not just mean moralising about what should or should not be done in a particular situation. Rather, it systematically links the concepts of morality, responsibility and decision-making in organisations.

Business ethics consists of business principles and standards that guide behaviour in the world of business (Ferrell et al., 2011). Ethics is the thought process that comes into play when we are deciding between right and wrong, or, more typically, about weighing two rights. It's establishing the process of using appropriate principles of decision-making when differing values come into conflict with each other (Driscoll & Hoffman, 1999).

Making ethical decisions

There are many ways of studying and analysing management decision-making and action from an ethical perspective. An important aspect is to realise that decision-making involves three separate components, each having ethical dimensions.

1. Intent: this is a critical aspect of decision-making – the why. What is the reason, drive or purpose for the decision? As noted earlier in this chapter, moral accountability is predicated on the actions or decisions that are undertaken with knowledge or consciousness – in other words, intent.
2. Action: this is the process of making the decision or the undertaking of the action. It is the 'how' of decision-making, which is sometimes referred to as the means.
3. Outcome: this is the consequence or the impact of the decision or action.

We would normally consider holding a person morally accountable for their actions by considering why they made the decision, the decision itself and the consequences of the decision.

What is important to keep in mind is that by introducing these perspectives, we are increasing the quality and scope of our decision. While there are numerous ethical theories or approaches to thinking, we can summarise these into three distinct categories, which involve determining ethics by focusing on:

1. the outcome or consequences of a decision;
2. principles or processes that guide the decision; and
3. the characteristics or virtues of those making the decision.

The first step in analysing moral issues is obvious, but not always easy: Get the facts. Some moral issues create controversies simply because we do not bother to check the facts. This first step is also among the most important and the most frequently overlooked (Velasquez, 2006). We now discuss each of the three ethical approaches in detail.

Ethics by outcome: egoism, altruism and utilitarianism

This group of theories is perhaps the most attractive to the business community because it uses an analytical approach that parallels the cost benefit analysis used in most business decision-making. The objective of this approach is to generate the greatest possible benefit for the largest number of people while minimising the damage or harm to others. The issue here is not how these outcomes are achieved, but rather the cost or benefit that is incurred. Because they focus on the outcome of a decision, these approaches are often referred to as consequentialism. The approaches are also linked to economic analysis, with the most common method, utilitarianism, encompassing the word 'utility', which in economics means value. Thus, this approach is concerned with measuring the value of a particular outcome relative to another. Utilitarianism holds that the moral evaluation will depend on the good or bad consequences produced for everyone by the action. The primary way of determining the moral worth of an action is to evaluate all the social cost or benefit associated with it.

Consequentialism also applies to individuals, as egoism and altruism suggest. Both are concerned with evaluating the cost and benefits of a decision; however, egoism focuses on the benefits to the self, whereas the altruist is concerned with maximising benefits to others. Its application to marketing decisions should be clear – the decision that generates the greater potential for distribution, promotion and attractiveness of a product or service to consumers for the least cost would be the most favoured one.

Problems with consequentialism

The major problem with outcome theories is that they hold that the moral or ethical worth of an action or practice is determined solely by the consequences of the practice or action, and not by the intent of the action. Thus, how we arrive at a decision is not considered relevant, providing the benefit is considered moral. This raises the possibility of a business decision advancing the interests of the business, but in an unethical manner – for example, using questionable promotion strategies, or including false or misleading statements about a product or service so as to attract customers.

Two other problems can be immediately identified: whose interests are evaluated, and what is actually measured.

It is often difficult to identify all the parties and stakeholders affected by a decision; therefore, utilitarianism – in particular – is often restricted to those of immediate interests. In the business world, this is often limited to shareholders, consistent with the objective of maximising shareholder wealth. This has the danger of excluding key stakeholders with the potential to affect a business from consideration – to the organisation's detriment.

The other problem is that of measurement. An often-quoted phrase in management is that if it is measurable, it is valued. Unfortunately, the converse is also true – if we cannot quantify it, we ignore it. Thus major omissions in consequentialism are those issues that are by nature nebulous, such as emotional well-being, psychological harm and business reputation. As the marketing professional provides a key link between the organisation and the external environment, the decisions and strategies advanced by marketers have the greatest potential to enhance or destroy business reputation.

Ethics by process: rights, justice and fairness, and due process

The second branch of ethics addresses the inadequacies of consequentialism by arguing that actions and practices cannot be justified solely in terms of the consequences or outcomes, but rather that the actions and practices have intrinsic moral or ethical value, for example, some actions and practices may be morally wrong, no matter how good their outcomes might be. This group of theories includes concepts related to duty and obligation (deontology), using rights as a moral guide, using principles as the basis for decision-making, and following a rational and clear decision-making process.

Deontologists suggest that the business world is complex and characterised by uncertainty, making it extremely difficult (if not impossible) to identify all stakeholders and the impacts our decisions would have. Therefore, the ethical decision should be determined by ensuring that the decision does not violate the rights of individuals, is consistent with an accepted principle such as fairness and/or follows a transparent and agreed decision-making process.

These approaches are also very common in business. Organisations are required to follow the law, while policies and procedures can be viewed as organisational laws. Decision-making and problem-solving use rational analytical approaches enabling verification of justification of the process. Many societal and organisational laws are based on principles of justice and fairness, such as equal employment opportunity. We also consider people's rights, particularly when purchasing products and services; we expect to be fully informed about a product and that it is safe – that it will not cause harm.

The relevance of these approaches to the marketing function should similarly be clear. As discussed earlier in this chapter, the professional associations to which marketers belong typically have codes of ethics, conduct or practices to which members must adhere. These are forms of rules and duties of the profession as distinct from those of the organisation. Similarly, laws exist in most countries regarding advertising and communication, which must also be followed as a form of duty. Thus, process is critical for marketing professionals to ensure that the way they make their decisions is also ethical.

Problems with process

Following codes, laws, principles and processes blindly without question may not necessarily result in an ethical outcome. Consider unfair dismissal laws, when an employee may have committed a serious offence worth of dismissal, yet because they have not taken through an approved performance management process, an industrial court may rule in favour of the employee. Or consider the collection of data on customers' needs and behaviour – while within the laws, if it is excessively done and without consideration of privacy issues, then concerns of unethical practices may be raised and regulations may be imposed on marketers. Similarly, one of the consequences of articulating individual rights is that when they are violated, an individual has the right to compensation or justice – this can lead to an extremely litigious environment, even for frivolous matters.

Another potential problem is the interpretation of principles and in particular law – the concept of the spirit versus the intent of law comes to mind. For example, are organisations that explore tax laws for loopholes to reduce taxation acting in the spirit or the letter of the law?

Ethics by virtue or character

The third ethical perspective is that of virtue ethics, which seeks to emphasise the concept of character rather than a calculus or the following of a principle. Its origins lie in the tradition of Greek philosophers, such as Plato and Aristotle; indeed the area is sometimes called Aristotelian ethics. However, there are also many parallels to Eastern thinking, including Vedantic principles and Confucianism.

Essentially, the virtue approach argues that people should act in a manner consistent with the advancement of specific characteristics that we would all agree are characteristics of ethical people. Virtues include honesty, integrity, truthfulness, courage and so on. Conversely, we should actively discourage characteristics or vices that are undesirable, such as lying, stealing, cheating and licentious behaviours.

According to Hinman (2010), Aristotle suggests that the objective is to achieve a 'strength of character', which involves finding the proper balance between the two extremes of excess and deficiency. This is often referred to as the 'Golden Mean'. Aristotlean virtue is a characteristic that needs to be practised, so that it becomes a learned habit. Thus, for Aristotle, you can teach people to be virtuous. We can see the application of virtue ethics in many organisations in their mission and value statements – terms such as 'integrity', 'trustworthy' and 'caring' are often used to establish the sort of characteristics that the organisation wishes to promote. The application of virtue ethics to decision-making is somewhat similar to principle-based approaches, but rather than asking if the decision is consistent with the principles (such as fairness), the virtue approach asks us to consider the person making the decision and whether their decision displays the characteristic of fairness. Virtue ethics ask us to consider whom we want to be and if the decision is something that will contribute to the flourishing of society.

While some people maintain that the virtue approach lacks a rigid paradigm, in many ways this is also its strength. Although we may debate details of a definition of integrity, there is a general agreement as to what the general characteristics of a person with integrity would be. Again, the application of virtue approaches to the marketing professional should be fairly clear. The task of communicating the benefits of a product or service to potential customers is a key responsibility of the marketing function. Virtues such as trust and honestly are critical in this communication process.

Vietnam

As of 2013, Vietnam ranked 112 of 182 countries in the Transparency International's Corruption Perception Index, well behind countries like Thailand and China. According to Global Times (2014), Vietnam's Government Inspectorate of Vietnam detected 45 corruption cases in 2013, with the involvement of 99 people. The Government Inspectorate revealed that, in 2013, a total of 354 billion Vietnamese dong (US$16.7 million) was found to have been embezzled (Global Times, 2014). The Government Inspectorate said that corruption and waste in Vietnam mainly occurred in fields of land use, credit, banking, asset management and capital, causing huge economic losses and public discontent.

The international community is supporting Vietnam's efforts to tackle corruption. For example, Australia has developed a three-year training programme that is targeting 275 members of the Vietnamese Communist Party – Vietnam's most powerful political institution – with training in national integrity systems and factors contributing to corruption. The programme provides high-level policy training and operational training to tackle corruption. Topics included in the training encompass corruption diagnosis and monitoring, financial accountability, a legislative and institutional framework to help prevent and deal with corruption, and investigation methods (Australian Department of Foreign Trade and Affairs, 2014).

Vietnamese Prime Minister Nguyen Tan Dung instructed closer inspection of the performance of ministers and chairpersons of people's committees across Vietnam, especially in exercising state management of land, capital construction investment, state-owned enterprises and implementation of national target programmes. According to Inspector General Huynh Phong Tranh, in 2013, the agency conducted a total of 8,921 administrative inspections. They detected the misuse of 326.5 trillion Vietnamese dong (US$15.5 billion) and 4,520 hectares of land. Consequently, more than 25 trillion Vietnamese dong (US$1.2 billion) and 3,653 hectares of land have been reclaimed, while more than 1,580 collectives and 2,675 individuals were fined for administrative violations. The inspection sector also transferred 72 cases and 75 individuals to investigation agencies.

This case presents grave concerns with corruption in Vietnam, with cases permeating multiples industries. With such a presence of unethical practices, Vietnam is damaging its reputation as a place for conducting business. From a marketing perspective, the case may highlight that support from the both the government and international community can assist Vietnamese businesses, and in particular marketers, to improve their procedures, outcomes and, not least, their virtue and morality. Awareness and training are needed; however, on many levels, ethics by virtue and character are also warranted in order to improve the reputation of Vietnam further. With time, and proper institutional frameworks, marketers in Vietnam may join various associations and adhere to their code of ethics. In that way, companies and customers alike will be better off.

Cambodia

In Cambodia, there is little written on the topic of ethical marketing. However, there is evidence that it is practised to great extent. According to StartSomeGood.com, a crowd-funding platform for non-profits and social entrepreneurs, campaigns using ethical marketing approaches are evidenced. For example, a project by the Cambodian Children's Trust (CCT) proposes teaching children not what to think, but how to think. They note that 'if we teach children everything we know, their knowledge is limited to ours. If we teach children to think, their knowledge is limitless'(CTT, 2014). The focus in the CCT's approach involves studying ethics and philosophy at an early age, as they believe that such knowledge will give children the necessary skills to use good thinking as the guide by which they live.

At the Cambodian Children's Trust, the emphasis is on giving vulnerable Cambodian children the best chance at leading a happy, fulfilling and successful life. Succeeding in life depends on our ability to solve the problems we encounter along the way. The campaign aims to teach the children to question and how to work out what is ethical or unethical (or somewhere in between). The teachings include giving the children the ability to identify flaws in arguments. Through education, the children will learn about the major religions and, with the skills they develop, will be able to make up their own minds.

According to the Atheist Alliance International (2014), Theravada Buddhism is practised by around 95 per cent of the Cambodian population. In reality, however, behind the doors of Khmer temples there lies belief in superstitions, with rituals, spirits, ghosts, gods and sorcerers, which, it can be argued, injects immeasurable stress and fear into the lives of most Cambodians. In a country where corruption is widespread and 40 per cent of the population live below the poverty line, it is vital that Cambodia's children – its future leaders – learn how to think for themselves, how to reason and how to be ethical and moral citizens. For marketers, early education in ethics, fairness and morality may foster greater awareness and improved ethical marketing skills. The future of Cambodia depends on this.

The Philippines

In the Philippines, business ethics are greatly influenced by the plurality of languages and ethnicities, geographic fragmentation and the predominant Roman Catholic religion, together with the still relatively short experience in nationhood (Sison & Angeles, 1997). In addition, the rapid growth and liberalisation of the economy, coupled with the inequitable distribution of wealth, the destruction of the environment and corruption (Sison & Angeles, 1997), account for the main ethical concerns. Among the four countries in this chapter, the Philippines has probably the most advanced stage of implementation of different professional bodies related to code of ethics, including the marketing society MORES (Marketing and Opinion Research Society). MORES is an association of qualified research practitioners from advertising agencies, advertisers, media, research agencies and individuals.

In their pursuit to promote and ensure that high standards, MORES (2014) has established principles of ethical practice of marketing and opinion research for the guidance of its members. The following is from their website (http://www.mores.com.ph/about-us/code-of-ethics):

1. Section 1.1 – The purpose of marketing and opinion research is the objective collection and analysis of information willingly provided by respondents on products and services. In line with this objective, MORES members shall endeavour to uphold the principles of impartiality and objectivity, fair competition, driving high standards of quality, the advancement and development of research methods and ensure the use of market research to obtain unbiased information and not a disguised selling activity.
2. Section 1.2 – Since the purpose of marketing and opinion research is the obtaining of information and not the direct creation of roles or the influencing of respondents opinion or behaviour, a research company, therefore, shall not engage in any activity directly or indirectly presented as market research while having as its real purpose the attempted sale of commodities or services.
3. Section 1.3 – All market research work shall be undertaken in a spirit of complete impartiality, and the research company shall not allow itself to be influenced in the conduct of its own surveys by any other consideration than the adoption of procedures which will redound to the interest of the client. For this purpose, marketing research companies should be responsible for the development of necessary research techniques and also for the maintenance of high standards of operation.
4. Section 1.4 – Marketing and opinion research should be conducted not only according to accepted principles of fair competition but also according to standards based on generally accepted scientific methods.

The above illustrates an example of a marketing code of ethics. It includes all three levels of ethics, as previously discussed. Such code of ethics provides integrity and trust to the marketing profession in the Philippines, which is an excellent starting point to improve the reputation of marketing. However, as with any other country, problems are also demonstrated. Recently, Philippines-based pharmaceutical companies have been urged by a coalition of health professionals and health advocates to follow a voluntary international code of business ethics in the biopharmaceutical industry seeking to ensure the best interest of patients (Mateo, 2014).

The Medicines Transparency Alliance (MeTA) Philippines, a multi-stakeholder coalition composed of agencies and organisations in the government, private sector, civil society, academe and health professional associations, together with its international development partners, stated that drug companies in the Philippines must adhere to 'The Mexico City Principles for Voluntary Code of Business Ethics in the Biopharmaceutical Sector'. This document spells out standards for the ethical promotion of medicines aiming to ensure that medical decisions are made in the 'best interest' of patients. Roberto M. Pagdanganan, chairman of MeTA Philippines, said, 'ethical conduct by the pharmaceutical companies and their transparent and accountable actions are crucial in improving healthcare delivery to the Filipino people.' He continued:

> The time is now ripe to forge the inherent link with the issues of ethics, ethical conduct, and marketing ethics, and to rally support for advocacies for adherence to voluntary codes of responsible business practices, and for a stronger regulatory framework for medicines promotion that would focus on putting patients first.
>
> *(Mateo, 2014)*

It seems that the Philippines are on the right track towards marketing ethics, and its influences are fruitful for their international reputation as a place to conduct business and for foreign investors, tourists and other stakeholders.

Indonesia

In an article entitled: 'Is there an ethics crisis in Indonesia?', Primanita (2011) outlines issues with corruption and other unethical concerns in Indonesia. An official, Busyro Muqoddas (quoted in Primanita, 2011), notes that in the wake of revelations about many government officials with suspiciously large bank accounts, ethics had not quite taken hold among public servants.

According to the Financial Transaction Reports and Analysis Center (PPATK), since 2002, there have been 1,800 cases of suspected corruption by civil servants, many of whom have bank accounts with billions of rupiah. Busyro stated: 'In the various studies and measurements undertaken by the KPK [Corruption Eradication Commission], it is apparent that the code of ethics, as an instrument against corruption, is not yet a main object of attention in the majority of government institutions' (Primanita, 2011).

Busyro calls for the development of a code of ethics to prevent corruption, but notes that such awareness among heads of ministries or government institutions to build is still very low. A 2004 government regulation requires government institutions to develop a code of ethics; however, of 18 central institutions, eight of them did not have a code of ethics, as required. Busyro added that his institution had submitted a list of suspicious bank accounts, belonging to low- and middle-ranking civil servants, that contained large amounts of money, so that the KPK could follow up. The support from Vice President Boediono, who also heads the presidentially appointed National Guiding Committee for Bureaucratic Reform, assists in the eradication of corruption. Specifically, he called for cooperation between the KPK and the government.

The case illustrates how important the codes of ethics and standards for behaviour are as instruments for enforcing discipline in state institutions. For marketers, this is not an exemption either. From the case, several guidelines can be gathered:

1. The implementation of a code of ethics among civil servants would help enhance the integrity of the individual members and assist in the safeguarding of their institutions' integrity.
2. When state personnel work according to ethics, all the potential for corruption can be minimised.
3. Collaboration between different organisations and all the components of the nation is necessary to eradicate corruption and unethical behaviour.
4. Sustainable results will only be achieved if corruption eradication efforts are improved through a better institutionalised framework — that is, only if a government bureaucracy is capable of closing opportunities for corruption and is immune to corrupt practices.
5. Corrupt officials will attempt to circumvent the system by moving funds into their private accounts. Thus, a review of the state financial management system is necessary to close loopholes, and tighter supervision by superiors is also important.
6. Finally, if subordinates are engaging in glamorous lifestyles and suddenly becoming rich, their superiors should accord them more attention.

New research directions

Ethical marketing in South East Asia remains mostly unexplored in the literature due to the difficulty in collecting data, and the few resources available. However, like anywhere else, many examples of unethical marketing practices are evidenced, and to some extent, more cases may be found in developing countries due to higher environmental uncertainty, a less developed institutional and legal framework, and increasing power of market competition. We recommend the following areas for future studies:

- exploring differences between developing and developed countries in managers' perception and implementation of ethical marketing;
- linking ethical marketing with ties with government, often considered essential in developing countries;
- from a consumer perspective, focusing on social values, such as family unity, hierarchies, religion and spirituality, in ethical marketers' decision-making processes;
- examining corruption practices and loopholes, and identifying ways in which they can be eradicated;
- understanding the marketers' role in this connection; and

- comparing and contrasting ethical marketing across different sectors and industries (retail, corporate, government, NGOs, higher education, etc.) in Vietnam, Cambodia, the Philippines and Indonesia, with the aim of developing a comprehensive ethical marketing framework.

Practising ethical marketing: Vietnam, Cambodia, the Philippines and Indonesia

Responsible decision-making

As suggested above, one of the problems with integrating ethical perspectives into business decision-making is that we use some of these principles unconsciously or in a restricted fashion. Rarely do we seek to integrate the three categories of ethics as filters to our decision-making, yet doing so will help improve the quality of our decisions, but alerting us to possible violations of individual rights or duties, ignoring key stakeholders or acting in a way that others would see as unacceptable. Ronald Francis, Professor of Business Ethics at the Centre for International Corporate Governance in Melbourne, Australia, suggests that the first reference point in resolving ethical questions are these key principles in ethics.

He puts forward a decision tree which business people can use as a 'quick guide' when confronted with ethical dilemmas. This decision tree seeks to establish the ethical validity of the question or action. Velasquez (2006) puts forward a similar series of questions that seeks to articulate the ethical dimension of a decision or action. If it fails at any point, it should alert us to possible ethical challenges and we should revisit the decision or action.

1. What benefits and what harms will each course of action produce, and which alternative will lead to the best overall consequences?
2. What are the rights of those involved, and does the proposal involve risk or harm to persons, animals or property?
3. Is the proposal consistent with the law?
4. Is the action consistent with professional codes of ethics?
5. Which course of action treats everyone the same, except where there is a morally justifiable reason not to, and does not show favouritism or discrimination?
6. Which course of action is and will be seen as consistent with virtues or characteristics such as integrity, honesty and so on?
7. Am I prepared to have my decision and the reasons for it made public?

Duties of a marketing professional

Koehn (1994), Sagar (1995), May (1989) and Burger (1995) suggest that true professions are bound by a duty to act within the limits of their knowledge. Beauchamp and Bowie (1997) state that professional practice standards hold that obligations and other standards of moral conduct are determined by the customary practice of the professional community. They suggest that proponents of such positions argue that individuals are charged with various responsibilities or duties − for example, avoiding harm, honouring warranties, avoiding conflicts of interest and obeying legal requirements. Beauchamp and Bowie also highlight that such individuals must use professional criteria for determining appropriate actions. They specifically state that any person without expert knowledge is unqualified to determine what needs to be done. This suggests that professionals have a duty to act within the limits of their expert knowledge.

As we have identified a number of marketing associations in the region, each would have slightly different contexts and thus may have slightly different expectations of marketers in terms of their duties and responsibilities. However, several key duties can be identified that would apply to all marketing professionals, including:

1. to provide expertise and knowledge within the limits of the marketing function;
2. not to knowingly advance information about a product or service that is untrue;
3. not to use their expertise to knowingly manipulate consumers into purchasing a product or service; and
4. not to use their expertise to target specific groups who are not in a position to make a purchasing decision.

An examination of the Australian Marketing Institute Code of Ethics reveals a number of key duties consistent with the concept of marketing as a profession. Firstly, the existence of the Institute and a Code of Ethics are requirements of an occupation being considered as a profession. The first three statements of the Code relate to the public or social duties that the marketing professional has to the broader community. Some statements address the duties of the marketer to the employer or client and the requirement to act within the limits of knowledge and the law. Other statements relate to the duties of the professional with regard to other marketing professionals and the need to advance the interests of the profession, while the remaining statements clarify the duties of the marketing professional with respect to the professional body.

Marketing regulation

The emergence of a discourse of marketing ethics can be sought in the way legislators regulate the marketing practice.

The first attempt to regulate the advertising in Vietnam dates back to 2001, with the enactment of the Ordinance on Advertising (No. 39-2001-PL-UBTVQH10). The Ordinance was replaced by the first Law on Advertisement passed by the National Assembly on 21 June 2012 (6/2012/QH13), which came into effect on 1 January 2013. Decree No. 181/2013/ND-CP (Decree 181) was passed on 4 November 2013 and came into force on 1 January 2014. This last decree sets very specific requirements on the advertising of special goods such as pharmaceutical products, food, cosmetics and medical equipment, and so on. The law prohibits advertising of a number of goods (article 7), namely cigarettes, wine that contains 15 per cent alcohol or above, dairy being breastmilk substitute for children under 24 months old, prescription drugs, some OTC drugs, pornographic products and products that might incite violence.

The ban of advertising of breastmilk substitute is a direct consequence of Vietnam's embracing the International Code of Marketing of Breastmilk Substitutes adopted by the World Health Assembly in 1981. The Code does not prohibit the production and sale of breastmilk substitutes. However, it covers the improper marketing and promotion of food products that compete with breastfeeding, as they are important factors that often negatively affect the choice and ability of a mother to breastfeed optimally. More interestingly, article 8 stipulates a number of acts prohibited in advertising. One of the most controversial prohibitions deals with any content that is contrary to the customs and traditions of Vietnam. Clearly, this is a clause open to broad interpretation. The law also bans comparative advertising and any form of communication denigrating competitors. One provision bans 'spamming' or any form of unsolicited advertising communication.

No joint industry commissions to self-regulate the advertising industry exist in Vietnam. This somewhat reflects what is happening in other areas of the economy. For example, while in many jurisdictions, corporate governance codes are mostly developed by private councils of publicly traded companies, in Vietnam, the corporate governance code for listed company comes in the form of a decree of the Ministry of Finance. However, the new law on advertising lays the foundations for the formation and recognition of associations of advertising professionals.

Practice case study

Public discourse on marketing ethics

In Vietnam, the general public showed their sensitivity towards marketing communications, which were perceived to violate traditional social values. As a consequence, lively debate and criticism occurred on social networks. Two cases illustrate the types of communication that can stir discussion.

The first case has to do with a commercial promoting a popular shampoo brand, Rejoice. In the commercial a young woman – portrayed by Miss Vietnam 2006 Mai Phuong Thuy – visits her boyfriend's family. The detail causing a lot of online controversy was about the wording of her answering to her future mother-in-law. In the TV advertisement, when asked about her beautiful long hair by her future mother-in-law, she answers '*à không, chỉ là Rejoice*' (No, just Rejoice). However, in Vietnam, the younger woman was supposed to say '*Dạ, chỉ là Rejoice thôi bác ạ*', using an expression respectful of the age difference with the interlocutor. Many pages of social media were filled with mostly negative comments.

Another commercial that was seen as controversial was meant to promote Maggi 3, a Nestlé brand. The commercial narrative portrays a man having dinner with a seductive woman, but suddenly the man remembers that he has to run home, as his wife is cooking there using Maggi 3. Although the idea behind the commercial is that using Maggi 3 in cooking will keep the family united, the explicit reference to a possible affair stirred a lot of controversy among commentators on social media. An additional layer of complexities that attracted commentators' attention had to do with the use of the words '*phở*' (a popular Vietnamese noodle dish) and '*cơm*' (rice) in the commercial to stress the opposition between the two women. In Vietnamese language, '*phở*' is used to allude to the mistress of a married man while '*cơm*' refers to a bona fide wife.

These cases may seem harmless when compared to provocative advertising styles seen in many more developed economies, but they clearly show a growing attention of the general public towards the messages spread through marketing.

One last example shows how public discourse can lead to government intervention. In 2011, advertising posters promoting the upcoming blockbuster *Rise of the Planet of the Apes* were displayed prominently in major cities across the country (the poster was regularly licensed by the Ministry of Culture). By pure coincidence, the opening day of the movie displayed on the posters was 19 August. This is also the date on which, in 1945, the Việt Minh under Hồ Chí Minh began a revolution against French colonial rule in Vietnam. Soon, the poster became the object of caricatures and was shared on social media with an ironic tongue-in-cheek connotation referring to Vietnam as the 'Planet of the Apes'. Posters were pulled down and in some cases left with the date erased.

Questions

1. In the case of Rejoice shampoo, what would you have done, as the marketing manager, to ensure damage control on such negative publicity?
2. Are there any examples from developed economies where marketers have violated ethical and social values and caused public discourse?
3. In the case of Maggi 3, how would you use ethical marketing approaches to communicate the idea of 'family unity'?
4. Are there any examples of crossing the line in terms of ethical and social values in Cambodia, the Philippines and Indonesia?
5. In the final case of the *Planet of the Apes* posters, which laws permitted the Vietnam government to pull down all the posters? Do you think this is fair? Would this have happened in more developed economies, and if so, under what regulations?

References

Ardagh, D. (2010). *Business as a profession: A bridge too far or fair way to go?* Saarbrucken: Lambert Academic Publishing.

Atheist Alliance International. (2014). <https://startsomegood.com/Venture/atheist_alliance_international/Campaigns/Show/critical_thinking_and_secular_ethics_in_cambodia>.

Australian Department of Foreign Trade and Affairs. (2014). <http://aid.dfat.gov.au/countries/eastasia/vietnam/Pages/other-init3.aspx>.

Beauchamp, T. L., & Bowie, N. (1997). *Ethical theory and business* (5th ed.). Upper Saddle River, NJ: Prentice-Hall.

Buchholz, R. (1989). *Fundamental concepts and problems in business ethics*. Englewood Cliffs, NJ: Prentice-Hall.

Burger, W. E. (1995). The decline of professionalism. *Fordham Law Review*, *63*(4), 949–958.

Camenisch, P. F. (1983). *Grounding professional ethics in a pluralistic society*. New York, NY: Haven Publications.

Child, J. (1984). *Organization: A guide to problems and practice*. New Jersey: Prentice-Hall.

Child, J. (2005). *Organization: A guide to problems and practice*. Malden, MA: Blackwell Publishing.

Cogan, M. L. (1953). Toward a definition of profession. *Harvard Educational Review, 23,* 33–50.

CTT (2014). Cambodian Children Trust. <http://www.cambodianchildrenstrust.org> Accessed 27.05.14.

De George, R. (1999). *Business ethics* (5th ed.). Englewood Cliffs, NJ: Prentice-Hall.

De George, R. T. (2010). *Business ethics* (7th ed.). Massachusetts, USA: Pearson.

Driscoll, D. N., & Hoffman, W. M. (1999). *Ethics matters: How to implement values-driven management*. Massachusetts: Bentley College Center for Business Ethics.

Eraut, M. (1994). *Developing professional knowledge and competence*. London: The Falmer Press.

ESOMAR. (2014). <http://www.esomar.org>.

Ferrell, O. C., Fraedrich, J., & Ferrell, L. (2011). *Business ethics: Ethical decision making and cases* (8th ed.). Boston, MA: Houghton Mifflin.

Flexner, A. (1910). *Medical education in the United States and Canada: A report to the carnegie foundation for the advancement of teaching*. Stanford, CA: The Carnegie Foundation.

Global Times. (2014). 55 Corruption Cases Detected in Vietnam in 2013. Available from <http://www.globaltimes.cn/content/836540.shtml#.U0oOhRZx2ZY> Accessed 13.04.14.

Gold, J., Rodgers, H., & Smith, V. (2002). The future of the professions: Are they up for it? *Foresight, 4*(2), 46–53.

Grinter, L. E. (2006). Vietnam's thrust into globalization: Doi Moi's long road. *Asian Affairs: An American Review, 33*(3), 151–165.

Hinman, L. (2010). Ethics matters. Available from <http://ethicsmatters.net/index.shtml>.

International Business Publications (2009). *Vietnam business law handbook*. Washington, DC: International Business Publications.

Khurana, R., Nohria, N., & Penrice, D. (2005). Management as a profession. In J. W. Lorsch, L. Berlowitz, & A. Zelleke (Eds.), *Restoring trust in American business*. MA: American Academy of Arts & Sciences, MIT Press.

Kim, A. M. (2008). *Learning to be capitalists: Entrepreneurs in Vietnam's transition economy*. Oxford and New York: Oxford University Press.

Koehn, D. (1994). *The ground of professional ethics*. London: Routledge.

Lennertz, J. E. (1991). Ethics and the professional responsibility of lawyers: A commentary. *Journal of Business Ethics, 10,* 577–579.

Lusch, R. F., & O'Brien, M. (1997). Fostering professionalism. *Marketing Research, 9*(1), 24–30.

Mateo, I.C. (2014) PHL drug firms urged to follow int'l code of business ethics. *GMA News,* 18 February. Available from <http://www.gmanetwork.com/news/story/348977/economy/business/phl-drug-firms-urged-to-follow-int-l-code-of-business-ethics>.

May, W. (1989). *Vocation, career and profession. Monograph Series*. Brisbane: The Australian Institute of Ethics and the Professions.

Middlehurst, R., & Kennie, T. (1997). Leading professionals: Towards new concepts of professionalism. In J. Broadbent, M. Dietrich, & J. Roberts (Eds.), *The end of the professions?* London: Routledge.

Mintzberg, H. (1979). *The structuring of organizations: A synthesis of the research*. Englewood Cliffs, NJ: Prentice Hall.

MORES. (2014). <http://www.mores.com.ph>.

Morgan, G. (1998). *Images of organizations*. California: Sage.

Preston, N. (1996). *Understanding ethics*. Annadale, NSW: Federation Press.

Primanita, A. (2011). Is there an ethics crisis in Indonesia? *Jakarta Globe*, 8 December. Available from <http://www.thejakartaglobe.com/archive/is-there-an-ethics-crisis-in-indonesia>.

Raelin, J. A. (1991). *The clash of cultures: Managers managing professionals*. Boston, MA: Harvard Business School Press.

Reader, W. J. (1966). *Professional men*. London: Routledge.

Sagar, W. (1995). Characteristics of a profession. *The National Public Accountant*, *40*(3), 6−8.

Sison, A. J. G., & Angeles, A. P. (1997). Business ethics in the Philippines. *Journal of Business Ethics*, *16*(14), 1519−1528.

Velasquez, M. (1998). *Business ethics: Concepts and cases* (4th ed.). Upper Saddle River, NJ: Prentice Hall.

Velasquez, M. (2006). *Business ethics: Concepts and cases* (5th ed.). Upper Saddle River, NJ: Prentice Hall.

Wall, A. (1998). Ethics and management: Oil and water. In S. Dracopoulou (Ed.), *Ethics and values in health care management* (pp. 13−28). London: Routledge.

Wilensky, H. L. (1964). The professionalization of everyone. *American Journal of Sociology*, *70*, 137−158.

Winch, C. (2004). What do teachers need to know about teaching? A critical examination of the occupational knowledge of teachers. *Journal of Educational Studies*, *52*(2), 180−196.

Part Two

Social Marketing

Social marketing in China, Taiwan, Japan and South Korea

Stephan Dahl

Introduction

Chapter 6 will introduce social marketing as 'seeking to develop and integrate marketing concepts with other approaches to influence behaviour that benefits individuals and communities for the greater social good'. This chapter expands on the definition by examining how cultural factors influence social marketing practice and research, using the Framework for Cross-Cultural Social Marketing Research (Dahl, 2009). The chapter examines the difference in issues addressed by social marketing campaigns and message framing based on examples of social marketing campaigns and research in relation to China, Taiwan, Japan and South Korea.

Learning objectives

After reading this chapter, you should be able to:

- understand, define and conceptualise social marketing and its theoretical base;
- outline the social marketing issues prevalent in China, Taiwan, Japan and South Korea; and
- demonstrate the application of the Framework for Cross-cultural Social Marketing Research across the Asian region.

The state of the art in social marketing in China, Japan and South Korea

Despite claims that marketing can frequently be globalised, little empirical support for this conjecture has been presented (Dahl, 2004). In fact, cultural aspects significantly influence different parts of marketing. Consumers' underlying cultural values influence their reactions to and interpretations of marketing cues. For instance, colours are interpreted as having different meanings in different cultures. Similarly, some cultures place greater emphasis on the 'hidden' meanings of colours used in marketing, while others rely explicitly on what is said. Especially in marketing communications, cultural values are considerably influencing the interpretation of the communication. While there is extensive research showing the influence of culture on commercial marketing, there is relatively sparse research in relation to

Ethical and Social Marketing in Asia.

social marketing specifically, and very few studies are published on social marketing from an Asian perspective. Most of the published cases are based on case studies from a health promotion point of view, and virtually no systematic research on social marketing in East Asia is accessible in the international literature. In the case of broader cross-cultural studies examining social marketing, nearly all have supported the finding linked to general marketing: that social marketing is highly affected by culture. We therefore briefly review in this section the most important cultural constructs in relation to marketing and social marketing activity, before examining social marketing activities as part of the wider cross-cultural framework.

Cross-cultural frameworks and marketing

Most studies into commercial marketing rely on Hofstede's cultural dimensions. These are based on work carried out in the 1970s, although they are extended to include further dimensions and data from more countries. The model distinguished five cultural dimensions:

1. Power distance;
2. Individualism/collectivism;
3. Masculinity/femininity;
4. Uncertainty avoidance; and
5. Long-term orientation.

Data for most countries is readily available, and frequently used in consumer behaviour and marketing communications research as country-level indicators of cultural values. We shall now briefly review the five dimensions and where each of the countries this chapter is concerned with stand in relation to countries with more published research, such as Australia, the USA and the UK.

Power distance − This is the extent to which members of the society with less power accept that power is distributed unequally. High power distance countries, such as Japan, are characterised by relative respect for authority, while in lower power distance countries, such as the UK, authority can have a negative connotation, and hierarchical power structures are often regarded with suspicion.

Individualism/collectivism − Individuals in individualistic societies tend to put greater emphasis on looking out for themselves and their immediate families, rather than the wider community. Conversely, in collectivist countries greater emphasis is placed on the needs of the wider group than the individual constituent of the group. Individualist countries are often characterised by small family units, such as those frequently found in the UK or the USA, while countries scoring higher on this dimension, such as many Latin American countries, tend to have larger family units.

Masculinity/femininity − Achievement and success are highly valued in masculine societies, while quality of life and caring for others are more emphasised in feminine societies. Gender roles are often very strongly differentiated in masculine societies. Envy of success and rewards are also common − for example, programmes like the 'Employee of the Month' programme work well in masculine societies. Typical examples of strongly masculine societies include the USA and Japan, while examples of feminine societies include the Netherlands and Sweden.

Uncertainty avoidance – Uncertainty is perceived as potentially threatening in countries with high uncertainty avoidance and hence it is avoided where possible – for example, through the introduction of strict rules or formality. Countries such as Germany, which is seen as relatively high on uncertainty avoidance, have explicit rules, laws and regulations for many areas of life.

Long-term orientation – This is the extent to which a society collectively holds conventional, historic continuum-oriented views, or emphasises short-term, future orientation. This dimension is derived from the work of Michael Bond related to Chinese Values, and is therefore the most 'Asian' of the five Hofstede dimensions. Countries that score highly on long-term orientation tend to have strong order systems; they value perseverance highly, and they often place a greater importance on concepts such as shame and face. For short-term oriented societies, the emphasis is more on the immediate, often individual, pursuit of happiness.

Figure 6.1 shows a comparison of the country scores of this chapter's countries with the USA, the UK and Australia. While there is significant criticism of Hofstede's methodology, and individual values can never be a reflection of individual circumstances, the scores nevertheless show that strong cultural differences exist between the countries where much of the social marketing thought originates from and the countries this chapter is concerned with on all dimensions. Specifically, the countries in this chapter score significantly higher on power distance, relatively low on individualism (i.e. they are mostly collectivist) and high on long-term orientation. But even among the countries with which this chapter is concerned, there are some notable differences: Uncertainty avoidance is relatively high in Taiwan, Japan and Korea, but significantly lower in Hong Kong and China. Similarly, Japan scores extremely highly on masculinity, while the other countries score more moderately on this dimension. Given this culturally diverse context, it is therefore important to remember the often subtle but highly impactful influences that cultural differences can have on general marketing and marketing communication in particular.

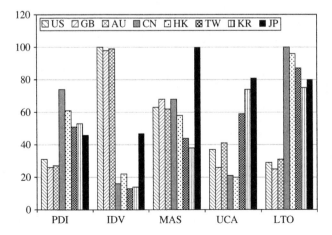

Figure 6.1 Comparison of the country scores of China, Taiwan, South Korea and Japan with the USA, the UK and Australia.

The impact of culture can be easily seen in terms of customer reaction to specific marketing programmes. Specifically, targeted audiences' self-construal and self-referencing are theoretically important constructs for creating and maintaining customer relevance of social marketing programmes. Self-construal describes an individual's view of themselves and related self-concepts. Relational-interdependent self-construal (RISC) focuses explicitly on how an individual self-defines in relation to other people around them, focusing specifically on close relationships (Cross, Bacon, & Morris, 2000). Individuals with a high RISC emphasise close relationships, and regard these relationships as crucial aspects of their self-definition and self-expression. For high-RISC individuals, such relationships can extend to generalised others, such as wider community groups. Conversely, low-RISC individuals tend to focus more on immediate and close relationships, but tend to put less emphasis on wider relationships such as ethnic groups or other generalised groupings.

While RISC emphasises an individual's self-construal rather than a cultural norm, RISC levels have an explicit relationship with cultural dimensions. High RISC tends to be more frequently found in areas that also score highly on Hofstede's collectivism, while low RISC individuals are more frequently observed in countries that score highly on Hofstede's individualism (Cross et al., 2000). Consequently, high-RISC individuals are more likely to be encountered in all countries this book and this chapter are concerned with, as Asian countries, broadly speaking, score highest on Hofstede's collectivism index (Hofstede, 2001): China scores as one of the most collectivist countries in Hofstede's data set, suggesting culturally strong loyalty to in-groups and a large proportion of high-RISC individuals. Consistent with this data, Hong Kong and Taiwan (for which separate data is available in Hofstede's data set) score highly in terms of collectivism. South Korea scores similarly highly on the collectivism scale used in Hofstede's research. Japan, on the other hand, scores only moderately strong on the collectivism scale. This suggests that although Japanese culture displays many of the traits associated with a collectivist society, such as strong in-group relationships and emphasis on in-group harmony, these are moderated by traits more often associated with individualist countries. For example, Hofstede argues that Japanese society depends less on larger and extended families, typically found in Chinese and Korean society (Hofstede, 2001). Rather, Japanese individuals tend to place greater emphasis on, and live and engage to a greater degree with, their immediate family. However, while Japan is less collectivistic than most of its neighbours, it is certainly relatively collectivistic when compared to most 'Western' countries such as the UK, the USA or Australia, where much of the current ideas and thinking about social marketing originates.

Reverting back to the notion of RISC, it is therefore likely that a greater number of high-RISC individuals are found amongst the population in China and South Korea, with a more diverse, though leaning towards high-RISC individuals, population being found in Japan. Self-referencing further mediates how individuals reactions likely to occur in response to social marketing campaigns, especially social advertising. Self-referencing as a construct explains how and under which circumstances individuals relate observed persuasive messages to their individual self structures (Burnkrant & Unnava, 1995). Specific to an Asian context, Martin, Lee, and Yang (2004) showed the importance of self-referencing in advertising, showing that Asian consumers, albeit residing outside of Asia, display higher self-referencing in relation to advertisements featuring Asian models, and develop more positive attitudes towards advertising and purchase behaviour intentions in response to advertising with Asian models. Moreover, even for culturally incongruent products, if Asian models were used in the advertising, self-referencing and purchase intention was higher for Asian consumers. Although the original study was not related to social marketing, Martin, Veer, and Pervan (2007) further demonstrated self-referencing in relation to weight-perception: Examining advertising showing either larger or slimmer models, they demonstrated that people believing that they can control their own weight have higher levels of self-referencing when being exposed to slimmer models.

More specifically in relation to social advertising, and examining binge drinking and road safety issues, Martin et al. (2013) demonstrate that individuals scoring highly on RISC respond more favourably to advertising showing two models than a single model, while individuals scoring low on RISC respond more favourably to adverts featuring a single model. Moreover, the effect of RISC is mediated further by self-referencing. As can be seen from the above discussion, cultural factors can have a potentially significant impact on social marketing campaigns, which is important to consider specifically when relying on frameworks developed in culturally very distinct countries (e.g. the USA, the UK or Australia) and these are being applied in countries that this book, and particularly this chapter, is dealing with.

The framework for cross-cultural social marketing

Although cultural factors in the sense of cultural dimensions are important aspects when considering cross-national application of marketing principles, it is nevertheless also important to consider further other factors that may influence marketing campaigns. The 'Framework for Cross-cultural Social Marketing' (see Figure 6.2) introduces a number of different points to consider, and therefore

Figure 6.2 Framework for Cross-cultural Social Marketing.

contextualises social marketing interventions in the wider cultural and social context in which they occur.

The social marketing intervention itself is displayed as a circle uniting five external contexts that have direct influence on the intervention and four internal aspects of the intervention that are likely to be influenced as a result of the wider cultural and social context in which the intervention takes place. The external contexts are as follows.

1. The *historical* context, describing the historical development and resultant self-conceptualisation of the target population or culture. Historical events may have shaped attitudes or beliefs in the target population about health-related or other social marketing relevant factors. For example, traditionally, believes in yin and yang as health promoting concepts have been common in China, and continue to be regarded as important aspects of health behaviour (Chen, 2001).
2. The *cultural* context refers to the broader cultural dimensions prevalent in the target population. For example, in our case, we find that China, Taiwan and Korea are highly collectivist, with Japan more moderately so. Similarly, all countries score relatively highly on masculinity and power distance using the Hofstede framework (Hofstede, 2001).
3. The *economic* context of the target population has a further direct influence on the social marketing intervention. For instance, access to health care is often more difficult for target populations from an economically disadvantaged background, and particularly so in developing countries. Similarly, the wider economic context of the country may have a significant impact on health-related spending. For example, as a percentage of GDP, health care spending in China is nearly half (5.2 per cent) that of Japan (9.5 per cent) (World Bank, 2012).
4. The *social* context in which a social marketing intervention occurs clearly has a strong influence on the intervention. For instance, family life, religion and other social factors have a direct influence on attitudes and behaviours linked to health and social marketing objectives.
5. Finally, the *psycho-social values* interact with the social marketing intervention. For instance, in China, psycho-social beliefs linking the caring for others, seeking of peace and happiness with improved health are common (Chen, 2001).

Clearly, the external contexts are interconnected symbiotic, rather than dyadic. For instance, cultural elements are likely to influence psycho-social elements, historical factors are likely to influence current economic factors, and so forth.

From the external influence factors, social marketing intervention connects to four internal aspects, which are influenced by the five external contexts. The internal aspects are as follows:

1. The *content*, i.e. the messages used in a social marketing intervention, framing of messages and so forth. For instance, choosing appeals consistent with collectivist cultures is likely to be more successful in Asian countries.
2. The *methods* used as part of the social marketing campaign − for instance, use of advertising or reliance on social media, direct interventions or grass-roots activism.
3. The *interpretation* of a message is likely to be different depending on the target audience and the attitudes and believes held. For instance, cultural meaning attached to colours may influence the interpretation of messages.
4. Finally, the *outcome* and evaluation is subject to the wider context in which the social marketing intervention has occurred. For instance, different outcomes may be necessary depending on specific target groups, and evaluation methods may need to be adjusted.

Issues in social marketing

The importance and choice of issues addressed by social marketing interventions heavily depends on the country and external factors. For example, in developed and Western countries, much emphasis is placed on issues such as energy consumption, safer driving, anti-smoking and prevention of alcohol and drug abuse, while in developing countries, much of the social marketing focus centres on basic health issues, such as sanitation, family planning, maternal and child health, and HIV/STI prevention (Saini & Mukul, 2012). The countries discussed in this chapter are a mixture of developing and developed countries, as per the IMF classification (International Monetary Fund, 2012). Despite the controversial nature of such classification system, it may nevertheless give some insights into the likely impact of using the framework classification, and of economic contexts for issues that are likely to arise in the different countries: Taiwan, South Korea, Hong Kong and Japan are classified as a highly developed countries with advanced economies, while mainland China is classified as a developing country. Echoing the classification by the IMF, the Human Development Index takes into account a broader set of variables, including health and inequality. This index, similar to the IMF index, classifies South Korea, Hong Kong and Japan as very highly developed countries, while mainland China is classified as a medium developed country (Malik & United Nations Development Programme, 2013).

Much progress has been made in the provision of universal health care in China, especially through wide-ranging reform plans launched in 2009 with the aim of achieving universal health coverage by 2020 (Yip et al., 2012). However, despite this progress, wide inequalities remain, including a health care system that has been describes as 'hindered by waste, inefficiencies, poor quality of services, and scarcity and maldistribution of the qualified workforce' (Yip et al., 2012, p. 833). Similarly, social issues in China, such as urban migration on an unprecedented scale, has resulted in significant issues related to environmental quality, including air and water pollution in urban centres (Gong et al., 2012). Moreover, increases in road traffic and vehicle ownership have resulted in a increase of road-safety issues in urban and rural areas, which are pressing issues potentially addressable by social marketing interventions (Gong et al., 2012).

Similarly, reactions to issues may be significantly different depending on cultural and sociological factors. For instance, sustainable behaviours, such as purchasing of organic food, responsible use of transportation and giving to charity have been found to be significantly more common in South Korea than in the USA and Germany (Minton et al., 2012). However, the motives for engaging in such behaviours were also reported as highly different in South Korea than in Germany and the USA, suggesting that responses to issues are equally dependent on wider contextual factors, which Minton et al. (2012) argue to be culture related. Similarly, relative conservative attitudes of policymakers, the wider population and especially target audiences have been found to hamper needle-exchange programmes in semi-urban China, leading to disappointing results of social marketing campaigns focusing on the issue (Yap et al., 2002).

Other issues with varying responses and likely reactions include the dramatic rise of obesity in China, largely attributable to the consumption of fashionable Western-style fast food (Curtis, McCluskey, & Wahl, 2007). This increase in obesity is not mirrored in the same way in Korea or Japan, and the motives for consumption of fast food are likely to be different in these countries in comparison to China.

Message framing in China, Taiwan, Japan and South Korea

Despite being widely debated in relation to social marketing, the relationship between culture and message framing remains largely under-researched (Biener et al., 2008). Using the wrong message in health and social marketing campaigns can, however, have potentially serious consequences: it can turn the audience off the advocated behaviour (Slater, 2006). Several potential issues related to message framing have been identified in the extant literature, though most of the research has not specifically looked at the implications in relation to Asia, and China, Korea and Japan in particular.

For instance, messages can be either loss- or gain-framed. Gain-framed messages focus on the benefits resulting from adopting a specific behaviour, or alternatively ceasing an undesired behaviour. Conversely, a loss-framed message emphasises the potential negative consequences of not ceasing or not engaging in a desired behaviour. For example, anti-smoking messages can either emphasise the potential health benefits derived from ceasing smoking (gain-framed) or warn people about the dangers of not giving up smoking (loss-framed). Based on Regulatory-Focus Theory (Higgins, 1998), individuals holding collectivist messages have been found to be more responsive to loss-framed messages, while individuals holding individualistic vales are more likely to respond to gain-framed messages (Uskul, Sherman, & Fitzgibbon, 2009). Consequently, based on the previous discussion, messages designed for the countries covered by this chapter are most likely to be effective when they use loss-framed messages.

In a similar vein, for commercial messages, soft-sell messages have been found to be more appealing for customers in collectivist countries (Lin, 2001). In contrast to the commercial findings, social marketing-related advertising messages in China rely heavily on hard-sell messages, establishing clear behavioural principles.

Source credibility

Source credibility is an important aspect of social marketing campaigns, as they often have to convey relatively complex messages in simple arguments. However, source credibility can vary depending on the cultural and social/historical contexts in which a message is transmitted. This chapter has already briefly touched on source credibility, which is likely to be enhanced when the same ethnicity as the target group is used in communication campaigns (Martin et al., 2004). However, simply relying on ethic background when adopting social marketing campaigns may be too simplistic, because of the potential interaction of distinctiveness theory and power distance.

Distinctiveness theory (McGuire, 1984) posits that an individual's distinctive traits in relation to other people in their environment are more salient, and result in greater identification with persuasive messages, than commonly found traits in the environment. Consequently, someone from an ethnic minority is more likely to attribute greater trustworthiness to an advertising spokesperson from the same ethnic background as them. Deshpandé and Stayman (1994) have shown that this effect is significant in advertising, and this observation is congruent with the results of Martin et al.'s (2004) later studies in relation to self-reference. However, as distinctiveness theory posits that the distinctive traits are the most salient, it implies also that studies that involve ethnic minorities overseas cannot be readily relocated to the home country. For instance, Martin et al.'s (2004) study draws on samples from New Zealand, where Asians are an ethnic minority, and consequently Asian ethnicity is likely to be a salient feature based on Distinctiveness Theory postulation. However, the same is evidently not true in Asian countries, and thus merely relying on ethnic clues as the most distinctive features may not be enough, nor is it likely to cause self-referencing in itself.

Moreover, as previously pointed out, all of this chapter's countries are relatively high on power distance. While, again, there is no specific social marketing-related research, research from commercial marketing would suggest that in countries with relatively large power distance, expert status and appropriate terminology and symbolism is highly important. However, many of the social marketing campaigns developed in the West, and consequently more countries with lower power distance, rely not on experts but on lay spokespeople to convey messages. Such choices of spokespeople may not be appropriate in high power distance countries, where expert advice may be regarded as more persuasive.

Consequently, identifying source credibility and messaging strategy issues requires extensive testing. Careful testing may be especially important in contexts where social marketers have experience of adopting a campaign to ethnic minorities in one country – and are trying to transfer these campaigns to the home country.

Media and integration issues

It has been noted that media choice for social marketing campaigns is different across cultures. Saini and Mukul (2012), after examining social marketing campaigns in South Asia, point out that many campaigns differ significantly from social marketing campaigns in the USA. In terms of media choice, most American social marketing campaigns depended heavily on conventional advertising as a major campaign vehicle, while in South Asia, campaigns relied heavily on non-conventional media. Some of the non-conventional media use was driven by availability and access issues, but also cost issues. Consequently, many South Asian social marketing campaigns faced the need to be significantly more innovative and explore more imaginative ways of bringing their message across than the American social marketing campaigns included in their study. While Saini and Mukul's study explicitly focused on South Asia (e.g. India, Pakistan and Bangladesh), similar differences may emerge when studying social marketing campaigns across China,

Japan and South Korea, not least as there are large differences between different regions, availability and usage of specific media, and targeted populations. For instance, large parts of China are heavily rural, and while local media is available, their media usage may be more similar to media usage in some rural areas of South Asia. Similarly, media ownership and the availability of international programmes in China is largely state regulated, while in Japan commercial broadcasting is notably important and there are few restrictions on content. Similarly, some of the highest Internet penetration rates in the world are held by South Korea (84.1 per cent), Japan (79.1 per cent) and Taiwan (76 per cent). However, China has a significantly lower, albeit rapidly rising, Internet penetration rate (42.3 per cent) (ITU, 2012). Similar to traditional media channels, Internet content in South Korea, Hong Kong, Taiwan and Japan is relatively unregulated, while there is significant censorship of Internet content in China — for example, some of the best-known social networking sites such as Twitter and Facebook are unavailable in most areas.

A further difference to consider when designing social marketing programmes may be the relative influence of media channels. Social media has been found to be highly influential in South Korea, where many people are avid users of Twitter (Minton et al., 2012). But Twitter is used only rarely in Hong Kong, and media in general is less effective. For example, Lee (2008) showed that peer pressure was the top predictor of environmentally friendly consumption behaviour among young consumers in Hong Kong.

Summary

Despite large cultural and other differences making social marketing campaigns in East Asia most likely to be substantially different to those in Western countries, there are few publications that have systematically examined this. Drawing on material examining a commercial perspective, it is likely that social marketing campaigns will be drastically different, not only on strictly cultural but also on other social marketing-relevant external and internal levels. The Framework for Cross-cultural Research in Social Marketing offers an explanatory basis on which to base future research, specifically dividing the external factors and internal factors that are likely to be affected when conducting social marketing campaigns across different countries.

New research directions

There is substantial need to examine social marketing from a cross-cultural angle, and this naturally includes countries such as China and Japan, which have traditionally been frequently researched in cross-cultural commercial advertising and marketing research. The framework presented in this chapter, together with other areas, such as differences in message perception/framing effectiveness, and media usage and media effectiveness research, are areas of further research that are likely to yield promising results.

Practising social marketing in China, Japan and South Korea

The chapter can be used to identify cultural and other aspects of a social marketing campaign that may need to be adjusted when carrying out campaigns in East Asia, specifically in China, Japan and South Korea. While the literature on specific campaigns in this area is embryonic, given the need for social marketing campaigns, more specific literature is bound to arise based on case studies in this area.

These types of campaigns can encompass a wide variety of different campaigns. For instance, they might examine and apply principles from this chapter to developing and adopting international campaigns in one of the countries. Alternatively, there is a need for more social marketing campaigns to engage local audiences around issues specifically pertinent to countries such as China, which are rapidly developing. For instance, a recent television advertising campaign run on CCTV in China focused on the complexities of parents dealing with having a disabled child – an issue that, while pertinent throughout the world, has special relevance in a country with relatively strict family planning regulations. Similarly, in 2008 Greenpeace faced a challenge in Japan when activists were arrested for their role in highlighting an embezzlement scandal with whale meat in Japan. In this case, Greenpeace relied on international and national newspapers in Japan to highlight the issue. Some other issues may be more global. For instance, Green Korea United relied on guerrilla marketing techniques to highlight the issue of deforestation. The organisation used pictures of cut tree trunks on walkways and between trees in streets to showcase the extent of the problem.

Practice case study

Waste management is a serious problem in densely populated Hong Kong: With more than 6 million tons of solid waste being produced each year, the government of Hong Kong Special Administrative Region needs to act quickly to reduce the waste disposed of, as the three landfills of Hong Kong are likely to be filled up in a matter of a few years. As land is in short supply in Hong Kong, additional landfills will be costly and are likely to destroy precious green space.

Faced with this dilemma, the government of Hong Kong has created the 'Hong Kong Blueprint for Sustainable Use of Resources 2013–2022' Programme, which aims to tackle the problem through a three-pronged approach:

1. The blueprint envisages policies and legislation to encourage behavioural changes to reduce waste at consumer level;
2. Territory-wide awareness campaigns to educate the public; and
3. An update of the existing waste-related infrastructure to cope more effectively with the ever increasing waste produced in the territory.

Prior to the launch of the blueprint, the government has already engaged in some awareness raising campaigns, including a campaign to encourage waste recycling.

The aim of the programme was to explain which types of waste should be collected in which coloured bins, enabling the authorities to separate waste more readily, and reduce the amount of waste taken to landfill sites.

While the campaign has been widely visible in recent years, there has been no reduction in overall waste produced in Hong Kong, which is acknowledged in the new blueprint. Comparing waste-production rates between different cities, the blueprint document emphasises the success of waste fees in Taipei and South Korea, which have dramatically reduced the amount of waste produced. While the document does not explicitly endorse waste fees for private households, the government of Hong Kong does suggest that an existing scheme for building waste reduction, based on waste fee, might be expanded to cover more areas. Thus, legislation and the fee for producing waste are seen as potential ways forward, including a food waste-recycling fee proposed for 2013.

However, apart from fees and legislation, a key cornerstone is social mobilisation. The document proposes consultation meetings and focuses specifically on food waste reduction; however, it remains silent on other measures. Based on the campaign above, and after consulting the blueprint document (http://www.enb.gov. hk/en/files/WastePlan-E.pdf), suggest ways in which the government of Hong Kong can move forward.

Further investigation

Key areas to focus on:

- Cultural impact on message framing and social marketing design;
- Social and political aspects of social marketing campaigns in East Asia;
- The different roles of media, including social media as a means to achieve behaviour change; and
- Motivators for different behaviours and how they differ or indeed are similar to motivators in other parts of the world.

References

Biener, L., Wakefield, M., Shiner, C. M., & Siegel, M. (2008). How broadcast volume and emotional content affect youth recall of anti-tobacco advertising. *American Journal of Preventive Medicine*, *35*(1), 14.

Burnkrant, R. E., & Unnava, H. R. (1995). Effects of self-referencing on persuasion. *Journal of Consumer Research*, *22*(1), 17−26.

Chen, Y. (2001). Chinese values, health and nursing. *Journal of Advanced Nursing*, *36*(2), 270−273.

Cross, S. E., Bacon, P. L., & Morris, M. L. (2000). The relational-interdependent self-construal and relationships. *Journal of Personality and Social Psychology*, *78*(4), 791−808.

Curtis, K. R., McCluskey, J. J., & Wahl, T. I. (2007). Consumer preferences for western-style convenience foods in China. *China Economic Review*, *18*(1), 1−14.

Dahl, S. (2004). Cross-cultural advertising research: What do we know about the influence of culture on advertising? Available at <http://ssrn.com/paper=658221>.

Dahl, S. (2009). A framework for cross-cultural social marketing research. < http://dahl.at/wordpress/2009/04/17/a-framework-for-cross-cultural-social-marketing-research > Accessed 01.08.14.

Deshpandé, R., & Stayman, D. M. (1994). A tale of two cities: Distinctiveness theory and advertising effectiveness. *Journal of Marketing Research*, *31*(1), 57−64.

Gong, P., Liang, S., Carlton, E. J., Jiang, Q., Wu, J., Wang, L., & Remais, J. V. (2012). Urbanisation and health in China. *The Lancet*, *379*(9818), 843−852.

Higgins, E. T. (1998). Promotion and prevention: Regulatory focus as a motivational principle. *Advances in Experimental Social Psychology*, *30*, 1−46.

Hofstede, G. (2001). *Culture's consequences: Comparing values, behaviors, institutions, and organizationsacross nations*. London: Sage Publications.

International Monetary Fund (2012). *World Economic Outlook, April 2012: Growth resuming, dangers remain*. Washington, DC: International Monetary Fund.

ITU. (2012). International Communication Union. < http://www.itu.int/net/pressoffice/index.aspx?lang = en#.U9uW0hbnKao > .

Lee, K. (2008). Opportunities for green marketing: Young consumers. *Marketing Intelligence & Planning*, *26*(6), 573−586.

Lin, C. A. (2001). Cultural values reflected in Chinese and American television advertising. *Journal of Advertising*, *30*(4), 83−94.

Malik, K., & United Nations Development Programme (2013). *Human Development Report 2013: The Rise of the South: Human Progress in a Diverse World*.

Martin, B. A., Lee, C., & Yang, F. (2004). The influence of ad model ethnicity and self-referencing upon attitudes: Evidence from New Zealand. *Journal of Advertising*, *33*(4), 27−37.

Martin, B. A., Veer, E., & Pervan, S. J. (2007). Self-referencing and consumer evaluations of larger-sized female models: A weight locus of control perspective. *Marketing Letters*, *18*(3), 197−209.

Martin, B. A. S., Lee, C. K.-C., Weeks, C., & Kaya, M. (2013). How to stop binge drinking and speeding motorists: Effects of relational-interdependent self-construal and self-referencing on attitudes toward social marketing: Binge drinking and speeding motorists. *Journal of Consumer Behaviour*, *12*(1), 81−90.

McGuire, W. (1984). Search for the self: Going beyond self-esteem and the reactive self. In R. A. Zucker, J. Aronoff, & A. I. Rabin (Eds.), Personality and the prediction of behavior.. Orlando: Academic Press. The Michigan State University Henry A. Murray lectures in personality.

Minton, E., Lee, C., Orth, U., Kim, C.-H., & Kahle, L. (2012). Sustainable marketing and social media: A cross-country analysis of motives for sustainable behaviors. *Journal of Advertising*, *41*(4), 69−84.

Saini, G. K., & Mukul, K. (2012). What do social marketing programmes reveal about social marketing? Evidence from South Asia. *International Journal of Nonprofit and Voluntary Sector Marketing*, *17*(4), 303−324.

Slater, M. D. (2006). Specification and misspecification of theoretical foundations and logic models for health communication campaigns. *Health Communication*, *20*(2), 149−157.

Uskul, A. K., Sherman, D. K., & Fitzgibbon, J. (2009). The cultural congruency effect: Culture, regulatory focus, and the effectiveness of gain-vs. loss-framed health messages. *Journal of Experimental Social Psychology*, *45*(3), 535−541.

World Bank (2012). Health expenditure, total (% of GDP). Available at <http://data.worldbank.org/indicator/SH.XPD.TOTL.ZS> Accessed 12.02.14.

Yap, L., Wu, Z., Liu, W., Ming, Z., & Liang, S. (2002). A rapid assessment and its implications for a needle social marketing intervention among injecting drug users in China. *International Journal of Drug Policy*, *13*(1), 57−68.

Yip, W. C., Hsiao, W. C., Chen, W., Hu, S., Ma, J., & Maynard, A. (2012). Early appraisal of China's huge and complex health-care reforms. *The Lancet*, *379*(9818), 833−842.

Social marketing: Singapore, Malaysia and Thailand

7

Sharyn Rundle-Thiele

Introduction

A marketing philosophy centres on satisfying customers – and more importantly, satisfying customers better than competitors can. Companies such as Diageo and Lion Nathan are frequently criticised for the role they play in increasing consumption of alcohol. These companies have created value by delivering products at a time and place that is convenient for their customers over decades. The products delivered by companies such as Diageo and Lion Nathan offer benefits desired by their consumers. For example, ready-to-drink types of alcohol, such as Vodka Cruisers, were created to target adolescents by offering a sweeter version of alcohol, and brands of wine were developed to target women and increase their consumption of alcohol. Marketers, whether commercial or social, seek to create value via a mutually beneficial exchange between one party and another.

The ability of marketers to change behaviour is increasingly being recognised by local, state and federal governments across the globe. Today, governments are faced with many social problems at great cost to the community. Tobacco offers an excellent case in point. Tobacco remains the only legal and easily obtainable consumer product that harms users (World Health Organization, 2011). Tobacco contains more than 4,000 chemicals and it is considered to be the leading cause of preventable death worldwide (Altamirano & Bataller, 2010). Smoking kills 5.4 million people across the globe annually and tobacco is responsible for one in ten adult deaths (Loncar & Mathers, 2006). Smoking causes more deaths than illegal drug use, automobile crashes, homicides, suicides and AIDS put together (Loncar & Mathers, 2006). Reducing deaths from tobacco-related illness remains one of the key global health challenges, and further actions are needed to reduce smoking.

Australia is one of the global leaders in this area, having devoted more than two decades of effort to combating high smoking rates. Changes to government policy have included tax increases, tobacco advertising bans and graphic warnings on cigarette packaging, while public health campaigns have involved the use of education to increase awareness of the effects of tobacco on health. These multifaceted strategies and comprehensive tobacco control programmes have led to positive results in decreasing tobacco consumption and reducing smoker numbers (Wilson, Erika Avila, & Chander, 2012). While policy and education will always remain important behaviour change tools, a further one is available: social marketing. This has proven

Ethical and Social Marketing in Asia.

itself effective in encouraging people to voluntarily change smoking behaviour (Stead, Ross, & Angus, 2007).

This chapter introduces the concept of social marketing as a means to change voluntary behaviour in individuals and to influence policy. This chapter explores the formal definition of social marketing: 'Social Marketing seeks to develop and integrate marketing concepts with other approaches to influence behaviour that benefit individuals and communities for the greater social good'[1] and explains how this definition is adopted in practice by social marketers today. Examples from Singapore, Malaysia and Thailand are used to demonstrate how social marketing is being implemented in practice.

Social marketing employed to its full extent is a credible approach to behaviour change. While reading this chapter, think about how the ideas discussed can be applied to the things you encounter in your everyday life. You will realise that there are some common elements to each instance of social marketing. How these factors come together to provide a value offering that leads to behaviour change is what differentiates good social marketing efforts from bad social marketing efforts.

Learning objectives

After reading this chapter, you should be able to:

- discuss how social marketing aims to change behaviour for social good; and
- understand the social marketing benchmark criteria.

What is social marketing?

Since social marketing was first defined by Kotler and Zaltman in 1971, there has been much debate surrounding the definition of social marketing. Various definitions have been proposed by authors over the past 40 years and some are listed in Table 7.1.

The term 'social marketing' is often confused with social media. It is important to start by saying social marketing is not Twitter, Facebook and other social media platforms. Social marketing was first defined by Kotler and Zaltman (1971, p. 5) as 'the design, implementation and control of programmes calculated to influence the acceptability of social ideas and involving considerations of product planning, pricing, communication, distribution, and marketing research'.

Over time, the definitions of social marketing have changed and today our understanding is that social marketing represents a lot more than promotion. Professor Jeff French led a global initiative in 2012 to develop a consensus definition of social marketing. This definition reflects how social marketing scholar (researchers) and practitioners understood social marketing in 2012. A working

---

[1] This definition was adopted by the American Marketing Association in October 2007.

Table 7.1 **Social marketing as defined by leading authors over time**

Author	Social marketing is...
Kotler and Zaltman (1971)	the design, implementation and control of programmes calculated to influence the acceptability of social ideas and involving considerations of product planning, pricing, communication, distribution and marketing research.
Brown (1986)	a natural outgrowth of several developments in and out of marketing, including: 1. increased needs of non-business organisations or marketing services; 2. attacks on marketing's negative impact on society; 3. the emergence of exchange theory; 4. the coalescence of social marketing-oriented theory; and 5. the decline of consensus-oriented perceptions of social reality.
Andreasen (1994)	the adaptation of commercial marketing technologies to programmes designed to influence the voluntary behaviour of target audiences to improve their personal welfare and that of the society of which they are a part.
Rothschild (1999)	the offering of voluntary choices within an environment that encourages and supports responsible and progressive choices.
Donovan and Henley (2003)	the application of commercial marketing technologies to the analysis, planning, execution and evaluation of programmes designed to influence the voluntary and involuntary behaviour of target audiences in order to improve the welfare of individuals and society.

group comprised of representatives from top social marketing bodies – the Australian Association of Social Marketing (AASM), the International Social Marketing Association (iSMA) and the European Association of Social Marketing (ESMA) – was formed to develop the consensus definition. A consensus definition was published in 2013 and this definition has been endorsed by all leading social marketing bodies – the Australian Association of Social Marketing (www.aasm. org.au), the International Social Marketing Association (iSMA) and the European Association of Social Marketing (ESMA).

The 2013 definition of social marketing is as follows (e.g. French, 2013):

> *Social marketing seeks to develop and integrate marketing concepts with other approaches to influence behaviour that benefit individuals and communities for the greater social good. Social Marketing practice is guided by ethical principles. It*

seeks to integrate research, best practice, theory, audience and partnership insight, to inform the delivery of competition sensitive and segmented social change programmes that are effective, efficient, equitable and sustainable.

Table 7.2 outlines some of the key factors that were deemed to be essential or important by the 167 social marketing experts that completed the survey in 2012. For the full list of factors, please go to http://www.i-socialmarketing.org/assets/social_marketing_definition.pdf.

Population Development Associates (PDA) are a private organisation based in Thailand who market a range of products and services through community development centres (Andreasen, 1988). A water tank project run by PDA builds water tanks in villages to help improve the quality of life for villagers. The water tank project was not designed to provide revenue, but it does provide some overhead to PDA (Andreasen, 1988). Many commercial marketing concepts do not easily translate to social marketing, and these areas are being examined currently by social marketing scholars. For example, there is a lot of debate around the four Ps of marketing.

Table 7.2 Summary of social marketing activities deemed to be important or essential

Description	Essential + important (% total responses)	Rank
Set and measure behavioural objectives	83	1
Uses audience insight and research	81	2
Focus on the production of social good	79	3
Use audience segmentation to understand and target interventions	76	4
Apply data, research, evidence and behavioural theory in developing programmes	73	5
Rigorous evaluation and reporting of short-term impacts, ROI and longer-term outcomes	73	6
Use systematic planning and marketing management methodology	68	7
Undertake competition analysis and develop competitor intervention strategies	67	8
Apply and be guided by an ethical analysis and standards	66	9
Apply commercial marketing theory and practice to social challenges	61	10
Focus on up-stream, mid-stream and down-stream audiences	58	11
Analyse communication channels and other forms of influence	57	12
Inform and shape the total social policy intervention mix	54	13

Many social marketing scholars (researchers) believe the four Ps of commercial marketing do not apply to social marketing. Note that in Table 7.2 the four Ps of marketing was ranked as number 21 by the 167 social marketing experts surveyed in 2012. Some scholars believe ideas such as the four Cs of marketing (consumer, cost, convenience and communication) proposed by Schultz, Tannenbaum and Lauterborn (1993) may be more applicable in social marketing, offering a clearer framework, than the four marketing Ps of place, price, promotion and product.

Benchmark criteria for social marketing

Various authors have proposed a number of different frameworks to give social marketing a clear structure. The frameworks proposed offer a better understanding of core social marketing concepts and principles, and help us to understand better what is (and is not) social marketing. Alan Andreasen in his 2002 paper titled 'Marketing social marketing in the social change marketplace' put forward six social marketing criteria to distinguish social marketing from other change disciplines such as public health and education.

Andreasen's six criteria act as a check that an intervention has a consumer focus, as each criteria redirects the focus back to the goals of both the programme sponsor and the consumers the intervention seeks to influence – a behavioural objective reminds social marketers that their goal is to change behaviour, not just educate or inform. Additionally, audience segmentation requires clear thoughts about who the efforts are aimed at, while formative research helps ensure an understanding of the consumer and orientation of the social marketing intervention towards the target market. Next, creating an exchange requires consideration of what has to be given up by the target audience in order for them to undertake the desired behaviour while the marketing mix pushes social marketers to present holistic solutions that are attractive and valuable, helping to induce both trial and repeat behaviour. Finally, consideration of the competition provides social marketers with the awareness that they must consider the competing pressures faced by consumers (many of which are far more appealing than the behaviour social marketers are attempting to change) when planning to understand how the offering they create will reduce some of those pressures in favour of the behaviour they are trying to influence (Carins & Rundle-Thiele, 2014).

Over time, other authors (for example, Lefebvre & Flora, 1988; National Social Marketing Centre, 2012; Walsh, Rudd, & Moeykens, 1993) have provided frameworks for social marketing. These frameworks have many similarities, but also some differences (see Figure 7.1). For example, the Lefebvre et al. and Walsh et al. frameworks have a different emphasis on consumer orientation and evaluation when compared to Andreasen's framework, while the UK National Social Marketing Centre eight benchmark criteria extend Andreasen's framework (see http://www.thensmc.com/sites/default/files/benchmark-criteria-090910.pdf). Figure 7.1 illustrates the various criteria, indicating areas of common understanding.

| Walsh et al., 1993 | LeFebvre et al., 1988 | Andreasen, 2002 | French et al., 2010 (adapted from Andreasen, 2002) |

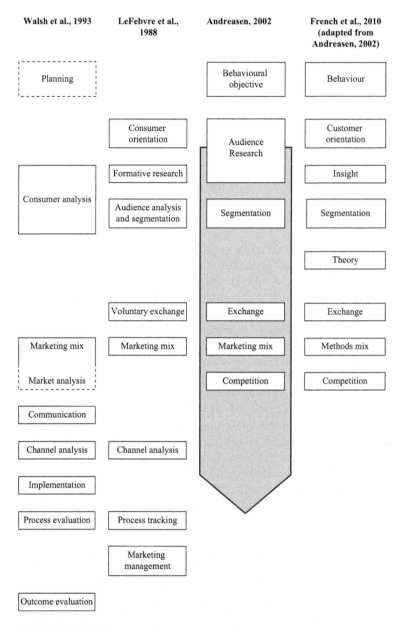

Figure 7.1 Social marketing processes.
Source: Carins, 2012.

Each of the frameworks illustrated in Figure 7.1 indicates an involved and considered social marketing process, which typically starts with an understanding of the consumer. There is also a consistent focus in all frameworks featured in Figure 7.1 on having a marketing mix, or mix of strategies within the intervention. Process management and evaluation feature heavily in the first two frameworks

(Lefebvre and Walsh). Andreasen discusses the importance of evaluation, and the challenges associated with evaluating social marketing campaigns, but he does not include evaluation as a separate benchmark in his framework. The UK's National Social Marketing benchmark criteria also stress the criticality of planning, review and evaluation. The iSMA board unanimously approved a list of 12 competencies at their 22 April 2014 board meeting for social marketing. The competencies are:

1. Describe social marketing to colleagues and other professionals and differentiate it from other approaches to behaviour and social change.
2. Work with colleagues and stakeholders to identify community or national priorities and identify those to which a social marketing approach may be usefully applied.
3. Identify and segment affected populations and select appropriate segments to give the greatest priority to programme planning.
4. Prioritise and select measurable behaviours of individuals, organisations and/or policy-makers to influence.
5. Design and conduct a situational analysis and formative research needed to understand current audience barriers and benefits, and inform an integrated marketing mix strategy.
6. Select and apply relevant behavioural and social science theories, models, frameworks and research to inform development of a social marketing strategic plan.
7. Create an integrated social marketing mix strategy with consideration of all appropriate evidence-based tools needed to influence adoption of a desired behaviour.
8. Test the potential effectiveness of draft social marketing strategies with representatives of target audiences and stakeholders.
9. Manage and lead implementation of social marketing interventions.
10. Design and implement a programme evaluation plan, including a monitoring system to ensure programmes are on track to achieve goals.
11. Apply ethical principles to conducting research, and developing and implementing a social marketing plan.
12. Document and communicate the results of the programme and its evaluation to colleagues, stakeholders, communities and other relevant organisations and groups.

However, these are not included as separate criteria for benchmarking social marketing campaigns, because they do not distinguish social marketing from other behaviour change disciplines. Social marketing evaluation is vital for funding bodies and governments to determine whether interventions are successful, and calculations of return on investment (ROI) are essential to demonstrate the case for continued support of programmes (Carins, 2012).

It is important to note that while all elements of the criteria are not required for a programme to be labelled social marketing, the use of all six benchmark criteria proposed by Alan Andreasen has been shown to increase a social marketer's chance of changing the targeted behaviour (Carins & Rundle-Thiele, 2014). Let's consider each of Andreasen's six benchmark social marketing criteria in more detail.

Behaviour change

The key aim for social marketers should be behaviour as a change outcome — that is, the targeted behaviour should be the focus of any social marketing campaign design, implementation and evaluation. Social marketers want people to increase a desired behaviour (e.g. increased physical activity or eating of healthy foods) or to decrease an undesirable behaviour (e.g. smoke less, take less drugs or drink less alcohol). Behaviour change is mentioned in most social marketing frameworks (see Figure 7.1), as it is fundamental to intervention success.

In practice, many social marketing practitioners and researchers often aim to change attitudes, awareness, and behavioural intentions rather than focusing on the actual behaviour itself. Social marketing interventions should be monitored to assess their effectiveness in changing targeted behaviours to understand whether the intervention is achieving its aims. Evaluation is used by social marketers to identify how interventions can be improved. Best practice evaluation of social marketing interventions should involve the inclusion of baseline measurement and a control group, to effectively evaluate change in the desired behaviour. The use of a control group permits confounding factors to be examined, ensuring that a comprehensive understanding of what caused the behaviour change is gained. Social marketers should employ multiple evaluation methods including a pilot test, as well as pre- and post-tests to identify improvements to be made to the intervention. For example, evaluation can enable a social marketer to alter the target audience once evaluation data shows that those interested in the intervention were younger than originally intended during intervention planning. By repositioning the intervention to appeal even more to a younger audience, the intervention can reach a target audience that is more responsive and engaged with the intervention.

A study by Sajahan et al. (2012) evaluated the 'Anti Drug Campaign' carried out by the National Drug Agency (AADK), District of Kuala Muda Kedah, Malaysia. A non-probability sampling (convenience sampling) method was used with 300 surveys given to respondents who visited the Anti-Drug Campaign. Results of the survey indicated that only 2.5 per cent of respondents were not aware of the campaign and 25.5 per cent of respondents also agreed that anti-drug campaign organised by AADK led them to turn away from drugs. The study authors concluded that anti-drug campaigns conducted at Kuala Muda District, Kedah obtained a positive response from the community; however, the campaign alone did not change drug-taking behaviour. Insights from the evaluation would be useful to further develop the campaign to ensure that drug taking behaviour is minimised.

Audience research

Audience research is essential in social marketing just as market research is essential in commercial marketing (Andreasen, 2002). Audience research is the use of market research to (a) understand target audiences before developing interventions, (b) routinely test interventions elements before they are implemented and (c) monitor interventions as they are implemented in the field. Consider research findings from Singapore in relation to obesity where the problem of obesity is not caused by a lack of knowledge among individuals. Audience research (see http://www.wpro.who.int/noncommunicable_diseases/about/HealthierFoodCentreProgramme-Singapore.pdf) indicates that 66 per cent of Singaporeans would like to lose weight and 62 per cent acknowledged the importance of regular exercise. Yet knowing that one should eat a balanced diet and exercise regularly is not the same as actually doing it. Many individuals who have vowed to lose weight have found it challenging to modify their existing lifestyles. Research indicates that those who have lost weight have found it difficult to maintain the weight loss. Audience research provides an opportunity for the social marketer to learn about the target audience and to understand how best to design an intervention for that specific audience. Mixed methods should be used when undertaking audience research, including both qualitative and quantitative methods. Qualitative approaches include focus groups, interviews and/or literature reviews, while quantitative methods consist of surveys, observations and/or analysis of previously collected data.

Segmentation

Andreasen's third benchmarking criteria states that segmentation should be used to maximise efficiency and effectiveness. In short, segmentation should be used to make decisions about who to target, in order to maximise scarce budget resources. Segmentation is based on the principal understanding that populations are comprised of different people who have different needs and wants (heterogeneous) and that groups with similar needs and wants can be identified using complex analytical techniques such as cluster analysis. Segmentation is a process that involves dividing a total market (population) into groups with relatively similar needs to design a social marketing intervention to meet the needs of one or more targeted groups. Segmentation analysis can be based on one or more of demographic, psychographic, geographic and behavioural factors.

A social marketing campaign encouraging pregnant women to give up alcohol during pregnancy segmented a market into two different ethnic groups in California, USA. The two groups were African American women and a group of Latina adolescent women. Although the campaign message of not consuming alcohol during pregnancy was consistent for the two segments, the message and delivery was altered to better suit the intended audiences and their unique characteristics. Two different campaigns and slogans were developed. For the African American women, the campaign slogan was 'Drinking and babies don't mix' with a graphic image of an ill baby in an intensive care unit with the word 'nonreturnable' stamped in the corner. The text that accompanied the image put attention on the harm that even a small amount of alcohol can cause to an unborn baby. The intervention materials for the Latina adolescents were delivered in both English and Spanish, and were framed differently from the other segment, with an emphasis on 'what drinking can do and... lasts a lifetime' (Glik, Halpert-Schilt, & Zhang, 2001; Kubacki et al., 2013).

Exchange

Exchange describes the something that a person has to give up in order to get the proposed benefit. In the case of healthy eating campaigns, clear cases of exchange exist when social marketers offer immediate benefits in the form of food samples, coupons, vouchers, prizes or extra time off (Carins & Rundle-Thiele, 2014). Exchange can be difficult to detect when analysing social marketing campaigns. The application of commercial marketing's exchange principle in social marketing can be highlighted using the Team Up social marketing campaign launched by VicHealth in 2013. A consumer who finds a sporting team that needs a player on Team Up may join the team and exercise once a week. Over time, this increased level of activity may lead to weight loss resulting from the sustained higher levels of physical exertion. The act of registering on Team Up may not deliver an immediate benefit to the consumer, but over time the benefits (e.g. weight loss) may accrue. The long-term benefits are costly and time consuming for a social marketer to measure when compared to the ease a commercial marketer experiences with direct measurement such as product sales.

A good example of exchange in social marketing is the Road Crew Campaign that was delivered in the United States to prevent drink driving. To reduce drink driving, the Road Crew Campaign (Rothschild, Mastin, & Miller, 2006) introduced luxury taxis that would take people home after a night out drinking. In exchange for money, the target audience could enjoy a ride home in a limousine and this led to an outcome of reduced drink driving. Exchange can be difficult to achieve when the desired behaviour is to decrease or stop a pre-existing behaviour. Understanding what the alternatives to the desired behaviour are can provide insight into what would represent a valuable exchange to the target audience.

Marketing mix

Social marketing is more than communication and social media, and on 22 April 2014 the iSMA competencies approved made this clear. Competencies 5 and 7 clearly state a full marketing mix, suggesting that social marketing is more than communications or promotion. Social marketers develop, test and implement a solution that is attractive to the target market. Many social marketing textbooks remain set out around a traditional four Ps marketing mix of product, price, place and promotion. It is increasingly being recognised in social marketing that the four Ps framework does not always apply, and this framework can often confuse people as they try to explain a social marketing campaign that is little more than a communications campaign.

A review of studies that state they relate to social marketing can uncover many social marketing efforts that do not extend beyond communication − e.g. advertisements, posters, pamphlets, public relations, social and mobile media. Social marketing efforts should involve a full marketing mix and they need to offer more than messages communicated across different media (Lefebvre, 2011). Social marketers need to adopt a full marketing mix of techniques that includes (but is not limited to) pricing, sensory appeal, product bundling, promotions, packaging and retail displays to influence behaviour change.

Population Services International (PSI), a non-profit organisation dedicated to improving the health of low-income people worldwide, created a social marketing campaign in 2003 that focused on HIV/AIDS and STD prevention in Thailand to promote the 'One' condom brand during the Songkran water festival (marking the Thai New Year) in the Chiang Mai and Chiang Rai provinces. The target population was 'underserved high-risk groups, including indirect sex workers and their clients; men who have sex with men; migrant populations; low-income youth aged 15–25; and current and former drug users' (PSI Thailand, 2014). One hundred and fifty PSI staff and trained volunteers, dressed in green condom-shaped raincoats, distributed condom samples and promotional materials on the streets of Chiang Mai during the day and entertainment venues at night. The 'One' brand condoms were also sold at non-traditional outlets such as 24-hour convenience stores, entertainment spots, guesthouses, migrant and student dormitories, and sales points frequented by populations most at risk for HIV/AIDS (PSI Thailand). Logos for the One brand were placed on more than 350 buses and *tuk-tuks* (three-wheel taxis). More than 100,000 print advertisements were distributed, and giant banners were placed in key locations all over the city. Radio advertisements and branded trucks with loudspeakers heralded the arrival of 'The One You've Been Waiting For' (PSI Thailand). During this campaign, PSI used every possible media outlet they could to try to establish sustainability of the 'One' condom brand in Thailand. PSI partnered with local and national Thai organisations, including the Center for Communicable Disease Control (Region 10), the Chiang Mai provincial health office, drug treatment facilities, local law enforcement, Chiang Mai University and Thai nongovernmental organisations.

Image taken from the PSI case study. Available online at http://academic2.american.edu/ ~zaharna/Thailand/Case.htm.

Competition

A key ingredient to success for social marketers centres on recognising and addressing the competition of the behaviour targeted by an intervention remains. Competitive analysis was undertaken in the ANGELO (Simmons, Mavoa, & Bell, 2009) healthy eating social marketing campaign to determine what was (and was not) available, both in terms of foods (too many high-fat snacks available, mainly high-fat, low-vegetable meals, too many high-sugar drinks at home, junk food for lunchboxes) and the economic, policy and sociocultural influences present to design a campaign that could counteract the competition.

Social marketers have to understand what other behaviours are competing for the chosen target audience's time and attention, in order to develop strategies that minimise the impact of the competition. For example, the Road Crew social marketing campaign identified that direct competition included other types of transportation such as taxis. By considering direct competition, Road Crew could create a superior product offering, in the form of luxury limousines, to reduce the incidence of drink driving after a night out in the bars and clubs. In order to compete with commercial market offerings, social marketing needs to offer unique and meaningful benefits, which represent better value than the competing behaviours to take advantage of consumer self-interest.

Conclusion

Social marketing is a professional craft, which seeks to create programmes designed to influence human behaviour. Commercial marketing targets choice and purchase behaviours. People are asked to buy products, switch brands, and recommend products and services to others. Social marketers are given the responsibility of targeting complex social behaviours and to work with an audience that doesn't always recognise it has a problem. Social marketers are often faced with marketing the least desired option, and for this reason, social marketing is different from commercial marketing, where the options marketed are cheaper, bigger, faster, new and/or improved. Social marketing, when employed to its full extent, offers a credible approach to behaviour change. This chapter has outlined 12 competencies that a practising social marketer should have; it has presented social marketing using Andreasen's six social marketing benchmark criteria and offered a range of best practice examples of social marketing from Singapore, Thailand and the USA. The chapter has outlined how a programme is planned, tested and implemented to provide a value offering that leads to behaviour change, and this is what differentiates good social marketing efforts from bad social marketing efforts.

References

Altamirano, J., & Bataller, R. (2010). Cigarette smoking and chronic liver diseases. *Gut*, *59*, 1159—1162.

Andreasen, A. R. (1988). Alternative growth opportunities for contraceptive social marketing programs. *Journal of Health Care Marketing*, *8*(2), 38—46.

Andreasen, A. R. (1994). Social marketing: Its definition and domain. *Journal of Public Policy & Marketing*, *13*(1), 108−114.

Andreasen, A. R. (2002). Marketing social marketing in the social change marketplace. *Journal of Public Policy & Marketing*, *21*(1), 3−13.

Brown, B. (1986). *Social marketing and the construction of a new policy domain: An understanding of the convergence which made social marketing possible,* doctoral thesis. Virginia Commonwealth University.

Carins, J. (2012). *Healthy eating in the Australian Defence Force (ADF): A pilot social marketing study,* unpublished doctoral confirmation paper. Griffith University, Department of Marketing.

Carins, J., & Rundle-Thiele, S. R. (2014). Eating for the better: A social marketing review (2000−2012). *Public Health Nutrition*, *17*(7), 1628−1639. Available from http://dx.doi.org/10.1017/S1368980013001365.

Donovan, R., & Henley, N. (2003). *Social marketing: Principles and practice*. Melbourne: IP Communications.

French, J. (2013). The iSMA, ESMA and AASM Collaborative programme to develop a Consensus Definition of Social Marketing <http://www.strategic-social-marketing.vpweb.co.uk/free-tool-box.html>.

French, J., Blair-Stevens, C., Merritt, R., & McVey, D. (2010). *Social Marketing and Public Health: Theory and Practice*. Oxford: Oxford University Press.

Glik, D., Halpert-Schilt, E., & Zhang, W. (2001). Narrowcasting risks of drinking during pregnancy among African American and Latina adolescent girls. *Health Promotion Practice*, *2*(3), 222−232.

Kotler, P., & Zaltman, G. (1971). Social marketing: An approach to planned social change. *Journal of Marketing*, *35*(3), 3−12.

Kubacki, K., Rundle-Thiele, S. R., Buyucek, N., Pang, B., Palmer, J., Parkinson, J. (2013). A systematic literature review: Social marketing interventions aiming to minimise harm from alcohol. *VicHealth Report no. 03/2013*, 102.

Lefebvre, R. C. (2011). An integrative model for social marketing. *Journal of Social Marketing*, *1*, 54−72.

Lefebvre, R. C., & Flora, J. A. (1988). Social marketing and public health intervention. *Health Education Quarterly*, *15*, 299−315.

Loncar, D., & Mathers, C. D. (2006). Projections of global mortality and burden of disease from 2002 to 2030. *PLoS Med*, *3*(11), e442.

National Social Marketing Centre. (2012). *Social Marketing Benchmark Criteria*. Available from <http://thensmc.com/sites/default/files/benchmark-criteria-090910.pdf> Accessed 04.05.12.

PSI Thailand. (2014). <http://www.psi.org>.

Rothschild, M. L. (1999). Carrots, sticks, and promises: A conceptual framework for the management of public health and social issue behaviors. *Journal of Marketing*, *63*(4), 24−37.

Rothschild, M., Mastin, B., & Miller, T. W. (2006). Reducing alcohol-impaired driving crashes through the use of social marketing. Available online at <http://www.roadcrewonline.org/files/researchpaper.pdf>.

Sajahan, M. S., Khir, M. R. M., Johari, N. R., & Jaafar, E. (2012). Social marketing practice in 'anti drug campaign' as an alternative of continuous improvement in public awareness. *Interdisciplinary Journal of Contemporary Research in Business*, *3*, 58−70.

Schultz, D. E., Tannenbaum, S. I., & Lauterborn, R. F. (1993). *Integrated Marketing Communications: Putting it together and Making it Work*. Illinois, USA: NTC Business Books, McGraw-Hill.

Simmons, A., Mavoa, H. M., Bell, A. C., De Courten, M., Schaaf, D., Schultz, J., & Swinburn, B. A. (2009). Creating community action plans for obesity prevention using the ANGELO (Analysis Grid for Elements Linked to Obesity) framework. *Health Promotion International, 24,* 311–324.

Stead, M., Ross, G., & Angus, K. (2007). A systematic review of social marketing effectiveness. *Health Education, 107,* 126–191.

Walsh, D. C., Rudd, R. E., & Moeykens, B. A. (1993). Social marketing for public health. *Health Affairs 25 (Millwood), 12,* 104–119.

Wilson, L. M., Erika Avila, T., & Chander, G. (2012). Impact of tobacco control interventions on smoking initiation, cessation, and prevalence: A systematic review. *Journal of Environmental and Public Health,* Article ID 961724.

World Health Organization. (2011). *WHO Report on the Global Tobacco Epidemic,* Geneva.

Social marketing: India, Pakistan and Bangladesh

Dilip S. Mutum, Ezlika Ghazali and Anvita Kumar

Introduction

India, Pakistan and Bangladesh share more than boundaries; they also share a similar heritage and history. The partition of the British Indian Empire led to the creation of Pakistan and India, which gained independence on 14 August 1947 and 15 August 1947, respectively. India is the seventh largest country in the world and covers an area of approximately 3.3 million km². The country is rightly called a sub-continent and is comprised of a multi-ethnic, multi-religious and multi-lingual society. It is made up of 28 states and seven union territories, each with their own culture and official languages – even though Hindi and English are the official languages of the country, 22 official languages are recognised by the constitution of India (Ministry of Law and Justice, 2014).

Pakistan is the 36th largest country in the world with an area of approximately 803,940 km². The official language is Urdu, but other languages are also spoken here, with Punjabi spoken by 48 per cent of the population. In terms of administration, the country is divided into four provinces and four federal territories (World facts and figures – Pakistan, 2014). Officially known as the Islamic Republic of Pakistan, the World Bank describes the country as having 'important strategic endowments and development potential' due to its strategic geographic location between South Asia, Central Asia, China and the Middle East (World Bank, 2014c).

Bangladesh seceded from Pakistan and became independent on 26 March 1971. It covers an area of 144,000 km² and the official language is Bangla. Since its independence, the country has made impressive improvements in human development, especially with regards to advancing women's and children's health (UNDP, 2014b). Highlighting the progress made by the country, the UN Secretary-General Ban Ki-moon said: 'risen from great hardship to build a thriving economy, a vibrant civil society and a dynamic future' (UN News Centre, 2011). All three countries are members of the South Asian Association for Regional Cooperation (SAARC).

Learning objectives

After reading this chapter, you should be able to:

- understand the importance of social marketing and comprehend the challenges and barriers to social marketing campaigns in India, Pakistan and Bangladesh;

Ethical and Social Marketing in Asia.

- demonstrate how to organise and manage social marketing in different parts of this region; and
- appreciate the application of the concepts of social marketing and marketing mix in a case study.

Challenges

One of the major challenges faced by all three countries is poverty. For example, if we look at India, it is a country of contradictions. In the 67 years since its independence from the British on 15 August 1947, India has seen tremendous growth and human development. The Indian economy is the world's eleventh largest by nominal GDP and fourth largest economy in purchasing power parity terms (PPP) (IMF, 2013; World Bank, 2014a). Several Indians are now among the richest in the World (Forbes, 2014). However, despite this impressive economic growth and wealth creation, there are huge disparities in human development. Thirty-seven per cent of India's population (about 410 million people) falls below the poverty line, which translates to roughly one-third of the world's poor (World Bank, 2014b).

Human development in Pakistan has also become a critical concern for sustainable economic growth especially in the light of the high infant and under-fives mortality rates in the country. Of interest, perhaps, for the current discussion, is that the country is currently ranked as one of the lowest spenders on education and health in the region (at about 2 per cent of GDP) (World Bank, 2014c). However, on the bright side, Pakistan has made impressive reductions in poverty rates, which currently stands at an estimated 17.2 per cent in 2007/08 as compared to around 34.5 per cent in 2001/02. Of the three countries, Bangladesh has an impressive track record in terms of growth and development with poverty reduction in both urban as well as rural areas, with nearly a third moving out of poverty since 1992. However, around 47 million people are still below the poverty line and Bangladesh remains one of the most densely populated countries in the world (World Bank, 2014d).

Poverty is closely related to the fast population growth experienced by all three countries. Soon after Independence, the Indian government recognised their country's 'population problem', which was seen as an impediment to the country's development. Consequently the government launched a family planning programme supported by various international organisations. In fact, social marketing was first introduced in India in the 1960s to tackle this 'problem'. However, experts are quite divided on the success rates of social marketing campaigns targeted at tackling this problem. This is highlighted by the fact that despite impressive improvements in food production, the country has still not been able to meet the nutritional needs of the growing population (Hopper, 1999). With a population of 1.21 billion (as on 1 March 2011) and growing at an average of 1.64 per cent annually, it is the second most populous country in the world after China (623.7 million males and 586.4 million females) (Govt. of India website, 2014). Pakistan has a population of 179.2 million and a population growth rate of 1.69 per cent (World Bank, 2012b), while Bangladesh has a population of 154.7 million and a population growth rate of

1.19 per cent. Pakistan and Bangladesh have the world's sixth and eighth largest populations in the world, respectively (World Bank, 2012c). They are also among the world's most densely populated countries. Figure 8.1 shows the population growth rate across the three countries.

Among the other major social challenges facing the three countries are the HIV/AIDS epidemic (UNDP, 2014a). According to the World Bank, there are 2.40 million HIV infected Indians are living with HIV. Although recent studies show a declining trend, the epidemic still remains one of the major issues of concern, and government efforts are focused on preventing new infections (World Bank, 2012a). The threat of AIDS/HIV facing Pakistan was highlighted by Rodrigo and Rajapakse (2009), who reported that although most of the South Asian countries are in the low HIV prevalence category, the numbers are increasing in Pakistan. Of the diagnosed cases, males predominate (87 per cent), with most belonging to the 20—40 age group. (Husain & Shaikh, 2005; UNAIDS, 2002). Bangladesh has managed to contain the HIV/AIDS epidemic in the country and the reasons for relatively low levels is believed to be due to their 'HIV prevention programs targeting high risk groups backed by a state-of-the-art surveillance system' (World Bank, 2012d).

Among all the challenges faced by these three countries, the unsustainable population growth remains one the biggest areas of concern. It affects and is related to a number of other social issues as well. The HIV/AIDS epidemic is also another major challenge facing all three countries. This chapter will thus focus on the contraception and family planning as well as HIV/AIDS social marketing programmes in these three countries. We will first take a brief look at the history of social marketing in these countries and then examine some of the major issues and challenges faced by various social marketing campaigns.

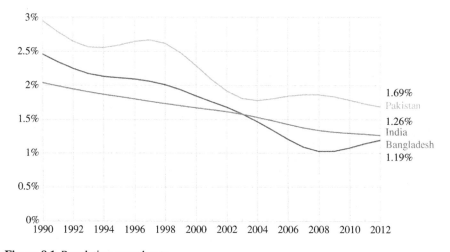

Figure 8.1 Population growth rate.
Source: Based on World Bank data (Google, 2014).

Route map: social marketing: India, Pakistan and Bangladesh

Social marketing in India

Most scholars agree that the first documented use of social marketing — employing marketing theories, tools and techniques to address social issues — was in India in 1964, when a marketing plan to promote family planning was proposed by the Indian Institute of Management (IIM), Calcutta. Targeted primarily at married couples, the proposal called on the private sector 'to consider ways of extending the distribution of contraceptive services, especially the condom, through commercial channels' (Chandy et al., 1965, p. 7). Their objective was to make their preferred contraceptive product, condoms, a normal household item.

The IIM model was considered the most viable for delivering family planning (Harvey, 2008). The social marketing of contraceptives was subsequently implemented as part of the national family planning programme. To meet the growing demand of condoms, the Ministry of Health and Family Welfare set up HLL Lifecare Limited (HLL), then called Hindustan Latex Limited, in the south Indian state of Kerala, for the production of condoms. Their first plant was built at Peroorkada in Trivandrum (now Thiruvananthapuram), with technical help from Okamoto Industries of Japan. Nirodh condoms were officially launched by the government in 1968. Two more plants were added at Trivandrum and Belgaum in 1985. The company is now one of the world's largest manufacturers of condoms, with an annual production of around 800 million pieces (as of December 2012). Besides Nirodh, other brands include Zaroor, Masti and the upmarket Moods. Subsequently, the social marketing of marketing planning continued with other contraception methods and products. Mala D — an oral contraceptive pill brand available over the counter without a prescription — was launched in 1987.

The early 1990s saw the launch of numerous Social Marketing Organisations (SMOs), which were involved in the implementation of social marketing programmes with funding from government and other organisations. HLL Lifecare Limited has established itself as the leading SMO in the country. Other leading SMOs in India today include Hindustan Latex Family Planning Promotion Trust (HLFPPT) (promoted by HLL Lifecare Limited), Population Services International, India (PSI) and Population Health Services, India (PHSI), among others. Under the Ministry of Health and Family Welfare, India's government-led contraceptive social marketing programme is now the largest in the world (Deshpande, Balakrishnan, Bhanot, & Dham, 2011), and has recognised social marketing as key to 'providing accessible and affordable contraceptive products' (FHI 360, 2011).

However, despite the fact that the population growth rates in India have slowed down, they are nowhere near the Indian government's targets, and according to the French National Institute for Demographic Studies (INED), India will overtake China as the world's most populous nation by 2050 (Pison, 2013). So what happened?

Social marketing in Pakistan

A review of literature reveals that several studies on social marketing in Pakistan have focused on the HIV/AIDS issue. Studies looking at the implementation of social marketing to contain the threat of HIV/AIDS in Pakistan observed that non-governmental organisations (NGOs) in Pakistan provide information and free access to condoms and clean needles. A case in point is Greenstar Social Marketing Pakistan, a non-profit NGO. They use the franchising model and are one of the first health franchisers in the world. Targeting the low-income and non-users, they use a 'total market approach which has different price points for each segment of the population' (Bhattacharyya et al., 2010). Greenstar targets truck drivers in Karachi, the capital of Pakistan, providing HIV counselling services and condoms, as well as medical treatment facilities for the drivers(Husain & Shaikh, 2005). Their marketing campaign to promote their brand of condoms, called Touch condoms, involved ads on TV, newspapers, posters and billboards, and the organisation was praised for communicating their message openly in a country where a conservative approach is commonly used when communicating topics considered culturally 'sensitive' (Butt, 2009).

Highlighting the importance of social marketing, Husain and Shaikh (2005) emphasise the importance of preventive strategies, which are culturally acceptable. According to them:

> these strategies must logically address the known mechanisms of spread and should integrate biomedical and behavioural approaches. However, the application of a single isolated strategy will undermine the purpose of a preventive programme by laying stress on one aspect of complicated human behaviour.
>
> *(Husain & Shaikh, 2005, p. 294)*

Similarly, Qureshi and Shaikh (2006) highlighted the need to address cultural misconceptions and societal barriers, which had an impact on healthy behaviour in Pakistan. They emphasised the importance of using social marketing in motivating low-income and high-risk groups, which were susceptible to the myths, fallacies and misconceptions pertaining to health. One of their recommendations was the setting up of 'health promotion committees' at village levels to reduce these myths and fallacies. They also highlighted the successful implementation of social marketing strategies to promote the use of iodised salt (Qureshi & Shaikh, 2006).

Several papers have also looked at the use of social marketing of insecticide-treated mosquito nets in Pakistan (Howard et al., 2003; Qazi & Shaikh, 2006; Rowland et al., 2002). It was found that Howard et al. (2003) did not really talk about social marketing, but merely pointed out that subsidies for the nets should be targeted at the most poor, who could not afford the nets. Looking at condom social marketing campaigns, Harvey (1994) pointed out that one of the most successful countries was Pakistan (looking at sales of condoms), differentiating it from Bangladesh, which had a long-established, multi-method, heavily subsidised government programme. This was because in Pakistan, competition from other methods was considered minimal. A study undertaken to evaluate the effectiveness of the 2009 marketing communication campaign on thematic condom indicated that approximately 15 per cent of urban married men were aware of Touch condom advertising. The study further found that the advertising campaign led to greater degree of discussion on family planning, condom use and an improved perception of the effectiveness of condom use (Agha & Beaudoin, 2012). This indicates a promising possibility of adopting advertising to educate the public on contraceptive and other important health issues. Husain and Shaikh (2005) point out that the public sector is also actively involved in the process including advertisements in both the electronic and print media; however, much of the initiative and in this field appears to be led by the NGOs.

Social marketing in Bangladesh

As mentioned earlier, Bangladesh has been quite successful in improving the social conditions in the country as compared to its two neighbours. A lot of the credit goes to the effectively run social marketing campaigns. Schellstede and Ciszewski (1984) analysed the success of the Social Marketing Project (SMP), which was managed by Population Services International (PSI). This contraceptive and family planning programme was launched on a national scale in 1975.

A few studies have also looked at the social marketing of oral contraceptives and it was revealed that most of the users were higher in socioeconomic terms. They had higher educational qualifications and were more affluent (Boone, Farley, & Samuel, 1984; Davies, Mitra, & Schellstede, 1986) than users of socially marketed condoms (Ciszewski & Harvey, 1994).

With funding from the Global Fund, the organisation Save the Children used drop-in centres to increase condom use by female sex workers (FSWs) in Bangladesh. Save the Children provided free condoms, education, counselling and testing services besides sexually transmitted infection (STI) clinics and general health services. A survey in 2012 found that condom use increased tremendously from 66.7 per cent to 95.5 per cent, from 2008 to 2012 (Hossain, Sultana, Amin, & Siddiqua, 2013). Hossain et al. (2013) concluded that strong motivational support and peer education would help to keep up this high rate of condom use among FSWs. This was essential to prevent the spread of HIV.

Among the various NGOs involved in social marketing in Bangladesh, one organisation that stands out is the Social Marketing Company (SMC) which was established in 1974 as a Family Planning Social Marketing Project under an agreement between the Bangladesh government, Population Services International (PSI), a US-based NGO and USAID. The SMC later became a company with a voluntary board of directors in 1990 (SMC, 2014a). It is now the largest and one of the most successful privately managed not-for-profit organisations for a single country in the world. Besides focusing on family planning and maternal and child health, they are also involved in the prevention of sexually transmitted diseases (STDs)/AIDS as well as education programmes. The SMC began addressing the issues of STDs and HIV/AIDS in 1995 by targeting high-risk populations, in particular the FSWs.

The SMC story is really impressive and the organisation is moving towards 100 per cent self-reliance with independence from donations, due to their social franchise model comprising of a private sector network of branded providers (Gonsalkorale, 2010). Later, we will examine the successful BlueStar Programme, which was launched in June 1998.

Looking at the Bangladesh experience, what has emerged is the importance of community-based approaches and partnerships in implementation of social marketing campaigns. El Arifeen et al. (2013) have identified three distinctive strategies that have resulted in improved health service coverage and outcomes in Bangladesh, which are:

1. experimentation with community-based approaches to health service delivery;
2. experimentation with partnerships for health service delivery; and
3. early adoption of innovations.

According to El Arifeen et al., these approaches were responsible for the success of a number of high-priority programmes in Bangladesh and have evolved over time to meet the different challenges.

The state of the art in social marketing: India, Pakistan and Bangladesh

Challenges and barriers to social marketing campaigns in India

Given the diversity of India, barriers to effective social marketing are bound to vary from region to region and also between urban and rural areas. The following are some specific challenges and barriers, focusing specifically on the contraceptive social marketing campaigns.

Effects of coercive policies

India has the unsavoury distinction of being one of only two countries where coercion has been used in family planning programmes (the other being China). With increasing pressure from international organisations, in 1975 the then Prime Minister of India, Indira Gandhi, introduced a national population policy. Some overzealous states instituted forced sterilisations, which resulted in 8.3 million sterilisations in 1976–7 against a forecasted 4.3 million (Veron, 2006). This led to widespread resentment, especially among the poorer sections of society and minorities targeted. Largely due to the unpopularity of the forced sterilisations, the Congress Party was defeated at the elections in 1977 and this ended the population policy. Although successive governments made several efforts to make the family planning campaigns friendlier, this has damaged the credibility of government organisations and anybody involved in family planning programmes. It has also undoubtedly hurt social marketing campaigns and it will take a long time to regain the trust of the people. This underlines the importance of instituting voluntary family planning programmes, if we want to have sustainable population control. As highlighted by Connelly (2008), there are other factors that are more effective than coercion in the long run. Connelly noted that birth rates fell as women became more educated and had more rights. This means that family planning programmes would be more effective and sustainable where women had a choice.

Selling-focused approaches

A look at the various population control social marketing campaigns reveals that these campaigns are still focused on selling; they are product-focused approaches. These information-intensive campaigns focus on informing, making use of intensive media advertising and printed materials. We are now talking about the need to build long-term customer relationships (Rust, Moorman, & Bhalla, 2010) and the consumer-centred approach, where positive social change is the main objective, rather than fiscal targets. It is essential to remember that in this approach, the consumer is an active participant and partner in the whole process of behaviour change.

Barriers to contraceptive social marketing

A study by the Urban Health Initiative (UHI) (2010) identified four main barriers to effective social marketing of contraceptives in the North Indian state of Uttar Pradesh. The barriers were:

1. lack of convenient access to retail outlets for the poor;
2. lack of incentive for retailers to stock and sell the socially marketed brands because of lower profits;
3. lack of up-to-date information among many pharmacists and chemists about contraceptive methods, which meant that they were unable to provide guidance to women about their safety and efficacy; and
4. unfavourable impressions about condoms among men. This was probably the only internal barrier and related to embarrassment while buying condoms, decrease in sexual pleasure or belief that condom use indicated a lack of trust.

The UHI reported two programmes: Innovations in Family Planning Services Project II (IFPS II) and Sadhan Social Marketing Network. Both programmes focused on increasing the use of birth-spacing (i.e. the time interval from one child's birth date until the next child's birth date) methods, especially condoms and pills, for family planning.

Challenges and barriers to social marketing campaigns in Pakistan

Although specific targeted strategies such as counselling services provided by Greenstar HIV to truck drivers have been proven successful, these are quite restricted. Promoting preventive activities within the general population was the most challenging issue (Husain & Shaikh, 2005). This may be due to the fact that organisations involved in sexual health campaigns are too culturally sensitive and thus do not get their message across effectively. As Butt (2009) has pointed out,

'Organisations involved in the field of reproductive and sexual health are guilty of being too conservative in their approach and appear to place a higher value on our comfort levels rather than the clarity of their message.'

Agha (2010) also highlighted the importance of convincing other family members, especially husbands and mothers-in-law. In fact, it was revealed that support of family planning use by in-laws was the strongest determinant of a woman's intentions to use contraceptive methods. Agha (2010) pointed out that one of the biggest challenges was the fear that IUDs and sterilisation would make women sterile and harm their wombs, and therefore recommended that these concerns should be addressed using social marketing.

Challenges and barriers to social marketing campaigns in Bangladesh

Schellstede and Ciszewski (1984) highlighted some of the issues facing contraceptive and family planning programmes, especially the fact that like Pakistan, Bangladesh had a religious (Islamic) and conservative society. It was realised from the start that in order to be effective, the campaign needed to be more explicit, especially in the advertising of contraceptives. The importance of husbands in implementing family planning programmes was also highlighted in another study, particularly with regard to 'obtaining supplies from the commercial sector and acting as instructors' (Davies et al., 1986). This was similar to the results of the study in Pakistan (Agha, 2010). Here Agha (2010) pointed out the dominant role that men play in communication networks.

However, the main challenge facing Bangladesh is sustaining the successes achieved in health service coverage and health outcomes. As identified by El Arifeen et al. (2013), a key challenge is the provision of training, support and supervision of the largely unregulated community-level workers. For a lot of poor people in the country, these workers are the 'first line of care'. El Arifeen et al. point out that the government needs to 'clearly define its roles as a policy maker, regulator and implementer if Bangladesh is to meet these future challenges' (El Arifeen et al., 2013, p. 2022).

New research directions

McKenzie-Mohr (2000) highlights the advantages of community-based social marketing as opposed to information-intensive programmes in fostering sustainable behaviour. According to him, media advertising can be effective in creating awareness and understanding of issues, but are limited in their ability to foster behaviour change. The foundation of community-based social marketing is the uncovering of and understanding the perceived barriers that prevent people from engaging in the desired behaviour. It has been observed that social marketing is instrumental in changing the 'health behaviour of individual citizens' (Hastings, MacFadyen, & Anderson, 2000).

Practising social marketing: IIM contraceptive social marketing campaign proposal in India

As an example of the application of the chapter topic in action/practice, we examine the marketing mix analysis of the IIM contraceptive social marketing campaign proposal in India. We analyse the proposal using the 'four Ps' of marketing — product, price, place and promotion — as a social marketing framework.

Product

The IIM recommended focusing on high-quality and well-packaged condoms. Branding was considered important and the IIM recommended branding the condoms using a term familiar to Indians, and thus Nirodh, meaning protection, was born. Initially the condoms were imported and subsidised by the government. Branding was essential in order to position the condom as a higher-quality product and to appeal to consumers more than the generic no name products.

Price

It should be remembered that when *Nirodh* was launched, the Government of India were already distributing condoms free of charge. The commercially available brands were much costlier, which priced them out of the hands of poorer consumers. The IIM recommended an affordable retail price of Rs. 0.30 (approximately £0.003) for a packet of six condoms, or Rs. 0.50 each, which would be subsidised by the government and distributed through commercial channels. This was about 85 per cent lower than the commercial prices at that time (e.g. the 1960s). There is also a body of literature that shows that lower prices for socially marketed products does lead to increased uptake among low-income sections of society. The opposite holds true as well (Price, 2001). The IIM came to this price based on an estimated average consumption of six condoms per month per family. Their rationale for charging a price was that this would cover wholesale and retail selling costs as well as some costs of their promotions. It would also eliminate the additional need to maintain inventories. Although the IIM did not highlight it, products distributed free are often perceived by consumers as low in quality. Thus costing them at an affordable price resulted in a higher perceived quality than giving them away for free would achieve.

Place

Regarding the distribution channels, the IIM estimated that more than 200,000 outlets would be required in urban areas, with a further 200,000 relatively large shops in rural areas. They highlighted the importance of *kiranas* (or dry grocers, e.g. grocery stores selling non-perishable, unrefrigerated packaged products), as these were the local shops where most of the household shopping was done (Chandy et al., 1965, p. 7). The intimate knowledge of *kirana* shopkeepers and their friendly social relationships was considered highly important.

Promotion

Finally, the IIM proposed an increase of the family planning promotional activities by at least 20 times in terms of the scale (and range) in order to facilitate the social marketing strategy's success. This was to be carried out by a massive government-led national campaign to promote various family planning programmes and methods. Interestingly, they recommended that about 10 per cent should go to promotions of the condoms in retail outlets, and about five per cent should go directly to promoting the use of condoms. The use of mass media and print was highlighted.

Practice case study: the BlueStar Programme

One of the most successful programmes launched by the Social Marketing Company (SMC) of Bangladesh was the BlueStar Programme (BSP). This programme was launched in June 1998 and used the social franchise model comprising of a private sector network of branded providers, in order to increase the utilisation of public health services. This was done by using community-based private health providers to improve the quality, awareness, accessibility and affordability of these services.

BlueStar providers

There are non-formal private health practitioners who are recruited based on set criteria and trained by the SMC. The providers agree to deliver a defined package of services. They also keep detailed records, which are sent to the SMC. Although only graduate providers were initially accepted, non-graduate medical practitioners have been accepted since 2000. The SMC currently has 4,000 providers nationally. According to the SMC, each of these providers serves an average of 200 patients per week, which includes 80 per cent women and approximately 14 per cent were children. A programme evaluation study of 1,379 private sector health service providers indicated that the knowledge level of BlueStar providers was significantly higher than that of non-BlueStar providers with regard to contraception, including knowledge of side effects (SMC, 2014b).

Segmentation and targeting

The SMC markets a variety of contraceptives under its family planning programme. Each of these products is positioned differently and targeted at different price segments. For example, the SMC launched its branded injectable contraceptive SOMA-JECT in March 2003. This was positioned as a high quality contraceptive and targeted at low and middle-income families. The number of administrations of SOMA-JECT in 2013 was 1,236,747, compared to 8,500 in the first year of marketing in 1999.

User satisfaction

According to the Bangladesh Demographic and Health Survey (BDHS) in 2008, four out of ten modern contraceptive users, six out of ten condom users and two out of ten injectable users reported that they used SMC brands. The SMC have also reportedly captured 81 per cent share of the condom and 90 per cent of the oral contraceptive pill retail market (sources: CHMI, 2014; Gonsalkorale, 2010; SMC, 2014b).

Further investigation

Social marketing has a long history in India, Pakistan and Bangladesh. The contraceptive and family planning social marketing campaigns have had some successes − with the lowering of population growth rates. Clearly there are some barriers, which are hampering the campaigns. The model proposed by the IIM in India has been analysed using the marketing mix. We believe that it is crucial to systematically identify, understand and then eliminate the barriers to the desired sustainable behaviour changes, namely the adoption of contraceptives described in this chapter.

Future studies need to focus on appropriate evaluation methods and approaches. Here are some key questions/projects that require further investigation:

1. Would be accurate to say that social marketing campaigns in these three countries are still very much selling focused and there needs to be a move towards a more consumer-centric approach?
2. Are the campaigns focusing too much on meeting family planning targets? For example, targets such as number of condoms distributed, etc., which are easier to meet compared to the complexities associated with measuring and evaluating large-scale behaviour changes.
3. Husain and Shaikh (2005) emphasised the importance adopting specific and culturally acceptable strategies (in the context of HIV/AIDS programmes). However, the question is that whether organisations in these countries are too conservative in their approach − as Butt (2009) puts it, 'going for the whole nudge nudge wink wink approach'. By being too culturally sensitive, is there a risk of diluting the message that the organisations are trying to communicate?
4. Looking at the various social marketing campaigns in these three countries, it appears that some of the most successful ones are those led by private NGOs (Pakistan) while others are spearheaded or strongly supported by the government (Bangladesh) and government linked companies (India). What are the factors for their successes while other efforts failed?

References

Agha, S. (2010). Intentions to use contraceptives in Pakistan: Implications for behavior change campaigns. *BMC Public Health*, *10*(1), 450.

Agha, S., & Beaudoin, C. E. (2012). Assessing a thematic condom advertising campaign on condom use in urban Pakistan. *Journal of Health Communication: International Perspectives*, *17*(5), 601−623.

Bhattacharyya, O., Khor, S., McGahan, A., Dunne, D., Daar, A. S., & Singer, P. A. (2010). Innovative health service delivery models in low and middle income countries-what can we learn from the private sector. *Health Research Policy and Systems*, *8*(1), 24.

Boone, M. S., Farley, J. U., & Samuel, S. J. (1984). A cross-country study of commercial contraceptive sales programs: Factors that lead to success. *Studies in Family Planning*, *16*(1), 30−39.

Butt, A. (2009). Advertising sexual and reproductive health in Pakistan: The Touch condom song. Available at <http://asiancorrespondent.com/36272/advertising-sexual-and-reproductive-health-in-pakistan-the-touch-condom-song> Accessed 20.03.14.

Center for Health Market Innovations (CHMI). (2014). BlueStar Bangladesh. Available at <http://healthmarketinnovations.org/program/bluestar-bangladesh> Accessed 22.03.14.

Chandy, K. T., Balakrishman, T. R., Kantawalla, J. M., Mohan, K., Sen, N. P., Gupta, S. S., et al. (1965). Proposals for family planning promotion: A marketing plan. *Studies in Family Planning*, *1*(6), 7−12.

Ciszewski, R. L., & Harvey, P. D. (1994). The effect of price increases on contraceptive sales in Bangladesh. *Journal of Biosocial Science*, *26*(1), 25−35.

Connelly, M. J. (2008). *Fatal misconception: The struggle to control world population*. Harvard, MA: Harvard University Press.

Davies, J., Mitra, S. N., & Schellstede, W. P. (1986). Oral contraception in Bangladesh: Social marketing and the importance of husbands. *Studies in Family Planning*, *18*(3), 157−168.

Deshpande, S., Balakrishnan, J., Bhanot, A., & Dham, S. (2011). Successful contraceptive social marketing attempts in India. In H. Cheng, P. Kotler, & N. Lee (Eds.), *Social marketing for public health: Global trends and success stories* (pp. 327−355). Massachusetts: Jones and Bartletts Publishers.

El Arifeen, S., Christou, A., Reichenbach, L., Osman, F. A., Azad, K., Islam, K. S., et al. (2013). Community-based approaches and partnerships: Innovations in health-service delivery in Bangladesh. *The Lancet*, *382*(9909), 2012−2026.

FHI 360. (2011). Improving access to family planning: Is social marketing the answer? India e-FP Issue Brief #6 Topic: Family Planning and Social Marketing. Available at <http://www.fhi360.org/sites/default/files/media/documents/india-efp-forum-background6.pdf> Accessed 25.02.14.

Forbes. (2014). The world's billionaires. K. A. Dolan & L. Kroll, (Eds.). Available at <http://www.forbes.com/billionaires> Accessed 24.02.14.

Gonsalkorale, R. (2010). *Review of Procurement Management Capacity of the Social Marketing Company, Bangladesh*. Submitted to the U.S. Agency for International Development by the Strengthening Pharmaceutical Systems (SPS) Program. Arlington, VA. Management Sciences for Health. Available at <http://pdf.usaid.gov/pdf_docs/PNADX090.pdf> Accessed 22.03.14.

Google. (2014). Population growth rate. Available at <https://www.google.co.uk/publicdata/explore?ds=d5bncppjof8f9_&met_y=sp_pop_grow&hl=en&dl=en&idim=country:PAK:IND:BGD> Accessed 20.03.14.

Govt. of India website. (2014). Available at <http://india.gov.in/india-glance/profile> Accessed 24.02.14.

Harvey, P. D. (1994). The impact of condom prices on sales in social marketing programs. *Studies in Family Planning*, *25*(1), 52−58.

Harvey, P. D. (2008). Social marketing: No longer a sideshow. *Studies in Family Planning*, *39*(1), 69−72.

Hastings, G., MacFadyen, L., & Anderson, S. (2000). Whose behaviour is it anyway? The broader potential of social marketing. *Social Marketing Quarterly*, *6*(2), 46−58.

Hopper, G. R. (1999). Changing food production and quality of diet in India, 1947−98. *Population and Development Review*, *25*(3), 443−477.

Hossain, Z., Sultana, F., Amin, M., & Siddiqua, Y. (2013). P4. 036 Condom use among female sex workers (FSWs) increased through drop-in center (dic) based service delivery approach in Bangladesh. *Sexually Transmitted Infections*, *89*(Suppl. 1), A299.

Howard, N., Chandramohan, D., Freeman, T., Shafi, A., Rafi, M., Enayatullah, S., et al. (2003). Socio-economic factors associated with the purchasing of insecticide-treated nets in Afghanistan and their implications for social marketing. *Tropical Medicine & International Health*, *8*(12), 1043−1050.

Husain, S., & Shaikh, B. T. (2005). Stalling HIV through social marketing: Prospects in Pakistan. *Journal of Pakistan Medical Association*, *55*(7), 294−298.

IMF. (2013). World economic outlook database. Available at <http://www.imf.org/external/pubs/ft/weo/2013/02/weodata/index.aspx> Accessed 24.02.14.

McKenzie-Mohr, D. (2000). Promoting sustainable behavior: An introduction to community-based social marketing. *Journal of Social Issues*, *56*(3), 543−554.

Ministry of Law and Justice. (2014). Constitution of India. Eighth Schedule, Articles 344 (1) and 35. Available at <http://lawmin.nic.in/coi/coiason29july08.pdf> Accessed 24.02.14.

Pison, G. (2013). The population of the world. *Population & Societies*, *503*. (September) Available at <http://www.ined.fr/fichier/t_publication/1653/publi_pdf2_population_societes_2013_503_world_population.pdf> Accessed 13.03.14.

Price, N. (2001). The performance of social marketing in reaching the poor and vulnerable in AIDS control programmes. *Health Policy and Planning*, *16*(3), 231−239.

Qazi, S., & Shaikh, B. T. (2006). Social marketing of insecticide-treated bednets: The case for Pakistan. *Eastern Mediterranean Health Journal*, *13*(2), 449−456.

Qureshi, N., & Shaikh, B. T. (2006). Myths, fallacies and misconceptions: Applying social marketing for promoting appropriate health seeking behavior in Pakistan. *Anthropology and Medicine*, *13*(2), 131−139.

Rodrigo, C., & Rajapakse, S. (2009). Current status of HIV/AIDS in South Asia. *Journal of Global Infectious Diseases*, *1*(2), 93−101.

Rowland, M., Webster, J., Saleh, P., Chandramohan, D., Freeman, T., Pearcy, B., et al. (2002). Prevention of malaria in Afghanistan through social marketing of insecticide-treated nets: Evaluation of coverage and effectiveness by cross-sectional surveys and passive surveillance. *Tropical Medicine & International Health*, *7*(10), 813−822.

Rust, R. T., Moorman, C., & Bhalla, G. (2010). Rethinking marketing. *Harvard Business Review*, *88*(1/2), 94−101.

Schellstede, W. P., & Ciszewski, R. L. (1984). Social marketing of contraceptives in Bangladesh. *Studies in Family Planning*, *15*(1), 30−39.

SMC. (2014a). About SMC. Available at <http://www.smc-bd.org/index.php/page/view/98> Accessed 18.03.14.

SMC. (2014b). BlueStar Program. Available at <http://www.smc-bd.org/index.php/page/view/46> Accessed 18.03.14.

UNAIDS. (2002). Epidemiological fact sheets on HIV/AIDS and sexually transmitted infections: Pakistan. Available at <http://www.unaids.org/en/other/functionalities/View Document.asp> Accessed 18.03.14.

UNDP. (2014a). About India: Challenges. Available at <http://www.in.undp.org/content/india/en/home/countryinfo/challenges.html> Accessed 13.03.14.

UNDP. (2014b). About Bangladesh. Available at <http://www.bd.undp.org/content/bangladesh/en/home/countryinfo> Accessed 18.03.14.

UN News Centre. (2011). Ban lauds Bangladesh's progress on women's and children's health (15 November). Available at <http://www.un.org/apps/news/story.asp/story.asp?NewsID=40399&Cr=maternal&Cr1=#.UzAea_l_uPY> Accessed 18.03.14.

Urban Health Initiative (UHI). (2010). Expanding contraceptive use in urban Uttar Pradesh: Quality of care (March). Available at <http://www.uhi-india.org/index.php?option=com_docman&task=doc_download&gid=355&Itemid=80> Accessed 13.03.14.

Veron, J. (2006). Stabilising India's population: Easier said than done. *Population & Societies*, *423*(May), 1–4 Available at <http://www.ined.fr/fichier/t_publication/1172/publi_pdf2_pop_and_soc_english_423.pdf> Accessed 13.03.14.

World Bank. (2012a). HIV/AIDS in India (10 July). Available at <http://www.worldbank.org/en/news/feature/2012/07/10/hiv-aids-india> Accessed 13.03.14.

World Bank. (2012b). Pakistan. Available at <http://data.worldbank.org/country/pakistan> Accessed 20.03.14.

World Bank. (2012c). Bangladesh. Available at <http://data.worldbank.org/country/bangladesh> Accessed 20.03.14.

World Bank. (2012d). HIV/AIDS in Bangladesh (10 July). Available at <http://www.worldbank.org/en/news/feature/2012/07/10/hiv-aids-bangladesh> Accessed 20.03.14.

World Bank. (2014a). IDA and India. Available at <http://www.worldbank.org/ida/country/india.html> Accessed 24.02.14.

World Bank. (2014b). India: Country results profile. Available at <http://web.worldbank.org/WBSITE/EXTERNAL/NEWS/0,, contentMDK:22888405 ~ menuPK:141310 ~ pagePK:34370 ~ piPK:34424 ~ theSiteP-K:4607,00.html> Accessed 13.03.14.

World Bank. (2014c). Pakistan overview. Available at <http://www.worldbank.org/en/country/pakistan/overview> Accessed 18.03.14.

World Bank. (2014d). Bangladesh overview. Available at <http://www.worldbank.org/en/country/bangladesh/overview> Accessed 20.03.14.

World facts and figures – Pakistan. (2014). Available at <http://www.worldfactsandfigures.com/countries/pakistan.php> Accessed 20.03.14.

Social marketing: Cambodia, Indonesia, the Philippines and Vietnam

Lukas Parker, Linda Brennan and Dang Nguyen

Introduction

This chapter evaluates social marketing in the context of four dynamic and diverse countries within South East Asia: Cambodia, Indonesia, the Philippines and Vietnam. Diversity, social and cultural issues, and other macro-environmental factors are explored. The aim is to enable readers to comprehend how social marketers can organise and manage social marketing activities in different parts of the South East Asian region. Theories of social marketing applicable to the region are reviewed and extant research presented.

The unique characteristics of the four individual countries are explored in order to draw out the implications for social marketers within this dynamic and diverse region. Key themes explored include the impact of the behavioural ecological environment on developing social marketing strategy. These themes are described at the theoretical level and then explained using practical examples. The case examples include health and sanitation programmes in Vietnam and Indonesia, oral health in the Philippines, road safety campaigns in Cambodia and Vietnam, and sexual and reproductive health campaigns throughout the region.

Learning objectives

After reading this chapter, you should be able to:

- understand the impact of the socio-cultural behavioural ecology on designing social marketing strategy;
- locate exemplar social marketing strategies and campaigns in the region; and
- understand how to differentiate social marketing strategy according to various levels of social marketing (upstream, midstream, downstream).

Route map: social marketing in Cambodia, Indonesia, the Philippines and Vietnam

The future is not ahead of us. It has already happened. Unfortunately it is unequally distributed among companies, industries and nations.

(Kotler, 2002)[1]

Social marketing is a complex enterprise that often aims to rectify the perceived wrongs of global society by creating positive social change (Kotler, 2013; Spotswood, French, Tapp, & Stead, 2012; Wood, 2012). Kotler's opening quote is an example of how difficult marketing and therefore social marketing is in a globalising world where nations, industries and companies compete for unequally distributed resources in order to maximise their own well-being, sometimes at the expense of the 'others', whoever they may be. The world faces a number of challenges, not least of which is sustainability (economic, social and environmental), and social marketing has a role to play in responding to these challenges. Figure 9.1 illustrates marketing from a conceptual point of view. A *marketing* organisation considers three key areas in the development of their offering (programme, product, service,

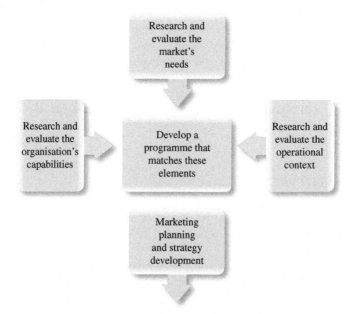

Figure 9.1 Principles of marketing.

[1] And also available on http://www.pkotler.org/kotlers-quotes.

idea or concept). The first key area, and that which has the greatest priority, is research and evaluation of the market (or customer) needs. The market and the social marketing issue must be at the centre of the social marketing organisation's activities. Secondly, the organisation will research and evaluate its own capability in matching the needs of the market. Thirdly, the operating environment and context is taken into account, particularly in relation to the changes taking place that will affect the organisation or the market.

Theoretically, a social marketing organisation develops their offering (programme product, service, idea or concept) only *after* considering these three areas. Note that the arrows feeding into the programme development stage of marketing are formative research and evaluation. The marketing planning and strategy development stage come after formative research takes place. In reality, this does not always occur and many organisations have limited flexibility in adapting the core offering in response to the three key areas. However, some flexibility can be gained if we consider the offering in terms of its total effect on the market using the levels of social marketing presented in Figure 9.2. The actual market in any programme might comprise more than one level and each level may view things differently from the organisation (and each other) and this is the key to effective marketing; look at yourself from the *market's* point of view, even if there are multiple levels, motivations and activities required for each type of market identified. That is, any particular programme may have multiple markets to deal with when it comes to creating social change.

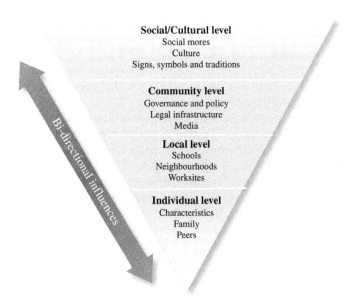

Figure 9.2 The Behavioural Ecological Model.
Source: Adapted from Hovell, Wahlgren, & Gehrman (2002).

To create social change, social marketing draws on a wider variety of theoretical frameworks and disciplines than commercial marketing does. The International Association for Social Marketing (http://www.i-socialmarketing.org) defines social marketing as follows:

> Social Marketing seeks to develop and integrate marketing concepts with other approaches to influence behaviours that benefit individuals and communities for the greater social good.
> Social Marketing practice is guided by ethical principles. It seeks to integrate research, best practice, theory, audience and partnership insight, to inform the delivery of competition sensitive and segmented social change programmes that are effective, efficient, equitable and sustainable.
>
> (accessed 10 January 2014)

There is a wide-ranging debate about the efficacy of commercial marketing practices surrounding the use of mainstream tools of marketing such as the four Ps, or one of the many other 'marketing mix' conceptualisations, segmentation and targeting in social settings where upstream, midstream and downstream social marketing strategies are used in interventions (Lefebvre, 2011). Traditionally, commercial marketing practice has focused on downstream activities and there have been many successful campaigns designed to influence individual behaviour for the social good such as smoking cessation, safe sex, exercise, pro-environmental behaviour and other beneficial outcomes. However, social change is increasingly required and social marketing is working more closely with public policy in engendering positive social outcomes. In these situations, social marketing principles need to be adapted for the context and in consideration of the social system in which the social marketing problem is embedded. Of particular importance are factors relating to culture and social mores; however, economic, political and technological circumstances must be adapted to. Figure 9.2 shows the various levels that that must be adapted to when developing social marketing strategy.

In the countries in question in this chapter, social marketing occurs at each of the levels of activity depicted in Figure 9.2. Social marketers usually practise in the middle two layers of influence, either at the community or local levels. Upstream social marketing occurs when the flow of activity is designed to influence the upper (larger) portion of the triangle. Downstream is to influence the individuals and their normative reference groups such as family and friends. When the issue is one of public policy, then upstream social marketing will be necessary. External agencies such as the United Nations, the World Bank and the Asian Development Bank often work at the socio-cultural level in order to address wide-ranging issues of poverty, population health and vulnerable populations such as children. Sample campaigns at each level of the Behavioural Ecological Model have been listed in Table 9.1.

Table 9.1 Levels of social marketing activity selected examples by country

Level	Vietnam	Cambodia	Indonesia	Philippines
1. Socio-cultural	UNICEF and Vietnamese Government ethnic minority support via school scheme and immunization (Nettleton, 2006; Thanh Nga & Thanh Huong, 2013) Wider public policy with protecting rights to breastfeed (UNICEF, 2012)	UNICEF, the Cambodian Government and 17 Triggers stopping orphanage tourism by creating a viral campaign (17 Triggers, 2014)	The ILO and the Indonesian improving work practices such as child labour and sustainable workplace practice (International Labour Organization, 2012)	United Nations and Disaster resilience in reaction to Typhoon Haiyan and building strategic sustainability for vulnerable coastal areas in the Philippines (United Nations, 2013)
2. Community	Global Helmet Vaccine and Asia Injury Prevention Foundation (Asia Injury Prevention Foundation, 2013a)	UNICEF living with HIV/AIDS and Buddhist monks – creating a religious network support (UNICEF Cambodia, 2012)	Bill and Melinda Gates Foundation with DKT Indonesia, clinics for better family planning (Olson, 2013)	Philippines' Department of Health and Oral Health Program for people across health cycles (Department of Health, 2011)
3. Local	Hand-washing in the Mekong with locals through education and infrastructure building (Australian Government, 2009; Parker, 2013)	PSI working with local NGOs on promoting condom use among high-risk groups (Population Services International, 2014)	Rare and Ecosystem reservation through the family, with children as ambassadors (Boss, 2008)	Department of Health-National Center for Disease Prevention and Control and Smoking cessation (Department of Health, 2013)
4. Individual	Green ribbon campaign in raising awareness on anti-littering and the LIN Center for Community Development (Ruy Băng Xanh, 2013)	Hand washing and sanitation improvement through adoption of three desirable behaviours (Water SHED, 2013)	Coalition for a Healthy Indonesia/John Hopkins University and Handwashing with soap campaign with mothers as early adopters of new behaviour (Goodwin, 2011, 2013)	Philippines Open University and Cosmetic toxic awareness – encouraging use of 'green' cosmetic products (Philippine Star, 2013)

Level 1 campaigns – socio-cultural

Level 1 campaigns are characterised by the need for social and cultural change in order to bring about some positive social outcome. In some cases the outcome will be enhanced population health, for example, for wider societal level social, economic or environmental well-being. These strategies are necessary when the type of issue or potential solutions require a national or regional effort in order to approach a resolution.

In Level 1 – socio-cultural – the example case studies are principally from the United Nations. In Vietnam the case study is one where UNICEF has been working on providing equitable education and healthcare to children of ethnic minority groups in Vietnam.[2] They have done this through providing bilingual programmes and free immunisation. Another campaign is that of promoting breastfeeding for new mothers by working with Vietnam's National Assembly on legislative frameworks that enable women to work and continue to breastfeed. 17 Triggers created a viral campaign to raise awareness against orphanage tourism in Cambodia in protection of children's right to privacy and from possible sexual abuse by providing information on their webpage and prompting the online global community to share the message.[3] The International Labour Office and its office in Jakarta launched a social marketing campaign with an educational nature to promote responsible workplace practice to both protect the rights of Indonesian workers and to ensure sustainable economic development.[4]

Disaster resilience is a critical issue in all of these countries, especially the Philippines as a coastal country. When the Philippines was severely devastated by the historical Typhoon Haiyan, the United Nations vowed to provide assistance especially for children by supporting back-to-learning efforts, developing a child protection system, rebuilding water systems for sanitation, providing safe vaccines for prevention of communicable diseases and providing services to children threatened by malnutrition.[5] On top of these disaster-responsive initiatives, efforts towards sustainable disaster management with long-term programmes on infrastructure support as well as lifestyle and behaviour change are critical to preparing communities and the country as a whole against natural adversity.

Level 2 campaigns – community

Level 2 campaigns are those where the issue or the solution resides at the community level and where there is a requirement for multiple stakeholders to be engaged in the resolution process. These stakeholders will be those that control public policy frameworks such as legislators and government as well as community level organisations that have or will have an impact on the issue. It is at this level that the media become critical partners in the social change process.

[2] http://www.unicef.org/vietnam.
[3] http://www.17triggers.com.
[4] http://www.ilo.org/global/lang--en/index.htm.
[5] http://www.un.org.ph.

The Asia Injury Prevention Foundation (AIPF) successfully put a helmet on the vast majority of Vietnamese on a motorbike both by lobbying for the passing of a helmet law and by public education using mainstream media, as well as by working with designers to provide helmets suitable for use in the Vietnamese context.[6] This multi-layered approach with a focus on the community level transformed the desired behaviour into a ubiquitous norm, hence going beyond the mechanical process of law enforcement for change of behaviour (Hill et al., 2009). This case is fully explored at the end of this chapter.

In another Level 2 case, by taking into account the significance of Buddhism as the national religion in Cambodia, UNICEF sought cooperation with numerous pagodas throughout Cambodia to form a support programme for HIV/AIDS sufferers and their families through building a sense of community.[7]

The Bill and Melinda Gates Foundation funded DKT Indonesia to establish clinics for Indonesian midwives in order to improve capacity to safely insert and remove intrauterine devices, and create an environment whereby Indonesian women gain increased access to family planning.[8] In the Philippines, the government takes a leading role in initiating and supporting numerous health programmes, including one that cuts across the whole life-cycle in improving oral health in the country for children, adolescents, pregnant women, and elderly people, with a mixture of oral service provision, oral sanitary product provision, oral health education, and development of relevant policies and protocols.[9]

Level 3 campaigns – local

Level 3 campaigns are those where the issue and the solution can be tackled at a more local level. That is one where the partnerships and stakeholders are more intimately connected to the interpersonal relationships with the affected individual(s). These are relationships such as schools, workplaces and neighbourhoods. Understanding how people engage and interact in these local communities is critical to the success of social marketing strategy.

In Vietnam, the Australian Government (via AusAid) helped children adopt a healthy habit of washing their hands frequently to improve overall sanitation standards after building the necessary water supply infrastructure[10] in various projects throughout the Mekong Delta (Parker, 2013). This campaign combined an individual with a local strategy. Firstly by providing the infrastructure to local communities and secondly by working with children to teach them the necessary skills to effectively make use of the new water and sanitation system. Another local campaign is that of PSI which is well-known for its initiatives in promoting safe sex

---

[6] http://asiainjury.org.

[7] http://www.unicef.org/infobycountry/cambodia.html.

[8] http://www.dktinternational.org/country-programs/indonesia.

[9] http://www.doh.gov.ph.

[10] http://aid.dfat.gov.au/countries/eastasia/vietnam/Pages/home.aspx.

and its 100% Condom use campaign in South East Asia, together with its partnership with United Health Network to support local NGOs in Cambodia on health issues.[11]

In Indonesia, the exemplar local campaign is Rare's initiative in Indonesia to conserve the Togean Islands. This campaign was conducted by targeting village children, who became ambassadors for environmental conversation and actively persuaded their parents into the initiative, which resulted in a national park being built in the area.[12] In the Philippines, a targeted local campaign was to encourage smoking cessation by raising awareness and providing the necessary services for smokers with an intention to quit. This was combined with a non-smoking norm creation campaign on a national level. In addition to training health personnel, No Tobacco Month and No Tobacco Day celebrations, the campaign also provided health education for smokers and their immediate families.[13]

Level 4 campaigns – individual

Individual campaigns are those where both the issue and the solution can be tackled at the individual level; where individuals are both responsible for and able to act in relation to the problem. Individual behaviour change is often necessary for social marketing. However, unless the individual is motivated and able to act and has the opportunity to do so (Binney, Hall, & Oppenheim, 2006), then social marketing will not be successful. The social marketing campaigns at this level tend to focus on creating the motivation to act; creating the infrastructure around opportunity and ability usually needs to be dealt with at the other levels.

Examples at this level include the Green Ribbon (Ruy Băng Xanh) Campaign's partnership with LIN Center for Community Development to raise awareness and persuade urban residents in Ho Chi Minh City to stop littering.[14] By encouraging people to tie green ribbons onto the motorbikes, bags and accessories of those who pledged never to litter as a reminder against littering, the campaign took a personal and soft approach to generating awareness and aiming to establish intrinsic motivation. Meanwhile, the Cambodian Ministry of Rural Development initiated the Stop the Diarrhea Campaign in collaboration with multiple international and local non-profit organisations to help Cambodians adopt three tangible and healthy habits: use latrines, wash their hands with soap and drink treated water.[15] On the same issue, the Fantastic Mom campaign by the Coalition for a Healthy Indonesia and John Hopkins University targeted a decrease in infant mortality rate from diarrhoea by getting mothers and caregivers to wash their hands with soap through a community-based approach involving a sense of sisterhood[16] (Goodwin, 2013).

[11] http://www.psi.org/cambodia.
[12] http://www.rare.org/blog/tag/indonesia.
[13] http://www.doh.gov.ph.
[14] http://ruybangxanh.org.
[15] http://www.mrd.gov.kh.
[16] http://goodwincollaboration.files.wordpress.com/2011/06/insm2010-presentation-goodwin-sydney.pdf.

With public health programmes being prominent in social marketing initiatives in the Philippines, an individual and small-scale example from the Philippines would be the University of Philippines Open University's campaign to promote the switch to organic and organic-based personal care products by raising awareness about toxic chemicals in cosmetic products and involving celebrity endorsement in 'setting the example' for the new behaviour adoption.[17]

The types of social marketing activities undertaken at each level

The levels of social marketing depicted in Table 9.1 have different foci on social marketing practice depending on the objectives of the programme, the target audience for the change and the type of change being sought. Table 9.2 illustrates the relationship between the levels and the type of social marketing activity. In any particular social marketing strategy, any or all of the activities may be required, from working with governments by providing financial and technical assistance, to working with families and individuals to ensure that they understand and can behave in the manner that the social marketing intervention is aiming to achieve. For example, in providing clean water and sanitation to populations, the entire supply chain including treatment and availability of clean water to households and individuals may require a whole-of-system approach. Individuals hand-washing on their own is not enough, clean water supplies are not enough on their own without the individual washing their hands, and so on. Each element that is present or not present in the supply chain impacts on the outcome. If clean water is not feasible within the context, then there are interventions that can be applied at the local and individual levels that can mitigate risk. However, no intervention can work in isolation of the factors that contribute to the issue and the problem. Formative research is always required that enables the social marketer to design strategies that are appropriate to the level and the context.

Each of the levels of influence have different types of objectives for social marketing, seek alternative types of change, and have varied audiences with diverse motivations and methods of decision-making. As a result, the typical social marketing activities required at each level will need to be adapted accordingly. For example, social marketing objectives range from broader social and cultural change to individual behaviour change. Social change objectives might be to empower women to participate in their societies and be in control of their fertility (see PLAN, http://plan-international.org). Individual-level objectives might be to encourage women to use birth control. Dealing with women on their own will not be as successful as using mid-stream organisations to facilitate access to said women and to give the social support that leads to empowerment and control. The objectives for each level will be commensurate with the motivations of the audience. For example, governments want high-level outcomes such as enhanced population health, and economic and social well-being for their constituents. However, there are many trade-offs that must be made in the achievement of these goals, and social marketers must learn to

---

[17] http://www.philstar.com/business/2013/09/23/1237007/safe-cosmetics-drive.

Table 9.2 Levels of social marketing and typical marketing activities

Level	Type of SM objectives	Type of change sought	Typical audience	Type of decision-making	Typical focus of social marketing activities
1. Socio-cultural	• Social change • Long-term generational change	• Economic, political, cultural or traditional practice	• Government policymakers and NGOs operating at a national or regional level	• Group • Political • Policymaking	• Advocacy • Public policy negotiations • Public relations • Technical assistance • Financial assistance
2. Community	• Permission to act in the country or on the issue • Establishment of legal framework	• Organisational-level decision-making • Either active participation or non-interference in activities at next levels	• Business and provincial or local government • NGOs operating at within a specific SM context	• Group • Corporate • Pragmatic	• Public communications • Publicity • Strategic partnerships and alliances • Seminars, consultations and meetings • Conferences and exhibitions
3. Local	• Access to and support for affected community members	• Referrals • Local support systems • Structural intervention • Programme development	• Groups and communities • Mass organisations such as unions, cooperatives	• Group • Participation • Inclusive	• Sponsorships • Community participatory action • Training and education resource development • 'Sales' promotions • Online social marketing (information) • Fremiums and giveaways
4. Individual	• Prevention of, encouragement for or cessation of behaviours	• Individual behaviours	• Individuals (usually at risk)	• Individuals within their social system (e.g. collectivism, family decision-making dynamics)	• Advertising • Social media • Mobile applications • Interpersonal interactions • Direct media such as notice boards, flyers, brochures, wearable marketing

work collaboratively alongside governments and not in competition with them. A social marketing campaign at the individual level will be useless if the campaign conflicts with government policy and women are jailed for using contraceptives (Truong & Quesada-Bondad, 2014). Social change takes time and decision-making at each level has its own complexities. The amorphous 'audience' does not actually exist except inasmuch as it describes a group of individuals. Each group of individuals undertakes decision-making in slightly different ways.

Decision-making at the social-cultural level is characterised by the word 'political'. This term is used to include the processes by which nations and global or regional organisations such as the United Nations and ASEAN make decisions in relation to each other and in accordance with their own specific objectives. It may consist of bureaucracy, democratic procedures and legislative systems, for example. In addition, there will be informal and formal processes that facilitate joint decision-making and agreements on outcomes such as public policy statements and resource allocations. These decision-making processes (and their sub-processes) are not usually transparent to 'outsiders', although those on the 'inside' will understand how they work and be able to use them to their advantage (Ryan, 2014). Organisations such as the UN make concerted efforts to be transparent but the large amount of information available can obscure the message for someone who does not know how to interpret it (an outsider).

The audience motivations and decision-making dynamics in each of the levels leads directly to selection of social marketing 'tools' and activities designed to implement the social marketing/social change strategy. The final column in Table 9.2 is a selected set of tools that can be used at each of the levels. It is presented as an indicative list of things that social marketers can do and it is not meant to be exhaustive. There is a vast array of activities taking place in social marketing and social change settings. Table 9.3 is a description of each of the tools and a selected set of references for where these tools have been used in social marketing and social change.

The state of the art in social marketing in Cambodia, Indonesia, the Philippines and Vietnam

Within the region, there are a number of key issues that are unique and create challenges for social marketers. The key issues that face the region when it comes to social marketing can be categorised under the following headings:

1. sustainable development and the unintended consequences of increasing material well-being on sustainability;
2. poverty and issues associated with alleviating poverty such as the divide between rich and poor and rapid urbanisation of agrarian populations;
3. population health including economic, social, emotional and environmental well-being;
4. access to water and sanitation; and
5. side effects of modernisation and development such as road safety, waste disposal, and water and airborne pollution.

Table 9.3 Social marketing activities at each level and selected literature

Level	Typical focus of social marketing activities	Description	Selected social marketing literature using these tools
1. Socio-cultural	• Advocacy • Public policy negotiations • Public relations • Technical assistance • Financial assistance	Tools at this level are designed to facilitate political decision-making. Either by providing in country assistance (technical or financial) or by promoting the desired social or public policy change.	Wallack and Dorfman (1996) Lang and Rayner (2007) Labonte (1998) Thabrany (2003) Schaub-Jones (2010)
2. Community	• Public communications • Publicity • Strategic partnerships and alliances • Seminars, consultations and meetings • Conferences and exhibitions	Tools at this level are designed to facilitate partnerships and alliances between entities that will empower, enable and inform social change.	Bauman, Walker, McLean, Shilton, and Bellew (2014) Samu and Wymer Jr (2013) Lefebvre (2013) Novelli (1984) Bissell (2006) Liston-Heyes and Liu (2013) Leenaars, Jacobs-van der Bruggen, and Renders (2013) Moodie et al. (2013)
3. Local	• Sponsorships • Community participatory action • Training and education resource development • 'Sales' promotions • Online social marketing (information) • Fremiums and giveaways	Tools at this level are designed to facilitate access to individuals where required and to provide communities and individuals with the necessary means to effect the social change.	Bates et al. (2012) Madill et al. (2014) Babor, Higgins-Biddle, Higgins, Gassman, and Gould (2004) Roche et al. (2010) Jalleh, Anwar-McHenry, Donovan, and Laws (2013) Bowers and Arlington (2013) Haq, Cambridge, and Owen (2013) Dann (2011)
4. Individual	• Advertising • Social media • Mobile applications • Interpersonal interactions • Direct media such as notice boards, flyers, brochures, wearable marketing	Tools at this level are designed to facilitate individuals within their social system and provide them with the knowledge and wherewithal they need to enact social change.	Brennan and Binney (2010) Dann and Dann (1998) Boehm and Itzhaky (2004) Bhat-Schelbert et al. (2012) Neiger et al. (2012) Schuster, Drennan, and Lings (2013) Drennan, Brown, and Mort (2011) Beratan (2007) Macklem (2014)

Each of the countries in this chapter has their own unique challenges when it comes to societal change. These challenges range from educating people to behave in ways that are not traditional to creating public policy frameworks that are inclusive of a myriad of customs and cultures. The countries in the region are as different to each other as East and West are different. Furthermore, within the countries in question there are substantive differences internally between sub-cultures (mostly ethnic minorities), provinces and states, urban and rural, rich and poor. Table 9.4 is a summary of the main differences between the countries that affect the social marketing landscape.

As lesser-developed but quickly developing nations, Cambodia, Indonesia, the Philippines and Vietnam must grapple with the concept of sustainable development and the unintended consequences of the impact of increasing material well-being on sustainability (Binney & Brennan, 2007). As middle classes grow in these countries, the investment in material well-being increases the strain on environmental resources. However, sustainability is often not the greatest priority for a rapidly developing country, with population health and poverty alleviation usually being more salient goals (Brennan, Parker, & Aleti-Watne, 2013). In some cases, ensuring access to clean water and sanitation in the face of upstream pollution requires an international collaboration to be facilitated by a 'neutral' third party such as that of the Greater Mekong region (Asian Development Bank, 2012). Social marketing campaigns can be found addressing these issues across the region and in each of the four countries. An excellent example of a grass-roots, individual-level campaign is the Vietnam 'Green Ribbon' Campaign designed to get people to advocate against littering, mentioned earlier. However, to be successful, they will need to work with community-level and provincial entities to ensure that the infrastructure is in place to 'follow through' on the behaviours of the passionate individuals who aim to change the face of Vietnamese roadsides with their anti-littering activities.

Evidence-based advocacy is key to this issue (UNICEF, 2009; World Health Organization, 2014), but the authorities in question have priorities such as anti-corruption, improving education standards, narrowing income gaps, decreasing pollution, improving the standards of health care systems, as well as increasing the population's overall income and the number of affordable houses (Ministry of Justice, 2011). Creating salience for the issue will require upstream and midstream social marketing in addition to this downstream-focused communications campaign. Vietnam is not unique when it comes to grappling with these concerns. Cambodia, Indonesia and the Philippines all face similar problems, and yet tackling these problems is essentially different because of the nature of the society and the dynamics of the country.

The 'correct' way to address any issue is not known. Each approach has to potential to be 'the' magic bullet if you believe the rhetoric of the web pages of those purporting to tackle the next big issue. Unfortunately, the evidence is simply not available with which these programmes can be independently assessed. Evidence based organisations such as those where we derived the statistics in Table 9.5 cannot agree on something as 'simple' as what the population of a given country is, let alone how best to approach endemic poverty or prevailing population

Table 9.4 Social marketing landscape

Country	Population	Major religions	Languages	Average age	Birth rate	Infant mortality rate	Population in urban areas	GDP per capita	Political system
Cambodia	15,205,539 (July 2013 est.)	Two (Buddhism and Islam)	Khmer (official) 95%, French, English	24.1	24.4/1000	52.7 deaths/ 1,000 live births (2013 est.)	20% (2011)	$2,400 (2012 est.)	Multi-party democracy under a constitutional monarchy
Indonesia	251,160,124 (July 2013 est.)	Islam, Protestantism, Roman Catholicism, Hinduism	Bahasa Indonesia (official, modified form of Malay), English, Dutch, local dialects (of which the most widely spoken is Javanese)	29.2	17.04/1000	26.06 deaths/ 1,000 live births	50.7%	$4,900 (2012 est.)	Multi-party democratic republic state
The Philippines	105,720,644 (July 2013 est.)	Five (Catholic (Roman Catholic, Aglipayan), Muslim, Evangelical, Iglesia ni Kristo and other Christian branches)	Filipino (official; based on Tagalog) and English (official); eight major dialects – Tagalog, Cebuano, Ilocano, Hiligaynon or Ilonggo, Bicol, Waray, Pampango and Pangasinan	23.5	24.24/1000	18.19 deaths/ 1,000 live births (2013 est.)	48.8% (2011)	$4,400 (2012 est.)	Multi-party democratic republic state

Vietnam	92,477,857 (July 2013 est.)	Six (Buddhism, Catholicism, Hoa Hao, Cao Dai, Protestantism, Islam)	Vietnamese (official), English (increasingly favoured as a second language), some French, Chinese and Khmer, mountain area languages (Mon-Khmer and Malayo-Polynesian)	29.2	16.26/1000	19.61 deaths/ 1,000 live births (2013 est.)	30% (2011)	$3,800 (2012 est.)	Single-party communist state

Source: Selected statistics from the CIA World Factbook (2014).

Table 9.5 Statistics in four countries – why triangulation is important

Country	Demographic statistic	World Bank	CIA World Factbook	Government's official statistics
Cambodia	Population	14,864,646 (2012)	15,205,539 (July 2013 est.)	13,395,682 (2008)
	Median age of population	Not available (*Data on group age percentage available*)	**total:** 23.7 years **male:** 23 years **female:** 24.4 years (2013 est.)	Not available (*data on age group distribution available*)
	Average income per annum $US	$880 (2012)	Not available	Not available
	Average number of years in education or literacy rate	74% (2009)	**total population:** 73.9% **male:** 82.8% **female:** 65.9% (2009 est.)	77.6% (2008)
Indonesia	Population	246,864,191 (2012)	251,160,124 (July 2013 est.)	243,740,000 (2011)
	Median age of population	Not available (*Data on group age percentage available*)	**total:** 28.9 years **male:** 28.4 years **female:** 29.5 years (2013 est.)	Not available (*data on age group distribution available*)
	Average income per annum $US	$3,420 (2012)	Not available	Not available (*data on workers under supervisory level's wages available*)
	Average number of years in education or literacy rate	93% (2011)	**total population:** 92.8% **male:** 95.6% **female:** 90.1% (2011 est.)	93.25%

The Philippines	Population	96,706,764 (2012)	105,720,644 (July 2013 est.)	92,340,000 (2010)
	Median age of population	Not available (*Data on group age percentage available*)	**total:** 23.3 years **male:** 22.8 years **female:** 23.8 years (2013 est.)	Not available (*data on age group distribution available*)
	Average income per annum $US	$2,500 (2012)	Not available	Not available (*data family average income available*)
	Average number of years in education or literacy rate	95% (2008)	**total population:** 95.4% **male:** 95% **female:** 95.8% (2008 est.)	92.3% (2000)
Vietnam	Population	88,775,500 (2012)	92,477,857 (July 2013)	88,526,883 (April 2012)
	Median age of population	Not available (*Data on group age percentage available*)	**total:** 28.7 years **male:** 27.6 years **female:** 29.7 years (2013 est.)	Not available (*data on age group distribution available*)
	Average income per annum $US	$1,550 (2012)	Not available	$2,551 (2012) (*calculation from average monthly income in VND*)
	Average number of years in education or **literacy rate**	93% (2011)	**total population:** 93.4% **male:** 95.4% **female:** 91.4% (2011 est.)	94%

health issues. Further to this is often an inability to be able to obtain reliable data in the first place.

The consequence of this lack of agreement about the evidence is continual argument about what needs to be done, whether or not it needs to be done at all, and who it needs to be done with, or for. The problem then becomes intractable (Lee, Schultz, & Kotler, 2011) and 'wicked' (Kennedy & Parsons, 2012) to the point where scalable solutions seem to be impossible (Domegan, Collins, Stead, McHugh, & Hughes, 2013). This is also evident in discourse about what constitutes research evidence in the region, as there are differences in what is valued as evidence of the need for social change, even amongst global organisations such as the World Health Organization and UNICEF (Brennan, Voros, & Brady, 2011). Furthermore, sometimes those educated in the hard sciences traditions find it difficult to trust fully the ethnographic and qualitative research of the type conducted by, for example, UNICEF C4D[18] evaluators such as Tacchi and colleagues (see for example, Lennie & Tacchi, 2013; Watkins & Tacchi, 2013) (Table 9.6).

New research directions

Social marketing research is often conflated with the other disciplines that it works alongside with to affect social change (Berzins, Greb, Young, & Hardee, 2014; McAuley, 2014). As a result, social marketing research can be 'anything' that needs to be done to resolve the social problem being addressed (McAuley, 2014, Brennan et al., 2014). The three types of formative research delineated in Figure 9.1 are all important directions and suggestions for new research; simply not enough is known about anything in particular for anyone to be fully informed. Most importantly, the research must be made publicly available so that others in the region can use the knowledge in informing their strategies. International nongovernmental organisations (INGOs) have a role to play in providing the underpinning infrastructure to ensure that local knowledge is not lost and useful ideas can be transferred from one context to another where appropriate (Brennan & Fien, 2013). Understanding customer or market needs on their own are insufficient to address the large-scale social problems that exist in some countries in the region. For example, it is self-evident to suggest that sex workers in Cambodia need access to condoms. It is naive to posit that condoms are the solution to HIV/AIDS transmission when the larger structural contributors are endemic to the region (Hardee, Gay, Croce-Galis, & Peltz, 2014). The ecology of the sex trade in Cambodia is not known; only components are available and even then that knowledge is often unverified and anecdotal.

The following list is generated from the authors' experience in developing social marketing strategies in the region. They have been categorised under the levels where they would be considered to have the most impact.

---

[18] Communication for Development: http://www.unicef.org/cbsc.

Table 9.6 Summary of issues, opportunities and social marketing solutions

Issue	Opportunity	Social marketing solution
Sustainability	Increase infrastructure to support activities such as recycling, decrease pollution, waste reduction, sustainable agriculture/aquaculture	Mid-stream and upstream social marketing, technical and financial assistance, green life-cycle supply chain (reduce, reuse, recycle).
Poverty alleviation	Increase accessibility and availability of sustainable development resources to affected populations and communities	Midstream and downstream strategies such as social enterprise development, equitable and sustainable micro-finance, training and education, technical assistance
Population health and well-being (social, emotional, economic and environmental)	Empowering disadvantaged groups and giving 'voice' to communities and marginalised groups	Mid-stream and downstream strategies including communication for development style campaigns
Access to water and sanitation	Create the social, physical, technical and environmental infrastructure to support a healthy water and sanitation system	Whole-of-system strategies incorporating up-stream technical and financial assistance to downstream hand-washing and personal hygiene communication campaigns.
Side effects of development	To improve potential for sustainable and safe development of lesser developed countries.	Depending on the particular issue each side effect may require a different strategy. For example to reduce the impact of pollution will require upstream for legislation, mid-stream for communication to enterprises and enforcement of laws. Improved housing for people without land may require financial and technical assistance (mid-stream) in addition to assistance with community support and social infrastructure development. Lowering the road toll on urban roads might require upstream and midstream for physical infrastructure and downstream communications for individuals to behave safely.

Socio-cultural-level research

- Understanding the ecological system of the behaviour starts at this level (Cherrier & Gurrieri, 2014; Lindridge et al., 2013). Reliable data on regional issues: development, veracity checking and verification by an independent source; combined with a list of 'known-unknowns' so that when research is conducted it can be done in a cost effective and collaborative manner (and it is shared with others).
- Geographical problem mapping and highlighting locales where targeted interventions will have the most impact. Using new technologies such as Geographic Information Systems (GIS), a much more technical and evidence-based system can be developed, providing community and local partnerships with the knowledge base they need to work together on addressing social issues. Importantly, GIS can be used to map qualitative data in addition to quantitative data; capturing attitudes, intentions, behaviours and so on.

Community-level research

- The ability for people to work collaboratively on creating positive social change requires a deep understanding of the social-behavioural ecology in which the social marketing issues arise. Furthermore, there is a need to research the potential for public and private partnerships: how to find and establish partnerships, how to manage them and how to disseminate knowledge within the ecological system for the benefit of all (Madill, O'Reilly, & Nadeau, 2014).
- There is a need to understand governance systems and legal infrastructure for social marketing in the region: how to get things done in each country; primarily to allow outsiders an ability to navigate the system if need be, or to assist insiders on achieving their goals.
- In order to understand the 'competition', there needs to be a publicly and centrally available list of programmes and projects underway.

Local-level research

- What the best methods are of addressing social marketing issues within local and community systems.
- The role of community and social support systems in social marketing — how best to use community participation in fostering sustainable social change.
- Appropriate 'marketing mix' strategies to address audiences at this level — not individuals, but groups and organisations.

Individual-level research

- Understanding how people make decisions, not only for themselves but also within their social system is important, especially in Confucian heritage and collectivist traditions. Theories of social change developed in the West are not 'cut-and-paste' into the region or countries described in this book.
- Communication and media infrastructure; how best to reach targeted individuals within each of the countries in the region.
- The level of concern about specific social marketing issues — the premise being that if there is no concern, awareness-building may be required before behaviour change can be established.

Practising social marketing in Cambodia, Indonesia, the Philippines and Vietnam

As evidenced in the earlier sections of this chapter, social marketing is a widely applied tool for addressing social change issues in the region. There are case studies in every country. Choosing exemplar case studies is therefore difficult, as many are worthwhile and are making positive differences to their respective markets. We have selected the following cases as being indicative of programmes that are successfully working across and between the various levels of the framework. The case studies were introduced in Table 9.1 at the outset of this chapter. Table 9.7 summarises why these cases are examples of best practice in social marketing. The outcomes of the social marketing strategy or campaign have been included in the final column. One of the factors that contributes to these campaigns being exemplars is that of transparency and applicability of tools to other contexts and social problems.

Practice case study: helmets and beyond: the Asia Injury Prevention Foundation in Vietnam

One of the most striking aspects of daily life in Vietnam is the ubiquity of the seemingly chaotic traffic and never ending streams of motorbikes on the roads in the major cities, towns and highways. In Vietnam the motorcycle is king, with 96.1 motorbikes for every 100 households, compared to 1.3 cars (General Statistics Office, 2010). Along with this very high motorcycle ownership comes a high number of accidents. There are over 30 deaths per day on Vietnamese roads (World Health Organization, 2013). Back in 2007 it was also estimated that there were around 30,000 cases of severe brain injury per year attributed to road crashes. At that time motorbike helmets were mandatory on national highways only, but optional on town and city streets and highways.

Upstream social marketing

An intervention was required, but the problem was complex and huge. Driving and motorcycle behaviour is typically seen as an individual behaviour problem, and is largely tackled in other countries at the individual level. However, other countries usually have a legal infrastructure in place in which they can shift the onus to the individual. Often social marketing and social change campaigns focus too heavily on the downstream individuals who are carrying out 'bad' behaviours (Wallack, 1990), rather than influencing government and policymakers to help bring about change. Increasingly social marketing strategies are going upstream and social marketing is used much more strategically to inform policy formulation and strategy development (Andreasen, 2006). In the case of upstream social marketing, the focus is less on the individual or community, but instead the focus in

Table 9.7 Examples of best practice

Level	Case	Focus	Outcome
1. Socio-cultural	Safe sex in Cambodia – 100% Condom campaign	Upstream and later downstream	Increase in condom use from 43% to 93% in Sihanoukville after full implementation Passing of 'Regulation on 100% condom use in Sihanoukville' Drop in the percentage of men purchasing commercial sex Decrease in HIV prevalence Decrease in STI prevalence (Chaya, 2006; World Health Organization, 2000)
2. Community	Helmet vaccination in Vietnam	Upstream	Introduction of new legislation on use of helmets in Vietnam Introduction of the tropical helmet 89% of all Vietnamese adults wear helmets when travelling on motorbikes (Asia Injury Prevention Foundation, 2014)
3. Local level	Oral health in the Philippines	Midstream	Development of the Outpatient Dental Health Care Finance Package Development of the Orally Fit Child (OFC) standard for national measurement Development of the Revised Rules and Regulations and Standard Requirements for Private School Dental services in the Philippines, Guidelines in the Implementation of Oral Health Program for Public Health Services in the Philippines, and National Policy on Oral Health (Department of Health, 2011)
4. Individual	Hand-washing with soap in Indonesia	Downstream	Health message reached 10 million people in two major provinces Increase in awareness of hand-washing benefits from 45% to 85% Increase in people hand-washing with soap from 35% to 56% (Goodwin, 2013)

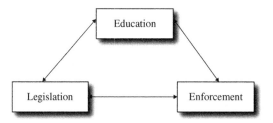

Figure 9.3 The tripartite model of behavioural compliance for effective social marketing campaigns (Snitow & Brennan, 2011).

on using strong target 'market' insight to inform and develop effective policy and strategy. Part of this is achieved through the effective use of media advocacy. The goal of media advocacy is to influence and lead changes in government policies (see Table 9.3) (Wallack, 1990). This is particularly critical given that government are the gatekeepers of the three important fundamentals of behavioural compliance (see Figure 9.3). Well-designed education and training programmes, combined with effective legislation and proper enforcement, are critical to behavioural compliance in social marketing campaigns, particularly when it comes to those aimed at reducing child or adolescent injury (Harvey, Towner, Peden, Soori, & Bartolomeos, 2009).

The strategy

The Asia Injury Prevention Foundation recognized the need for an upstream social marketing strategy in addressing concerns about the carnage on Vietnamese roads. Beginning in 1999 with the passion of founder Greig Craft, it has now grown to include Cambodia and Thailand (Asia Injury Prevention Foundation, 2013b). The Asia Injury Prevention Foundation continues to work upstream with the Vietnamese government in order to provide advocacy, education and support about safe driving practice including helmet use. One of the core activities of the Asia Injury Prevention Foundation has been global and legislative advocacy. Their fundamental belief is that:

> It is the responsibility of government agencies to develop national traffic legislation, appropriate helmet standards, and traffic safety curricula for schools. We build relationships with governments to advocate for progressive legislation and regulatory tools, combine with enforcement and communication activities, to effect sustainable behaviour change.
>
> *(Asia Injury Prevention Foundation, 2013c)*

Their campaigning often focuses on changing people's behaviour, creating 'talkability' in the general public, raising funds, but also, importantly, influencing legislation. This influence and 'talkability' is facilitated by working upstream and also includes the training of policymakers and journalists on helmet usage

(Asia Injury Prevention Foundation, 2013a). As part of this process, they have been working directly with the police, who are the face of the enforcement of helmet laws. However, they have also involved the police in the education process in street-based awareness events, and also involve police directly in the education process within schools in Cambodia and Vietnam (Asia Injury Prevention Foundation, 2012).

An education programme has been running in schools since 1999 called 'Helmets for Kids'. This programme both includes an educational component and provides helmets for free to students within participating schools. To maximise the likelihood of long-term wearing of helmets, 'tropical' helmets have also been designed and manufactured by the foundation. These helmets are well-suited to the hot and often humid conditions of South East Asia, reducing the excuse not to wear the helmets. They are also funky, stylish and fun in a uniquely Asian way, not mirroring the 'heavy metal' tough style worn in other countries, thus maximising the motivation to wear the helmets as a fashion item.

The outcomes

One of the success stories of the Asia Injury Prevention Foundation was the introduction of the first universal mandatory helmet law in Vietnam on 25 June 2007, which, when it took effect on 15 December 2007, covered all riders and passengers on all roads. At that time, official penalties for not wearing helmets when required were increased tenfold (Passmore, Phuong Nam, Lan Huong, & Trong Ha, 2010). Within the first year of the law taking effect, 680,000 recorded infringements were issued for non-wearing of helmets (Passmore et al., 2010). More importantly, since that time the number of road deaths annually have dropped, with the latest statistics showing a 5.19 per cent drop in the total number of road accidents, 0.5 per cent drop in road deaths and 9.4 per cent drop in road injuries from 2012 to 2013 (National Traffic Safety Committee, 2014).

While the new laws, combined with targeted education and enforcement are widely recognised as successful, there is still room for improvement, particularly in terms of wider education and better enforcement (Nguyen, Passmore, & Nguyen, 2012). It is estimated that there are still over 4,000 children killed on the roads very year. Under the 2007 helmet laws, all children over the age of five must wear a helmet, but there is still a low level of compliance — sometimes as low as 16 per cent in some areas (Brondum, Truong, & Dinh, 2012; Nguyen et al., 2012). The Asia Injury Prevention Foundation continues to work hard with their ongoing Helmets for Kids programme and also on advocating better helmet safety legislation and standards to bring about further positive change (Boufous et al., 2012). The Asia Injury Prevention Foundation is now working in neighbouring Cambodia, China and Thailand to build upon its success in Vietnam.

Further investigation

The issue of road safety is an ongoing global concern, with populations worldwide struggling with keeping their people safe at the same time as increasing their mobility. The following key questions arise as a result of this case:

1. How does road safety in Vietnam move beyond behaviour change?
2. At what point is there likely to be a diminishing return on individual behaviour change strategies?
3. How does a lesser-developed country afford a greater investment in physical infrastructure such as roads and traffic lights?
4. How do you create a sustainable enforcement infrastructure incorporating policing, fines and ticketing, collections and enforcement of fines and penalties?
5. In a lesser-developed country where there are so many calls on the public purse, what are the next steps for the AIPF in terms of supporting Vietnam, Cambodia and Thailand in reducing their respective road tolls and increasing public safety on the roads?

Conclusion

This chapter has used the behavioural ecological model to classify and explain social marketing interventions applicable at each level of the system. We have used the four countries as examples of social marketing practice that might be applicable to other South East Asian countries. The four countries – Cambodia, Indonesia, the Philippines and Vietnam – all face slightly different challenges when it comes to tacking their social problems. In creating their futures, each of the countries has their own priorities and is approaching issues in their own culturally and socially appropriate manner. The role of social marketing in this context can be to assist governments and non-government organisations to initiate, establish, develop and maintain programmes that will have multi-level impact. The issues faced in developing countries where rapid social change is taking place are unique and need to be examined in further depth. This chapter provides a very brief insight into an exciting region where social marketing can be instrumental in producing positive social change.

References

17 Triggers. (2014). *17 triggers homepage.* Available from <http://www.17triggers.com> Accessed 14.01.14.

Andreasen, A. R. (2006). *Social marketing in the 21st century.* Thousand Oaks, CA: Sage.

Asia Injury Prevention Foundation. (2012). *Annual Report 2012.* Available from <http://issuu.com/makingroadssafe/docs/aipfoundationannualreport2012>. Accessed 14.01.14.

Asia Injury Prevention Foundation. (2013a). *AIPF in Vietnam.* Available from <http://asiainjury.org/our-reach/vietnam> Accessed 14.01.14.

Asia Injury Prevention Foundation. (2013b). *History*. Available from <http://asiainjury.org/about-us/history>. Accessed 14.01.14.

Asia Injury Prevention Foundation. (2013c). *Global and legislative advocacy*. Available from <http://asiainjury.org/our-work/global-legislative-advocacy>. Accessed 14.01.14.

Asia Injury Prevention Foundation. (2014). *Children are in danger. ChildHelmet.Org*. Available from <http://childhelmet.org/vi/thuc-trang/tre-em-dang-gap-nguy-hiem>. Accessed 14.01.14.

Asian Development Bank. (2012). *Greater Mekong Subregion Atlas of the environment* (2nd ed.). Manila: Asian Development Bank.

Australian Government. (2009). *Vietnam's Mekong Delta water and sanitation project recognised as Australia's top 2009 engineering achievement*. Available from <http://aid.dfat.gov.au/LatestNews/Pages/Vietnams-Mekong-Delta-water-and-sanitation-project-recognised-as-Australias-top-2009-engineering-achievement.aspx>. Accessed 14.01.14.

Babor, T. F., Higgins-Biddle, J. C., Higgins, P. S., Gassman, R. A., & Gould, B. E. (2004). Training medical providers to conduct alcohol screening and brief interventions. *Substance Abuse*, *25*(1), 17−26.

Bates, M. A., Glennerster, R., Gumede, K., & Duflo, E. (2012). The price is wrong. Field actions science reports. *The Journal of Field Actions* 30−37 [Special issue 4].

Bauman, A., Walker, S., McLean, G., Shilton, T., & Bellew, B. (2014). Mass media campaigns to promote physical activity: Australia and New Zealand as case studies. In R. Pate, & D. Buchner (Eds.), *Implementing physical activity strategies* (pp. 1−90). Thousand Oaks, CA, USA: Human Kinetics.

Beratan, K. K. (2007). A cognition-based view of decision processes in complex social−ecological systems. *Ecology and Society*, *12*(1), 27. Available online at: <http://www.ecologyandsociety.org/vol12/iss1/art27/>. Accessed 9.02.15.

Berzins, K., Greb, H., Young, M. H., & Hardee, K. (2014). Urbanization, population, and health myths: Addressing common misconceptions with strategic health communication. In C. Okigbo (Ed.), *Strategic urban health communication* (pp. 25−36). New York, USA: Springer.

Bhat-Schelbert, K., Lin, C. J., Matambanadzo, A., Hannibal, K., Nowalk, M. P., & Zimmerman, R. K. (2012). Barriers to and facilitators of child influenza vaccine − perspectives from parents, teens, marketing and healthcare professionals. *Vaccine*, *30*(14), 2448−2452.

Binney, W., & Brennan, L. (2007). Social change and sustainability − An oxymoron? *Paper presented at the fourth international nonprofit and social marketing conference: Social entrepreneurship, social change and sustainability* (pp. 27−28) September, Brisbane, Australia.

Binney, W., Hall, J., & Oppenheim, P. (2006). The nature and influence of motivation within the MOA framework: Implications for social marketing. *International Journal of Nonprofit and Voluntary Sector Marketing*, *11*(4), 289−301.

Bissell, M. (2006). Chlamydia screening programs: A review of the literature. Part 2: Testing procedures and educational interventions for primary care physicians. *Canadian Journal of Human Sexuality*, *15*(1), 13−22.

Boehm, A., & Itzhaky, H. (2004). The social marketing approach: A way to increase reporting and treatment of sexual assault. *Child Abuse & Neglect*, *28*(3), 253−265.

Boss, S. (2008). *The cultural touch. Stanford social innovation review*. Available from <http://www.ssireview.org/articles/entry/the_cultural_touch>. Accessed 14.01.14.

Boufous, S., Ali, M., Nguyen, H. T., Stevenson, M., Vu, T. C., Nguyen, D. T. Y., et al. (2012). Child injury prevention in Vietnam: Achievements and challenges. *International Journal of Injury Control and Safety Promotion*, *19*(2), 123−129.

Bowers, P. H., & Arlington, T. (2013). Community based participatory research and youth tobacco control: A qualitative interpretive meta-synthesis. *Perspectives on Social Work*, *9*(1), 58−76.

Brennan, L., Binney, W., Parker, L., Aleti Watne, T., & Nguyen, D. (2014). *Social marketing and behaviour change: Models, theories and applications*. Cheltenham UK: Edward Elgar.

Brennan, L., & Binney, W. (2010). Fear, guilt and shame appeals in social marketing. *Journal of Business Research*, *63*(2), 140−146.

Brennan, L., & Fien, J. (2013). Where to from here? Lessons for sustainable community development. In L. Brennan, L. Parker, T. Aleti-Watne, J. Fien, D. T. Hue, & M. A. Doan (Eds.), *Growing sustainable communities: A development guide for Southeast Asia* (pp. 254−264). Prahran Vic. Australia: Tilde University Press.

Brennan, L., Parker, L., Aleti-Watne, T., Fien, J., Duong, T. H., & Doan, M. A. (Eds.), (2013). *Growing sustainable communities: A development guide for Southeast Asia* Prahran Vic. Australia: Tilde University Press.

Brennan, L., Voros, J., & Brady, E. (2011). Paradigms at play and implications for validity in social marketing research. *Journal of Social Marketing*, *1*(3), 100−119.

Brondum, L., Truong, T. N. T., & Dinh, K. P. (2012). *Helmets for Kids programme increases helmet use among students*. http://dx.doi.org/10.1136/injuryprev-2012-040590d.52.

Chaya, N. (2006). Cambodia and HIV: Winning round two in a preventive fight. *Population Action International Research Commentary*, 1(7). Available from <http://populationaction. org/wp-content/uploads/2012/01/Cambodia_and_HIV.pdf>. Accessed 14.01.14.

Cherrier, H., & Gurrieri, L. (2014). Framing social marketing as a system of interaction: A neo-institutional approach to alcohol abstinence. *Journal of Marketing Management*, *30*(7-8), 607−633. http://dx.doi.org/10.1080/0267257X.2013.850110.

CIA World Factbook. (2014). <https://www.cia.gov/library/publications/the-world-factbook/ docs/didyouknow.html>.

Dann, S. (2011). *The marketing mix matrix. ANZMAC paper*. Available from <http://www. anzmac.org/conference/2011/Papers%20by%20Presenting%20Author/Dann,%20Stephen %20Paper%20016.pdf>. Accessed 14.01.14.

Dann, S., & Dann, S. (1998). Cybercommuning: Global village halls. *Advances in Consumer Research*, *25*, 379−385.

Department of Health. (2011). *Oral health program*. Philippines' Department of Health. Available from <http://www.doh.gov.ph/content/oral-health-program.html>. Accessed 14.01.14.

Department of Health. (2013). *Smoking cessation program*. Philippines' Department of Health. Available from <http://www.doh.gov.ph/content/smoking-cessation-program-0. html>. Accessed 14.01.14.

Domegan, C., Collins, K., Stead, M., McHugh, P., & Hughes, T. (2013). Value co-creation in social marketing: Functional or fanciful?. *Journal of Social Marketing*, *3*(3), 239−256.

Drennan, J., Brown, M. R., & Mort, G. S. (2011). Phone bullying: Impact on self-esteem and well-being. *Young Consumers: Insight and Ideas for Responsible Marketers*, *12*(4), 295−309.

General Statistics Office. (2010). *Result of the Viet Nam household living standards survey 2010*. Ha Noi, Vietnam: Tống Cục Thống Kê (General Statistics Office).

Goodwin, N. (2011). The role of social marketing in international development: Lessons from the 'Fantastic Mom' project in Indonesia. *Presentation at the 2010 International Nonprofit and Social Marketing Conference*. Available from <http://goodwincollaboration.files.word-press.com/2011/06/insm2010-presentation-goodwin-sydney.pdf>. Accessed 14.01.14.

Goodwin, N. (2013). Sustainable change marketing: An approach to development and communications programs in Indonesia and beyond. In L. Brennan, L. Parker, T. Aleti-Watne, J. Fien, D. T. Hue, & M. A. Doan (Eds.), *Growing sustainable communities: A development guide for Southeast Asia* (pp. 155–166). Prahran Vic. Australia: Tilde University Press.

Haq, G., Cambridge, H., & Owen, A. (2013). A targeted social marketing approach for community pro-environmental behavioural change. *Local Environment, 18*(10), 1134–1152.

Hardee, K., Gay, J., Croce-Galis, M., & Peltz, A. (2014). Strengthening the enabling environment for women and girls: What is the evidence in social and structural approaches in the HIV response? *Journal of the International AIDS Society, 17*. (1). Available from http://dx.doi.org/10.7448/IAS.17.1.18619.

Harvey, A., Towner, E., Peden, M., Soori, H., & Bartolomeos, K. (2009). Injury prevention and the attainment of child and adolescent health. *Bulletin of the World Health Organization, 87*, 390–394.

Hill, P. S., Ngo, A. D., Khuong, T. A., Dao, H. L., Hoang, H. T. M., Trinh, H. T., et al. (2009). Mandatory helmet legislation and the print media in Viet Nam. *Accident Analysis and Prevention, 41*, 789–797.

Hovell, M. F., Wahlgren, D. R., & Gehrman, C. (2002). The behavioral ecological model: Integrating public health and behavioral science. In R. J. DiClemente, R. Crosby, & M. Kegler (Eds.), *New and emerging theories in health promotion practice & research* (pp. 347–385). San Francisco, CA: Jossey-Bass Inc.

International Labour Organization. (2012). *Launch of social marketing campaign for responsible working practices.* International Labour Organization. Available from http://www.ilo.org/empent/Projects/score/WCMS_226323/lang--en/index.htm>. Accessed 14.01.14.

Jalleh, G., Anwar-McHenry, J., Donovan, R. J., & Laws, A. (2013). Impact on community organisations that partnered with the Act-Belong-Commit mental health promotion campaign. *Health Promotion Journal of Australia, 24*(1), 44–48.

Kennedy, A.-M., & Parsons, A. (2012). Macro-social marketing and social engineering: A systems approach. *Journal of Social Marketing, 2*(1), 37–51.

Kotler, P. (2002). *Marketing management.* New Delhi: Prentice Hall.

Kotler, P. (2013). The larger context for social marketing. *Paper presented at the World Social Marketing Conference*, Toronto, Canada.

Labonte, R. (1998). Healthy public policy and the World Trade Organization: A proposal for an international health presence in future world trade/investment talks. *Health Promotion International, 13*(3), 245–256.

Lang, T., & Rayner, G. (2007). Overcoming policy cacophony on obesity: An ecological public health framework for policymakers. *Obesity Reviews, 8*(Suppl. 1), 165–181.

Lee, N. R., Schultz, P. W., & Kotler, P. (2011). *Social marketing to protect the environment: What works.* Thousand Oaks, CA: Sage.

Leenaars, K., Jacobs-van der Bruggen, M., & Renders, C. (2013). Peer reviewed: Determinants of successful public–private partnerships in the context of overweight prevention in Dutch youth. *Preventing Chronic Disease, 10*. Available from http://dx.doi.org/10.5888/pcd10.120317.

Lefebvre, R. C. (2011). An integrative model for social marketing. *Journal of Social Marketing, 1*(1), 54–72.

Lefebvre, R. C. (2013). *Social marketing and social change: Strategies and tools for improving health, well-being, and the environment.* San Francisco, CA: Jossey-Bass.

Lennie, J., & Tacchi, J. (2013). *Evaluating communication for development: A framework for social change.* USA & Canada: Routledge.

Lindridge, A. M., MacAskill, S., Ginch, W., Eadie, D., & Holme, I. (2013). Applying the social ecological model to social marketing communications. *European Journal of Marketing, 47*(9), 1399–1420.

Liston-Heyes, C., & Liu, G. (2013). A study of nonprofit organisations in cause-related marketing: Stakeholder concerns and safeguarding strategies. *European Journal of Marketing*, *47*(11/12), 1954−1974.

Macklem, G. L. (2014). Providing preventive services in schools (pp. 1−18). *Preventive mental health at school*. New York, USA: Springer.

Madill, J., O'Reilly, N., & Nadeau, J. (2014). Financing social marketing programs through sponsorship: Implications for evaluation. *Journal of Social Marketing*, *4*(1), 22−37.

McAuley, A. (2014). Reflections on a decade in social marketing. *Journal of Social Marketing*, *4*(1), 77−86.

Ministry of Justice. (2011). *Decision on Vietnam's five year plan of social and economic development. Vietnam Government Law Documentation Database*. Available from <http://vbqppl.moj.gov.vn/vbpq/_layouts/print.aspx?id = 27298>. Accessed 14.01.14.

Moodie, R., Stuckler, D., Monteiro, C., Sheron, N., Neal, B., Thamarangsi, T., et al. (2013). Profits and pandemics: Prevention of harmful effects of tobacco, alcohol, and ultra-processed food and drink industries. *The Lancet*. Available from http://dx.doi.org/10.1016/S0140-6736.

National Traffic Safety Committee. (2014). *Prime Minister Nguyen Tan Dung: Road accident rate has gone down, but we need to keep improving!* Available from <http://antoangiaothong.gov.vn/xa-lo-thong-tin/thu-tuong-nguyen-tan-dung-tai-nan-da-giam-phai-phan-dau-giam-nua-24783.html>. Accessed 14.01.14.

Neiger, B. L., Thackeray, R., Van Wagenen, S. A., Hanson, C. L., West, J. H., Barnes, M. D., et al. (2012). Use of social media in health promotion purposes, key performance indicators, and evaluation metrics. *Health Promotion Practice*, *13*(2), 159−164.

Nettleton, S. (2006). *Monthly immunization days save lives and build babies' health*. Vietnam: UNICEF. Available from <http://www.unicef.org/infobycountry/vietnam_30867.html>. Accessed 14.01.14.

Nga, T., & Huong, T. (2013). *Bilingual education programme provides equitable education for ethnic minority children in Viet Nam*. Vietnam: UNICEF. Available from <http://unicefvietnam.blogspot.com/2013/07/bilingual-education-programme-provides.html>. Accessed 14.01.14.

Nguyen, P. N., Passmore, J., & Nguyen, T. H. (2012). Motorcycle helmet wearing in children in Viet Nam − a comparison of pre and post law. *Injury Prevention*, *12*(Supp. 1), A195.

Novelli, W. D. (1984). Developing marketing programs. In L. Frederiksen, L. Solomon, & K. Brehony (Eds.), *Marketing Health Behavior* (pp. 59−89). New York, USA: Springer.

Olson, D. J. (2012). *How one non-profit social marketing agency funds health clinics, midwives*. Bill and Melinda Gates Foundation. Available from <http://www.impatientoptimists.org/Posts/2012/01/Innovation-at-Work-Non-Profit-Social-Marketing-Agency-Funds-Health-Clinics-Midwives>. Accessed 14.01.14.

Parker, L. (2013). Personal hygiene, environmental sanitation: A case of social marketing in the Mekong Delta. In L. Brennan, L. Parker, T. Aleti-Watne, J. Fien, D. T. Hue, & M. A. Doan (Eds.), *Growing sustainable communities: A development guide for Southeast Asia* (pp. 241−253). Prahran Vic. Australia: Tilde University Press.

Passmore, J., Phuong Nam, N., Lan Huong, N., & Trong Ha (2010). The development and implementation of mandatory motorcycle helmet legislation in Vietnam. *Injury Prevention*, *16*(Suppl. 1), A217.

Philippine Star. (2013). *Safe cosmetics drive*. Available from <http://www.philstar.com/business/2013/09/23/1237007/safe-cosmetics-drive>. Accessed 14.01.14.

Population Services International. (2014). *PSI in Cambodia*. Available from <http://www.psi.org/cambodia>. Accessed 14.01.14.

Roche, A. M., Bywood, P., Hughes, C., Freeman, T., Duraisingam, V., Trifonoff, A., et al., (2010). The role of schools in alcohol education. *Report to the Australian Government Department of Education.* Available from <http://www.decd.sa.gov.au/drugstrategy/files/links/RoleSchoolsAlcoholEd.pdf>. Accessed 14.01.14.

Ruy Băng Xanh. (2013). *Green ribbon program.* Available from <http://ruybangxanh.org/vi>. Accessed 14.01.14.

Ryan, M. E. (2014). Allocating infection: The political economy of the swine flu (h1n1) vaccine. *Economic Inquiry, 52*(1), 138−154. Available from http://dx.doi.org/10.1111/ecin.12023.

Samu, S., & Wymer, W. W., Jr. (2013). *Nonprofit and business sector collaboration: Social enterprises, cause-related marketing, sponsorships, and other corporate-nonprofit dealings.* New York: Routledge.

Schaub-Jones, D. (2010). Should we view sanitation as just another business? The crucial role of sanitation entrepreneurship and the need for outside engagement. *Enterprise Development and Microfinance, 21*(3), 185−204.

Schuster, L., Drennan, J. C., & Lings, I. (2013). Consumer acceptance of m-wellbeing services: A social marketing perspective. *European Journal of Marketing, 47*(9), 1439−1457.

Snitow, S., & Brennan, L. (2011). Reducing drunk driving-caused road deaths: Integrating communication and social policy enforcement in Australia. In H. Cheng, P. Kotler, & N. Lee (Eds.), *Social marketing for public health: Global trends and success stories* (pp. 383−403). Sudbury, MA: Jones and Bartlett Publishers.

Spotswood, F., French, J., Tapp, A., & Stead, M. (2012). Some reasonable but uncomfortable questions about social marketing. *Journal of Social Marketing, 2*(3), 163−175.

Thabrany, H. (2003) Social health insurance in Indonesia: Current status and the proposed national health insurance. *Paper presented at the Social Health Insurance Workshop by WHO SEARO*; 13−15 March 2003.

Truong, T.-D., & Quesada-Bondad, A. (2014). *Intersectionality, structural vulnerability, and access to sexual and reproductive health services: Filipina domestic workers in Hong Kong, Singapore, and Qatar* (pp. 227−239). *Migration, gender and social justice.* London: Springer.

UNICEF. (2009). *Evidence-based advocacy for gender in education: A learning guide.* Available from <http://www.unicef.org/eapro/advocacy_guide_FINAL4.pdf>. Accessed 14.01.14.

UNICEF. (2012). *Partnering with Viet Nam's National Assembly to protect breastfeeding.* Vietnam: UNICEF. Available from <http://www.unicef.org/eapro/media_18594.html> Accessed 14.01.14.

UNICEF Cambodia. (2012). *Buddhist monks and UNICEF join to improve the lives of vulnerable families.* Available from <http://www.unicef.org/infobycountry/cambodia_61571.html> Accessed 14.01.14.

United Nations. (2013). *One month on, UN renews pledge to help Philippines recover from deadly typhoon.* United Nations News Office. Available from <http://www.un.org/apps/news/story.asp?NewsID=46747&Cr=philippines&Cr1=#.UtYbdpHQxG4>. Accessed 14.01.14.

Wallack, L. (1990). Media advocacy: Promoting health through mass communication. In K. Glanz, F. M. Lewis, & B. K. Rimer (Eds.), *Health behavior and education* (pp. 370−386). San Francisco, CA: Jossey-Bass.

Wallack, L., & Dorfman, L. (1996). Media advocacy: A strategy for advancing policy and promoting health. *Health Education & Behavior*, *23*(3), 293−317.

Water SHED. (2013). *Stop the Diarrhea Campaign*. Available from <http://www.watershedasia. org/wash-social-marketing-campaign>. Accessed 14.01.14.

Watkins, J., & Tacchi, J. (2013). Mobile content and participatory communication for development. In K. Prasad (Ed.), *New media and pathways to social change: Shifting development discourses* (pp. 232−252). Delhi: B.R. Publishing Corporation.

Wood, M. (2012). Marketing social marketing. *Journal of Social Marketing*, *2*(2), 94−102.

World Health Organization. (2000). *100% Condom use programme in entertainment establishments*. World Health Organization Publications. Available from <http://www.wpro. who.int/publications/docs/condom.pdf>. Accessed 14.01.14.

World Health Organization. (2013). *Global status report in road safety: Supporting a decade of action*. Geneva, Switzerland: World Health Organization: Department of Violence & Injury Prevention and Disability. Available from <http://www.who.int/violence_injury_ prevention/road_safety_status/2013/en>. Accessed 14.01.14.

World Health Organization. (2014). *Finding evidence*. Available from <http://www.who.int/ evidence/library/en>. Accessed 14.01.14.

Further reading

Berzins, K., Greb, H., Young, M. H., & Hardee, K. (2014). *Urbanization, population, and health myths: Addressing common misconceptions with strategic health communication* (pp. 25−36). *Strategic urban health communication*. Springer.

Hastings, G., Angus, K., & Bryant, C. (2012). *Handbook of social marketing*. Thousand Oaks, CA: Sage Publications, Inc.

Part Three

Fairness Management

Fairness management: China, Taiwan, Japan and South Korea

Nikki Lee-Wingate

Introduction

It is imperative to understand how consumers perceive fairness, because consumer perceptions of fairness (or unfairness) produce significant attitudinal, affective and behavioural consequences (Tyler & Smith, 1998). Consumers both consume and value attitudes conforming to fairness concerns just as they do other commodities (Eckel & Grossman, 1996). Consumers show strong emotional reactions to unfairness and seek ways to resolve the emotions via disclosure (Lee-Wingate & Corfman, 2011). Consumers are driven to action by fairness concerns, even to a degree of acting contrary to self-interest (Montada, 1991). The powerful influence of consumer fairness perceptions has been widely demonstrated in psychology, economics, marketing and management literature.

Consumers consistently prefer outcomes that support normative expectations about fairness and strongly disfavour outcomes that deviate from them. This is why less than 1 per cent of the data from ultimatum and dictator games in experimental economics confirms the game-theory predictions of winner-takes-it-all (Camerer & Thaler, 1995). The real market data at a macro level corroborate the experimental data with individual participants. Concern about fairness has been invoked to explain such anomalous market occurrences as sticky prices, sticky wages and resulting unemployment (Akerlof & Yellen, 1988, 1990) and even employee theft (Greenberg, 1990). The influence of fairness on markets seems greatest when not all the terms of a transaction can be fully specified or enforced (Fehr, Kirchsteiger, & Riedl, 1998). This appears particularly of interest in the East Asian markets of China, Taiwan, Japan and South Korea, where an implicit set of transaction terms may be the norm.

Fairness concerns influence consumer satisfaction (e.g. Austin, McGinn, & Susmilch, 1980; Goodwin & Ross, 1992; Messick & Sentis, 1979; Oliver, 1997; Swan & Oliver, 1985, 1991; Szymanski & Henard, 2001), shopping intentions (Campbell, 1999) and willingness to pay (Ajzen, Rosenthal, & Brown, 2000). People are motivated to restore equity if they find themselves in an unfair situation. The means to restore equity may even include stealing (Greenberg, 1993). Because of consumer actions, companies with unfair business practices are marked with bad reputations and eventually lose business. These actions may be passive, such as decreasing repeat purchase behaviour, or aggressive, such as boycotting unfair companies (Kahneman, Knetch, & Thaler, 1986a). The case at the end of this chapter illustrates a consumer willing to destroy his own car to make a point against a corporation.

In this chapter, I first explain the important theoretical concepts of fairness management as applied to China, Taiwan, Japan and South Korea: comparison standards of fairness, fairness principles and moderators, facets of fairness, self-serving bias of fairness perceptions and fairness-related emotions. I then offer suggestions for future research directions and practical implications for practising marketing in China, Taiwan, Japan and South Korea. The chapter concludes with a case study from China and suggested discussion topics for the case study.

Learning objectives

After reading this chapter, you should be able to:

- understand how consumers perceive fairness;
- explain current research in fairness management in China, Taiwan, Japan and South Korea;
- demonstrate the concepts of fairness in a practice case study; and
- explore research directions for further study.

Current research in fairness management in China, Taiwan, Japan and South Korea

Comparison standards of fairness perceptions

The research on fairness began with studies of equity theory (Adams, 1965) and relative deprivation theory (Crosby, 1982). Both theories agree on the idea that fairness judgments are based on a comparison process, whereby the outcomes of the judge are contrasted with the outcomes received by a comparative referent (Martin & Murray, 1983). There is a variety in referent standards that are used in the comparison to produce the resulting judgment (Austin, 1977). The comparative referent may be external or internal. External or social comparison standards come from comparable others. Internal standards come from either one's own past experience or mental simulations.

Information on social comparison can be used to construct fairness perceptions. Generally we evaluate how fair our situation is by appraising the situation of another who is similar to us in most relevant aspects (Austin, 1977). This comparison refers to comparisons made by a participant to others in the immediate situation, those who are in an ongoing relationship with the person. The person will initially compare their outcome/input ratio directly with a partner following an interaction with the partner or after they have mutually interacted with a common third party. In this manner, consumers compare their outcomes with those of other consumers, after they have individually interacted with a common firm.

It is vital for firms to manage this process because fairness perceptions are more susceptible to social-comparison-based information than satisfaction judgments (van den Bos, Lind, Vermunt, & Wilke, 1997). The extent to which one has access to information of the others in the immediate situation is the key. When information on multiple social comparison referents is available, people may separately compare their focal outcome with each piece of comparison standard, rather than integrating available comparison information to form one reference point (Ordonez, Connolly, & Coughlan, 2000). In contrast, people may compare their outcome with the most superior other or the most inferior other (Fehr & Schmidt, 1999). Depending on which one is selected, consumers may change their fairness perceptions.

Internal comparison standards play an important role. Individuals will be satisfied with rewards that equal or exceed their expectancies and dissatisfied with rewards below their expectancies. This concept has been utilised as the expectation disconfirmation model in the satisfaction literature in marketing (e.g. Oliver, 1993, 2000). Consumers form these expectancies based on past experiences, whether in general form or as specific exemplars (Messe & Watts, 1983). An additional source of information comes from the simulation heuristics (Kahneman & Tversky, 1982). If people can imagine or mentally simulate what they could get (*a priori*) or have got (*post hoc*), then this mental image can be used for comparison with the actual outcome. This simulated image may be an image of a generalised other or 'mythical men' (e.g. Berger, Fisek, Norman, & Wagner, 1983; Berger, Zelditch, Anderson, & Cohen, 1972; Taylor, Wood, & Lichtman, 1983; Wood, Taylor, & Lichtman, 1985).

Likewise, social comparison referents may not necessarily be authentic. They can easily be fabricated (Goethals, 1986), to serve whatever goal the comparer has in mind, through a process termed as constructive social comparison (Goethals, Messick, & Allison, 1991). Rather than dealing with actual comparison data, people produce self-generated social comparison information, in order simply to imagine or make up information about what others are like, how they might perform and what they might think (Goethals & Klein, 2000; Suls, 1986).

Which standards are used more prominently in constructing fairness perceptions? On the one hand, several studies support the possibility that internal comparison standards may be primary, and social comparison standards secondary. Messe and Watts (1983) found that social comparison had little (if any) moderating effect on the impact of internal standards on fairness judgments. Their studies showed that social comparison appeared to magnify fairness judgments when subjects were paid an amount that was substantially lower than their own internal standards; but when the pay was consistent with their own internal standard of equity, social comparison did not affect fairness judgment. Only when one experiences gains are the outcomes of other persons important determinants of fairness judgments; in the case of losses, the outcomes of others have little influence over fairness perceptions (de Dreu, Lualhati, & McCusker, 1994).

On the other hand, some argue that the social comparison standards may dominate internal standards in influencing fairness judgments. In both business and personal situations, people are more concerned with the comparison of their own outcomes with those of another party than with the value of their own outcomes (Loewenstein, Thompson, & Bazerman, 1989). Knowing others' outcomes significantly influenced bargaining satisfaction (Corfman & Lehmann, 1993). Social comparison information may be perceived as more relevant and diagnostic than internal expectation information (van den Bos et al., 1997). With technological advances, it is becoming easier and easier to search for and observe a plethora of offers for other consumers. The availability of social comparison information in this manner will inevitably restrict the implementation of individual-level price discrimination or dynamic pricing because of fairness concerns (Bolton, Keh, & Alba, 2010).

Ultimately, whether social comparison information or internal expectation is used depends on the salience of the information in the particular situation (Austin et al., 1980). Salience may be determined by incorporating both accessibility and diagnosticity (Feldman & Lynch, 1988). If one piece of information is immediately accessible and perceived to be diagnostic, then this information will be more likely to be used − whether it is internal or external − to form a frame of reference with which to evaluate the fairness of a situation.

In East Asian countries, the degree of open sharing of the information may be larger within tighter in-groups, compared to the out-groups. It may depend on cultural characteristics in these countries related to Hofstede's individualistic-collectivistic tendencies and power distance measures. Because of the concerns about 'face', Chinese consumers are known to be more sensitive to in-group versus out-group differences than American consumers (Bolton et al., 2010). This is where in-group versus out-group memberships may play a role, especially in Asian countries with strong membership ties from various life-stage organisations (e.g. hometowns, schools, clubs, companies). Comparison within the relevant reference groups (in-groups) becomes more important and significant in determining fairness perceptions in East Asian countries with high collectivistic tendencies. Central to this process is managing the information available for consumers to actively use as the comparison standards for their fairness judgments. What information from which groups is readily available? Does the cultural norm dictate that participants should focus on their own efforts or to seek equal treatment among all? Information availability on social comparison standards or tendency regarding the usage of internal comparison standards both influence salience of each comparison standard. Managing such salience of particular comparison standards, if at all possible, is a goal to pursue for marketers in East Asian countries.

Fairness principles and moderators

There are two prominent principles of fairness: equality and equity (Deutsch, 1975). The simplest rule of fairness, equality, is often used in friendships and other solidarity relationships (Deutsch, 1985). This is the fairness rule found in economic experiments that employ ultimatum or dictator games, where everyone provides the same input while participating in an economic experiment (e.g. Loewenstein et al., 1989; Messick & Sentis, 1979).

The equity principle is less simple, requiring the ratios of inputs and outputs to be calculated. Equity involves notions of exchange, the dominating value in economic relations (Deutsch, 1985). Equity is typically defined as the equivalence of the outcome/input ratios of all parties involved in the exchange. The problem with employing the equity principle is that it is not always possible to calculate equity ratios, because information is often unavailable. Further, the way that inputs and outcomes are defined is subjective and often controversial (Tyler, Boeckmann,

Smith, & Huo, 1997). Even with sufficient information about the inputs, the information may be multidimensional and require complex rules for integrating the information to judge fairness (Cook & Yamagishi, 1983). The complexity of available information about attributes (status, investments) and contributions (inputs) may overwhelm cognitive resources. Thus, the selection and utilisation of expectations of fairness involve compromise for efficiency's sake (Mitchell, Tetlock, Mellers, & Ordonez, 1993). This is especially the case for consumers when they compare their outcome to those of other consumers. This fact suggests that consumers mainly use the equality principle as a default when arriving at fairness perceptions.

In East Asian countries, equality rather than equity may be preferred. Support is found from studies investigating on consumers' reactions to variable pricing or price increases. In one study involving hotel pricing tactic, Korean consumers perceived the variable-pricing practices to be less fair than did American consumers (Choi & Mattila, 1993).

If using the equity principle in East Asian countries, considerations should be given in defining what constitutes as valid input. For example, Koreans are more sensitive to differences in seniority, education and family size in determining fairness of pay, whereas Americans are more sensitive to variations in individual job performance and work effort (Hundley & Kim, 1997). Even within East Asian countries, there still exist national differences in preferring various types of inputs when calculating fairness judgments. Hong Kong Chinese and South Korean employees prefer emphasising maintenance inputs, whereas Japanese counterparts prefer task inputs (Kim, Weber, Leung, & Muramoto, 2009).

In addition to the overall country differences that may determine the type of fairness principles utilised, the following moderators should be considered. They include the goal of the task, justifiability of the actions and relationship among involved parties.

Goal of the task

Deutsch (1975) argued that the collective goal of a group or society influenced the selection of a dominant fairness principle. When economic productivity is a primary goal, equity will be the dominant principle; when fostering or maintenance of enjoyable social relations is the primary emphasis, equality is the principle typically selected. These goals are closely related to the nature of the situation: personal and non-personal situations. Unequal pay is acceptable in business settings, but equal payoffs are expected in personal settings (Loewenstein et al., 1989). This reasoning supports how Hong Kong and Taiwan differ. Although they are both of Chinese culture, the overriding goal of society in Hong Kong has always been more economic, thus changing the fairness perceptions and resulting quality-of-life perceptions (Liao, Fu, & Yi, 2005).

Deutsch (1982) proposed four dimensions to provide a typology of relationships and to illustrate which justice criteria will be selected: cooperative versus competitive, equal versus unequal power, task versus socio-emotional and formal versus informal. This categorisation seems to correlate with the amount of self-interest in the relationship. Cooperative, equal power, socio-emotional and informal relationships tend to depend on the equality principle because the primary goal of the relationship does not lie in pursuing self-interest. On the other hand, competitive, unequal power, task and formal relationships may rely on the equity principle, because the primary goal is in maximising self-interest. These distinctions are also correlated with the individualistic-collectivistic dimensions (Hofstede, 1980). In collectivist cultures of East Asian countries, there is a strong tendency to be more concerned with the consequences of one's behaviour for in-group members and to be more willing to sacrifice personal interests for the attainment of group goals (Triandis, 1989).

Given these considerations, the key to operating in East Asian markets to manage consumer fairness as best as possible is grounded in whether the corporations can successfully build the camaraderie with the customers as part of the same group, with a common goal. Successful customer relationship management in that regard is intricately linked with high consumer fairness perceptions (Lee-Wingate, 2011).

Justifiability of the actions

Assuming the usage of equity principle, two reference points are presumed in dual entitlement principle (Kahneman et al., 1986a; Kahneman, Knetsch, & Thaler, 1986b). Transactors (customers, tenants or employees) are entitled to the terms of the reference transaction, and firms (merchants, landlords or employers) are entitled to the terms of the reference profit. 'Reference transaction' refers to a pre-established price or wage and 'reference profit' refers to a pre-established profit level. It is unfair to prevent the other party from maintaining the reference profit or reference transaction. Firms are allowed to pursue their reference profit, and thus, certain price increases to protect their reference profit are not perceived as unfair, even at the expense of the customer's ability to maintain the reference transaction. These include inevitable changes in the cost structure, such as inflation (Bolton, Warlop, & Alba, 2003; Nunes, Hsee, & Weber, 2002). This also is universal in China: Chinese consumers accept a price rise because of cost increase, but regard as unfair the price remaining high even with decreased cost (Huangfu & Zhu, 2012).

Attempts to increase the profit without such 'legitimate' reasons were deemed unfair. In particular, it becomes troublesome if perceivers cannot justify intentions of other involved parties behind the actions that triggered perceptions of unfairness (Campbell, 1999; Rabin, 1993). Given the same outcome, if the perceivers can infer that the intentions are good or neutral, then they don't judge the situation as unfair in the way that they would have, had the inferred intentions been bad or personal. The same outcome rendered by someone who personally wanted to inflict harm will be judged to be less fair than the otherwise equal outcome rendered by someone with a neutral attitude. For example, if a rare item is auctioned off to contribute to a charity, the decision to hold the auction is perceived as fairer than if the motive had been to make profits off the rarity.

These facts underscore the importance of good public relations effort. Whenever possible, corporations must communicate the goodwill of their actions to consumers. Although the degree of understanding dual entitlement principle may be weak in consumers, firms must strive to disclose fully all relevant information regarding their good intentions behind their actions and ensure transparency and sincerity at all times.

Relationship between involved parties

The primary ordering dimension when viewing unfair situations is the nature of the social relationship among the parties involved (Mikula, Petri, & Tanzer, 1990). These are factors typically related to interpersonal attraction processes, such as similarity, proximity and degree of openness (Cook & Hegtvedt, 1983). When similarity between parties or proximity of future interaction is high, an equality rule is preferred over an equity rule (Greenberg, 1978). For example, business executives rated most business actions as fairer than did the general population (Gorman & Kehr, 1992). When decisions are made openly, the equality rule is preferred; when allocation decisions are made secretly, the equity rule dominates (Lane and Messe, 1971). Both the emotional quality and duration of the relationship may also influence rule preferences. Friends use the equality rule while non-friends use the equity rule (Austin, 1980). Equity is preferred for tasks and equality is preferred for socio-emotional functions (Tyler, 1994). Even in business situations, when the relationship of the negotiators became more personalised (with higher liking), and long-term oriented (with longer history and higher likelihood of future interactions), negotiators appeared to care more for equality in their outcomes (Corfman & Lehmann, 1993).

Dependency relations between the involved parties affect fair actions (van Dijk & Vermunt, 2000). When participants know that the other participants can retaliate and protect their own self-interest, they act more strategically and less fairly, seeking optimal payoff. However, when the other party is perceived as powerless, many feel that it is inappropriate to take advantage of the powerless party − hence they divide according to the equality principle. It is particularly true for Japan, where it is considered fair that the party with greater power earns a smaller portion of the surplus, sharing more of it with the weaker partner; This contrasts with the US participants, who believe that it is fair that the party with greater power takes a larger share of the surplus (Buchan, Croson, & Johnson, 2004). It also applies to China, where *guanxi* implicitly favours the weaker party of the relationship (Alston, 1989).

Firms are easier to blame for unfairness than individuals, given the same actions (Seligman & Schwartz, 1997). Firms are perceived as more motivated by profit, and people believe that wealthy or profitable firms can better afford to be fair. Consistent with this, Kahneman et al. (1986b) found that the profitability and the size of the firm influenced fairness judgments, such that larger firms were more likely to be perceived as unfair for the same actions than smaller firms. In China, even the type of firm ownership matters. Price hikes by state-owned monopolies are seen as more unfair than the same price increase by non-state-owned corporations (Huangfu & Zhu, 2012).

These facts may pose a substantial problem for a large multinational corporation entering the East Asian market, competing head-to-head against smaller local firms. Firms must acknowledge and mange consumer expectations for them to conform to the role of the larger, more powerful partner in an ongoing relationship: more benevolent and protecting of the weaker party, individual consumers. Signalling commitment may be key in managing worse fairness perceptions of international retailers (such as Wal-Mart and Carrefour) when compared to local retailers (Homeplus or E-mart) in South Korea (Suh, 2004).

Distributive and procedural fairness

There are two main different facets of fairness perceptions: distributive and procedural. Distributive fairness is about the fairness of specific, personal outcomes (Cook & Hegtvedt, 1983; Deutsch, 1985; Oliver, 1993; Oliver & Swan, 1989a,b). Distributive justice was related to overall fairness more strongly for Americans and Japanese than for Chinese and Koreans, because of the differences in materialism (Kim & Leung, 2007).

Procedural fairness involves the relative manner and procedures through which outcomes are delivered (Lind & Tyler, 1988; McFarlin & Sweeny, 1992; Thibaut & Walker, 1978). Two types of input must be incorporated into procedurally fair decisions: process control and decision control (Thibaut & Walker, 1975). These refer to the degree of participation in the process, whether to present evidence on their behalf or to have any say in the decision. Merely knowing that they, as a consumer, can contribute their voice is important in fairness determination. In particular, procedural preferences in Japan, a collectivistic country, are determined by the perceived probability of the procedures in achieving animosity reduction and in granting the disputants process control (Leung, Au, Fernandez-Dols, & Iwawaki, 1992).

If the outcomes are allocated unfairly, victims of unfairness seek retribution through confrontation with the responsible party (Tyler et al., 1997). The intentions of these victims stem from their hopes of punishing wrongdoing and deterring the same action in the future (Carlsmith, Darley, & Robinson, 2002; Nagin, 1998). Hence, procedures that allow such an opportunity are perceived as fair. Whether these opportunities are feasible is correlated with power distance (Hofstede, 1980). Korea is relatively high in power distance and Japan is relatively moderate (Kotabe, Dubinsky, & Lim, 1992).

Interactional justice, a subset of procedural justice that focuses on interpersonal aspects, has received special attention in the services marketing and organisational literatures (Bies & Shapiro, 1987; Greenberg, 1993) and signals the relative manner in which the consumer is treated in terms of respect, politeness and dignity. Further, there are two types of interactional justice (Greenberg, 1993): informational justice (a thorough explanation) and interpersonal justice (polite, caring, sensitive communication). In service marketing studies, it is important to study fairness perceptions in the recovery of a service failure. Explanation is often deemed more important than compensation for collectivist countries (Mattila & Patterson, 2004), suggesting that procedural fairness may be more important at times than distributive fairness in the East Asian countries. Consistent with this view, the interpersonal treatment considering social sensitivity is deemed crucial in producing heightened fairness perceptions in China (Tata, Fu, & Wu, 2003).

Self-serving bias of fairness perceptions

Concerns about fairness are influential to the degree that they often compromise selfishness. However, a self-serving tendency still exists, biasing fairness perceptions (Messick & Sentis, 1983). This is synonymous with egocentric bias, where people are more concerned with inequalities that favour others than they are with inequalities that favour themselves (Lane & Messe, 1971; Messe, 1971). When a situation is to their advantage, it is less likely for people to judge it as unfair. If the same amount of discrepancy occurs in the reverse direction (i.e. they receive less than others), it is more likely for people to perceive unfairness.

The self-serving bias is more prominent when people are direct participants rather than bystanders or observers of an unfair situation (Diekmann, Samuels, Ross, & Bazerman, 1997), and when people are allocators of outcomes rather than recipients (Diekmann et al., 1997). People report that they are fairer than others in expressing fairness concerns (van Lange, 1991). For example, when participants are asked to write sentences including the words 'fair' and 'unfair', sentences including the word 'fair' tend to include the pronoun 'I', whereas sentences including the word 'unfair' tend to include the pronoun 'they' (Messick, Bloom, Boldizar, & Samuelson, 1985).

Self-serving bias is what prompts many consumers to experience unfairness even in situations that may be objectively viewed as fair. The extent of egocentric fairness bias is considered less in East Asian countries, such as Japan, than individualistic countries, such as the United States (Gelfand et al., 2002). However, it does exist in Japan (Tanaka, 1993). Interestingly, Japanese participants who strongly believe in a just world display larger self-serving bias than those who weakly believe in a just world (Tanaka, 1999).

Emotions of fairness perceptions

Perceptions about what is 'just', 'fair' or 'deserved' cannot exist without feelings (Tyler et al., 1997). Naturally, feelings of happiness and pride, as well as satisfaction, ensue when justice is realised. In contrast, perceptions of injustice coexist with 'feelings of personal relative deprivation' (Tyler et al., 1997), anger (Homans, 1961), envy (Smith, Spears, & Oyen, 1994), psychological depression (Zohar, 1995), low self-esteem (Koper, Van Knippenberg, Bouhuijs, Vermunt, & Wilke, 1993) and guilt (Scher, 1997). Outrage, horror, shock and resentment join the list (Cahn, 1964). Betrayal and jealousy qualify as justice-related emotions as well (Feinberg, Krishna, & Zhang, 2002).

The typology of emotional responses to fairness perceptions consists of the two following: positive and negative reactions. The negative emotions can be further classified into two types: emotions in response to receiving less than is fair (such as anger or resentment) and emotions in response to receiving more than is fair (such as guilt or fear of retaliation). The common focus of the past research has been placed on the negative reactions to unfairness, and especially the reactions of anger, that result from disadvantageous inequity or inequality. In Japan, the closeness of the relationship and the perceived responsibility of the other involved party's needs were shown to be causal factors of fairness-related anger (Uehara, Nakagawa, Mori, & Ohbuchi, 2012).

There are theoretical distinctions on whether fairness concerns activate emotional responses, or emotional responses prompt fairness cognition. Regardless of the order of occurrence, the consensus is on the concomitant generation. In an iterative process, fairness perceptions and the emotions impact each other and may precede each other under certain circumstances. In an advantageous state for the fairness perceiver, the positive emotions that are concomitantly generated may not necessarily elevate the already high level of fairness perceptions any further. Conversely, when the generated emotions are negative, the sheer negativity of the emotions may act as a strong cue that negatively influences fairness perceptions. This is consistent with affect-as-information framework positing that affective feelings serve an important feedback function (e.g. Schwartz, 1990). When the experienced affect is perceived to originate from specific target objects, its influence on subsequent judgment regarding those target objects will only be greater. This is the case with most judgments of consumer fairness, since the target object that is perceived as responsible for the perceptions of unfairness to occur exists in the tangible forms of retailers, service providers, manufacturers and other marketers.

Emotional aspects of fairness management is challenging in East Asian countries of China, Taiwan, Japan and South Korea. In China and Taiwan, the emotional term is *guanxi*; in Japan, *wa*; in Korea, *inwha* (Alston, 1989). All three terms denote the informal, socio-emotional and obligational nature of the relationship imposed on to all involved parties within any business contexts. It is more than give and take. All three emphasise social obligations that each participant must execute in a tight-knit in-group, in order to ensure the group's success against other out-groups. What is inherently implied in these concepts is the notion of individual sacrifices for the greater good or goal of the in-group.

Another interesting phenomenon in East Asian countries of China, Taiwan, Japan and South Korea involves the notion of 'face'. It represents status earned in a social network (Ho, 1976). Face influences Chinese consumers (Li & Su, 2007). A similar construct exists in Japan and South Korea as well. The fairness emotion related to face concerns is shame. The mediator of Chinese fairness perceptions is shame, whereas it is anger for American fairness perceptions (Bolton et al., 2010). Japanese consumers showed similar susceptibility to shame rather than to anger (Kitayama, Mesquita, & Karasawa, 2006).

New research directions

It is evident that consumers' perceptions of fairness influence their relationships with firms, whether local or foreign, in East Asian countries. Knowing and predicting how differently East Asian consumers construct fairness perceptions contributes to planning effective marketing strategies. A great leap toward betterment has been taken in fairness research when cross-cultural differences appeared as a new topic. Research on American vs. East Asian differences related to fairness perceptions paved the way. Now is the time to pursue differences and similarities among the East Asian countries of China, Taiwan, Japan and South Korea.

Despite the preliminary assumption that all East Asians are alike, made in numerous cross-cultural studies using Hofstede's cultural dimensions, East Asian countries differ in several aspects of attitudes and behaviours (e.g. Abramson & Ingelhart, 1995; Alston, 1989; Kim & Leung, 2007; Paik & Tung, 1999). Future research should investigate deeper into why and how these differences originate, in order to offer businesses more insights on how to operate and manage consumer fairness perceptions better, and develop stronger customer relationships in these countries.

Practising marketing in China, Taiwan, Japan and South Korea

In East Asian countries, group affiliations and ties are deep-rooted. Thus, when managing information that could potentially be used in fairness judgments, marketers must note the significance of in-group versus out-group comparisons in fairness judgments (Bolton et al., 2010). Collectivist consumers experience a greater loss of face when a friend pays a lower price than when a stranger pays a lower price. Similarly, collectivist Chinese consumers experience a greater loss of face when paying a higher price to a vendor with which they have a long-term relationship than to a newly encountered vendor. As such, if dynamic pricing were to be implemented, marketers must ensure the equal level of prices for all members of each group, although differences between groups may exist.

Whether the equity or the equality rule is utilised to arrive at fairness perceptions depends on several moderators that shape the situation. When the specifics of the situations are clear, the following conclusion can be made. Those with a task-based goal, in non-personal (or business), short-term, dissimilar and distant relationship circumstances, may prefer the equity rule. Conversely, those with a relational goal, in personal, long-term, similar and close relationship circumstances may prefer the equality rule. If faced with ambiguous or insufficient information, or limited cognitive resources, it is more likely for equality to overrule equity (Deutsch, 1985). In Japan and South Korea, the overriding societal goal often emphasises unity and harmony. This fact suggests that equality rule may be preferred in general. Reconciling this general tendency and the equity rule often used in the business setting will be a challenge for fairness managers in the East Asian countries.

Emphasising procedural fairness, management must confirm that organisational and consumer procedures are implemented (a) consistently, (b) without self-interest, (c) on the basis of accurate information, (d) with opportunities to correct the decision, (e) with the interests of all concerned parties represented, and (f) following moral and ethical standards (Leventhal, Karuza, & Fry, 1980). It is impossible to prevent all negative outcomes, whether it is regarding service failure or product pricing. But it is feasible to install fair procedures to resolve complaints. Particularly in East Asian countries, it is crucial that interactional fairness is emphasised in this process − to offer a thorough explanation, in polite, sensitive and caring manners of communication. These aspects of interactional fairness contribute to signalling the sincerity of the business in its commitment to be a member of the in-group in a long-term relationship.

Self-serving biases in fairness perceptions still exist in these countries, albeit to a lesser degree than in Western countries. What is important is to acknowledge implicitly the existence of this bias, as no East Asian consumers will explicitly and openly admit to its presence. Management should be considerate when offering compensation to recover for a service failure. Although compensation is appreciated by consumers and is influential in determining fairness perceptions, offering compensation is going to backfire if it is done without thorough explanation, and if executed without politeness and sincerity. The point is to convey the sincerity of the businesses, in order to encourage customers to feel appreciated and respected, and to assist customers in saving their 'face', especially in public or in front of other customers.

Fairness-related emotions are extremely meaningful in East Asian countries. It goes beyond building rapport or camaraderie among employees. Building successful customer relationships in East Asian countries starts with managing fairness-related emotions well. It requires understanding the basic emotions that drive consumer behaviour − that the emotion of shame is stronger motivator than the emotion of anger − and putting the best foot forward in becoming a partner in preventing the negative emotions.

Although *guanxi* is cultivated by the exchange of gifts and favours, and is a common practice in China and Taiwan (Hwang, Golemon, Chen, Wang, & Hung, 2009), global marketers must be ethically conscious with the *guanxi* practices in managing fairness. Careful treading of the social relationship landscape is necessary, supported by deep understanding of the local consumer psychology.

Practice case study[1]

In 2001, Mr Sheng Wang openly and drastically protested against Mercedes-Benz based on his perception of unfair and insensitive treatment he received. Mercedes-Benz repeatedly failed to repair a problem with his car's fuel system, which started a few weeks after the purchase. Ultimately, Mr Wang demanded an exchange or return. Mercedes-Benz did not agree and insisted that the problem persisted not because of the engine defects but from the use of inferior low-octane fuel. It was to no avail with Mr Wang, who claimed that he owned four Mercedes-Benz vehicles in his company, all using the same fuel, but only this one had the problem.

Having already performed repairs worth US$160,000, including replacing oil spray nozzles, Mercedes-Benz decided against replacing the car, but offered to clean the fuel system at no charge even after the warranty expired. Mr Wang felt that this problem was not resolved to his satisfaction. As he had threatened Mercedes-Benz in his faxes, Mr Wang saw the public demonstration as his last resort.

[1] This is the case study discussed in Chen, Nguyen, and Klaus (2013), used here with the authors' permission.

He wrote 'No quality, no service' on his Mercedes SLK230 sports coupé. A water buffalo towed the car through his hometown of Wuhan. On the next day, he held a press conference, complaining of Mercedes-Benz's insensitivity towards the needs of Chinese consumers. At the end of the press conference, hired workers demolished the exterior of the car with sledgehammers and sticks. This event was highly publicised in popular media, creating a strong public opinion about Mercedes-Benz's customer satisfaction programme in China.

Mr Wang's expression of frustration based on perceived unfairness by foreign corporations is not uncommon in China. It is actually quite a popular tactic, to stage public destruction of faulty products, such as refrigerators, televisions, air conditioners and automobiles. Why do Chinese consumers resort to this kind of dramatic gesture? The poor quality of local complaint handling procedures is the norm, aggravating any complainants. Taking legal action is almost always extremely complicated and time-consuming, as well as expensive, with a low likelihood of winning. Thus it is an accepted fact that that emotional and dramatic publicity stints guarantee a news headline and, more importantly, the company's attention.

Indeed, the effect of the publicity stunt was clear. Coverage of the event in popular media included editorials commenting on the negative aspects of Mercedes-Benz products and service, some using vitriolic terms. Immediately afterwards, several other disgruntled Mercedes-Benz owners stepped forth to form the Association of Mercedes Quality Victims.

Mercedes-Benz responded by publicly attacking Mr Wang, saying that this was a publicity stunt for his company (an animal park). Mercedes-Benz management also attributed the problem to Mr Wang's driving habits, claiming that he drove too fast and steered too violently. They re-emphasised that the cause of problem was the low-quality fuel.

Naturally, Mercedes-Benz's response was construed as an implicit criticism of the state-owned petrol industry. Fuel providers in the area publicly issued countering statements, vouching for the fuel quality. Reactions from the Chinese public characterised Mercedes-Benz as insensitive and arrogant in dealing with Chinese customers. Public opinions bolstered the pre-existing view of how foreign corporations take advantage of Chinese consumers with deficient products, strengthening consumer resentment and distrust. Mr Wang's assistant was quoted giving his opinion of Mercedes-Benz as discriminating against Chinese customers in its services.

Despite the negative public opinion, Mercedes-Benz stood its ground, and threatened to sue Mr Wang for damaging its reputation. A letter of apology from Mr Wang was requested, and it was to be widely distributed in Chinese media. Mr Wang refused, and took the destroyed car to Beijing, the capital city, for more public demonstrations. Another Mercedes-Benz owner agreed to destroy his own car, citing the reason for his participation as protesting against Mercedes-Benz' discriminating and unfair treatment of the Association of Mercedes Quality Victims. Ultimately, Mercedes-Benz negotiated an out-of-court settlement, but only after months of visible public dispute, with significant damage to the Mercedes-Benz brand in China.

Case questions

1. What mistakes did Mercedes-Benz make, in considering how Chinese consumers arrive at fairness judgments? Review major theoretical concepts from the previous section to answer this question.
2. If you were in charge of Mercedes-Benz's corporate PR in China, what would you have done differently? Consider the characteristics of Chinese consumer as compared to European or American consumers, when constructing fairness judgments.

Further investigation

This case demonstrates how Mercedes-Benz did not consider the crucial underpinnings of fairness perceptions in the Chinese market. It is perfect material for discussion of the concepts discussed in this chapter. Below are some suggested points for discussions.

First, Mercedes-Benz did not consider what types of comparison standards were utilised for fairness judgments. Both external and internal standards existed very clearly in Mr Wang's case to argue otherwise. His perceptions of unfairness were only strengthened when his other Mercedes-Benz automobiles performed well with the same fuel supply. Unfairness was aggravated when other owners of Mercedes-Benz sympathised with him. Further, his simulated perception of how 'American' consumers would be treated in the same situation led him to believe that he was being discriminated against as a Chinese consumer.

Second, it is clear that Mr Wang and Mercedes-Benz were using different fairness principles. Mercedes-Benz was using the equity rule, calculating the costs of repairs and a goodwill offer to clean the engine at no charge and thinking that this was sufficient to compensate for the situation. Mr Wang insisted on replacement of the vehicle, so that he could get the equal quality and product that other Mercedes-Benz owners would. Mr Wang was using the equality principle.

Third, Mercedes-Benz fail to comprehend how importantly Mr Wang and Chinese consumers regard the procedural aspect of the fairness perceptions, especially interactional fairness. Neither a compelling explanation nor an acceptable level of sincerity seems to have been included in the communication with Mr Wang. In its effort to avoid admitting any wrongdoing necessary for future legal success, Mercedes-Benz may have deliberately excluded customary Chinese phrases signalling sincerity, politeness and good decorum. It is also likely that only written communication at the impersonal level was provided, not knowing that face-to-face interactions with higher levels of management are deemed to be more polite in Chinese culture.

Many additional country-specific moderators were not considered appropriately, including self-serving bias and emotional reactions to fairness. Proposed compensation may not have appeared sufficient to Mr Wang, presumably because of the manner with which the offer was presented. The same offer could have been presented in a way to capitalise on the *guanxi* aspect − to symbolise the longer-term relationship between Mercedes-Benz and Mr Wang, as a representative of his hometown, for example. Further, Mercedes-Benz did not appear to have attempted to assimilate into the Chinese in-group. Merely insisting on focusing on the rational and economic goal of the business relationship may have isolated Mercedes-Benz from the regional fuel suppliers' support and led the general public to perceive the company as arrogant. Had Mercedes-Benz focused on localising itself and truly attempting to be a company caring about Chinese consumers' well-being, this sort of situation might have been avoided.

References

Abramson, P. R., & Ingelhart, R. (1995). *Value change in global perspective*. Ann Arbor, MI: University of Michigan Press.

Adams, J. S. (1965). Inequity in social exchange. In L. Berkowitz (Ed.), *Advances in experimental social psychology* (Vol. 2, pp. 267–299). New York: Academic Press.

Ajzen, I., Rosenthal, L. H., & Brown, T. C. (2000). Effects of perceived fairness on willingness to pay. *Journal of Applied Social Psychology, 30*, 2439–2450.

Akerlof, G. A., & Yellen, J. (1988). The fair wage-effort hypothesis and unemployment. *The Quarterly Journal of Economics, 105*, 255–283.

Akerlof, G. A., & Yellen, J. (1990). Fairness and unemployment. *The American Economic Review, 78*, 44–49.

Alston, J. P. (1989). Wa, guanxi, and inwha: Managerial principles in Japan, China, and Korea. *Business Horizons, 32*, 26–30.

Austin, W. (1977). Equity theory and social comparison processes. In J. M. Suls, & R. L. Miller (Eds.), *Social comparison processes: Theoretical and empirical perspectives* (pp. 279–305). Washington DC: Hemisphere Publishing Corporation.

Austin, W. (1980). Friendship and fairness: Effects of type of relationship and task performance on choice of distribution rules. *Personality and Social Psychology Bulletin, 6*, 402–408.

Austin, W., McGinn, N. C., & Susmilch, C. (1980). Internal standards revisited: Effects of social comparisons and expectancies on judgments of fairness and satisfaction. *Journal of Experimental Social Psychology, 16*.

Berger, J., Fisek, M. H., Norman, R. Z., & Wagner, D. G. (1983). The formation of reward expectations in status situations. In D. M. Messick, & K. S. Cook (Eds.), *Equity theory: Psychological and sociological perspectives* (pp. 127–168). New York: Praeger.

Berger, J., Zelditch, M., Jr., Anderson, B., & Cohen, B. P. (1972). Structural aspects of distributive justice: A status value formulation. In J. Berger, M. Zelditch, Jr., & B. Anderson (Eds.), *Sociological theories in progress* (pp. 119–146). Boston, MA: Houghton Mifflin.

Bies, R. J., & Shapiro, D. L. (1987). Interactional fairness judgments: The influence of causal accounts. *Social Justice Research, 1*, 160–169.

Bolton, L. E., Keh, H. T., & Alba, J. W. (2010). How do price fairness perceptions differ across culture? *Journal of Marketing Research, 47*, 564–576.

Bolton, L. E., Warlop, L., & Alba, J. W. (2003). Explorations in price (un)fairness. *Journal of Consumer Research* (March), 474–491.

Buchan, N. R., Croson, R. T. A., & Johnson, E. (2004). When do fair beliefs influence bargaining behavior? Experimental bargaining in Japan and the United States. *Journal of Consumer Research, 31*, 181–190.

Cahn, E. (1964). *The sense of injustice.* Bloomington, IN: Indiana University Press. [Originally published in 1949 by New York university press].

Camerer, C., & Thaler, R. H. (1995). Anomalies: Ultimatums, dictators and manners. *The Journal of Economic Perspectives, 9,* 209−219.

Campbell, M. C. (1999). Perceptions of price unfairness: Antecedents and consequences. *Journal of Marketing Research, 36,* 187−199.

Carlsmith, K. M., Darley, J. M., & Robinson, P. H. (2002). Why do we punish? Deterrence and just desserts as motives for punishment. *Journal of Personality and Social Psychology, 83,* 284−299.

Chen, J., Nguyen, B., & Klaus, P. (2013). Public affairs in China: Exploring the role of brand fairness perceptions in the case of Mercedes-Benz. *Journal of Public Affairs, 13,* 403−414.

Choi, S., & Mattila, A. S. (1993). The role of disclosure in variable hotel pricing. *Cornell Hotel and Restaurant Administration Quarterly, 47,* 27−35.

Cook, K. S., & Hegtvedt, K. A. (1983). Distributive justice, equity, and equality. *Annual Review of Sociology, 9,* 217−241.

Cook, K. S., & Yamagishi, T. (1983). Social determinants of equity judgments: The problem of multidimensional input. In D. M. Messick, & K. S. Cook (Eds.), *Equity theory: Psychological and sociological perspectives* (pp. 95−126). New York: Praeger.

Corfman, K. P., & Lehmann, D. R. (1993). The importance of others' welfare in evaluating bargaining outcomes. *Journal of Consumer Research, 20,* 124−137.

Crosby, F. (1982). *Relative deprivation and working women.* New York: Oxford University Press.

de Dreu, C. W., Lualhati, J. C., & McCusker, C. (1994). Effects of gain-loss frames on satisfaction with self-other outcome differences. *European Journal of Social Psychology, 34,* 497−510.

Deutsch, M. (1975). Equity, equality, and need: What determines which value will be used as the basis of distributive justice? *Journal of Social Issues, 31,* 137−149.

Deutsch, M. (1982). Interdependence and psychological orientation. In V. J. Delilega, & J. Grzelak (Eds.), *Cooperation and helping behavior.* New York: Academic Press.

Deutsch, M. (1985). *Distributive justice: A social-psychological perspective.* New Haven and London: Yale University Press.

Diekmann, K. A., Samuels, S. M., Ross, L., & Bazerman, M. H. (1997). Self-interest and fairness in problems of resource allocation: Allocators versus recipients. *Journal of Personality and Social Psychology, 72* (May), 1061−1074.

Eckel, C. C., & Grossman, P. (1996). Equity and fairness in economic decisions: Evidence from bargaining experiments. In *Advances in economic psychology,* edited by G. Antonides, W. F. van Raaij, & S. Maital (Eds.), Chichester: John Wiley & Sons.

Fehr, E., & Schmidt, K. M. (1999). A theory of fairness, competition and cooperation. *Quarterly Journal of Economics* (August), 818−868.

Fehr, E., Kirchsteiger, G., & Riedl, A. (1998). Gift exchange and reciprocity in competitive experimental markets. *European Economic Review, 42,* 1−34.

Feinberg, F., Krishna, A., & Zhang, Z. J. (2002). Do we care what others get? A behaviorist approach to targeted promotions. *Journal of Marketing Research, 39* (August), 277−291.

Feldman, J. M., & Lynch, J. G., Jr. (1988). Self-generated validity and other effects of measurement on belief, attitude, intention and behavior. *Journal of Applied Psychology, 73,* 421−435.

Gelfand, M. J., Higgins, M., Nishii, L. H., Raver, J. L., Dominguez, A., Murakami, F., et al. (2002). Culture and egocentric perceptions of fairness in conflict and negotiation. *Journal of Applied Psychology*, *87*, 833–845.

Goethals, G. R. (1986). Fabricating and ignoring social reality: Self-Serving estimates of consensus. In J. M. Olson, C. P. Herman, & M. P. Zanna (Eds.), *Relative deprivation and social comparison: The ontario symposium* (Vol. 4, pp. 135–157). Hillsdale, NJ: Lawrence Erlbaum.

Goethals, G. R., & Klein, W. M. P. (2000). Interpreting and inventing social reality. In J. Suls, & L. Wheeler (Eds.), *Handbook of social comparison* (pp. 23–44). New York: Kluwer Academic/Plenum.

Goethals, G. R., Messick, D. M., & Allison, S. T. (1991). The uniqueness bias: Studies of constructive social comparison. In J. M. Suls, & T. A. Wills (Eds.), *Social comparison, contemporary theory and research* (pp. 149–173). Hillsdale, NJ: Lawrence Erlbaum.

Goodwin, C., & Ross, I. (1992). Consumer responses to service failure: Influence of procedural and interactional fairness perceptions. *Journal of Business Research*, *25*, 149–163.

Gorman, R. F., & Kehr, J. B. (1992). Fairness as a constraint on profit seeking: Comment. *American Economic Review*, *82*.

Greenberg, J. (1978). Allocator-recipient similarity and the equitable division of rewards. *Social Psychology*, *41*.

Greenberg, J. (1990). Organizational justice: Yesterday, today, and tomorrow. *Journal of Management*, *16*(2), 399–432.

Greenberg, J. (1993). Stealing in the name of justice: Informational and interpersonal moderators of theft reactions to underpayment inequity. *Organizational Behavior and Human Decision Processes*, *54*, 81–103.

Ho, D. Y. (1976). On the concept of face. *American Journal of Sociology*, *81*, 867–884.

Hofstede, G. (1980). *Cultures of consequences: International differences in work-related values*. Beverly Hills, CA: Sage.

Homans, G. C. (1961). *Social behavior: Its elementary forms*. New York: Harcourt, Brace, & World.

Huangfu, G., & Zhu, L. (2012). Do consumers' perceptions of price fairness differ according to type of firm ownership? *Social Behavior and Personality*, *40*, 693–698.

Hundley, G., & Kim, J. (1997). National culture and the factors affecting perceptions of pay fairness in Korea and the United States. *The International Journal of Organizational Analysis*, *4*, 325–341.

Hwang, D. B., Golemon, P. L., Chen, Y., Wang, T., & Hung, W. (2009). Guanxi and business ethics in confucian society today: An empirical case study in Taiwan. *Journal of Business Ethics*, *89*, 235–250.

Kahneman, D., & Tversky, A. (1982). The simulation heuristic. In D. Kahneman, P. Slovic, & A. Tversky (Eds.), *Judgment under uncertainty: Heuristics and biases*. New York: Cambridge University Press.

Kahneman, D., Knetsch, J. L., & Thaler, R. (1986a). Fairness as a constraint on profit seeking: Entitlements in the market. *American Economic Review*, *76*, 728–741.

Kahneman, D., Knetsch, J. L., & Thaler, R. (1986b). Fairness and the assumptions of economics. *Journal of Business*, *59*, 285–300.

Kim, T., & Leung, K. (2007). Forming and reacting to overall fairness: A cross-cultural comparison. *Organizational Behavior and Human Decision Processes*, *104*, 83–95.

Kim, T., Weber, T., Leung, K., & Muramoto, Y. (2009). Perceived fairness of pay: The importance of task versus maintenance inputs in Japan, South Korea, and Hong Kong. *Management and Organization Review*, *6*, 31–54.

Kitayama, S., Mesquita, B., & Karasawa, M. (2006). Cultural affordances and emotional experience: Socially engaging and disengaging emotions in Japan and the United States. *Journal of Personality and Social Psychology, 91*, 890–903.

Koper, G., Van Knippenberg, D., Bouhuijs, F., Vermunt, R., & Wilke, H. (1993). Procedural fairness and self-esteem. *European Journal of Social Psychology, 23*, 313–325.

Kotabe, M., Dubinsky, A. J., & Lim, C. U. (1992). Perceptions of organizational fairness: A cross-national perspective. *International Marketing Review, 9*, 41–58.

Lane, I. M., & Messe, L. A. (1971). Equity and the distribution of rewards. *Journal of Personality and Social Psychology, 20*.

Lee-Wingate, S. N. (2011). Managing consumer fairness perceptions to increase lifetime customer value. In R. Srinivasan, & L. McAlister (Eds.), *Marketing theory and applications: American marketing association winter educators' conference proceedings* (Vol. 22, pp. 183–193). Austin, TX: American Marketing Association.

Lee-Wingate, S. N., & Corfman, K. (2011). The effect of consumer emotional disclosure on fairness perceptions. *Psychology & Marketing, 28*, 897–908.

Leung, K., Au, Y., Fernandez-Dols, J. M., & Iwawaki, S. (1992). Preference for methods of conflict processing in two collectivist cultures. *International Journal of Psychology, 27*, 195–209.

Leventhal, G. S., Karuza, J., & Fry, W. R. (1980). Beyond fairness: A theory of allocation preferences. In G. Mikula (Ed.), *Justice and social interaction* (pp. 167–218). New York: Springer-Verlag.

Li, J. J., & Su, C. (2007). How face influences consumption: A comparative study of American and Chinese consumers. *International Journal of Market Research, 49*, 237–256.

Liao, P., Fu, Y., & Yi, C. (2005). Perceived quality of life in Taiwan and Hong Kong: An intra-culture comparison. *Journal of Happiness Studies, 5*, 43–67.

Lind, E. A., & Tyler, T. R. (1988). *The social psychology of procedural justice.* New York, NY: Plenum.

Loewenstein, G. F., Thompson, L., & Bazerman, M. H. (1989). Social utility and decision making in interpersonal contexts. *Journal of Personality and Social Psychology, 57*, 426–441.

Martin, J., & Murray, A. (1983). Distributive injustice and unfair exchange. In D. M. Messick, & K. S. Cook (Eds.), *Equity theory: Psychological and sociological perspectives* (pp. 169–205). New York: Praeger.

Mattila, A. S., & Patterson, P. G. (2004). Service recovery and fairness perceptions in collectivist and individualist contexts. *Journal of Service Research, 6*, 336–346.

McFarlin, D. B., & Sweeney, P. D. (1992). Distributive and procedural justice as predictors of satisfaction with personal and organizational outcomes. *Academy of Management Journal, 35*, 626–637.

Messe, L. A. (1971). Choosing among alternative distributions of rewards. In B. Lerberman (Ed.), *Social choice.* London: Gordon and Breach.

Messe, L. A., & Watts, B. L. (1983). Complex nature of the sense of fairness: Internal standards and social comparison as bases for reward evaluations. *Journal of Personality and Social Psychology, 45*, 84–93.

Messick, D. M., Bloom, S., Boldizar, J. P., & Samuelson, C. D. (1985). Why we are fairer than others. *Journal of Experimental Social Psychology, 21*, 480–500.

Messick, D. M., & Sentis, J. (1979). Fairness and preference. *Journal of Experimental Social Psychology, 15*.

Messick, D. M., & Sentis, K. (1983). Fairness, preference, and fairness biases. In D. M. Messick, & K. S. Cook (Eds.), *Equity theory* (pp. 61−94). New York: Praeger.

Mikula, G., Petri, B., & Tanzer, N. (1990). What people regard as unjust: Types and structures of everyday experiences of injustice. *European Journal of Social Psychology, 22,* 133−149.

Mitchell, G., Tetlock, P. E., Mellers, B. A., & Ordonez, L. D. (1993). Judgments of social justice: Compromises between equality and efficiency. *Journal of Personality and Social Psychology, 65,* 629−639.

Montada, L. (1991). Coping with life stress: Injustice and the question 'Who is responsible?'. In H. Steensma, & R. Vermunt (Eds.), *Social justice in human relations: Societal and psychological consequences of justice and injustice* (Vol. 2, pp. 9−30). New York: Plenum Press.

Nagin, D. (1998). Deterrence and incapacitation. In M. Tonry (Ed.), *The handbook of crime and punishment* (pp. 345−368). New York, NY: Oxford University Press.

Nunes, J. C., Hsee, C. K., & Weber, E. U. (2002). The effect of products' cost structures on consumer payment and purchase intentions. *Society for Consumer Psychology 2002 Winter Conference Proceedings.*

Oliver, R. L. (1993). Cognitive, affective, and attribute bases of the satisfaction response. *Journal of Consumer Research, 20* (December), 418−430.

Oliver, R. L. (1997). *Satisfaction: A behavioral perspective on the consumer.* New York: McGraw-Hill.

Oliver, R. L. (2000). Customer satisfaction with service. In T. A. Swartz, & D. Iacobucci (Eds.), *Handbook of services marketing and management.* Thousand Oaks, CA: Sage Publications.

Oliver, R. L., & Swan, J. E. (1989a). Consumer perceptions of interpersonal equity and satisfaction in transactions: A field survey approach. *Journal of Marketing, 53,* 21−35.

Oliver, R. L., & Swan, J. E. (1989b). Equity and disconfirmation perceptions as influences on merchant and product satisfaction. *Journal of Consumer Research, 16,* 372−383.

Ordonez, L. D., Connolly, T., & Coughlan, R. (2000). Multiple reference points in satisfaction and fairness assessment. *Journal of Behavioral Decision Making, 13,* 329−344.

Paik, Y., & Tung, R. L. (1999). Negotiating with East Asia: How to attain 'win-win' outcomes. *Management International Review, 39,* 103−122.

Rabin, M. (1993). Incorporating fairness into game theory and economics. *American Economic Review, 83,* 1281−1302.

Scher, S. J. (1997). Measuring the consequences of injustice. *Personality and Social Psychological Bulletin, 23*(May), 482−497.

Schwartz, N. (1990). Feelings as information: Informational and motivational functions of affective states. In E. Tory Higgins, & R. M. Sorrentino (Eds.), *Handbook of motivation and cognition: Foundations of social behavior* (pp. 527−561). New York: Guilford Press.

Seligman, D. A., & Schwartz, B. (1997). Domain specificity of fairness judgments in economic transactions. *Journal of Economic Psychology, 18,* 579−604.

Smith, H. J., Spears, R., & Oyen, M. (1994). 'People like us': The influence of personal deprivation and group membership salience on justice evaluations. *Journal of Experimental Social Psychology, 30,* 277−299.

Suh, S. (2004). Fairness and relationship quality perceived by local suppliers: In search of critical success factors for international retailers. *Journal of Global Marketing, 18,* 5−19.

Suls, J. (1986). Notes on the occasion of social comparison theory's thirtieth birthday. *Personality and Social Psychology Bulletin, 12,* 289−296.

Swan, J. E., & Oliver, R. L. (1985). *Automobile buyer satisfaction with the salesperson related to equity and disconfirmation.* Bloomington: Indiana University Press.

Swan, J. E., & Oliver, R. L. (1991). An applied analysis of buyer equity perceptions and satisfaction with automobile salespeople. *Journal of Personal Selling and Sales Management, 11,* 15−26.

Szymanski, D. M., & Henard, D. H. (2001). Customer satisfaction: A meta-analysis of the empirical evidence. *Journal of the Academy of Marketing Science, 29,* 16−35.

Tanaka, K. (1993). Egocentric bias in perceived fairness: Is it observed in Japan? *Social Justice Research, 6,* 273−285.

Tanaka, K. (1999). Judgments of fairness by just world believers. *The Journal of Social Psychology, 139,* 631−638.

Tata, J., Fu, P. P., & Wu, R. (2003). An examination of procedural justice principles in China and the U.S. *Asia Pacific Journal of Management, 20,* 205−216.

Taylor, S. E., Wood, J. V., & Lichtman, R. R. (1983). It could be worse: Selective evaluation on mental health. *Journal of Social Issues, 39,* 19−40.

Thibaut, J., & Walker, L. (1975). *Procedural justice: A psychological analysis.* Hillsdale, NJ: Lawrence Erlbaum.

Thibaut, J., & Walker, L. (1978). A theory of procedure. *California Law Review, 66,* 541−566.

Triandis, H. C. (1989). The self and social behavior in differing cultural contexts. *Psychological Review, 96,* 506−520.

Tyler, T. R. (1994). Psychological models of the justice motives: antecedents of distributive and procedural justice. *Journal of Personality and Social Psychology, 67* (November), 850−863.

Tyler, T. R., & Smith, H. J. (1998). Social justice and social movements. In D. T. Gilbert, S. T. Fiske, & G. Lindzey (Eds.), *The handbook of social psychology* (Vol. 2, pp. 595−629). New York: Oxford University Press.

Tyler, T. R., Boeckmann, R. J., Smith, H. J., & Huo, Y. J. (1997). *Social justice in a diverse society.* Boulder, CO: Westview Press.

Uehara, S., Nakagawa, T., Mori, T., & Ohbuchi, K. (2012). When does anger evoke self-interest and fairness motives? The moderating effects of perceived responsibility for nNeeds. *Japanese Psychological Research, 54,* 137−149.

van den Bos, K., Lind, E. A., Vermunt, R., & Wilke, H. A. M. (1997). How do I judge my outcome when I do not know the outcome of others? The psychology of the fair process effect. *Journal of Personality and Social Psychology, 72* (November), 1034−1046.

van Dijk, E., & Vermunt, R. (2000). Strategy and fairness in social decision making: Sometimes it pays to be powerless. *Journal of Experimental Social Psychology, 36,* 1−25.

van Lange, P. A. M. (1991). Being better but not smarter than others: The Muhammad Ali effect at work in interpersonal situations. *Personality and Social Psychology Bulletin, 17,* 689−693.

Wood, J. V., Taylor, S. E., & Lichtman, R. R. (1985). Social comparison in adjustment to breast cancer. *Journal of Personality and Social Psychology, 49.*

Zohar, D. (1995). The justice perspective on job stress. *Journal of Organizational Behavior, 16,* 487−495.

Fairness management: Singapore, Malaysia and Thailand

Bang Nguyen, Lyndon Simkin and S F Syed Alwi

Introduction

Like being admitted to the Bar and upon taking the oath to become an attorney, could marketing practitioners of the future be called before the members of a Marketing Council prior to calling themselves marketers? If marketing practitioners were required to be legally qualified to practise marketing management, more consumer fairness and trust should be evident (Nguyen et al., 2014). Consider issues of data collection, monitoring and storage and the mishandling of this information (Deighton, 2005), or issues of favouritism/discrimination of profitable customers over unprofitable ones (Frow, Payne, Wilkinson, & Young, 2011). For the managers who deal with customers on a daily basis, it is a well-known practice to treat some customers differently, but do those managers appreciate the consequences of such a strategy? Scholars suggest customer favouritism leads to unfairness perceptions (e. g. Boulding, Staelin, Ehret, & Johnston, 2005), but not always, as seen in the airline industry (Nguyen & Simkin, 2013). It is essential to consider issues of unfairness and distrust, as they may impact on the way in which regulations and further control are employed by laws and directives (Gershoff, Kivetz, & Keinan, 2012).

Scholars suggest that firms build customer relationships to learn about customers' behaviour (e.g. Boulding et al., 2005). Firms, knowing their customers, favour certain groups over others (Dibb & Meadows, 2004). Focusing on certain important customers can result in more efficient use of marketing resources (Payne, Storbacka, & Frow, 2009). Benefits include improved prospects for better meeting customers' needs, increased interaction and more intimate relationships (Nguyen & Mutum, 2012). However, researchers have recently proposed that treating customers differentially potentially provokes unfairness perceptions due to the unequal distribution of outcomes (Frow et al., 2011). This is the customer relationship management (CRM) paradox.

The purpose of this chapter is to present ways to overcome the customer relationship management paradox and to provide managers with a framework for fairer marketing practices. Specifically, we develop a conceptual framework, considering how to overcome the CRM paradox. Our findings echo the implementation of successful marketing schemes, namely ethical CRM, social marketing and corporate social responsibility (CSR). Our framework will assist firms to consider fairness issues in their organisation and improve the social well-being of customers, stakeholders and the broader markets.

We structure the present chapter as follows: first, we present a brief review of the literatures on the CRM paradox and fairness. Next, we discuss varying cases of unfairness in Singapore, Malaysia and Thailand. Subsequently, we discuss the managerial implications and present five steps for managing the CRM paradox. In our concluding section, we add final comments and present a series of mini-cases for further consideration.

Learning objectives

After reading this chapter, you should be able to:

- understand the relationship between the CRM paradox and fairness;
- explain fairness management in Singapore, Malaysia and Thailand;
- apply the concepts of fairness in order to overcome the CRM paradox; and
- explore fairness in mini case studies with directions for further study.

Route map – fairness management: Singapore, Malaysia and Thailand

In this chapter, we explore the role of fairness in managing customer relationships, and further link fairness with the CRM paradox. This paradox refers to 'the contradictory concept of treating customers individually, yet perceived as unfair due to differential customer treatment leading to inequitably outcomes' (Nguyen et al., 2014, in press). We begin with a theoretical discussion of the current marketing paradigm, followed by discussion on the managerial implications for fairness management in Singapore, Malaysia and Thailand. Next, we present the state of the art in fairness management and the implications for managers. Implementing fairness into the firm's practices is critical to overcome the inherent paradox, which is found in customer relationship management. It is an area that is significantly under-researched, despite its damaging outcomes, caused by negative word-of-mouth and customer retaliation.

The state of the art in fairness management: the CRM paradox

One of the great ideas in marketing is that firms should focus not merely on selling, but rather on meeting and fulfilling customer needs (e.g. Boulding et al., 2005). Meeting customer needs will require firms to think in terms of creating superior value (Luo, Wieseke, & Homburg, 2012). Firms must consider how they can tailor and personalise offerings for the individual customer, ensuring that they remain loyal to the firm's activities (Melnyk & Osselaer, 2012). Over the past decades, managers have pursued this relational approach in an attempt to create competitive advantages, by facilitating customised solutions to customers on an individual basis, most notably in segmentation (Dibb & Simkin, 2009) and relationship building schemes such as CRM (Nguyen & Mutum, 2012) and customer experiences (Klaus & Maklan, 2012).

For example, smartphone applications and other cellular devices connect customers with their vendors, easing not just the way purchases can be made, but also the way that firms collect customer behavioural data (Klaus & Nguyen, 2013). By using sophisticated customer tracking technologies, firms can direct their marketing efforts and attention to customers whom they estimate are able to yield the most profit over their customer-lifetime. These firms will select the customers they want to serve, favour those who are most profitable and devote little marketing budget to customers who do not fit their targeting criterions (Cao & Gruca, 2005). The development of data and tracking technologies is progressing. These technologies, with increased customer monitoring, make it possible to create offerings that no longer follow any particular standard pricing framework, but rather are determined by the individual situation and person (Nguyen & Mutum, 2012). Their marketing is on a one-to-one basis (Peppers & Rogers, 2012).

However, fundamental issues in the search for individual treatment of customers must be addressed. While there are clear benefits of a strategy that favour one customer over another (Fournier, 1998; Frow & Payne, 2009), such practices lead to discrimination against customers (Bolton & Alba, 2006). By targeting and favouring certain customers over others, firms increase the attractiveness of their offerings to one group, neglecting another. Recent research shows that such favouritism and differential treatment of customers may cause perceptions of unfairness (Bolton, Warlop, & Alba, 2003), resulting in buyers opting out of relationships (Dwyer, Schurr, & Oh, 1987), spreading negative information (Xia, Monroe, & Cox, 2004) or engaging in misbehaviour that may damage the firm (Grégoire & Fisher, 2008). Research continues to explain that the favoured and non-favoured customers have different perceptions towards various marketing schemes, and that these customers develop their unfairness based on comparative standards of what they feel that they were entitled to at the time of purchase (Nguyen & Simkin, 2013). In our study, we focus on developing such fairer marketing approaches. Based on the above, we warrant more research into advancing CRM applications in order to better meet customers' needs. However, with this process, careful consideration must be taken regarding the CRM paradox, and how such personalised experiences may affect customers and their perceptions of fairness. Therefore we next explain how fairness is determined.

Perceptions of fairness

Researchers suggest that fairness is 'a judgment of whether an outcome and/or the process to reach an outcome are reasonable, acceptable, or just' (Bolton et al., 2003, p. 474). Fairness is considered a prerequisite for improving relationship quality between buyers and sellers (Oliver & Swan, 1989) and acts as an antecedent of trust (Morgan & Hunt, 1994), increasing the potential for creating cross-sales, up-selling and increasing profits, and for developing a long-term relationship (Ernst, Hoyer, Kraft, & Krieger, 2011).

One of the main theories used to understand fairness is equity theory (e.g. Adams, 1965; Homans, 1961). Equity theory proposes that individuals in social exchange relationships compare each other the ratios of their inputs into the exchange to their outcomes from the exchange. Inequity exists when the perceived inputs and/or outcomes in an exchange relationship are psychologically inconsistent with the perceived inputs and/or outcomes of the referent (Huppertz, Arenson, & Evans, 1978). For example, a customer may feel that they have not received enough promotional deals, compared to the amount of time and money spent with a particular retailer. The customer therefore feels an inconsistent input versus output, and may feel unfairly treated (Haws & Bearden, 2006). Or if a travel customer travels first class, that customer may expect to receive better meals, more space and an overall better experience because of the high price. If these things are not fulfilled compared to those who are travelling business or economy class, or with the last visit, the customer will feel that there is an inconsistency between the perceived input and outcomes, and thus they will be inclined to have perceptions of unfairness.

Various scholars establish several standards to explain fairness, including factors such as: (a) with whom the customers compare each other, (b) the similarity of the previous transaction with the current one, (c) the attributions as to who is responsible for a sudden change in the purchase situation, and (d) general social norms and beliefs (for more, see Xia et al., 2004).

The role of social networking sites, online fora and blogs

The CRM paradox suggests that firms' attempts to build relationships with customers, in order to customise individual services, results in a strategy where one customer receives better treatment than another. These in turn, are the same inequality mechanisms, which may lead to perceptions of unfairness (Campbell, 2007). For example, Amazon's test use of dynamic pricing was a public relations nightmare for the organisation. As they launched their new pricing system, Amazon was quickly revealed to be selling the same DVD movies for different prices to different customers (Adamy, 2000). When customers uncovered the differential pricing, this attempt to implement a new differential pricing structure was met with extreme displeasure, eventually forcing the firm to end the trial. Chat boards were flooded with complaints against the organisation and negative word-of-mouth was widespread, damaging its brand reputation (Cox, 2001). As Feinberg, Krishna, and Zhang (2002) put it: 'Few things stir up a consumer revolt quicker than the notion that someone is getting a better deal. That's a lesson Amazon.com has just learned.' In this case, unfairness was evident because this differential pricing strategy and tracking methods were seen as a violation of society norms.

The idea that someone else is getting a better deal on the same offer can raise eyebrows and evoke dissatisfaction (Feinberg et al., 2002; Smith, Bolton, & Wagner, 1999). Nevertheless, foundations of CRM lie in the fact that separate customers have varying needs and want different products and services − even different prices and ways of promotion. Without careful consideration of any differential treatment of customers, inappropriate and incomplete use of CRM may put the firm at risk of long-term failure (Boulding et al., 2005). While there are no further details to the Amazon case, other than they had to close their discriminatory pricing and apologise, we can only assume that there was also damage to their sales/profit. Certainly, customers would be more suspicious of buying online and dealing with Amazon for some time into the future. The worst-case scenario for Amazon would be customers leaving the firm and developing distrust in the firm − while this is not evidenced in the Amazon case, researchers in unfairness have shown this link (e.g. Campbell, 1999).

To understand how to manage the CRM paradox, it is necessary to understand the concept of transparency. While still in the developing stages, we are moving towards a more perfect and transparent marketplace. Given the increasing use of social networking sites, various Internet fora, blogs, comparison websites, etc., more transparency in vendors' various offerings exists (Kim & Ko, 2012). As a result, customers have more comparative points, potentially leading to more perceptions of unfairness. The use of social media and mobile technologies has been an increasingly effective way for firms to interact with their customers through Facebook, Twitter and YouTube (Kaplan & Haenlein, 2010). Yet these same kinds of devices have revolutionised customers' market knowledge. So while customers are sharing their deals and shopping experiences with their friends and families on social media websites, the opposite may also occur. That is, web-based user-generated content allows customers an easy way to use these technologies − social media, blogs and mobile communication − to share quickly with many fellow peers their displeasure about how they have been poorly treated, damaging firms' brand reputation (Quinton & Harridge-March, 2010).

Next, each of the three countries of Singapore, Malaysia and Thailand will be reviewed with implications for fairness management.

Singapore

In Singapore, cases of unfairness, discrimination and public outcry are often found in several areas, such as nepotism, school admission for the wealthy, fast-track promotion, preferential hiring by nationality, etc. While not entirely unique to Singapore, these issues tend to be more prevalent in a country that greatly supports meritocracy (Singapore Armchair Critic, 2013). Influential bloggers such as the Singapore Armchair Critic (SAC) have published numerous articles on the topic, observing how meritocracy in Singapore has caused great unfairness among its citizens.

For example, American regulators recently opened a probe on the hiring practice of JPMorgan Chase in China. Ongoing investigation has sought to establish if the investment bank's recruitment practices have been favourable towards the offspring of high-ranking and influential Chinese officials ('princelings') as a quid pro quo for coveted business deals. Such practices are prohibited under the Foreign Corrupt Practices Act (FCPA) (SAC, 2013). One case involves the son of a former banking

regulator and the other, the daughter of a now-disgraced railway official. This has
led to speculations of similar practices in Singapore.

New York Times columnist Andrew Ross Sorkin stated that, according to him,
such hiring decisions did not seem unusual: '... given that many of the children of
the elite have some of the best educations and thriving networks of contacts, it is
hard to see how businesses are supposed to not seek them out, let alone turn them
away. As hard to defend as the phrase may be, it is a reality of life — it's not what
you know, but whom you know.'

SAC (2013) comments that the fallacies of Sorkin's argument may be illumi-
nated by the debate over meritocracy, asking: how is meritocracy unfair? Kenneth
Paul Tan, author of *Meritocracy and Elitism in a Global City*, explains that meritocracy, in trying to 'isolate' merit by treating people with fundamentally unequal
backgrounds as superficially the same, may already have allowed some to enjoy
unfair advantages from the very beginning, while others were ignored according to
the principle of non-discrimination. Sorkin notes that meritocracy can be a practice
that ignores and even conceals the real advantages and disadvantages that are
unevenly distributed to different segments of an inherently unequal society, and
suggests that it is a practice that perpetuates this fundamental inequality. Thus, meritocracy, defined as a system that rewards according to ability or achievement and
not birth or privilege, may be unfair precisely because it is blind to differences of
class, wealth and social status.

For example, under Singapore's education system, the concentration of good
schools in good neighbourhoods clearly favours the rich with tuition programmes
that are tailored to affluent families (Beauchamp, 2013). This suggests that if there
are two equally intelligent children, one from a poor family and another from a rich
background, the former has a lower chance of gaining entry into good schools.
SAC (2013) notes that such a passive blindness towards differences aggravates
inequality. It is further suggested that there are policies in place that actively reinforce inherited advantages. An example relates to the preferential access to good
schools given to children of alumni. Experts have thus found that Singapore's education system has the inclination to suppress intergenerational mobility.

Meritocracy, therefore, may be unfair and perpetuate inequality in two ways:
(1) by disregarding class, wealth or status differences on the principle of non-
discrimination; and (2) by deepening differences through discrimination against the
less privileged. Meritocracy is thus akin to giving the rich and privileged a head
start, and deliberately installs obstacles in the way of the disadvantaged.

The hiring practice of investment banks currently under scrutiny proves illustrative.
The *New York Times* reported that, in 2006, JPMorgan initiated a programme called
'Sons and Daughters' to impose proper standards when hiring relatives of China's rul-
ing elite on a separate track. However, the programme subsequently went awry:

> ... in the months and years that followed, the two-tiered process that could have
> prevented questionable hiring practices instead fostered them, according to the
> interviews as well as the confidential government document. Applicants from prom-
> inent Chinese families, interviews show, often faced few job interviews and relaxed

standards. While many candidates met or exceeded the bank's requirements, some
had subpar academic records and lacked relevant expertise.

(SAC, 2013)

The example shows how connections are more important than paper qualifications or relevant expertise. The best person for the job need not be the brightest. In this case, their merit lies in 'opening doors' or, more explicitly, bringing in business deals, and they are rewarded accordingly. Such a scenario can be exacerbated in the society of Singapore. SAC (2013) points out that the good society (supporting its idea of merit) is defined by meritocracy's winners. These must actively promote their own definition in order to gain widespread consensus and support, and control of future prospects for winning and staying in power.

The definition of merit in a self-serving manner, as illustrated with the situation in investment banks, is the flipside of a 'meritocratic' system. In Singapore, the winners possess the absolute control over the definition of merit via ideological state apparatuses such as the media and education, which are the dominant discourse that has been drummed into citizens (SAC, 2013). Their beliefs suggest that the system is inherently just and fair, but that inequality is but a reality of life and the inevitable outcome of globalisation. In addition, the poor are responsible for their own plight and therefore undeserving of help. This set of beliefs is branded as elitism. This is when society's brightest think that they have made good because they are inherently superior and entitled to their success, and do not credit their good fortune to birth and circumstance. Elitism occurs when economic inequality gives rise to social immobility and a growing social distance between the elite and the masses, and when these seek membership of a social class that is exclusive, and not representative of Singapore society (SAC, 2013).

Experts note that if the finance industry has to rely on connections to reap profits, then it does not engage with innovative products that will be rewarded in an open market. It is merely banking on access to the ruling elite to accumulate wealth. This implies that the financial market is a failing and therefore requires government intervention. In addition, the finance sector entrenches inequality by closing its doors to individuals who are not well connected by birth despite being talented and able (SAC, 2013)

Drawing from Wall Street in America, it is suggested that the

... upper crust passes on their connections to their kids, who then use said connec-
tions to acquire a position in finance or some other field where connections are
rewarded. The rare person from the middle or lower class who manages to get a
foot in the door quickly gets assimilated, using the connections he built during his
rise to help his children ... Finance becomes the near-exclusive playground of the
already-wealthy.

(Beauchamp, 2013)

The cost of this self-interested behaviour of one particular sector, is unfairly borne by the entire society. SAC (2013) notes that if nepotism in the guise of meritocracy in one sector already produces inequality, imagine the ramifications if the entire society embraces and even celebrates meritocracy in an uncritical manner. The privileged class' sense of entitlement means that it will resist any redistributive policies – a progressive tax system, more generous social handouts and higher government expenditure on education, etc. – to rein in widening inequality. SAC (2013) observes that this is already happening in Singapore.

Malaysia

In Malaysia, Amin (2013) notes that, in their everyday lives, consumers enter into various types of contracts for the supply of goods or services. However, in most cases these contracts contain terms that are more favourable to traders, and unfair to consumers. Unfair terms are typically found in the form of exemption clauses, which are seen or printed in the receipts, invoices and other sale documents. These standard form contracts are often designed by the traders, thus they are commonly created out of self-interest and are biased, leading to unfair terms for the consumers. These terms may be extremely harsh against consumers, because their rights may be limited or restricted or denied all together.

Malaysian consumers have been haunted with the issue of unfair contract terms for a long time. Despite the introduction of the Consumer Protection Act (CPA) in 1999, the issue remains and has not been properly tackled by the Act. Consumers feel unfairly treated due to a major loophole in Malaysian consumer protection law in the exemption clauses. In most cases, the terms and conditions are offered to consumers on a 'take it or leave it' basis.

Recently, the CPA (Amendment) Act 2010 has been rectified. It notes that the Amendment has adopted the Indian Law Commission Report on Unfair (Procedural and Substantive) Terms in Contract (2006), which divides unfairness into 'procedural' and 'substantive' unfairness. Such a division has not been done in any country so far (Amin, 2013). This case presents the extent to which procedural unfairness and substantive unfairness under a new CPA provide better protection to consumers in terms of getting a fair bargain, and what managers dealing with fairness management should become aware of. In the new law, unfairness is defined as 'a term in a consumer contract which, with regard to all the circumstances, causes a significant imbalance in the rights and obligations of the parties arising under the contract to the detriment of the consumer'. This general test of unfairness inevitably raises difficult issues of interpretation. Amin (2013) suggests that it does not mean that there should be a perfect symmetry between the parties' rights and obligations under the contract, but rather that the law is only concerned with a term that causes 'significant imbalance to the detriment of the consumer'. In other words, the contract should not appear to be too unbalanced towards one party after taking into consideration what the parties have promised to perform for each other.

In terms of the concepts of procedural and substantive unfairness, we note that it is not a new legal concept, and can be found in several literatures. The distinction between procedural and substantive unfairness has also been previously recognised by the court. The Indian Law Commission defines *procedural* unfairness as 'unfairness in the manner in which the terms of the contract are arrived at or are actually entered into by the parties' and states that substantive unfairness as 'a term by itself may be one-sided, harsh or oppressive or unconscionable and therefore unfair'. According to Willet, procedural fairness refers to fairness in the process leading up to the agreement, whereas substantive fairness concerns with fairness in the distribution of substantive rights and obligations under the contracts.

In simple terms, procedural unfairness looks at the process of making a contract, whereas *substantive* unfairness concerns the outcome of the process, that is, the content or substance of the contract. For example, if a consumer were not aware of a particular term due to its typography at the time of signing a contract, this would be an example of procedural unfairness. A good example of substantive unfairness is when a clause in a contract excludes one party from any liability for negligence. The concept is recognised under the common law and is found in the statute on contract law. Other examples of procedural unfairness include the doctrine of duress, undue influence, fraud and misrepresentation, whereas the substantive aspect of contractual fairness includes prohibition of certain contract terms such as restraint of trade. Nonetheless, Amin (2013) states that the two concepts may overlap and, in practice, it is not always easy to distinguish procedural unfairness from substantive unfairness, thus the court is to decide which one is more prevalent.

Substantive unfairness states that a contract or a term of a contract is substantively unfair if the contract or the term of the contract (Amin, 2013): (a) is in itself harsh; (b) is oppressive; (c) is unconscionable; (d) excludes or restricts liability for negligence; and (e) excludes or restricts liability for breach of express or implied terms of the contract without adequate justification. From the above points, it is reasonably clear that substantive unfairness should be focused on the wordings of the contract rather than on the procedure of making contracts.

As noted by Amin (2013), an overdue measure to protect consumers from extensive use of unfair terms in Malaysia has finally materialised with the introduction of the updated CPA (Amendment) Act 2010. It may be considered as major legislative intervention in contractual settings, which is deemed necessary to curb a widespread use of unfair terms in consumer contracts, especially those found in standard form contracts. In particular, the adoption of the Indian Law Commission's approach of dividing unfairness into procedural and substantive measures is unique, having never been done before.

For managers in Malaysia, the fundamental requirement of procedural fairness is to ensure transparency. Transparency requires contractual terms to be expressed in reasonably plain language, legible, and readily available and accessible to any consumer likely to be affected by the terms. Consumers must be provided with adequate information to enable them to make an informed decision. In addition, managers must be aware that the validity of a contract or a term of a contract can now be challenged by consumers on the ground of procedural unfairness or substantives unfairness, or both. Consequently, firms dealing with a standard form contract need to review their procedure before and at the time of signing a contract to ensure transparency and intelligibility. They further need to review all terms in their contracts to avoid contravention with the principles of substantive fairness (Amin, 2013). Overall, transparency should be seen as an incentive for firms to compete with one another more fairly by offering terms that better reflect consumer interest. While it remains to be seen whether this new law delivers significant practical improvement in protecting the legitimate interests of consumers, it does provide adequate means for preventing the continued application of unfair terms in consumer contracts. And in the case of Malaysian consumers, more fairness will be evidenced.

Thailand

In Thailand, examples of price discrimination between local residents and foreigners are not uncommon. As noted by Daoruang (2014), travel writer and editor, Thailand operates with a 'Dual Price System', in which many shopkeepers trick foreign tourists into paying more. Daoruang notes that in Thailand, there is a numbering system that is unique to the Thai language. When a tourist shops, they will often see the price written using Arabic numbers. While this is convenient for the tourist, especially at some tourist attractions in Thailand, many do not know that these places have a two-price system where they charge foreign visitors more than local people (Daoruang, 2014). He comments that:

> Usually the entrance fee is always written using Arabic numbers. If you spot the prices written in Thai numbers and Arabic numbers then for sure there are two prices. I think they do it this way because they are ashamed to let you know they are charging you double. I can't think of any other reason to hide the prices like this.

In other examples, shopkeepers are more cunning by having only one price list. However, reading the sign carefully (in Thai), it might say: '*lot ha-sib baht*' − this means reduce the price by 50 baht, and it will often clearly state that this is only for '*khon Thai*' or Thai people (Daoruang, 2014). Most shopkeepers at roadside stores have a calculator handy so that they can tap out the price for you.

Via various websites and blogs, many foreigners are stating their dissatisfaction. These tourists do not think it is fair that some tourist attractions disguise the fact that they have a dual price system. Daoruang (2014) comments that if they want to overcharge foreign tourists by as much as 200 per cent, then that is their decision. However, they should not do it in a way that is both sneaky and insulting. The case illustrates price unfairness well, and despite the example being in Thailand, it is not the only place in the world, which operates with a dual pricing system. In many ways, the dual pricing system is hurting the image of both the tourism industry and country itself. Thai people are internationally known for their kind and generous hospitality. But with such actions taken by those at a few tourist attractions, that reputation is being damaged. To overcome such discrimination, a more transparent pricing system in Thailand is required.

Conclusion

The propositions in our paper may serve as a guide for improved fairness management and fairer marketing practices, and help managers in implementing better offerings. Understanding unfairness with regard to customer management may equip managers with a better understanding of such issues so that they can deploy a fairer approach to customer management. That will help to minimise costly mistakes and support managers to utilise their resources better, so that they can achieve a sustainable competitive advantage.

Consequences of not addressing fairness in efforts to build relationships with customers are seen as a precursor to mistrust (Heath & Heath, 2008). Both fairness and trust are essential building blocks for successful customer management (Payne et al., 2009) and social marketing (Koschate-Fischer, Stefan, & Hoyer, 2012). If customers lose trust, there will be great problems in further developing applications to collect data in order to customise products and services. Regulations may just be one of the threats that could be imposed on unfair use of technological applications. On the one hand, an organisation would want to learn as much as possible about their customers as possible to fulfil customers' needs and desires, but at the same time, this individual treatment could result in discrimination, inequity and unfairness (Nguyen & Simkin, 2013). This is the paradox in customer relationship management. For managers, a warning follows, in order to emphasise the understanding of fairness and the consequences of how favouring certain customers may stir unfairness. Perhaps, if unfair marketing approaches continue, we may very well experience the rise of marketing practitioners, who are to be called before members of a Marketing Council. And once the marketing oath is taken, only then will they be able to call themselves marketers.

New research directions

Key areas for future research are:

* to empirically link fairness with the CRM paradox, individualisation, personalisation of adverts and the like;
* to link fairness with nepotism, favouritism and elitism;
* to link fairness management with legislative fairness; and
* to develop a multidisciplinary and multidimensional framework of fairness management.

Practising marketing

The following framework summarises the key elements from the present chapter and presents how brand fairness management can be successfully implemented in Singapore, Malaysia and Thailand.

Five steps to creating a fairer organisation

1. Are you ready for fairer one-to-one marketing?

In order to avoid a fairness fad or other disastrous outcomes, you must prepare the communications infrastructure and procedures for appropriate data handling in your organisation to create awareness about the consequences of unfairness. The first step for any organisation is to ensure that there are CRM systems to identify profitable customers, but, at the same time, to ensure sufficient communication about issues of fairness between all levels in the organisation, so that knowledge and information can be shared. A typical prerequisite to developing a fairer organisation is the use of knowledge management (KM) practices.

2. How well can your organisation adopt a fairer approach?

Make sure that you coordinate and convey the message to the involved parties or you could have a half-hearted effort, wasting both time and money. The second step is to identify the key groups within the organisation who deal with customers on a daily basis. Typically, this will be front-office; however, conveying the fairness message should not be limited to this group specifically. Since the creation of a fair organisation requires engagement and influence from senior management, a change in firms' philosophy towards fairer customer management may start from here with an overall strategic focus.

3. Can your organisation differentiate the fairness training from other corporate courses?

Implement training, but do not fall into the trap of inducing more corporate meetings and training that irritates your employees. As part of an ongoing effort for fairness, training must be implemented. The third step is to supplement the input from senior management with training for front-office. Depending on the nature of the organisation, a number of training and coaching sessions can be combined with customer service training and fairness. Fairness is not just a philosophy. Any practical marketing and sales training could incorporate advice into how the message of fairness may be passed on to end-customers in different ways. As far as we know, there are currently no training programmes like this; a new fairness-training programme should be developed. This 'gap' is nevertheless interesting in itself.

4. How well do you interact and develop interest in the implementation among your customers?

It is important that customers are involved in the implementation of the organisation's fairness efforts. Make them realise that your fairness efforts are changing the way business is done and that you are the leading power. The fourth step deals with specific efforts directed at generating further interest from customers. An example could be to conduct customer focus groups and surveys in order to understand how customers define fairness and what they expect from a fair organisation. Additionally, promotional activities such as leaflets or events may be organised to attract further interest. Involving customers is one of the best approaches for improving customer engagement. The aim must be on dual-value creation. Effectively, this means incorporating (and to some extent, partnering) with the customers in order to improve the learning relationship, understand the customers' needs better and create 'win-win' situations. In pragmatic terms, this means bringing customers into the firm, as a partner, to learn what their needs are. Subsequently, more personalised offers can be made to the benefit of the customers. For the firm, a clear benefit is increased customer data, decreasing customer switching and raising the fairness level and quality.

5. Does your organisation truly support fairness and effectively evaluate and monitor progress?

Wasted efforts are the number one enemy in any organisation. To avoid this, the final step is to monitor the implementation and address any issues that may have come up after the implementation. Ongoing checks with customers about their perceptions of fairness should be carried out and, possibly, benchmarked against a fairness scale that should have been developed in earlier stages. Remember that your customers and the community will appreciate your efforts. For example, using the FairServ scale (Carr, 2007) and FAIRQUAL scale (Nguyen & Simkin, 2012) may help benchmark the firm's own fairness quality with that of the competition. The FAIRQUAL measure is designed as an identification tool, so that companies can have a framework to consider and implement fairer approaches to their marketing efforts in areas that are perceived as unfair. As an instrument that looks into varying dimensions of fairness, it may be used to track customers' perceptions of (un)fairness more systematically. Each dimension can be analysed individually or to create an overall perceived level of unfairness. Consequently, it may be useful to categorise customers according to their perceived level of (un)fairness of the firm. The use of the FAIRQUAL is mainly to benchmark several clusters of companies in order to track their reputation and image from a customer perspective.

Practice mini cases

Examples of favouritism

- The super popular Thai beer Singha had promotional events by holding free beer-tastings exclusively for bartenders.
- Victoria's Secret distributed catalogues with different prices for the same goods based on the buyers' demographics and zip codes.
- Amazon experimented with different prices for different customers.
- Tesco provided discounts to loyalty card members but not to non-members.
- A local newspaper in Malaysia offered a 60 per cent subscription discount to residents of nearby community, but not to its other customers.

- Pillsbury (a grain producer) provided the option of buying a collector's plate at a reduced price to buyers of its product; this option is presumably valuable to collectors but not to others.

Examples of the CRM paradox – differential treatment

Same product, different environment and different prices: Coca-Cola once introduced a vending machine that could detect the outside air temperature and adjust prices accordingly (Leonhardt, 2005). While colder days stabilised regular prices, a hot day meant higher prices, as a computer chip automatically measured the temperature in the area. Soft drink enthusiasts were reeling at news that Coca-Cola Co. had developed the technology designed to boost prices automatically in Coke machines on hot days when demand went up. Such a cynical ploy to exploit the thirst of faithful customers when they were most susceptible to price gouging was seen as shameful and rejected immediately. When word of the scheme got out, Coca-Cola's PR agents denied plans to put such a machine in the marketplace. But the company's chief executive, Mr Douglas Ivester, had tipped his hand earlier that month when he told a Brazilian magazine that because the demand for a cold Coke increases on hot days, 'it is fair that it should be more expensive. The machine will simply make this process automatic.'

Same product, different customers and different prices: CRM systems can punish loyal customers, as they attempt to attract new customers with offers. This happens largely in mobile subscriptions and with service providers of broadband, gas and electricity. Such favouritism of certain customers over others is often perceived as unfair (by the loyal customers). An example is when high-priority customers are offered additional and superior services over other customers, because of their economic attractiveness. Such cases may or may not lead to fairness – it depends on other factors.

Same product, same customers and different prices: CRM systems can punish loyal and highly valuable customers whose circumstances temporarily change. This could be an airline gold cardholder, who often travels overseas on business. But due to a temporary reassignment to work that requires less travelling, this valuable customer may be demoted to the lowest level in a frequent flyer CRM scheme.

Examples of the CRM paradox – expert favouritism

- The manufacturer of Fastskin, a product designed to help competitive swimmers go through the water faster, gave away its product to all the Olympic teams, but not to other swimmers. Consumers – even though they are being disadvantaged – did not have feelings of unfairness, because they saw the professional swimmers as experts in their field, so the consumers actually preferred to be disadvantaged in this case.
- Many investors find financial offerings difficult to evaluate. Imagine an opportunity to create promotions that would appeal only to highly knowledgeable investors (experts) to signal the quality of the financial product. This could be a way to attract the non-targeted (non-expert) customers.

- Similarly, sellers of 'difficult-to evaluate' electronics may offer lucrative trade-ins to current owners, whom new customers consider informed users.
- In all these cases, sellers must decide between a promotion that has mass appeal and a promotion that attracts a niche segment. Research suggests that under certain circumstances, a niche promotion that fits targeted consumers can more effectively attract both the targeted and the non-targeted customers. This is contrary to the common consensus, which advocates equitable treatment to prevent consumer outrage.

Case study – SAS

In 2006, booking online for a seat on a flight from Copenhagen to Madrid with Scandinavian Airlines (SAS) cost around US$165 – that is, if you lived in the USA. If you lived in Denmark and booked via their online system, the same flight would have cost US$436. In other words, a Dane had to pay three times as much as an American for the same European flight and this was not even a one-time special offer for the Americans (Dukes, 2006). Rather, this differential treatment of customers and dynamic pricing initiative was part of the SAS online booking system, which quoted different prices depending on the customers' country of residence when they logged on. This was not received well by customers, and when the consumer advocacy groups in Denmark demanded an explanation, SAS claimed that there was a problem with the software and this 'glitch' was to blame.

The outcome of this case was embarrassment for the company. Such practices were not well received, creating complaints and outrage. The brand and reputation were damaged. Future purchases will be met with suspicion and it may take a long time before SAS will be able to restore the trust between itself and its customers.

Questions

1. Are similar examples found in other industries and countries? Name as many as possible.
2. What can fairness management do to overcome nepotism, elitism and discrimination?
3. In which way does fairness management incorporate laws and legislation?
4. Is marketing part of fairness management or is fairness management part of marketing? What is the relationship here between the two?

References

Adams, J. S. (1965). Inequity in social exchange. In L. Berkowitz (Ed.), *Advances in experimental social psychology* (Vol. 2, pp. 267–299). New York: Academic Press.

Adamy, J. (2000). E-tailer price tailoring may be wave of future. *Chicago Tribune, section 4* (25) September, 4

Amin, N. (2013). Protecting consumers against unfair contract terms in Malaysia: The consumer protection (amendment) act 2010. *Malayan Law Journal Articles, 1*, 1–11.

Beauchamp, Z. (2013). How Wall Street nepotism creates market failure. 20 August, <http://thinkprogress.org/economy/2013/08/20/2497591/wall-street-nepotism>.

Bolton, L. E., & Alba, J. W. (2006). Price fairness: Good and service differences and the role of vendor costs. *Journal of Consumer Research, 33*(2), 258–265.

Bolton, L. E., Warlop, L., & Alba, J. W. (2003). Consumer perceptions of price (un)fairness. *Journal of Consumer Research, 29*, 474–491.

Boulding, W., Staelin, R., Ehret, M., & Johnston, W. J. (2005). A customer relationship management roadmap: What is known, potential pitfalls, and where to go. *Journal of Marketing, 69*(4), 155–166.

Campbell, M. C. (1999). Perceptions of price unfairness: Antecedents and consequences. *Journal of Marketing Research, 36*(5), 187–199.

Campbell, M. C. (2007). Says who?! How the source of price information and affect influence perceived price (un)fairness. *Journal of Marketing Research, 44*(5), 261–271.

Cao, Y., & Gruca, T. S. (2005). Reducing adverse selection through customer relationship management. *Journal of Marketing, 69*(10), 219–229.

Carr, C. L. (2007). The FAIRSERV model: Consumer reactions to services based on a multidimensional evaluation of service fairness. *Decision Sciences, 38*(1), 107–130.

Cox, J. L. (2001). Can differential price be fair? *Journal of Product & Brand Management, 10*(5), 264–275.

Daoruang, P. (2014). Dual pricing system in Thailand – giving tourists the right to choose. Available from <http://www.2pricethailand.com/how-they-trick-foreign-tourists-into-paying-more>.

Deighton, J. (2005) Privacy and customer management. *Customer Management*, (MSI conference summary) (pp. 17–19). Cambridge, MA: Marketing Science Institute.

Dibb, S., & Meadows, M. (2004). Relationship marketing and CRM: A financial services case study. *Journal of Strategic Marketing, 12*, 111–125.

Dibb, S., & Simkin, L. (2009). Implementation rules to bridge the theory/practice in marketing segmentation. *Journal of Marketing Management, 25*(3/4), 375–396.

Dukes, A. J. (2006). Tailor-made prices. *Phi Kappa Phi Forum, 86*(3) <http://www.questia.com/magazine/1G1-151652179/tailor-made-prices>.

Dwyer, F. R., Schurr, P. S., & Oh, S. (1987). Developing buyer-seller relationships. *Journal of Marketing, 51*(2), 11–27.

Ernst, H., Hoyer, W. D., Kraft, M., & Krieger, K. (2011). Customer relationship management and company performance – the mediating role of new product. *Journal of the Academy of Marketing Science, 39*(2), 290–306.

Feinberg, F. M., Krishna, A., & Zhang, Z. J. (2002). Do we care what others get? A behaviourist approach to targeted promotions. *Journal of Marketing Research, 39*(3), 277–291.

Fournier, S. (1998). Consumers and their brands: Developing relationship theory in consumer research. *Journal of Consumer Research, 24*(4), 343–373.

Frow, P. E., & Payne, A. F. (2009). Customer relationship management: A strategic perspective. *Journal of Business Market Management, 3*(1), 7–27.

Frow, P. E., Payne, A., Wilkinson, I. F., & Young, L. (2011). Customer management and CRM: Addressing the dark side. *Journal of Services Marketing, 25*(2), 79–89.

Gershoff, A., Kivetz, R., & Keinan, A. (2012). Consumer response to versioning: How brands' production methods affect perceptions of unfairness. *Journal of Consumer Research, 39*(2), 382–398.

Grégoire, Y., & Fisher, R. J. (2008). Customer betrayal and retaliation: When your best customers become your worst enemies. *Journal of the Academy of Marketing Science, 36* (2), 247–261.

Haws, K. L., & Bearden, W. O. (2006). Dynamic pricing and consumer fairness perceptions. *Journal of Consumer Research, 33*, 304–311.

Heath, M. T. P., & Heath, M. (2008). (Mis)trust in marketing: A reflection on consumers' attitudes and perceptions. *Journal of Marketing Management*, 24(9−10), 1025−1039.

Homans, G. C. (1961). *Social behavior: Its elementary forms*. New York: Harcourt, Brace and World.

Huppertz, J. W., Arenson, S. J., & Evans, R. H. (1978). An application of equity theory to buyer-seller exchange situations. *Journal of Marketing Research*, 15(2), 250−260.

Kaplan, A., & Haenlein, M. (2010). Users of the world unite. The challenges and opportunities of social media. *Business Horizons*, 53(1), 59−68.

Kim, A. J., & Ko, E. (2012). Do social media marketing activities enhance customer equity? An empirical study of luxury fashion brand. *Journal of Business Research*, 65(10), 1480−1486.

Klaus, P., & Maklan, S. (2012). EXQ: A multiple-scale for assessing service experience. *Journal of Service Management*, 23(1), 5−33.

Klaus, P., & Nguyen, B. (2013). Exploring the role of the online customer experience in the firm's multichannel strategy − an empirical analysis of the retail banking sector. *Journal of Strategic Marketing*, 21(5), 429−442.

Koschate-Fischer, N., Stefan, I., & Hoyer, W. (2012). Willingness to pay for cause-related marketing: The impact of donation amount and moderating effects. *Journal Of Marketing Research*, 49(6), 910−927.

Leonhardt, D. (2005). Why variable pricing fails at the vending machine. *The New York Times*, 27.06.05. <http://www.nytimes.com/2005/06/27/business/27consuming.html?_r=0&adxnnl=1&adxnnlx=1407071067-KNdh2Y/JFROe3ZdiR38pKg>.

Luo, X., Wieseke, J., & Homburg, C. (2012). Incentivizing CEOs to build customer- and employee-firm relations for higher customer satisfaction and firm value. *Journal of the Academy of Marketing Science*, 40(6), 745−758.

Melnyk, V., & Osselaer, S. (2012). Make me special: Gender differences in consumers' responses to loyalty programs. *Marketing Letters*, 23(3), 545−559.

Morgan, R. M., & Hunt, S. D. (1994). The commitment-trust theory of relationship marketing. *Journal of Marketing*, 58(3), 20−38.

Nguyen, B., Lee-Wingate, N., & Simkin, L. (2014) The customer relationship management paradox: five steps to create a fairer organization. *Social Business*, 4(3), 207−230.

Nguyen, B., & Mutum, D. A. (2012). A review of customer relationship management: Success, advances, pitfalls and futures. *Business Process Management Journal*, 18(3), 400−419.

Nguyen, B., & Simkin, L. (2012). Fairness quality: The role of fairness in a social and ethically oriented marketing landscape. *The Marketing Review*, 12(4), 333−334.

Nguyen, B., & Simkin, L. (2013). The dark side of CRM: Advantaged and disadvantaged customers. *Journal of Consumer Marketing*, 30(1), 17−30.

Oliver, R. L., & Swan, J. E. (1989). Consumer perceptions of interpersonal equity and satisfaction in transactions: A field survey approach. *Journal of Marketing*, 53(2), 21−35.

Payne, A., Storbacka, K., & Frow, P. (2009). Co-creating brands: Diagnosing and designing the relationship experience. *Journal of Business Research*, 62(3), 379−389.

Peppers, D., & Rogers, M. (2012). *Managing customer relationships − a strategic framework*. New Jersey: John Wiley and Sons.

Quinton, S., & Harridge-March, S. (2010). Relationships in on line communities: The potential for marketers. *The Journal of Research in Interactive Marketing*, 4(1), 56−73.

Singapore Armchair Critic (2013). How meritocracy entrenches inequality. 9 September, <http://singaporearmchaircritic.wordpress.com/2013/09/09/how-meritocracy-entrenches-inequality>.

Smith, A. K., Bolton, R. N., & Wagner, J. (1999). A model of customer satisfaction with service encounters involving failure and recovery. *Journal of Marketing Research, 36*(4), 356–372.

Srinivasan, R., & Moorman, C. (2005). Strategic firm commitments and rewards for customer relationship management in online retailing. *Journal of Marketing, 69*(6), 193–200.

Xia, L., Monroe, K. B., & Cox, J. L. (2004). The price is unfair! A conceptual framework of price fairness perceptions. *Journal of Marketing, 68*(6), 1–15.

Fairness management: India, Pakistan and Bangladesh 12

Bang Nguyen, Lyndon Simkin and Sanjit Kumar Roy

Introduction

Research into the dark side of branding and marketing has grown substantially. This stream of research suggests that the marketing landscape today is dominated with suspicion and distrust as a result of practices that include hidden fees, deception, manipulation and information mishandling. In such a pessimistic economy, marketers are re-conceptualising the notion of brand fairness in marketing and customer management, so that the progress and advancements in marketing can flourish, avoiding further control and imposed regulation. Scholars suggest that to succeed in today's competitive markets, it is not enough to focus on customers' needs and wants, but rather, to recognise that over the long term, they must adopt a more ethical and social perspective. This approach has called for the emphasis on fairness management of brands in order to develop and enhance beneficial relationships with business partners, customers, communities, employees, governments and regulators, and investors (Ghoshal, 2005). The emphasis on fairness among stakeholders results in reinforcing trust, devotion and loyalty, and ultimately long-term success (Nguyen & Simkin, 2012). This, in turn, leads to the fair approaches of 'enlightened customer management' (Frow, Payne, Wilkinson, & Young, 2011) and 'enlightened market orientation' (Roy & Pratik, 2014).

Over the past two decades, marketing has undergone fundamental shifts (Boulding, Staelin, Ehret, & Johnston, 2005), from transactional to relational approaches. In the early 1990s, marketing academics and practitioners realised that there were inherent problems, such as negative societal consequences, which required the adoption of different approaches to marketing. The marketing profession thus shifted towards taking a more ethically and socially responsible perspective. The American Marketing Association's (AMA) Code of Ethics emphasises marketers' responsibility toward all stakeholders for example, customers, employees, investors, channel members, regulators and the community, highlighting that their actions and decisions should be of value to all. In response to the criticism of marketing as being unethical, research into fairness management has increased substantially.

In the present chapter, fairness is defined as 'a judgment of whether an outcome and/or the process to reach an outcome are reasonable, acceptable, or just' (Bolton,

Warlop, & Alba, 2003: 474). The focus is specifically on brand fairness, suggesting the management of fairness in the context of both consumer and firm level brands. Brand fairness is considered a prerequisite for improving consumer-brand relationship quality and acts as an antecedent of trust, commitment and loyalty (Morgan & Hunt, 1994). Consumers' brand fairness perceptions increase the potential for creating cross-sales, up-selling and profits, and developing a long-term relationship (Ernst, Hoyer, Kraft, & Krieger, 2011).

Learning objectives

After reading this chapter, you should be able to:

- understand the role and shift towards brand fairness management;
- explain criticism towards marketing and the role of fairness;
- describe brand fairness management in India, Pakistan and Bangladesh;
- apply the concepts of brand fairness management; and
- link fairness with enlightened market orientation (hereafter, EMO).

Route map — fairness management: India, Pakistan and Bangladesh

In this chapter, we explore the role of fairness in managing brands, and further link brand fairness with the concept of EMO — that is, firms' cares for consumer well-being and the incorporation of a higher purpose that transcends profit maximisation (George, 2014; Roy & Pratik, 2014). Linking fairness to EMO is a strong response to the current marketing paradigm, and could be the next source of competitive advantage. Following the theoretical discussion, we discuss the implications for fairness management in India, Pakistan and Bangladesh. Although brand managers implicitly emphasise the importance of fairness in branding strategies, brand management emphasising fairness and its impact on consumer behaviour is little researched, in particular in the Asian context (Chen, Nguyen, & Klaus, 2013). Scholars posit that fairness and unfairness are explained by the same set of underpinning theories, but may also be conceptually different constructs (Xia, Monroe, & Cox, 2004). Consumers often know when they see or experience unfairness, but it is more difficult to articulate what is fair. In the current chapter, we explore the roles of both fairness and unfairness in changing the marketing landscape. We subsequently develop a framework to manage unfairness in order to induce brand fairness. While the cases illustrate the contexts of India, Pakistan and Bangladesh, the framework may be applied to other Asian countries.

Next, we present the state of the art in brand fairness management and the implications for brand managers. Implementing fairness into the firms' branding practices increases the likelihood that consumers perceive the brand as being fairer, leading to desirable consumer behaviour, such as an increase in loyalty and positive word-of-mouth.

The state of the art in fairness management: a brand fairness perspective

Scholars suggest that the marketing function suffers from major problems related to both effectiveness and reputation-wise (Jost & Kay, 2010; Roy & Pratik, 2014). Sheth and Sisodia (2002) demonstrate that over the last decade, the marketing function has stagnated and declined in productivity. Roy and Pratik (2014) suggest that bad marketing is financially wasteful and has severe negative consequences for society. These authors note that the marketing profession, for example, has played a major part in the unconscionable denigration and objectification of women in society, and the ways in which women are portrayed in advertising has contributed to many serious problems among teenagers and young women, including eating disorders, feelings of worthlessness, depression, self-injury and suicide (Kilbourne, 2000).

Other accusations of marketing's negative influence on society include the following.

1. Irresponsible behaviour towards children. It is said that products are marketed to children aggressively, despite companies' knowledge of their harmfulness to the children's psyches or physical well-being. For example, scholars note that marketing aimed at children, is subversive and destructive to healthy development, as it promotes excessive materialism, the consumption of inappropriate products (such as video games with inappropriate content deliberately marketed to young children). In addition, many factors encourage and exploit what the industry calls 'the nag factor' and 'pester power' to get parents to buy things that their children have been conditioned to demand (Linn, 2005).
2. Obesity and type II diabetes afflicting countries all over the world. Instead of contributing to the social good, firms exploit the customers' needs and nurture their desires for good tasting but unhealthy food. These firms stimulate the consumption of foods that contain high levels of fat, sugar and chemicals, such as foods that lack nutrition – for example, soft drinks, juice drinks, energy drinks – while excessively large portions also are on the menu (Schlosser, 2001).
3. Marketing is further accused to contribute greatly to the cultural and environmental pollution, experienced worldwide. Cultural pollution include excessive amount of advertising, which drowns the beneficial messages that consumers would otherwise value. Excessive advertising has reduced the attention span of individual consumers. As marketer seeks to get as much attention span as they can, consumers have stopped paying attention to even beneficial communications (Sisodia & Backer, 2004). In addition, environmental degradation refers to the encouraging of excessive and mindless consumption, without concern to sustainability or negative environmental impact. The problem is inherent to marketing, as its objective is typically to maximise consumption, consequently disregarding the impact of the greater good.
4. More recently, researchers note that individual treatment of customers has caused concern for excessive favouritism, leading to unequal distribution of outcomes. For example, one of the great ideas in marketing is that firms should not merely focus on selling, but rather on meeting and fulfilling customer needs (e.g. Boulding et al., 2005). Meeting customer needs requires firms to think in terms of creating superior value (Luo, Wieseke, & Homburg, 2012) by tailoring and personalising offerings for the individual customer, making s/he remain loyal to their activities (Melnyk & Osselaer, 2012). However, individual treatment of customers

may potentially cause problems. By targeting and favouring certain customers over others, firms increase the attractiveness of their offerings to one group, neglecting another. Recent research shows that such favouritism and differential treatment of customers may cause perceptions of unfairness (Bolton et al., 2003), resulting in buyers opting out of relationships (Dwyer, Schurr, & Oh, 1987), spreading negative information (Xia et al., 2004), or engaging in misbehaviour that may damage the firm (Grégoire & Fisher, 2008).

5. Researchers find that the majority of consumers hold negative and even hostile views of marketing. Yankelovich (2014) conducted a study to determine contemporary consumer attitudes towards marketing practices and found that an overwhelming majority of respondents held negative attitudes towards marketing. Results suggested that over 60 per cent said that their opinion of marketing and advertising had declined over the previous years. Sixty-one per cent described the amount of marketing and advertising as 'out of control'. Nearly half the respondents said that the amount of marketing they were exposed to was detrimental to their experience of everyday life. In a different study, Sheth et al. (2006) found similar results when they surveyed consumers and business professionals about the image of marketing, with 65 per cent of consumers found to have a negative attitude towards marketing, 27 per cent being neutral and only 8 per cent positive. When asked to describe what they thought of when they heard the word 'marketing', respondents most commonly used words such as 'telemarketing', 'lies', 'deception', 'manipulative', 'gimmicks', 'exaggeration', 'invasive', 'intrusive' and 'brainwashing'.

Based on the above, we highlight the importance of more research conducted to advance different perspectives of marketing and how it should be managed. In the next section, we propose that adopting a fairness perspective to managing brands and marketing may lead to a more moral-based and enlightened approach to marketing (Frow et al., 2011).

Brand fairness

Fairness is one of the most important aspects in lasting customer relationships and desirable marketing outcomes. Fairness is conceptualised to include transparency, honesty and morality. The economic downturn has proved that opportunistic behaviour cannot be the agenda, where one party takes any opportunity to take advantage over another group. Instead, that just, trust, reason and fairness should be imposed in any business situation, starting with the way customers are handled and treated (Chapuis, 2012; Michell, Reast, & Lynch, 1998). Marketers must take responsibility. Next, each of the three countries of India, Pakistan and Bangladesh are reviewed with implications for brand fairness management.

India

The Alliance for Fair Trade with India (AFTI), headed by the National Association of Manufacturers (NAM), the US Chamber of Commerce and a dozen other industry groups in the USA, accused the government of India to discriminate systematically against a wide range of US innovative products and exports. The Alliance blames unfair actions and laws for benefitting India's business and industrial community at the expense of American jobs. They further note their support towards India's economic growth, but not through unfair trade practices that harm the USA (Minter, 2013).

India is accused of engaging in a variety of practices such as raising tariffs, imposing local content requirements, and revoking or denying patents and failing to respect global intellectual property (IP) standards. At a press briefing, Linda Dempsey, NAM's Vice President for International Economic Affairs, noted that several of its actions appear to violate rules set up by the World Trade Organization, as they have no other purpose than to give domestic corporations in India an unfair advantage over manufacturers and workers in the United States. NAM President and CEO, Jay Timmons, comments that India's recent discriminatory and unfair actions were harming American jobs and said his organisation was committed to ensuring that India abides by global trade rules to protect America's competitiveness (Minter, 2013).

With a US$1.8 trillion GDP and a rising middle class, India is considered a promising market for US exports. From 1992 to 2012, India's exports to the USA grew tenfold, to US$38 billion. India is now the fourth largest trading partner of the USA, with US$60 billion in annual trade volume. However, Linda Dempsey warned that India's current practices would harm its economy by discouraging foreign investment and impede its efforts to grow its manufacturing sector and promote innovation and sustainable development (Minter, 2013). Mark Elliot, Executive Vice President of the US Chamber of Commerce's Global Intellectual Property Center (GIPC), stated that Indian policies and recent judicial decisions regarding intellectual property rights have cast a daunting shadow over India's otherwise promising business environment.

Recently, the GIPC issued an international index designed to assess the intellectual property systems of 11 countries. The index revealed that India consistently ranked last behind Brazil, China and Russia on nearly every indicator.

Elliot state that India's IP policies affected a wide range of US industries, from motion pictures to telecommunications. For example, the rate of reported software piracy in 2010 in India was estimated to be 64 per cent, with a commercial value of US$1.4 billion (Minter, 2013). In addition, the pharmaceutical industry has been hit by a series of patent violations. In March 2012, an Indian agency granted a compulsory licence for an Indian company to manufacture a generic version of Bayer's Nexavar, a cancer drug, on the grounds that Nexavar was too expensive for Indian patients to afford. In another case, the Indian Supreme Court denied a patent to Novartis for Glivec, a leukaemia drug, despite the fact that its patent was recognised in more than 40 other countries (Minter, 2013). While the costs of Western drugs are frequently cited by Indian officials as a rational for local production, Novartis distributed Glivec to 95 per cent of leukaemia patients for free and the drug was heavily subsidised for the remaining group (Minter, 2013).

The above case indicates a perceived unfair situation at the international trade level. With regulations and restrictions, the government of India has created an unfair advantage, which is not well received by its competition. In this case, India is putting itself at risk by getting bad publicity and decreasing the goodwill of its partners, which in turn affects its country brand. The case illustrates how discrimination and favouring of one stakeholder over another, causes unfairness perceptions. To overcome these unfairness perceptions, the AFTI is calling for the Obama Administration to engage in high-level diplomatic efforts to put an end to these practices, suggesting that they wish a level playing field and a fair shake in India. At this strategic level, fairness may be achieved by responding purposefully, using all available trade tools and diplomatic engagement. Long-term fairness involves transparency, dual creation of value and increased consciousness among not only the customers but also all other stakeholders (Minter, 2013).

Drawing from the study of conscious capitalism (Sisodia, Wolfe, & Sheth, 2007) and customer advocacy (Urban, 2004), Roy and Pratik (2014) developed the concept of 'enlightened market orientation' in response to the extensive consumer criticism of marketing. Conscious capitalism has two key elements: (1) companies should articulate a higher purpose that transcends profit maximisation; and (2) companies should be managed for the benefit of all stakeholders in their ecosystem, not just shareholders. The rise of conscious capitalism (Aburdene, 2005; Mackey, 2007) reflects people's higher levels of consciousness about themselves and the world around them. This is due to natural evolution and the rapid aging of society, which have resulted in a higher proportion of people in mid-life and beyond. As consciousness is raised, people all over the world place great demands for transparency on companies using the Internet to accelerate this trend.

> *To be conscious means to be awake, mindful. To live consciously means to be open to perceiving the world around and within us, to understand our circumstances, and to decide how to respond to them in ways that honor our needs, values, and goals... A conscious business fosters peace and happiness in the individual, respect and solidarity in the community, and mission accomplishment in the organisation.*
>
> *(Kofman, 2006)*

In their working paper, Roy and Pratik (2014) note that marketing needs a new paradigm because 'business as usual' has its problems: public distrust is increasing; concerns are directed towards environmental sustainability; employees and customers are disconnected from the companies; suppliers are squeezed; and communities arrange to keep certain businesses out. The traditional approach to business is no longer adequate and needs to be replaced to the new market demands. This is in line with Urban (2004) as cited in Roy and Pratik (2014: p. 262), who state that:

> *'traditionally marketing has been based on the push/pull model whereby a manufacturer creates products/services and fulfils a need and then adopts aggressive communications and distribution strategies to convince customers to buy. However, the rise of customer power as a result of the growth of the internet and other newer technologies has altered the way in which companies target their customers.*

Researchers state that in the present times, customers can validate a company's marketing offerings and make informed decisions based on their own knowledge and peer-review groups. Customers are no more the passive recipients of company's offerings and marketing messages; they want to define value in their own terms and be a part of the whole process of value creation, delivery and ultimate use.

Sheth, Sisodia, and Barbulescu (2006) state that despite its deteriorating reputation, marketing has the capability to solve customers' problems, support their decisions and at the same time build higher levels of trust, accountability and transparency. Marketing has the power to enhance or to diminish overall well-being in society. With its power and influence, it is suggested that marketing embraces responsibility and 'stewardship'/trusteeship. The potential for companies to create value and make major contributions to solving some of society's problems are achieved with a greater sense of responsibility and consciousness.

Companies that practice enlightened market orientation embody the ideas of brand fairness and trust, and recognise that long-term survival links profit and prosperity with social justice and environmental stewardship. These firms operate with a systems view, recognising the connectedness and interdependence of all stakeholders. Companies practising EMO tap into deeper sources of positive energy and create greater value for all stakeholders, including customers, investors, suppliers, environment and societies. By utilising creative business models that are both transformational and inspirational, firms can help solve many of the social and environmental problems faced by the world today. For companies in India, we offer some EMO practices as follows.

1. Firms must identify a higher purpose than simply profit maximisation or shareholder returns. They must realise that it is not about creating and exploiting short-term desires, but rather to address important needs of society and individuals. A mission and purpose built around fairness, ethics and social will energise the firm, and develop passion and creativity among the employees. With an enlightened purpose, the firm may exist beyond its profit-making objective and creates meaning for all stakeholders. It further contributes to attract customers, motivate employees and inspire investors, who share common belief systems. Every firm must find, articulate and continually renew its unique mission and enlightened purpose through EMO.

2. Firms must exist and be managed for the benefit of all stakeholders. Managers must optimise the health of the overall 'ecosystem', recognising the connectedness and interdependence of all stakeholders in the society.

3. Managers must join and align the interests of each stakeholder and develop long-term relationships. This can be accomplished by emphasising value creation for all the involved parties, rather than working opportunistically to increase own profits. Such relational approach will create a win-win situation for both customers and firms alike.

4. Firms must not act opportunistically or engage in exploitation of any kind − that is, they should not take advantage of the stakeholders to advance their own interests by misusing people's fears and addictions. Instead, firms must adopt the mindset of stakeholder well-being in order to better serve them better.

5. Society must be considered as the ultimate stakeholder. Firms must realise that their responsibility is to advance the well-being of society as a whole. When firms are motivated and have the desire to help solve large societal problems in partnership with governments, other companies and non-governmental organisations, the resulting outcome can only be beneficial for everyone. Thus, firms are not costs but rather profitable to the society.

6. Firms must put emphasis on environmental sustainability to improve their goodwill. Hawken, Lovins, and Lovins (1999) suggest the notion of 'natural capitalism', referring to firms' responsibility for the environmental impact − such an approach must be adopted to achieve EMO. The objective is to 'do no harm' to the earth, and to strive to have a net *positive* impact on the environment.

7. Firms must approach the marketplace with a 'whole pyramid' model that seeks to uplift rather than ignore (or exploit) the poorer sections of the society.

8. Finally, firms must intrinsically believe that doing the right things ultimately brings improved results. While profit may be seen as a good measure and natural outcome success, the firm must adopt other measures and focus on the overall activities that benefit all stakeholders.

According to Roy and Pratik (2014), EMO recognises the connectedness and interdependence all the players in the company's ecosystem. Marketing, which incorporates fairness, has the power and force to benefit society. The larger the company, the more its marketing impact is on society and popular culture. EMO is defined as the practice of marketing with a higher level of consciousness about its purpose and its broader and long-term impacts on everyone involved in the process. It is the marketing with a conscience. It is about marketing that is driven by a primary concern for the customers' well-being, rather than with selling as much as possible. It advocates for the best interests of not only the customers, but all of the stakeholders involved.

Linking brand fairness to EMO is only sensible due to their common emphasis for the good. In combination, the two concepts advocate just and reason for customers, companies and societies. According to Davis (2002), EMO highlights 'healing' rather than a 'hucksterism' mindset of businesses. This is more important than ever, as people view marketing as consisting of gimmicks. EMO recognises its role in crafting and articulating a higher purpose for the firm. Fairness management embraces total transparency, and seeks to connect and integrate with customers around long-term mutual value creation. Thus, while EMO may be seen as the philosophical underpinning of doing good, brand fairness management is the actual execution of such ideas. If India is able to adopt these ideas, its US trading partners would feel fairly treated, increasing goodwill and improving their country's reputation.

Pakistan

In Pakistan, the American Embassy in Islamabad is receiving an increasing number of complaints from American companies due to unfair practices, many stemming from the caretaker government's actions. Examples include General Electric, Oracle and AES Eletropaulo, which have experienced problems in government tenders. Chevron and AES have yet to be paid millions of dollars for energy products and services rendered. Netsol and Microsoft have experienced non-compliance or interference in intellectual property rights (IPR) violations. These problems, totalling an estimated US$1.82 billion, present challenges for American businesses to compete fairly and survive in Pakistan. The government of Pakistan's cash crunch is the cause of the slow payments to the energy companies, and may further compli-cate bidding on government contracts (Patterson, 2014). Examples of each case are briefly presented next:

General Electric won a tender worth US$46 million (phase one) for a Railways Re-Signalling Project with the Ministry of Railways to re-signal the existing rail-way lines in Pakistan. Phases one and two were worth US$150 million. However, Pakistan Railways made technical changes in the contract so that the full contract could be awarded to another supplier using cheaper Chinese inputs. Feeling unfairly treated, the Ambassador sent a letter to the Chairman of the Pakistan Railways, requesting transparency in the tender process, and that GE's contract award for phase one of the project to be upheld. Neither GE nor the Embassy has received any replies (Patterson, 2014).

Oracle was interested in projects with Pakistan International Airways (PIA) worth US$23.5 million. PIA had been planning to implement Enterprise Resource Planning (ERP) and Maintenance Repair and Overhaul (MRO) solutions using pre-packaged applications software in order to automate its key business functions such as revenue accounting, inventory, aircraft maintenance, repair and overhaul. However, Samina Rizwan, Regional Director, reported that Oracle was structured out of the ERP project and could not fairly compete for the MRO project because the only competitor booked all costs under the ERP project to give away the ERP project for free. At the time of writing, Oracle does not plan to submit a tender due to their perceived unfairness in the procurement process (Patterson, 2014).

Microsoft Corporation has a case of pirated software use by the government of Pakistan. The government currently uses 90 per cent of pirated Microsoft software, worth US$10 million, for its operations. In a meeting with then Prime Minister Shaukat Aziz at the Economic Forum Summit in Boao, China, Microsoft's Bill Gates proposed that the government pay US$10 million over a five-year period for legal licences for government desktops, and asked that the Prime Minister respond within 45 days. The deadline passed without a response from the government. Bill Gates sent a letter to the former Prime Minister in June 2007 to follow up on their agreement, but Microsoft has yet to receive a response (Patterson, 2014).

The above examples illustrate the challenges in Pakistan, with the government neglecting its relationships with business partners. The Islamabad Embassy consid-ers the increased activity a troubling trend, with increased economic and financial problems continue to compound the government's political difficulties. The newly elected government, regardless of party, will have to face mounting economic chal-lenges. The Embassy continues to closely monitor each situation involving these and other American companies and raises each issue with the appropriate officials on a regular basis (Patterson, 2014).

It is highly unlikely that managers will abandon their current ideas of business prac-tices overnight, even though unfairness may arise due to the neglect of contracts and promises. The question for managers to consider is to ask what should be done to avoid the potential for such unfairness effect, and rather to be perceived as a fairer and more trustworthy organisation, in the minds of the customers. Although difficult at many levels, there are issues for managers to (re)consider, including those at a personal level. The main focus should be given to minimising the misuse (or over-use) of available marketing tools and make management decisions to maintain and enhance relationships for long-term success. Fairer marketing practices will aid managers in implementing better marketing schemes that are necessary in today's environment. Nguyen, Lee-Wingate, and Simkin (2014) propose four dimensions to develop fairness among marketers and within organisations. Each will now be discussed.

(1) Awareness and problem diagnosis

The first dimension identifies the importance of awareness and problem diagnosis. Organisations must create increased awareness of issues with unfairness so that managers can emphasise and deploy a fairer approach to their marketing efforts and practices. That will increase the likelihood for organisations to minimise costly mistakes, and support managers to focus their resources better, by allocating the right efforts to the right customer groups (Krasnikov, Jayachandran, & Kumar, 2009). More importantly, organisations should recognise that fairness is just as important as any other fundamental management considerations in the organisation and that creating a fair marketing management strategy is the final puzzle needed in order to achieve a sustainable competitive advantage. This is already evidenced to assist in the corporate social responsibility (CSR)-oriented organisation.

(2) Managing both the targeted and non-targeted stakeholders

To avoid unfairness, managers must understanding and manage all groups of stakeholders, including those that have been seen as unprofitable. For managers dealing with customer management, there is a need to distinguish between the two groups of customers with feelings of inequality, namely the targeted (favoured/desirable) and non-targeted (non-favoured/undesirable). This allows managers to develop a better grouping of their stakeholders; to identify the group which needs more attention; and to take appropriate action in order to retain those customers, keeping their loyalty (Verhoef, 2003). While it would be fairest to treat all groups similarly, there are efforts for managers to take, such as considering and incorporating issues of fairness in their targeting strategies (Feinberg, Krishna, & Zhang, 2002). This minimises the perceived unfairness intended by any differential treatment of stakeholders (Kumar, Scheer, & Steenkamp, 1995) and will give the manager a head start in creating a strategy to reduce the feelings of unfairness.

(3) Emphasis on positive associations and goodwill

The third dimension requires probing into the customers' behavioural traits and understanding the way they react to marketing and fairness management. For example, studies show that customers who believe that firms are exploiting their data will attempt to keep their data private, or distort their data (Deighton, 2005). This may decrease trust in a firm's activities (Morgan & Hunt, 1994), and cause dissatisfaction (Bolton & Lemon, 1999) and loss of potential key advantages. Consequently, firms need to recognise this causal effect and understand the importance of monitoring and managing customer perceptions of trust and fairness (Selnes, 1998). This is vital, because issues of fairness and trust are connected with a customer's willingness to provide data and their satisfaction with the ensuing relationship (Raithel, Sarstedt, Scharf, & Schwaiger, 2012).

Managers should strategically manage important variables leading to unfairness, including customers' negative inferences (e.g. Lewis, 2005). Managing negative inferences should be incorporated in any relationship-enhancing programme, considering issues of opportunistic behaviour and lack of transparency. These two issues must be considered as they have a direct impact on the way in which customers develop unfairness. Opportunistic behaviour concerns one party taking advantage over others (e.g. Xia et al., 2004). This is regarded as an element that relates to customers' negative inferences towards a firm's behaviour (Homburg, Hoyer, & Koschate, 2005). Opportunistic behaviour is defined as 'the practice of looking for and using opportunities to gain an advantage for oneself, without considering if this is fair or right' (e.g. Nguyen, 2011). Research shows that opportunistic behaviour and lack of transparency violate 'best practice' for good firm behaviour (Bull & Adam, 2011). Firms must incorporate these important variables in their strategic considerations when developing a fairer marketing strategy. A lack of transparency results in customers anticipating what a firm will do after it collects their data. If customers believe that firms for purposes of exploiting them by using their data, customers will attempt to keep their data private or only provide partially complete/ correct data. These inferences about a lack of transparency weaken marketing activities.

By improving transparency and communication, a firm can work towards preventing unfairness (Campbell, 1999). Managers can make a direct effort to build a successful relationship strategy because it shows that the firm is taking precautions for unfair treatment of customers. Being able to build goodwill should significantly improve the firm's competitive situation, as it shows the credibility of the firm (Thomas & Sullivan, 2005). This is an effective approach to diminish negative inferences and to encourage positive inferences about the organisation (Cox, 2001). To conclude on the case of Pakistan, more transparency and fairness are needed to develop goodwill and improve its reputation.

Bangladesh

In Bangladesh, rice millers are complaining about unfairness in new rice packaging norms. Local rice millers are concerned about facing uneven competition with private rice importers due to the new packaging norms imposed by the government. The Bangladesh government made it mandatory for local rice millers to sell rice in jute sacks from 1 January 2014. However, private importers are allowed to sell rice in polyethylene bags. Local rice millers say their costs have increased sharply due to the new norms. While the price of a jute sack is Tk 70 (around US$0.88), the price of a polyethylene bag is only Tk 13 (around US$0.16). Thus, the local rice millers have to invest more to buy jute sacks, consequently, giving importers an unfair advantage over the locals. The locals demand that the law should be binding on both millers and importers, to avoid unfair competition. Rice millers are already worried about the increasing private sector imports in the country due to high local prices. The Food Ministry data shows that the country imported 295,730 tons of rice up to 28 February 2014 in the FY 2013−14 (July 2013−June 2014) (Oryza. com, 2014). All the imports are by the private sector and the government stated it will not import any rice in this fiscal year. The country imported only 18,100 tons of rice during the same period in the FY 2012−13, of which about 20 per cent of rice was imported by the government, while the remaining was imported by the private sector. Data from Bangladesh's Customs Department branch in Benapole district of Jessore state shows that private importers shipped in 80 per cent of the rice from India. An official stated that imported rice is coming in polyethylene bags, but maize and wheat are being imported in jute sacks. He confirmed that the government has not specified whether rice should be imported in jute sacks. Benapole is the main land port for trade with India (Oryza.com, 2014).

In the case of Bangladesh, we note that the unfairness derives from unfair competition among local and foreign rice millers. It shows that unfairness may be found in anything beyond and above social norms. Often when someone finds something different or new to their current situation, or practices, unfairness perceptions are first to appear. This indicates that unfairness perceptions may be utilised by marketers to monitor and track existing perceptions towards greater social norms. To emphasise the education and re-education of marketing practitioners, we next draw from Nguyen et al.'s (2014) fourth dimension, highlighting the need to incorporate fairness in order to improve the well-being of firms and society alike.

(4) Highlight morality in marketing

Firms must link management with philosophical thinking about social and ethical responsibility. Philosophically speaking, there are many similarities in what has caused the current financial crises and with issues of unfairness in marketing. We suggest that the common denominator for the financial crisis and unfair marketing practices arise from managers' misbehaviours, including those of unfairness and unethical behaviour. Sub-prime mortgage lending meant creating loans for people who had difficulty maintaining their repayment schedule (Dibb & Simkin, 2009). These loans were characterised by higher interest rates and less favourable terms in order to compensate for higher credit risk. So, from the outset, problems were evidenced. However, had there been a stronger emphasis on fairness, integrity and good morals, such practices might have been avoided. The responsibility lies with the firm, and we suggest that fairer approaches to marketing and customer management will steer the firm away from unfair practices.

Scholars advocate that is a need to resolve these issues of unfair and unethical behaviour by emphasising honesty, impartiality, trustworthiness, uprightness and fairness (e.g. Britton & Rose, 2004; Nguyen & Mutum, 2012). Among other things, we suggest that companies need hearts and brains, as well as moral responsibility. Ultimately, it is every single individual's behaviour, as it is the individual's sense of moral responsibility, self-discipline and values that drive the direction a business takes.

It is important to acknowledge that running a two-week seminar in an attempt to educate business people in aspects of fairness will not achieve much. It would be like teaching a course in how to paint. People get the idea and the theory, but if they do not regularly practise, nothing much more will be achieved. The underlying issues will still be there. It is unrealistic to expect rapid changes in management values, and unrealistic to expect rapid systematic changes in the global economy. The changes must start with individuals, permeating inside organisations. Educating individuals starts from the beginning of their education, in kindergarten, and all the way through graduate school. A few weeks of introductory courses in fairness and ethics will not have a major impact.

Re-educating fairer ways for marketing and managers must be implemented early on. Fairness issues should be taught in books and classes in early stages, in order to achieve the true concept of relationship building and to obtain quality relationships between the involved parties (Zeithaml, Berry, & Parasuraman, 1996). Students must learn what the determinants of a good relationship are (Britton & Rose, 2004). The idea is not to eliminate these technologically advanced marketing applications, philosophies and approaches, but rather to find the causes of misbehaviour and work against them. If managers do not understand from where unfairness in marketing comes, it will continue to grow. This is why it is imperative to find and understand the causes, and to counteract them. This message is more relevant than ever in today's environment.

For example, all three governments of India, Pakistan and Bangladesh are seen to lack transparency, resulting in stakeholder revolt across nations and industries. The countries were not willing to follow procedures to act fairly and just; however, if the countries had been better at communicating their objectives, and been more transparent, they could have built goodwill with the stakeholders. Then, the outrage might have been avoided.

We recognise that a firm needs to rethink and develop fairer approaches. Whatever marketing schemes are being developed, it is imperative that consideration must be given to the ways in which a customer develops perceptions of unfairness and negative inferences (Campbell, 2007). The task is to generate *positive* inferences in the firms' offerings, so overall attributions are diminished. In that way, a customer will be able to differentiate between the various players and choose to build a relationship or remain in a relationship with the fairer firm. As Tapscott and Ticoll (2003) point out, the world that we live in today is characterised by an extraordinary degree of transparency, especially when it comes to business actions. This is due in large measure to the rise of the Internet as a pervasive technology that is accessible and affordable to virtually all. The authors suggest that if companies do not want to see certain of their actions publicised on the front page of the *New York Times*, they should not undertake those actions.

Conclusion

It is generally agreed that marketing's primary role is to represent the interests and perspectives of customers to companies. If the marketing function performs this essential task well, it has the potential to align the profit motive with what custo-mers truly need. However, the reality is often very different. In the aggregate, some scholars even suggest that the marketing function performs its role very poorly.

In this chapter, we proposed a fairer approach to marketing. In addition to allocating resources efficiently, other desirable fairness in the societal aspect include 'fair access to and fair distribution of society's benefits and burdens, along with the preservation of individual rights and of commonly shared resources' (Agle et al., 2008). Firms must realise that the institutional role of business in society is far broader than just generat-ing profits. Firms have value as community members, knowledge creators and agents of positive political change. Ignoring their institutional role and focusing solely on their own economic interest has deleterious consequences for society. Freeman (in Agle et al., 2008) highlights a fundamental precept of why businesses need to consider all their stakeholders in making decisions: they must take responsibility for the effects of their actions on all the groups and individuals that they impact. Any responsible business *must* therefore think about customers, employees, suppliers, communities and investors. 'Maximising profits' is not the purpose of the corporation; it is the outcome of a well-managed company. Stakeholder theory is a simple but powerful idea about what it means to be well-managed for the benefit of all. As Freeman says, 'Profits and purpose are two different ideas, and collapsing them is like concluding from the fact that I need red blood cells to live, that the purpose of my life is to make red blood cells.' Freeman concludes that the primary responsibility of an executive is to create as much value as possible for stakeholders because that's how you create as much value as possible for shareholders. This phenomenon is known as the 'stakeholder approach to management', and we encourage future studies to research and link this to fairness management, EMO and marketing. Above all, the outcome of good marketing is that customers, employees, suppliers and communities all feel like they have a stake in the company, even though they may not own any shares in it. When all of the stakeholders 'take ownership' of a company, it results in the creation of a strong ecosystem that helps protect the company from short-term fluctuations and even extreme external shocks in the marketplace. This is the true concept of brand fairness management.

New research directions

Key areas for future research are as follows.

- A number of scholars have applied stakeholder theory to marketing. Murphy, Stevens, McLeod, and Andersen (1997) contend that the fundamental change is the concept of the entire organisation contributing to create value for the customer, and it includes all the stakeholders who are associated with the organisation. Polonsky and Scott (2005) state that marketing is increasingly recognising that in order to be effective, companies need to satisfy a broader conception of stakeholders beyond just customers. Recognising the importance of other groups is an important first step, but, for the most part, marketing has failed to identify which stakeholders should be considered and how their needs should be fulfilled. Future studies should investigate the role of brand fairness in the stakeholder the-ory and link it with marketing.

- Murphy et al. (2005) proposed a holistic stakeholder relationship marketing model in which marketing performance is reflected in the delivery of long-term economic, social and environmental value to customers, employees, suppliers, communities and shareholders in order to enhance sustainable financial performance. How could such a framework be conceptualised? More research is needed to develop and test this model.
- Sisodia et al. (2007) argue that marketing has lost its way, consuming ever more resources but delivering less in terms of customer satisfaction and loyalty. What should marketing do in order to regain its effectiveness and develop a good reputation?
- How would a marketing model of handling all stakeholders look like, including those of brand fairness management and EMO?

Companies must treat all stakeholders as customers, as doing so increases the commodity that is in shortest supply in most business ecosystems: trust. What are the best ways to develop trust and fairness among different internal and external stakeholder groups, i.e. governments, non-profit institutions, universities, competitors, etc.?

Practice case study

Scholars suggest that transparency leads to increased fairness. Companies that are transparent find that their positive actions can achieve a high level of visibility and have many beneficial spillover effects. For example, the Indian Food Place, a special foods retail store in the capital of Mumbai, suffered a breakdown of its cash registers on the night of the Indian Diwali festival. Diwali, also called the 'festival of lights', is an ancient Hindu festival celebrated in autumn every year. Spiritually it signifies the victory of light over darkness, knowledge over ignorance, good over evil and hope over despair. In the Indian Food Place, the lines grew longer and customers were anxious to get home for their supper, so the store manager made an on-the-spot decision. He asked his employees to bag the groceries rapidly of all the waiting customers so they could then go home. When customers asked how much they owed, the answer was 'nothing'. As the employees explained, it was not the customers' fault that the cash registers were not working, and the Indian Food Place did not want to waste any more of their time. Some customers insisted that they would come back the next day and pay for the groceries, while others said that they would donate an equivalent amount of money to the local food bank. The Indian Food Place employees thanked them, but said that it was really not necessary for them to do so. The customers went home happy and filled with appreciation for this uncommonly generous gesture. The story would have ended here, except that on the day after Diwali, one of the customers contacted the local newspaper, and said, 'Do you know what happened at the Indian Food Place the other night?' The newspaper ran a story on the episode the next day, and the story soon started getting emailed around the country, which is how the store manager came to learn about the extent of his actions. The grocery giveaway had cost the store approximately US$2,000, but it resulted in positive publicity that was worth much more than that.

It strengthened the company's brand and improved upon the high level of trust that it already enjoyed with its customers and its employees. Note that the store manager did not need to get the permission of higher-ups within the company to do what he felt needed doing, nor did he do it for the express purpose of generating positive publicity. He simply did it because he felt it was the right thing to do. Given the greater level of transparency that exists today and the higher degree to which stakeholders are connected with one another and wear multiple hats, it is increasingly evident that a company's overall ecosystem is only as healthy as its weakest link. In other words, a successful company can eventually be felled by its failure to give adequate attention to any one of its stakeholders.

Questions

1. Why did the store manager feel compelled to give away the groceries?
2. Considering brand fairness management tactics, were there any alternative things he could have done?
3. In your opinion, was it the right decision to give away the goods for free?
4. Why did this turn out to be a success story for the Indian Food Place?

References

Aburdene, P. (2005). *Megatrends 2010: The rise of conscious capitalism*. Hampton Roads.
Agle, B. R., Donaldson, T., Freeman, R. E., Jensen, M. C., Mitchell, R. K., & Wood, D. J. (2008). Dialogue: Toward superior stakeholder theory. *Business Ethics Quarterly, 18*, 2.
American Marketing Association (AMA). <https://www.ama.org/Pages/default.aspx>.
Bolton, L. E., Warlop, L., & Alba, J. W. (2003). Consumer perceptions of price (un)fairness. *Journal of Consumer Research, 29*, 474−491.
Bolton, R. N., & Lemon, K. N. (1999). A dynamic model of customers' usage of services: Usage as an antecedent and consequence of satisfaction. *Journal of Marketing Research, 36*(2), 171−186.
Boulding, W., Staelin, R., Ehret, M., & Johnston, W. J. (2005). A customer relationship management roadmap: What is known, potential pitfalls, and where to go. *Journal of Marketing, 69*(4), 155−166.
Britton, J. E., & Rose, J. (2004). Thinking about relationship theory. In P. D. Rogers, & M. Rogers (Eds.), *Managing customer relationships − A strategic framework* (pp. 38−50). Hoboken, NJ: John Wiley and Sons.
Bull, C., & Adam, A. (2011). Virtue ethics and customer relationship management: Towards a more holistic approach for the development of 'best practice'. *Business Ethics: A European Review, 20*(2), 121−130.
Campbell, M. C. (1999). Perceptions of price unfairness: Antecedents and consequences. *Journal of Marketing Research, 36*(5), 187−199.
Campbell, M. C. (2007). Says who?! How the source of price information and affect influence perceived price (un)fairness. *Journal of Marketing Research, 44*(5), 261−271.

Chapuis, J. M. (2012). Perceived fairness and trust in consumer's reactions to revenue management. *International Journal of Revenue Management*, *6*(3), 145−157.

Chen, J., Nguyen, B., & Klaus, P. (2013). Public affairs in China: Exploring the role of brand fairness perceptions in the case of Mercedes-Benz. *Journal of Public Affairs*, *13*(4), 403−414.

Cox, J. L. (2001). Can differential price be fair? *Journal of Product & Brand Management*, *10*(5), 264−275.

Davis, M. (2002). *The new culture of desire: The pleasure imperative transforming your business and your life*. New York, NY: Free Press.

Deighton, J. (2005). *Privacy and customer management*. Customer Management, (MSI conference summary) (pp. 17−19). Cambridge, MA: Marketing Science Institute.

Dibb, S., & Simkin, L. (2009). Implementation rules to bridge the theory/practice in marketing segmentation. *Journal of Marketing Management*, *25*(3/4), 375−396.

Dwyer, F. R., Schurr, P. S., & Oh, S. (1987). Developing buyer-seller relationships. *Journal of Marketing*, *51*(2), 11−27.

Ernst, H., Hoyer, W. D., Kraft, M., & Krieger, K. (2011). Customer relationship management and company performance − the mediating role of new product. *Journal of the Academy of Marketing Science*, *39*(2), 290−306.

Feinberg, F. M., Krishna, A., & Zhang, Z. J. (2002). Do we care what others get? A behaviourist approach to targeted promotions. *Journal of Marketing Research*, *39*(3), 277−291.

Frow, P. E., Payne, A., Wilkinson, I. F., & Young, L. (2011). Customer management and CRM: Addressing the dark side. *Journal of Services Marketing*, *25*(2), 79−89.

George, J. M. (2014). Compassion and capitalism: Implications for organizational studies. *Journal of Management*, *40*(1), 5−15.

Ghoshal, S. (2005). Bad management theories are destroying good management practices. *Academy of Management Learning & Education*, *4*(1), 75−91.

Grégoire, Y., & Fisher, R. J. (2008). Customer betrayal and retaliation: When your best customers become your worst enemies. *Journal of the Academy of Marketing Science*, *36*(2), 247−261.

Hawken, P., Lovins, A., & Lovins, L. H. (1999). *Natural capitalism*. USA: Little, Brown and Company.

Homburg, C., Hoyer, W. D., & Koschate, N. (2005). Customers' reactions to price increases: Do customer satisfaction and perceived motive fairness matter? *Journal of the Academy of Marketing Science*, *33*(1), 36−50.

Jost, J. T., & Kay, A. C. (2010). Social justice: History, theory, and research. In S. T. Fiske, D. T. Gilbert, & G. Lindzey (Eds.), *Handbook of social psychology* (5th ed., pp. 1122−1165). Hoboken, NJ: John Wiley & Sons.

Kilbourne, J. (2000). *Killing us softly 3: Advertising's image of women*. Documentary produced by the Media Education Foundation. <http://www.mediaed.org>.

Kofman, F. (2006). *Conscious business: How to build value through values*. Sounds True.

Krasnikov, A., Jayachandran, S., & Kumar, V. (2009). The impact of customer relationship management implementation on cost and profit efficiencies: Evidence from the US commercial banking industry. *Journal of Marketing*, *73*(6), 61−76.

Kumar, N., Scheer, L., & Steenkamp, J. B. (1995). The effects of supplier fairness on vulnerable resellers. *Journal of Marketing Research*, *32*(1), 54−65.

Lewis, M. (2005). Incorporating strategic consumer behaviour into customer valuation. *Journal of Marketing*, *69*(6), 230−238.

Linn, S. (2005). *Consuming kids: Protecting our children from the onslaught of marketing and advertising*. New York, NY: Anchor Books.

Luo, X., Wieseke, J., & Homburg, C. (2012). Incentivizing CEOs to build customer- and employee-firm relations for higher customer satisfaction and firm value. *Journal of the Academy of Marketing Science*, *40*(6), 745−758.

Mackey, J. (2007). Conscious capitalism: Creating a new paradigm for business. <http://www.flowidealism.org/Downloads/JM-CC-1.pdf>.

Melnyk, V., & Osselaer, S. (2012). Make me special: Gender differences in consumers' responses to loyalty programs. *Marketing Letters*, *23*(3), 545−559.

Michell, P., Reast, J., & Lynch, J. (1998). Exploring the foundations of trust. *Journal of Marketing Management*, *14*, 159−172.

Minter, S. (2013). India's trade practices discriminatory and unfair, US businesses charge. Industry Week, 18 June, <http://www.industryweek.com/trade/indias-trade-practices-discriminatory-and-unfair-us-businesses-charge?page=2>.

Morgan, R. M., & Hunt, S. D. (1994). The commitment-trust theory of relationship marketing. *Journal of Marketing*, *58*(3), 20−38.

Murphy, B., Maguiness, P., Pescott, C., Wislang, S., Ma, J., & Wang, R. (2005). Stakeholder perceptions presage holistic stakeholder relationship marketing performance. *European Journal of Marketing*, *39*(9/10), 1049−1059.

Murphy, B., Stevens, K., McLeod, R., & Andersen, A. (1997). A stakeholder framework for measuring relationship marketing. *Journal of Marketing Theory and Practice*, 43−57.

Nguyen, B. (2011). The dark side of CRM. *The Marketing Review*, *14*(2), 137−149.

Nguyen, B., Lee-Wingate, N., & Simkin, L. (2014). The customer relationship management paradox: Five steps to create a fairer organization. *Social Business Journal*, *4*(3), 207−230.

Nguyen, B., & Mutum, D. S. (2012). A review of customer relationship management: Successes, advances, pitfalls and futures. *Business Process Management Journal*, *18*(3), 400−419.

Nguyen, B., & Simkin, L. (2012). Fairness quality: The role of fairness in a social and ethically oriented marketing landscape. *The Marketing Review*, *12*(4), 333−334.

Oryza.com (2014). Bangladesh rice millers complain about unfairness in new rice packaging norms. Oryza.com, 5 March, <http://oryza.com/news/rice-news/bangladesh-rice-millers-complain-about-unfairness-new-rice-packaging-norms>.

Patterson (2014). 2008: US companies risked losing $1.8bn due to Pakistan govt's unfair practices. Dawn.com, 19 March, <http://www.dawn.com/news/635961/2008-us-companies-risked-losing-1-8bn-due-to-pakistan-govts-unfair-practices>.

Polonsky, M. J., & Scott, D. (2005). An empirical examination of the stakeholder strategy matrix. *European Journal of Marketing*, *39*(9/10), 1199−1215.

Raithel, S., Sarstedt, M., Scharf, S., & Schwaiger, M. (2012). On the value relevance of customer satisfaction. Multiple drivers and multiple markets. *Journal of the Academy of Marketing Science*, *40*(4), 509−525.

Roy, S. K., & Pratik, M. (2014). Enlightened market orientation and consumer well-being. Working Paper.

Schlosser, E. (2001). *Fast Food Nation: The Dark Side of the All-American Meal*. New York, NY: Houghton Mifflin.

Selnes, F. (1998). Antecedents and consequences of trust and satisfaction in buyer-seller relationships. *European Journal of Marketing*, *32*(3/4), 305−322.

Sheth, J. N., & Sisodia, R. S. (2002). Marketing productivity: Conceptualization, measurement and improvement. *Journal of Business Research*, *55*(5), 349−362.

Sheth, J. N., Sisodia, R. S., & Barbulescu, A. (2006). The image of marketing with consumers and business professionals. In J. N. Sheth, & R. S. Sisodia (Eds.), *Does marketing need reform? Fresh perspectives on the future.* Armonk, NY: ME Sharpe.

Sisodia, R., & Backer, A. (2004). Cybermarketing and the tragedy of the commons: An environmental policy perspective. In: *Research reaching new heights, proceedings of the AMA marketing and public policy conference* (pp. 32–34). Salt Lake City, UT.

Sisodia, R. S., Wolfe, D. B., & Sheth, J. N. (2007). *Firms of endearment: How world class companies profit from passion and purpose.* Upper Saddler River, NJ: Wharton School Publishing.

Tapscott, D., & Ticoll, D. (2003). *The naked corporation: How the age of transparency will revolutionize business.* New York, NY: Free Press.

Thomas, J. S., & Sullivan, U. Y. (2005). Managing marketing communications with multi-channel customers. *Journal of Marketing, 69*(4), 239–251.

Urban, G. (2004). Customer advocacy – a new paradigm for marketing? In J. N. Sheth, & R. S. Sisodia (Eds.), *Does marketing need reform? Fresh perspectives on the future.* Armonk: M.E. Sharpe.

Verhoef, P. C. (2003). Understanding the effect of customer relationship management efforts on customer retention and customer share development. *Journal of Marketing, 67*(4), 30–45.

Xia, L., Monroe, K. B., & Cox, J. L. (2004). The price is unfair! A conceptual framework of price fairness perceptions. *Journal of Marketing, 68*(4), 1–15.

Yankelovich (2014). <http://thefuturescompany.com/what-we-do/us-yankelovich-monitor>.

Zeithaml, V. A., Berry, L. L., & Parasuraman, A. (1996). The behavioural consequences of service quality. *Journal of Marketing, 60*(2), 31–46.

Further reading

Akst, D. (2002). Ubiquitous ads devalue all messages. *The New York Times*, 2 June.

Arrow, K. J. (1984). *Individual choice under certainty and uncertainty.* Cambridge, MA: Belknap Press.

Barletta, M. (2006). *Marketing to women: How to understand, reach, and increase your share of the world's largest market segment.* Kaplan Business.

Conley, C. (2007). *Peak: How great companies get their Mojo from Maslow.* San Francisco, CA: Jossey-Bass.

Dunlap, A. J., & Andaman, B. (1997). *Mean business: How I save companies and make good companies great.* New York, NY: Fireside.

Egidi, M., & Marris, R. (1995). *Economics, bounded rationality and the cognitive revolution.* Brookfield, VT: Edward Elgar.

Elkington, J. (1997). *Cannibals with forks: The triple bottom line of 21st century business.* Oxford: Capstone Publishing. (The Conscientious Commerce Series).

Jensen, M. C. (2002). Value maximization, stakeholder theory, and the corporate objective function. *Business Ethics Quarterly, 12*(2), 235–247.

Kay, J. (1998). The role of business in society, 3 February. <http://www.johnkay.com>.

Maignan, I., Ferrel, O. C., & Ferrel, L. (2005). A stakeholder model for implementing social responsibility in marketing. *European Journal of Marketing, 39*(9/10), 956–977.

Payne, A., Ballantyne, D., & Christopher, M. (2005). A stakeholder approach to relationship marketing strategy: The development and use of the 'six markets model'. *European Journal of Marketing*, *39*(7/8), 855–871.

Simon, H. A. (1971). Designing organizations for an information-rich world. In M. Greenberger (Ed.), *Computers, communication, and the public interest*. The Johns Hopkins Press.

Smith, J. W. (2006). Coming to concurrence: Improving marketing productivity by reengaging resistant consumers. In J. N. Sheth, & R. S. Sisodia (Eds.), *Does marketing need reform? Fresh perspectives on the future*. Armonk NY: ME Sharpe.

Stone, A. (1982). *Regulation and its alternatives*. Washington, DC: Congressional Quarterly Press.

Fairness management: Vietnam, Cambodia, the Philippines and Indonesia

Allen Yu and Bang Nguyen

Introduction

This chapter covers studies exploring fairness from extant consumer behavioural and psychological theories and researches. Important aspects of cultural and social indicators that influence consumers' fairness perceptions are included in the Asian context. The chapter specifically focuses on the unique areas of Vietnam, Cambodia, the Philippines and Indonesia, contributing a much-needed framework in these little-researched areas. While the theoretical approach enables readers to understand the role of fairness, the practical examples and cases subsequently aids in understanding the application of fairness towards managing firms' marketing approaches. Thus the question is asked in this chapter: why do consumers sometimes believe that they are being treated unfairly?

Given increasing public concern, it seems appropriate to explore further the psychological and theoretical bases and findings about cultural and social indicators, to clarify what is known about the causes of perceived unfairness, and how these perceptions influence customers' behaviours. Various conceptualisations have been developed and adapted to explain the phenomenon of fairness. Each approach tends to address a specific reason for fairness perceptions. For example, the dual entitlement principle emphasises the influence of supply and demand changes and the sellers' profit orientation. Equity theory and distributive justice emphasise the importance of equality of outcomes between two parties in an exchange. In addition, procedural justice focuses on the influence of the underlying procedures used to determine the outcomes on fairness perceptions.

In this chapter, we present a conceptual framework for fairness that integrates the important aspects of cultural and social indicators in Vietnam, Cambodia, the Philippines and Indonesia, and organise existing fairness research to enlighten current practices about fairness management. First, we provide a route map that guides our understanding of fairness management in the marketing literatures. We then explore the state of art in fairness management, and present some new research directions. Finally, we show how fairness management and marketing are practised in each of the four countries, with an illustrative case study to help understand fairness management in depth.

We begin our chapter with defining what fairness management is, and why it is so important. Previously, fairness has been defined as a judgment of whether an outcome

Ethical and Social Marketing in Asia.

and/or the process to reach an outcome are reasonable, acceptable or just. In the context of marketing, researchers divide fairness into several concepts, each within their separate contexts, namely, general fairness, price fairness, service fairness, and retail fairness (in the next section, we describe these in more detail). While there are many factors that may influence unfairness perceptions, in this chapter, we pay more attention to how the concepts and indicators are related to cultural and social elements in each of the different countries, influencing consumers' fairness perceptions. We note that different cultures influence perceived fairness in different ways:

1. through comparisons of own interaction with another person's, or comparing current with previous interactions;
2. the attributions (or blame) for an unfair purchase situation; and
3. general social norms and beliefs.

These aforementioned points are briefly presented next relation to Vietnam, Cambodia, the Philippines and Indonesia.

Learning objectives

After reading this chapter, you should be able to:

- identify the focus and goals of fairness management;
- explain the role of fairness management in marketing;
- describe different directions of fairness theories and cases in Vietnam, Cambodia, the Philippines and Indonesia;
- discuss and understand the application of fairness management in a case study; and
- recognise further research streams in fairness management.

Route map: fairness management – Vietnam, Cambodia, the Philippines and Indonesia

Fairness management, which is the application and incorporation of fairness into the management process, links with a wider range of theories in the marketing literatures. This chapter explores the fairness management concept as an essential part of customer relationship management (CRM). CRM is defined as 'the purposive use of customer knowledge and technologies to help firms generate customised offerings on an individual basis based on fairness and trust in order to enhance and maintain quality relationships with all the involved parties' (Nguyen & Mutum, 2012, p. 413). In spite of the lack of consensus in the literature for a definition, as CRM increases in exposure, a growing number of scholars emphasise the need for a holistic approach and view CRM as a process reflecting integration of market orientation and information communication technology (Payne, 2001; Srivastava, Shervani, & Fahey, 1998). To create successful CRM implementation and long-lasting relationships, it is important to highlight four fundamental factors pertaining to a strong relationship: trust, relationship symmetry, satisfaction and fairness.

Trust is a feeling of security based on the belief that favourable and positive intentions towards welfare are on the agenda, as opposed to lying or taking advantage of the vulnerability of others (Moorman, Zaltman, & Deshpande, 1992; Morgan & Hunt, 1994). Trust is an essential component of commitment, and conceptually links with satisfaction and loyalty (Delgado-Ballester & Munuera-Aleman, 2001).

Relationship symmetry refers to the degree of equality between relationship members. Through various relationship elements, including information sharing, dependence and power, the balance of power determines the stability of a relationship. In a symmetric relationship, members have equivalent stakes in the relationship. In contrast, asymmetric relationships undermine the balance of power and create motivation for the stronger party to act opportunistically. With differing interests, this is a determinant of conflict and, eventually, a less stable relationship. Increased dependency by one party will result in a more asymmetric and less stable relationship, as one party may feel vulnerable and constantly look for more favourable relationships.

Satisfaction is essential in building long-term relationships. Satisfied customers are more inclined to remain in a relationship, whereas dissatisfied customers are likely to look for alternative options. The duration of the relationship depends on the customers' subjective assessment of the value of a relationship (Bolton & Lemon, 2007).

Fairness plays a critical role in the quality of relationships between consumer and firm. In marketing, the holistic concept of fairness has been conceptualised as general fairness (Huppertz, Arenson, & Evans, 1978), price fairness (Kahneman & Knetsch, 1986), service fairness (McColl-Kennedy & Sparks, 2003) and retail fairness (Nguyen & Klaus, 2013). According to Lee-Wingate and Stern (2007) general fairness is defined as equitable, fair dealing, honesty, impartiality and uprightness. General fairness can be explained in three dimensions: distributive, procedural and interactional justice (Alexander & Ruderman, 1987). Price fairness has been well researched, and researchers have offered varying directions about the concept. For example, Xia, Monroe, and Cox (2004) propose a framework of price fairness that includes the following dimensions:

1. transaction similarity and choice of comparison party (e.g. Bolton, Warlop, & Alba, 2003);
2. price comparison;
3. distribution of cost and profit (e.g. Frey & Pommerehne, 1993);
4. attributions of responsibility (Campbell, 2007); and
5. buyer—seller relationship stage (trust) (e.g. Ordóñez et al., 2000).

Referring to service fairness, several areas of research include: yield management, justification (Urbany et al., 1988), service failure (or poor-service recovery) (Mccoll-Kennedy & Sparks, 2003), interactional fairness (Nankung & Jang, 2010), accountability (Mccoll-Kennedy & Sparks, 2003) and systemic service fairness (Carr, 2007). While many scholars have researched the above fairness conceptualisations, more recently, retail fairness has been conceptualised (Nguyen & Klaus, 2013). This area differs from past conceptualisations of price and service fairness based on the context (Mccoll-Kennedy & Sparks, 2003; Xia et al., 2004). In addition, the emphasis on honesty, integrity, transparency and ethical behaviour, as part of a retailer's marketing tactics, are considered to be contemporary concepts that reflect an age where sophisticated technologies are advancing, and tracking/monitoring customers' needs and behaviours has become the norm. The retail fairness conceptualisation stresses the importance of the fair use of such technologies in retailing in order to foster customer caring treatment for the benefit of long-term relationships between retailers and customers alike.

Figure 13.1 shows the relationship between fairness management and other concepts in the wider marketing literature.

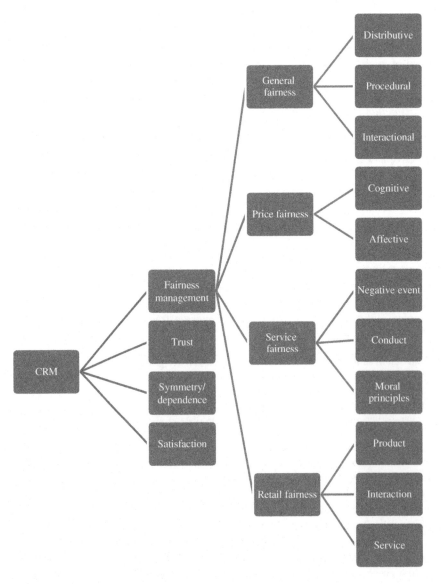

Figure 13.1 CRM and fairness management.

The state of the art in fairness management

Fairness management is a complex system. The key focus in fairness management is to understand how stakeholders' unfairness perceptions arise, so that efforts can be made to prevent and control the damages surrounding unfairness, using appropriate resources. Scholars posit possible explanations of how unfairness perceptions arise (see Figure 13.2), including:

1. customers' comparison of own interaction with another person's and previous interactions;
2. the attributions (or blame) for an unfair purchase situation; and
3. general social norms and beliefs.

In this chapter, we integrate these theories within a case study to explain how fairness management can be applied in practice.

Comparison

Research shows that when the degree of similarity between a comparative transaction is relatively high, buyers expect that they are entitled to the same as their comparison reference (for instance, past interactions or others buyers). Thus, if a transaction remains relatively similar, but the price is higher, buyers are likely to judge this as unfair (Rondan-Cataluña & Martin-Ruiz, 2011). In contrast, when the degree of similarity between transactions is low, the differences may explain the higher price, resulting in a judgment that it is less unfair or fair (Campbell, 1999). Transactions (or interactions) may vary in several ways:

1. They may occur at different times.
2. They may not vary in product category, but variation in terms of brands and models;
3. Offerings can be acquired through various channels.

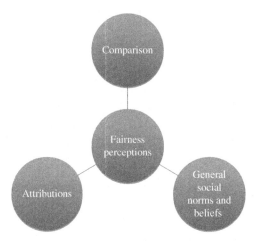

Figure 13.2 Determinants of unfairness perceptions.

4. Different terms and conditions will be involved.
5. Different people may be involved in the process.

Each of these elements influences the degree of similarity of a particular interaction. Thus, variations can disallow an exact comparison, possibly leading to unfairness perceptions.

For example, in recent years, e-commerce has stimulated an increasing number of consumers in the Philippines to do shopping online, providing a platform for a lower price for online users. However, other consumers, who may not like shopping online, or do not have access to these services, will have to spend more money on the same purchases by buying from retail stores. When comparisons are made to the online consumers, these others may feel that they are disadvantaged. In this case, both dissonance and inequity are evidenced, causing perceptions of unfairness.

Attributions

To understand why a situation may be different from a previous situation, consumers may make attributions as to who is responsible for a particular case of discrepancy (Helson, 1948). Consumers may seek information to determine whether the seller is responsible for the situation of inequality, because an explanation provides them with feelings of control over their environment and serves as an adaptive function. Weiner (1985) states that consumers are less motivated to seek attributions when they perceive the inequality is to their advantage than when they perceive it is to their disadvantage. For example, when buyers need to assess whether a price or an increase in a price is acceptable or fair, attributions towards the sellers' costs play an important role. A perception of unfairness may result from the consumers' understanding of why the higher price was set (Johnson, Holladay, & Quinones, 2009). An increase in price for the consumer, without a corresponding increase in the seller's costs, is perceived to be unfair, as this would be seen as an act of self-interest or a misuse of either an increase in demand or a scarcity of supplies. Thus, buyers will perceive inequality as more unfair if they perceive that the seller profits from the buyer's loss.

General social norms and beliefs

Fairness may be judged at an aggregate level across an interaction space that consists of multiple dimensions. Consumers may draw on their general knowledge about the marketplace to judge whether an exchange is fair, or not. Consumers may also rely on their own beliefs about the exchange norms to refine their price fairness judgments (Maxwell, 1999). Their ability to develop knowledge of marketers' tactics comes from buying experiences as well as the general flow of information. Research suggests that this meta-knowledge, whether accurate or not, guides consumers' fairness judgments (Xia et al., 2004). For example, a consumer may claim that a price is unfair without a particular reference to another point. However, although it seems that the claim may be based on a single point, it is nevertheless a comparison to an unspecified, but expected lower price that the consumer believes they are entitled to because of, for example, limited income. The general sense is also an important element to unfairness perceptions. For example, in Vietnam, many local companies can offer goods that are the same quality as the foreign products, but the general belief and social norms is that the local companies' products are inferior compared to the foreign company. So if the local company sets their prices at the same level as their foreign counterparts, consumers may believe that the local company is cheating their customers with substandard products and services, or overly inflated prices. Many consumers will thus find this unfair, and not buy their goods.

Vietnam, Cambodia, the Philippines and Indonesia

Fairness in marketing is typically studied from a consumer behavioural perspective. Consumer behaviour is defined as the study of psychological, social and physical actions when people buy, use and dispose products, services, ideas and practices (Blackwell, Szeinbach, Barnes, Garner, & Bush, 1999). Consumer research questions people's buying reasons, by exploring in which circumstances people purchase and consume. The research of consumer behaviour in South East Asia has received scant attention in the literature, due to the difficulty of access and collecting data, and focuses even less on consumers' unfairness perceptions. In the next section, the chapter presents cases from Vietnam, Cambodia, the Philippines and Indonesia, and explains the underlying theoretical bases of unfairness.

In Vietnam, fish farmer Doan Van Vuon became a folk hero when he used homemade landmines and guns to stop local officials, police and soldiers from forcibly taking his land in northern Vietnam. In another case, near the capital, Hanoi, thousands of police overwhelmed villagers who were trying to protect a 70-hectare (170-acre) plot of land, slated for use in a satellite city development (Win, 2012). These are two examples of conflicts over land that are a major source of friction between the public and officials in Vietnam, where rising land prices have led officials to move farmers off their land for more lucrative projects, often with little compensation.

All land in Vietnam belongs to the state, and usage rights are not always clear or protected. Government statistics show there were 700,000 land-related complaints in the last three years (2009–2012), 70 per cent of which were about land appropriation and compensation decisions that experts say are not only opaque and prone to corruption, but also inequitable and discriminate against farmers – a crucial sector of Vietnam's economy and an important base for the ruling Communist Party (Win, 2012).

To recover on the farmers' unfairness perceptions, the government is now working towards a revision of the Vietnam Land Law, to ensure increased transparency and, subsequently, fairness. Farmers and foreign analysts are cautiously optimistic that a revision of the Land Law now under way will make the law fairer, impartial and more transparent. According to Win (2012), 20-year leases for agricultural land issued in 1993 will expire in 2013, and the revision of the Land Law is expected to be approved soon after. A senior governance specialist at the World Bank in Vietnam mentions that 'If the revisions afford more rights to farmers and others who lose land and if the new system is perceived to be more fair, the number of conflicts will be reduced' (Win, 2012, p. 2). The example illustrates the important role of incorporating fairness management by the Vietnamese government, highlighting transparency and reducing inequity. When transparency is shown, people do not feel the need to make attributions as to who is responsible for an unfair situation. They feel a greater sense of control over the situation, which subsequently decreases unfairness perceptions. At the same time, procedural justice is achieved, as people gain increased knowledge, and are not feeling left in the dark, consequently leading to increased fairness. The government of Vietnam may, thus, work on revising on the Land Law, but also consider employing other fairness management schemes, such as building goodwill and increasing its reputation among the people.

In Cambodia, British actress Minnie Driver highlighted issues of exploitation and unfairness by urging multinationals to change their buying practices, so poor workers could have better lives. Following a fashion show at Oxfam's riverfront UK head-quarters, Cambodian garment workers sang tearful songs to create awareness about unfair treatment of workers, who are underpaid and overworked (Kate, 2004). Minnie Driver used the occasion to say that she visited Cambodia not as a global economist or an expert on Cambodia, but as a Western consumer. She further made a passionate plea to the heads of large corporations to consider their buying and outsourcing prac-tices. In particular, she emphasised how every time the corporations squeeze their employees to get lower production costs or faster production, the working women and their families back home suffer from such unfair treatment.

A global report entitled 'Trading away our rights: women working in global supply chains', by Oxfam, called on companies to make labour standards a key sourcing criterion. Minister of Commerce, Cham Prasidh, welcomed Minnie Driver's presence and hailed the Oxfam report as one that could pressure companies to keep orders in the increasingly labour-friendly country. Cham Prasidh also said that Minnie Driver should make a new movie called *Good Will Job Creator*, to follow *Good Will Hunting*, a film she co-stared in. He noted that Minnie Driver's presence in Cambodia served the purpose of making the heads of multinational corporations become responsible. In addition, he stated that celebrities with a noble mission can make companies understand that it is time to pay for the workers who are producing their products, and not just pay the price they want to pay (Kate, 2004).

As already mentioned, at the Oxfam event, a group of garment workers shared stor-ies about the hardships they face with the crowd. The women sang: 'The voice of gar-ment workers must be used to shout to tell all Cambodian women that to be a servant is very difficult. They curse, they blame us, and say we are bad girls, but we have no freedom and no rights' (Kate, 2004). At one point during the event, the music was turned down and Driver read testimonials of poor workers. Later, the worker-models walked down the catwalk with cutout-silhouettes of a woman's face emblazoned with phrases like 'Exploited', 'Narrowing Opportunities' and 'Not Valued'.

The case focuses attention on perceived exploitation, and perceptions of unfair-ness. In this case, managers used traditional marketing channels, such as a celebrity and events, to create awareness about unfairness, with the overall objective to man-age fairness from an emotional perspective. By stirring emotions among the audi-ence, the managers' efforts and event continue to have great effect, as the US and

Cambodian governments began inspecting factories in cooperation with the Garment Manufacturers Association of Cambodia. Since then, there have been significant improvements, although problems remain with respect to payment of wages and the length and frequency of overtime (Kate, 2004). Thus, as part of the fairness management scheme, continuous monitoring is needed in the hopes of making the inspection system sustainable. The monitoring process produces a safer working environment and more equitable working conditions, which in turn helps to improve the international credibility of Cambodian factories. The impact of fairness management is significant here, as the government is now branding itself as a labour-friendly nation and expects entry into the World Trade Organization in order to keep orders and factories in the country.

In the Philippines, there were strong reactions towards a pension provider when consumers felt unfairness treated. As Ocampo (2013) wrote an article about his experiences, the case quickly spread across the Internet, gathering the support of many other consumers, who together spread their complaints and negative word-of-mouth via social media and *The Philippine Star*, a national news outlet. The case started when Ocampo detailed how Pryce Plans, Inc. tried to induce him into accepting only 40 per cent of the cash value of his P300,000 pension plan that had matured five years ago, or taking 80 per cent equivalent in liquefied petroleum gas or memorial plots (Ocampo, 2013). It was seen as a clear violation of social norms, and an unfair deal by the company.

At least nine other victims expressed their outrage through email, which were subsequently posted publicly on various websites. The consumers had a common demand for fair treatment by Pryce Plans and other pre-need funeral establishments. Several of them expressed the following (Ocampo, 2013):

> '*I've been frustratingly dealing with [Pryce Plans] for the past years with the same result.*'
> '*What are you going to do? If in your stature you cannot do anything, the rest of us cannot do anything. Let us know what happens next.*'

The comments illustrate how perceptions of unfairness may arise when consumers feel exploited and taken advantage of. Price Plans had in this case acted opportunistically – a recurrent theme, which stirs unfairness perceptions. Three others provided details of their experiences as follows (Ocampo, 2013):

> '*I fully agree with your comments on the way Pryce Plans attends to your claim. UNFAIR! But that seems to be how pre-need and insurance plans have been doing business.*'
> '*I hope you can get a good chance of recovering a major portion of your investment soon. As a columnist, you can also speak on behalf of the countless condominium buyers who, after deciding to back out, cannot get a sizeable portion of their paid amounts ASAP.*'
> '*My discontent is due to the following: 1) the company is not insolvent; 2) it used my money interest-free for a year; 3) no damage to the developer as it can sell the unit to another at a higher price.*'

'The primary reason for backing out was that my wife had cancer and we needed the refund for her treatment. My wife died in 2011.'
'Thank you for exposing the nefarious activities of that plan company. That is what happened to the CAP (College Assurance Plan) pension plan.'
'. . . have them (lined up before) a firing squad? More exposés!'

The comments illustrate how unfairness leads to anger among consumers. When consumers are angry, many will express their complaints to others leading to negative word-of-mouth and damage to the company brand. This is why fairness management is an essential part of any organisation. Unfairness is particularly prevalent when the victims are sensitive groups like the elderly or children, which is in line with the ethical and social marketing literatures. For example:

'Take the case of a special program for elderly members of a fraternal association. Instead of looking after the welfare of senior members, the program has made them victims.'

As consumers continue to express their dissatisfaction, several psychological associations are made towards other related issues, such as dissatisfaction with the country's laws and lack of regulation.

'Filipino businessmen cannot be trusted. Foreign investors are at risk partnering with Filipinos. If they cheat their own kind, how much more they would cheat foreigners? Your misfortune isn't unique. Where is justice in the Philippines?'

The negative comments continued to lead to other associations and attributions:

'Under capitalism, cheating has been historically proven worldwide. The worst is what the biggest US banks and investment houses have done to their clients, big and small alike, that spurred the current prolonged global financial-economic crisis.'

The above comments suggest a crucial link between fairness and morality, and subsequently, the necessity in considering the adoption of more conscious-related marketing efforts. With fairness management efforts, solutions may be provided to the above case. Several consumers revealed their own solutions (Ocampo, 2013). For example, a consumer urges taking 'this ploy of pre-need and insurance companies to the attention of the Insurance Commissioner for appropriate action'. Another consumer, who claimed to have been jobless for five years now, called for amending some provisions of the law to put a stop to the short-changing of customers. Enacted in 1972, the Maceda law provides protection to buyers of real estate, including condos, on instalment basis.

'I think we need to correct the system of accountability and responsibility. There have been many companies like the one you wrote about and we (all stakeholders) haven't learned (lessons from their bad practices). For instance, there is no obligation to disclose important information about the company and its financial health to the potential investors/consumers.'
'Please continue writing on issues such as this...'

If unfairness issues get out of control, firms may face increased control and regulation. It is therefore essential that fairness is managed systematically. As shown in the final comments, successful fairness management often simply involves the inclusion of consumers into the company to build relations, create dual value, develop transparency and develop solutions. These fair practices link well with the concepts of CRM.

In Indonesia, many women and girls face unchallenged social attitudes, unfair laws and stereotyped gender roles in their struggle for fair and equal treatment (Jakarta Post, 2010a). Salil Shetty, the Secretary General of Amnesty International, comments that some of the barriers women face are a direct result of laws and policies that discriminate against them. The latest report by Amnesty International states that these discriminatory laws and bylaws in Indonesia have altered the personal lives of poor and marginalised women by denying them full control of their reproductive systems. Shetty continues: 'Other barriers are a result of discriminatory attitudes and practices among health workers and members of the community.'

In the reproductive health sector, discriminatory laws and attitudes have influenced decisions that women make. For example, the Amnesty report (Jakarta Post, 2010a) includes case studies of Miriana (21) and Susun (34), highlighting how they were married and delivered their first child before they reached their 18th birthdays. According to the report, both women's lives were influenced by stereotypical social views of women as wives and child-bearers codified in the 1974 Marriage Law. This law positions women as household caretakers and stigmatises those who cannot have children or want to delay pregnancy. Isabelle Arrandon, an Amnesty researcher focusing on Indonesia, comments that laws also discriminated between married and unmarried women, by providing uneven access to certain reproduction services, such as contraceptives (Jakarta Post, 2010a).

For example, the 2009 Population Law and Family Development and the 2009 Health Law stipulate that sexual and reproductive health services, such as family planning and contraception, may only be given to legally married couples. In addition, the family development law also requires a formal agreement between a husband and wife before access can be provided to certain types of contraception that carry health risks. Isabelle states that such laws make things difficult for young women. Due to the absence of legal access to contraceptives, many unmarried girls are forced to stop schooling or undergo unsafe abortions.

Isabelle comments that the government needs to decriminalise abortion to guarantee that all women − not only those who suffer from medical conditions − have access to safe abortions. Most women and health workers are largely unaware of a provision in the law that does not consider an abortion a crime in the case of pregnancy resulting from rape. Transparency of this law is often difficult, as the Criminal Code criminalises people who provide information or treatment that terminates pregnancy. Overall, Amnesty's report urged the government to repeal and review discriminatory laws and regulations at national and regional levels to ensure that women and girls received their rights. They suggest that government was responsible for correcting discriminatory views (Jakarta Post, 2010a). Below, a number of Indonesian laws considered discriminatory are shown (Jakarta Post, 2010b).

Sri Danti of the Women's Empowerment and Child Protection Ministry mentions that a few of the central government's laws are biased at the expense of women, citing the 1974 Marriage Law. The Marriage Law still allows teenage girls to marry and allows men to practise polygamy. The law says the minimum age for women to marry is 16 and for men, 19. Other laws that contradict the convention include the Blasphemy and Pornography Laws (Yuniyanti Chuzaifah, Chairwoman of the National Commission on Violence against Women, in Jakarta Post, 2010b). The Blasphemy Law can cause a woman to lose her constitutional rights as a citizen if she is a member of a religious group considered deviant by the law. The pornography law is against Article 5 on elimination of gender stereotype and prejudice and Article 13C, which regulates the freedom of culture. The law limits women's cultural expression and is open to interpretation.

The case illustrates the close associations between discrimination, unfairness and regulation. Fairness management is a complex issue that requires an inherent understanding of laws and regulations in order to achieve the desirable outcome of fairness. Fairness management in Asia, considered an emerging concept, still warrants much research, and we propose the more research into the associations between unfairness and discrimination, and the perceptions towards these. It is especially interesting to understand the point at which one becomes the other.

Overall, the cases illustrate that cultural and social indicators greatly influence the way in which perceived unfairness are judged, which in turn influence on consumers' behaviours. Consumers know what is fair and have clear ideas about what is unfair. Thus, the role of fairness managers is to monitor these, and if possible, influence these to the best of their abilities, in order to induce fairness for all stakeholders. In other examples, we view the great effects of fairness management efforts. For example, as a country with rich and unique tourism resources, Vietnam must focus on fairness efforts in the development of the tourism industry. It is generally recognised that service fairness impacts on satisfaction, hence if service fairness is improved, satisfaction will be improved, leading to increased loyalty and a positive nation brand. Recent research has suggested that a customer's overall satisfaction is influenced by their assessment of not only service fairness (e.g. courtesy, responsiveness,) but also product features (e.g. size of hotel room) and price.

In Cambodia, when making purchases, customers consider not only prices, but also quality and the social relationship between the buyer and seller. That is, relationships are a social indicator that influences consumers' decision-making in purchasing products and services. This perspective requires marketers to look at fairness in each of the consumer buying decision-making process over the duration of the relationship, and focus on the factors that determine the fairness of both the relationship itself and the fairness of the different product attributes. In the case of the Philippines, perceived fairness may be achieved with increased focus on the social indicators, such as economic resources, social class and political development. Indonesia, an increasingly popular destination for low-cost labour, must focus on developing its own brand fairness in order to attract quality investors, who are fairer and more just. Only with increased morality, responsibility, reliability and stability can any of the four South East Asian countries achieve fairness and, subsequently, trustworthiness as an important destination for investment and tourism.

New research directions

Since the present chapter is at the very end of the book, the following section on new research directions is expanded, as there is much more research that needs to be done in the areas of fairness and fairness management. There are five new research directions of fairness management. Some are related to practice, while others are important for theoretical development.

Transaction fairness

Researchers suggest that more research is needed to examine the issue of perceived price fairness in ways that go beyond the present and the pioneering findings on dual entitlement (Xia et al., 2004). For example, Xia et al. (2004) suspect that in addition to comparisons to past prices, competitor prices and perceived costs, fairness perceptions are driven by prices paid by other consumers. Consumers are often sensitive to this reference point when price discrimination exists — for instance, at a movie (senior versus adult ticket prices), at a car dealership (as a result of negotiation) and in the air (full fare versus economy tickets). The key for managers is to explore when the price discrimination is acceptable to the consumer, and on what basis. In other words, managers must consider under what conditions consumers are sensitive to comparison(s) across consumers, products, firms and/or time, and how fairness is effected if multiple reference points are important to the consumer. The transaction space should be expanded to emphasise the importance of the frame of reference when consumers judge price fairness for a single transaction (Xia et al., 2004). The importance of understanding consumers' reference point(s) and how they judge price fairness should be self-evident so that marketers, who develop pricing strategies, are better equipped to manage fairness. Such knowledge is useful to fairness management, and managers should be particularly interested in consumer knowledge, purchase satisfaction, and public welfare.

Aggregate fairness

Researchers should continue to examine the case of aggregation in which pricing for repeated rental of a good is constrained. In this instance, fairness may limit the price that can be charged, and profits that can be made, over the product's lifetime. Xia et al. (2004) speculate that fairness constraints also exist for goods and services over the lifetime of the customer. That is, the firm's profit, earned over multiple transactions, with a single customer may be limited by fairness considerations. Research shows that fairness decline over repeat transactions for both goods and services (Xia et al., 2004). Contrary to existing research, long-time customers are more sensitive to price and therefore less profitable to firms (e.g. Reinartz & Kumar, 2000). When a customer's repeat purchases constitute the *set of transactions* (i.e. a line transaction), fairness constraints in the aggregate should have important implications for loyalty pricing. When a customer purchases *a bundle of products* from a firm (i.e. a set of transactions), fairness constraints in the aggregate should have important implications for bundled pricing. In both cases, sensitivity to the total amount of profit extracted from a single customer may drive aggregate fairness judgments. These, in turn, may have implications for relationship marketing, CRM and customer lifetime value. While loyalty and bundling illustrate aggregation's potential usefulness, other situations often involve aggregation across multiple dimensions. For example, a consumer may hold perceptions of price fairness at the industry level (e.g. that gasoline prices are unfair), but perceptions of unfairness for a specific product. Such complexity with aggregation is little researched. Surveys that measure consumer perceptions of fairness across firms and products at a point in time provide a snapshot of fairness, and may not tell what fairness is at the multidimensional levels. Future research could investigate the formation of fairness judgments at these aggregate levels and, in turn, their relationship to aggregate or cumulative indices of customer satisfaction (Xia et al., 2004).

Consumer knowledge

Although consumer research has historically investigated product knowledge and expertise (Alba & Hutchinson 1987), Wright (2002) has recently called for consumer research on 'marketplace met cognition' (i.e. everyday market-related thinking). In Xia et al.'s (2004) view, research on price fairness bridges the gap between product- and market-level knowledge, inasmuch as judgments about transaction fairness reflect consumer beliefs about marketplace dynamics. For example, research suggests that consumers have a schema for judging price fairness. Higher prices are attributed to profit (rather than quality or other costs), and price differences arising from some marketing strategies are judged as relatively unfair. Moreover, consumers appear to have a poor appreciation of the costs faced by firms. Many costs are ignored and some costs are viewed as unfair, leading to high and sticky profit estimates that contribute to perceptions of unfairness. Therefore, more research is needed to demonstrate appropriate scepticism regarding marketers' tactics and motivations, and to understand how consumer scepticism may derive from inappropriate beliefs about the competitive marketplace. Finally, additional research is needed to understand marketplace cognition, to learn the links between fairness and the potential for buyer—seller conflict, mistrust and consumer dissatisfaction.

Fairness management implementation

More research is needed to understand the systematic adoption of fairness management implementation processes. A consumer is able to differentiate between the different firms and choose to build a relationship or remain in a relationship with the fairest firm. To induce fairness, research must explore what the enterprises should do in order to build long-lasting relationships that are equitable and fair. While fairness in marketing is traditionally researched within the consumer behavioural realm, more research is needed to examine the role of fairness management in the broader strategic, operational and tactical divisions of an enterprise. There is need to integrate fairness management into the overall operations of the firm in order to enhance firms' performances. The questions that should be asked is how the firms implement fairness management, linking both internal and external organisational environments, and how managers control this process of fairness management implementation.

Management of emotions

Finally, more research is warranted to understand emotions and fairness perceptions in order to develop a more holistic view of fairness. Existing research has suggested that price fairness is a different concept from that of price unfairness. Consumers are clearer and more articulate about what they perceive as unfair than they are about fairness. Indeed, price fairness may not even be an issue until consumers perceive a price as unfair. In this case, affect is an important element, which may differentiate the varying levels of fairness and unfairness. Scholars suggest that there are different types of negative emotions associated with fairness perceptions. For example, a truly unfair perception is accompanied by strong negative emotions, such as anger and outrage, which may lead to severe actions toward the seller. Using different emotions as anchors and the cognition of inequality, many of the existing conceptualisations of unfairness can be systematically measured and categorised. In addition, researchers need to define these categories more specifically, and not use unfairness interchangeably with 'less fair'. Although consumers may believe that it is less fair that a department store sells a similar product at a higher price than a discount store, this 'less fair' price perception may not prevent them from shopping at the department store, whereas the term 'unfair' may do so. Thus there are important differences in the terms that should be taken into consideration. Conceptually distinguishing between less fair and unfair, and different types of emotions associated with inequality, helps us focus on the real unfair price situations, which are receiving more and more attention in marketing research.

Practice case study

The hotel industry

Machcud Sastroamidjojo is Marketing Manager for a large telecoms company in Indonesia. As part of his duties, he frequently goes on business trips to meet with clients and to attend conferences and meetings. One day, what was supposed to be a routine business trip to Jakarta, he requested his assistant to make a booking at a hotel in accordance to his preferences. Unfortunately, for whatever reasons, the hotel's CRM system was not working, and they were unable to retrieve Machcud's previous details, stating his history with the hotel and his personal preferences.

They, not knowing that he was a loyal customer, decided to set up a new account. When Machcud arrived at the hotel and was confronted with the higher price, which greatly exceeded his normal budget, he was furious. The hotel staff still did not recognise him, and told him that the increased price was due to the reason that it was during a holiday season, and rooms were limited, and demands were high. According to Machcud, the hotel even changed the price from the initial quote with another 20 per cent compared to the actual hotel bill. He felt that the price was not reasonable, and, despite expressing his anger, there was no solution. With the glitch in their CRM system, no one was able to recognise him as a loyal customer, nor were they able to identify the initial price. Despite complaints, Machcud did not feel satisfied and was still angry several days after. He was dissatisfied with both the way his complaints were handled, and the outcome, as he had to pay full fees. In addition, he felt unfairly treated, being dealt with as a new customer, and by the fact that the hotel simply raised their fees due to increased demand — he could not believe that was how they treated their new customers, and saw this as dishonest. Finally, as no one recognised him at his usual hotel, he felt frustrated. Consequently, to vent his anger, he proactively spread his feelings on various social media websites and among his friends and colleagues.

What does the case study mean for fairness management?

In the above case, there are several drivers of Machcud's unfairness perceptions. First, we note that transaction similarity drives perceptions of fairness. Machcud, being a frequent traveller, had a good sense about the hotel prices and comparative standards in general. While transactions may be different for multiple reasons — service characteristics, food quantity, purchase method, timing, etc. — for Machcud, these did not matter, because he was a regular customer and by comparing the new price with the previous transaction, he found a similar experience, with the only difference being the increased price. While he could understand the seasonal changes, he was still not satisfied with the price. In his mind, he expected the price to be the same as his comparison reference (his past experiences), thus developing unfairness perceptions. Rondan-Cataluña and Martin-Ruiz (2011) note that if a transaction remains relatively similar, but the price is higher, buyers will be likely to judge this as being unfair. This is well illustrated in the above case.

For the hotel, the objective is to make the customers' experiences as personalised as possible, responding to individual customers' preferences and needs. However, as the hotel's CRM failed in this instance, they did not manage to achieve this objective, adding further fuel to the fire when they were unable to recognise Machcud. Campbell (1999) notes that when the degree of similarity between interactions is low, the differences between may explain the higher price, resulting in a judgment that it is less unfair or as fair. Thus, if the hotel is able to personalise experiences to the customer, they may be able to charge a higher price, without a corresponding perception that the price is less fair. The example above shows how customer comparisons leading to increased unfairness perceptions are important.

These comparisons come in many forms, and the manager, working with fairness, must identify all aspects and risks associated with fairness judgments. Managers must pay attention to customers' attributions toward their cost−profit distribution, and whether there are associations of inequality. These must be dealt with immediately, since a perception that a price is unfair results not only from a perceived higher price, but also from consumers' understanding of why the higher price was set. Bolton et al. (2003) note that the seller's cost plays an important role in buyers assessing whether a price is acceptable and fair. Customers typically perceive a given price increase as fairer if it is a consequence of an increase in the seller's costs, but as unfair if it is linked to increased consumer demand. The latter is illustrated in this case, which is why Machcud felt unfairly treated. In many ways, the hotel would want transparency in its transactions to increase fairness, but at the same time, it would not want consumers to have a clear picture of the hotel's cost structures. This presents a dilemma, which needs to be carefully balanced. Machmud did not think the reason for increasing prices due to the festival season as acceptable. This led to his increased unfairness perceptions.

Helson (1948), referring to attributions theory, suggests that consumers may make attributions as to who is responsible for a particular perception of discrepancy. He notes that buyers may seek information to determine whether the seller is responsible for the situation of inequality because an explanation provides people with feelings of control over their environment and serves as an adaptive function. In the above case, we note that Machcud, in his opinion, reasonably thought that the hotel had to be responsible for his loss, due to their CRM failure. He felt greater anger when the hotel failed to accept his complaints and dealt with them unsatisfactorily. Thus he was not happy with either the hotel's procedures for complaints or the outcome, in that way affecting both procedural and distributive justice theories. In this case, the consequences were to the great detriment of the hotel, which, we suggest needs to implement fairness management as part of its CRM system.

Finally, while seasonal price adjustments are common in the hotel sector, and especially during the great festivals in Jakarta, Machcud did not accept this. He identified that as a loyal customer, he should not be affected by such seasonal price changes. Such beliefs, whether accurate to social norms or not, depend entirely on an individual's experiences, and can thus be much harder for the hotel to identify. It is therefore difficult to overcome such preconceptions, as these depend on the customers' experiences and their beliefs. As noted by Maxwell (1999), fairness may be judged at an aggregate level across an interaction space that consists of multiple dimensions. Consumers may draw on their general knowledge about the marketplace to judge whether an exchange is fair. Consumers may also rely on their own beliefs about the exchange norms to refine their price fairness judgments. This is one of the most challenging aspects of fairness management, and more research is needed to understand how the influence of such social norms and general beliefs may affect unfairness perceptions, in order to develop a framework for fairer marketing approaches.

What can managers do to overcome unfairness?

Customers' perceptions of fairness influence perceived value and customer satisfaction, and produce different emotions and behavioural responses. Specifically, the dissatisfied customer often takes different actions in response as follows:

- *Exit*: the customer changes supplier or stops buying the service (temporarily or permanently).
- *Voice*: the client complains to the provider and/or spreads negative word-of-mouth.
- *Loyalty*: the customer continues the relationship because of a lack of alternative suppliers or high switching costs.

It is vital to note the importance of both macro- and micro-environmental influences, such as economies and competition among suppliers in the development of the equity judgments and in the choice of consumers' behavioural responses. For instance, all things being equal, we may posit that in a monopolistic market, the consumers may have no other alternatives, and fewer comparison points, thus leading to weaker perceptions of unfairness.

In the following section, we will focus on the managerial implications and company applications, using the above case as an illustrative example. As our purpose is to reduce the risk of unfairness perceptions, we will analyse the critical elements and describe some useful methods.

Hotels often endeavour to increase occupation rates by selling rooms to different kinds of customers and segments. Most often, certain customers are preferred over others, perhaps because one group is more profitable than the other, or because the latter groups may not fit well with the overall positioning of the hotel or brand. However, unfairness may be displayed by the non-preferential group, as they may be seen as less important, and thus neglected. To manage the 'customer mix' correctly (Martin & Pranter, 1989), it is therefore important that these non-targeted groups are also managed, to some extent, so that they will avoid spreading negative word-of-mouth or other damaging misbehaviour.

Furthermore, other problems may stem from the practice of overbooking. In the hospitality industry, overbooking is the practice of intentionally selling more reservations for a date than the actual room availability of the hotel. Hotels use overbooking to offset the effects of clients' cancellations and no shows. Overbooking is based on forecasts. However, in the event that the forecasts turn out to be inaccurate or the firm overstretches the booking limit, the hotel then has to deal with excess clients. The displacement decision may be based on time of arrival, frequency of use, perceived importance or on a voluntary basis. In these cases it is important to set up appropriate service recovery strategies by the hotel (McColl-Kennedy & Sparks, 2003). In effect, problems may emerge when demand exceeds the optimal capacity level, especially in hospitality services. So it is important to set and to respect optimal capacity limits.

Hotel companies, by offering multiple prices for essentially the same service, can increase revenue by extracting consumer surplus. However, as customers are used to comparing their prices with those paid by other clients as well as with the rates they themselves had paid in the past, it is necessary that the reasons for the varying price levels are transparent. In fact, perceptions of price unfairness can be mitigated by a decrease in the similarity of the transactions, due to rate fences. These are the rules that hotels use to segment customers and justify why different people pay different prices. Correctly designed rate fences let hotel guests self-segment on the basis of their willingness to pay and can help companies to effectively target lower prices to those clients who are disposed to accept certain restrictions on their purchase and consumption experiences (Hanks et al., 1992; Kimes & Wirtz, 2003b). Therefore, fences and penalties (Fram and McCarthy, 1999) must be established with great care. In other words, to overcome perceived price discrimination, demand may be divided into different price buckets and customer segments according to price sensitivity. Finally, it is also important to consider consumer psychology in pricing decisions (Shoemaker, 2005) in order to anticipate negative reactions of customers to price differences. Studies have shown that offering customers preventive information on hotels' pricing practices can substantially enhance their perceptions of fairness (Choi & Mattila, 2008).

References

Alba, J. W., & Hutchinson, J. W. (1987). Dimensions of consumer expertise. *Journal of Consumer Research*, *13*, 411–454.

Alexander, S., & Ruderman, M. (1987). The role of procedural and distributive justice in organizational behavior. *Social Justice Research*, *1*, 177–198.

Ballester, E. D., & Aleman, J. L. M. (2001). Brand trust in the context of consumer loyalty. *European Journal of Marketing*, *35*(11/12), 1238–1258.

Blackwell, S. A., Szeinbach, S. L., Barnes, J. H., Garner, D. W., & Bush, V. (1999). The antecedents of customer loyalty: An empirical investigation of the role of personal and situational aspects on repurchase decision. *Journal of Service Research*, *1*(4), 362–375.

Bolton, L. E., Warlop, L., & Alba, J. W. (2003). Consumer perceptions of price (un)fairness. *Journal of Consumer Research*, *29*(March), 474–491.

Campbell, M. C. (1999). Perceptions of price unfairness: Antecedents and consequences. *Journal of Marketing Research*, *XXXVI*(May), 187–199.

Campbell, M. C. (2007). Says who?! How the source of price information and affect influence perceived price (un)fairness. *Journal of Marketing Research*, *XLIV*(May), 261–271.

Carr, C. L. (2007). The FAIRSERV model: Consumer reactions to services based on a multidimensional evaluation of service fairness. *Decision Sciences*, *38*, 107–130.

Choi, S., & Mattila, A. S. (2008). Perceived controllability and service expectations: Influences on customer reactions following service failure. *Journal of Business Research*, *61*(1), 42–54.

Delgado-Ballester, E., & Munuera-Aleman, J. L. (2001). Brand trust in the context of consumer loyalty. *European Journal of Marketing*, *35*(11/12), 1238–1258.

Frey, B. S., & Pommerehne, W. W. (1993). On the fairness of pricing — an empirical survey among the general population. *Journal of Economic Behavior and Organization*, *20*(3), 295–307.

Helson, H. (1948). Adaptation-level as a basis for quantitative theory of frames for reference. *Psychological Review*, *55*, 297–313.

Huppertz, J. W., Arenson, S. J., & Evans, R. H. (1978). An application of equity theory to buyer-seller exchange situations. *Journal of Marketing Research*, *XV*(May), 250–260.

Jakarta Post (2010a). Amnesty: RI women continue to face unfair laws, prejudice. *The Jakarta Post*5 November, <http://www.thejakartapost.com/news/2010/11/05/amnesty-ri-women-continue-face-unfair-laws-prejudice.html>.

Jakarta Post (2010b). Progress, challenges in elimination of unfairness. *The Jakarta Post*4 May, <http://www.thejakartapost.com/news/2010/05/04/progress-challenges-elimina-tion-unfairness.html>.

Johnson, S., Holladay, C., & Quinones, M. (2009). Organizational citizenship behavior in performance evaluations: Distributive justice or injustice? *Journal of Business and Psychology*, *24*(4), 409–418.

Kahneman, D., & Knetsch, J. L. (1986). Fairness as a constraint on profit seeking entitle-ments in the market. *The American Economic Review*, *76*(September), 728–741.

Kate, D. T. (2004). Film star Minnie Driver sows fairness for garment workers. *The Cambodia Daily*9 February, <http://www.cambodiadaily.com/archives/film-star-minnie-driver-sows-fairness-for-garment-workers-38119>.

Lee-Wingate, S. N., & Stern, B. B. (2007). Perceived fairness: Conceptual framework and scale development. *Advances in Consumer Behavior*, *34*, 400–402.

Martin, C. L., & Pranter, C. A. (1989). Compatibility management: Customer-to-Customer relationships in service environments. *Journal of Services Marketing*, *3*(3), 5–15.

Maxwell, S. (1999). The social norms of discrete consumer exchange: Classification and quantification. *American Journal of Economics and Sociology*, *58*(4), 999–1018.

McColl-Kennedy, J. R., & Sparks, B. A. (2003). Application of fairness theory to service failures and service recovery. *Journal of Service Research*, *5*(3), 251–266.

Moorman, C., Zaltman, G., & Deshpande, R. (1992). Relationships between providers and users of market research: The dynamics of trust within and between organisations. *Journal of Marketing Research*, *29*(3), 314–328.

Morgan, R. M., & Hunt, S. D. (1994). The commitment-trust theory of relationship market-ing. *Journal of Marketing*, *58*(3), 20–38.

Namkung, Y., & Jang, S. C. (2010). Effects of perceived service fairness on emotions, and behavioral intentions in restaurants. *European Journal of Marketing*, *44*(9/10), 1233–1259.

Nguyen, B., & Klaus, P. (2013). Retail fairness: Exploring consumer perceptions of fairness towards retailers' marketing tactics. *Journal of Retailing and Consumer Services*, *20*(3), 311–324.

Nguyen, B., & Mutum, D. S. (2012). A review of customer relationship management: Successes, advances, pitfalls and futures. *Business Process Management Journal*, *18*(3), 400–419.

Ocampo, S. C. (2013). Other victims outraged by Pryce Plans unfairness. *The Philippine Star*, 27 April, <http://www.philstar.com/opinion/2013/04/27/935449/other-victims-outraged-pryce-plans-unfairness>.

Ordóñez, L. D., Connolly, T., & Coughlan, R. (2000). Multiple reference points in satisfac-tion and fairness assessment. *Journal of Behavioral Decision Making*, *13*(3), 329–344.

Payne, A. (2001). *Customer relationship management*. Keynote address to the inaugural meeting of the Customer Management Foundation, London.

Reinartz, W., & Kumar, V. (2000). On the profitability of long-life customers in a noncon-tractual setting: An empirical investigation and implications for marketing. *Journal of Marketing*, *64*, 17–35.

Rondan-Cataluña, F. J., & Martin-Ruiz, D. (2011). Moderating effects in consumers' perceptions of price unfairness. *Journal of Consumer Behaviour*, *10*, 245–254.

Srivastava, R. K., Shervani, T., & Fahey, L. (1998). Market-based assets and shareholder value: A framework for analysis. *Journal of Marketing*, *62*(January), 2–18.

Weiner, B. (1985). An attributional theory of achievement motivation and emotion. *Psychological Review*, *92*(4), 548–573.

Win, T. L. (2012) *Vietnam Land Law revision should improve fairness transparency – analysis.* <http://www.so.undp.org/content/dam/vietnam/docs/UNDP-in-the-News/31294_Vietnam_Land_Law_revision_should_improve_fairness.pdf>.

Wright, P. (2002). Marketplace metacognition and social intelligence. *Journal of Consumer Research*, *28*(March), 677–682.

Xia, L., Monroe, K. B., & Cox, J. L. (2004). The price is unfair! A conceptual framework of price fairness perceptions. *Journal of Marketing*, *68*(4), 1–15.

Part Four

Conclusion

Conclusion to ethical and social marketing in Asia: incorporating fairness management?

Bang Nguyen and Chris Rowley

Introduction

The growing interest in ethical and social marketing and fairness management approaches by organisations among academics and practitioners alike has been demonstrated in our book. We covered 14 diverse economies in three regions: North East (China, Taiwan, Japan and South Korea), South East (in two blocks: Singapore, Malaysia and Thailand; and Vietnam, Cambodia, the Philippines and Indonesia) and South (India, Pakistan and Bangladesh) Asia.

The sheer diversity of Asia provides a difficult environment to the development and management of ethical and social marketing and fairness management. Differing cultures, economic development stages, resources, politics and consumption behaviours requires variable emphasis in different markets. Nevertheless, ethical and social marketing and fairness management have been shown to be particularly well received by some Asian firms and consumers due to emphasis on the greater societal good and Confucianism, often promoted by countries. Our book addressed the following areas.

1. *Ethical marketing*: Readers will have gained insights into ethical marketing issues. Our book enables readers to compare, contrast and comprehend how firms organise and manage ethics variably across Asia. Furthermore, our book presented important aspects of decision-making processes, influencing consumer perceptions towards ethical marketing.
2. *Social marketing*: Readers were exposed to differing perspectives of social marketing and its effects on consumption behaviour. We presented a wide-range of cases across diverse sectors. Readers were exposed to differing management approaches, which, once applied to their business, might well increase their chances for successful implementation of social marketing.
3. *Fairness*: Our book explored fairness management from extant consumer behavioural and psychological theories and research. This enabled readers to understand the role of fairness and its subsequent application in managing their marketing approaches.

The rest of this chapter considers the managerial implications of ethical and social marketing and fairness management in Asia. This provides some guidelines for 'best practice', despite the limitations to such approaches (Rowley & Wei, 2011). As illustrated throughout our book, all the countries face different, complex issues, which require diverse approaches to ethics, social and fairness. We explore these in detail next.

Managerial implications in Asia

Our book treated the nature of ethical and social marketing and fairness management in the Asian context comprehensively. By drawing from varying perspectives, it explored research and practices in very different sectors and organisations. We shall now briefly go through each of the chapters in terms of key implications for management and practice.

In the first part of the book, ethical marketing guidelines were recommended across Asia. Chapter 2 gave suggestions about the application of ethical marketing in China, Taiwan, Japan and South Korea. These were as follows. Firstly, marketers should learn how to integrate ethics into the planning and strategy formulation processes. Ethics should be coordinated throughout the whole marketing process, from product development (e.g. avoid potentially dangerous, malfunctioning and environmentally harmful products, use quality assurance), price setting schemes (e.g. do not engage in price fixing, predatory price, price gouging), developing advertising and promotion strategies (marketing communications about products should not be intentionally deceptive and misleading) to choosing places to launch products (e.g. protection of consumers' personal information online). Secondly, understanding consumer culture and their perceptions of marketing ethics motivates marketing managers to establish codes of ethics relied on in consumer evaluations. Marketing strategies should be aligned with consumer culture values and variations in consumers' ethical evaluations of marketing practices for different marketing segments (e.g. children, elders, women). Thirdly, the increasing diversity of the international marketplace has significant and complex implications for marketing practices. In the past, multinational corporations (MNCs) experienced ethical dilemmas with their marketing strategies in other countries. For example, the French retailer Carrefour entered China in 1995 and in 2011 was accused by China's National Development and Reform Commission of overcharging customers in 11 stores (Enderle & Niu, 2012). Specifically, they used normal prices as sales prices, misleading customers with price figures. As a result, the stores were fined up to US$79,365, the highest ever fine of its sort imposed in China. Thus, how local communities of the global marketplace evaluated the marketing practices of MNCs has become an important subject for marketers.

Chapter 3 considered ethical marketing's managerial implications in Singapore, Malaysia and Thailand. Firstly, for tourism marketers and policymakers a useful finding was the adaption of ethical marketing towards country-branding. The identification of ethical concerns and the broad and holistic view of ethics allow organisations to detect public opinion on important elements within the country's state of affairs. This enabled marketers to develop systems and adjust campaigns based on both the characteristics of the population and their corresponding views towards that of the country-branding elements. This indicates that the best way to portray Singapore, Malaysia and Thailand is through physical, human capital, export, culture and heritage, politics, social and ethical aspects. These elements were important to foster positive emotions among a country's citizens and were considered key tools to build competitive advantage. They had important implications for tourism marketers and policymakers, by highlighting the importance of branding with an ethical perspective towards a country's citizens and investors, revealing elements relevant for country-branding and competitive advantage.

The key was to recognise the uncertainties related to ethical marketing from a branding perspective and to identify the factors associated with the perceptual differences among the countries that could help to manage these uncertainties. The chapter equips managers with a better understanding of ethical issues so that they can deploy a more moral-based approach to marketing ethics. This will minimise costly mistakes and help managers to manage their resources better regarding fair use of their resources.

Specifically, identifying cross-cultural differences is key to understanding marketing strategy that uses customer segmentation and favouritism. The feelings associated with status, face and each of the country elements allows managers to develop a better grouping of their stakeholders to identify the group which needs more attention and to take action in order to keep their customers loyal. This identification and awareness of the cultural differences will assist marketers to develop more appropriate approaches for targeting customers who are sensitive to perceptions concerning face, status and other country-brand elements. A company operating in these countries with this information will be able to take action and improve their reputation and goodwill (Xia, Monroe, & Cox, 2004) regarding ethical issues.

Chapter 4 presented guidelines for ethical marketing practices in India, Pakistan and Bangladesh. A holistic marketing framework (Kotler, Keller, Koshy, & Jha, 2013) of four pillars of internal, integrated, relationship and performance marketing was applied. This found the following.

1. *Internal*: Major ethical issues involving employees are their competency, attitude, awareness levels of company policy and motivation to follow it and certain degree of identification with the organisation. Other critical ethical issues were: fair and inclusive recruitment, treatment of employees, gender equity, wages or just meeting legal requirements, dealing with whistle blowers, contract employees and restructuring and involuntary retirement, etc.
2. *Integrated*: This dealt with both integration within (among brand management, market research, sales, post-sales-service) and without (among marketing, finance, production, systems, etc.), but still within an organisation. Major ethical issues were: promises made but not fulfilled due to lack of coordination, power struggles, personal reasons, etc. Poor response to customer grievances and complaints are due to 'turf' issues or red tape, or simply poor processes and lack of a culture of ownership. Blatant unethical practices include making false promises, unsubstantiated claims, fine print in warranties, short-changing customers, and bribing through associates or partners while meeting legal requirements.
3. *Relationship*: This is mainly about the long term, involving mutuality and trust. As many companies survive on a short-term basis in a highly competitive, uncertain environment − aided by poor governance and unorganised and somewhat less demanding customers − this aspect of marketing is the greatest casualty in this region. Some of the most unethical practices on targeting and positioning fall in this domain. These are: political parties targeting voters based on religion, caste, sect, etc., with divisive and consolidation

agendas; communal overtones in appeals to voters; neglect of the poor and vulnerable by health and education providers through premium pricing; and targeting children when selling junk food and beverages.
4. *Performance*: This consists of three major aspects of performance with regard to: (a) customers (including intermediaries and the regulators) in terms of satisfaction and delight; (b) companies in terms of sales, profit, growth, brand equity and customer acquisition and retention; and (c) society and environment in terms of equity, justice and sustainability.

Chapter 5 offered ethical marketing recommendations in Vietnam, Cambodia, the Philippines and Indonesia. The international community supported Vietnam's efforts to tackle corruption. For example, Australia has developed a three-year training programme targeting 275 members of the Vietnamese Communist Party – the most powerful political institution – with training in national integrity systems and factors contributing to corruption. The programme provides high-level policy training and operational training to tackle corruption. Topics included in the training encompass corruption diagnosis and monitoring, financial accountability, and legislative and institutional frameworks to help prevent and deal with corruption and investigation methods (Australian Department of Foreign Trade and Affairs, 2014). To make ethical decisions, Velasquez (2006) put forward a series of questions that sought to articulate the ethical dimension of a decision or action. If it failed at any point, it should alert us to possible ethical challenges and we should revisit the decision or action. These were as follows.

1. What benefit and harm will each course of action produce and which alternative will lead to the best overall consequences?
2. What are the rights of those involved and does the proposal involve risk or harm to persons, animals or property?
3. Is the proposal consistent with the law?
4. Is the action consistent with professional codes of ethics?
5. Which course of action treats everyone the same, except where there is a morally justifiable reason not to and does not show favouritism or discrimination?
6. Which course of action is and will be seen as consistent with virtues or characteristics such as integrity, honesty, etc.?
7. Am I prepared to have my decision and the reasons for it made public?

In Cambodia, behind the doors of Khmer temples lies belief in superstitions, with rituals, spirits, ghosts, gods and sorcerers, which, it can be argued, injects immeasurable stress and fear into the lives of most Cambodians. In a country where corruption is widespread and 40 per cent of the population live below the poverty line, it is vital that Cambodia's children, its future leaders, learn how to think for themselves, how to reason, and how to be ethical and moral citizens. For marketers, early education in ethics, fairness and morality may foster greater awareness and improved ethical marketing skills. Ethical decision-making in Cambodia may involve developing professional practice standards that hold obligations and other standards of moral conduct, determined by the customary practice of the professional community. Individuals are charged with various responsibilities or duties – for example, avoiding harm, honouring warranties, avoiding conflicts of interest and obeying legal requirements. It is also highlighted that such individuals must use professional criteria for determining appropriate actions. A good start would be to develop various professional bodies and marketing associations with codes of ethics.

In the Philippines, marketers were on the right track towards marketing ethics and its influences were fruitful for their international reputation as a place to conduct business and for foreign investors, tourists and other stakeholders. Several key duties can be identified that would apply to all marketing professionals.

1. To provide expertise and knowledge within the limits of the marketing function.
2. Not to knowingly advance information about a product or service that is untrue.
3. Not to use their expertise to knowingly manipulate consumers into purchasing a product or service.
4. Not to use their expertise to target specific groups who are not in a position to make a purchasing decision.

In Indonesia, codes of ethics and standards for behaviour were highlighted as instruments for enforcing discipline in state institutions. For marketers this is not an exemption either. Several guidelines can be gathered to overcome corruption.

1. The implementation of a code of ethics among civil servants would help enhance the integrity of the individual members and assist in the safeguarding of their institutions' integrity.
2. When state personnel work according to ethics, potential for corruption can be minimised.
3. Collaboration between different organisations and all the components of the nation is necessary to eradicate corruption and unethical behaviour.
4. Sustainable results will only be achieved if corruption eradication efforts are improved through a better institutionalised framework − that is, only if a government bureaucracy is capable of shutting down opportunities for corruption and is immune to corrupt practices.
5. Corrupt officials will attempt to circumvent the system by moving funds into their private accounts; thus a review of the state financial management system is necessary to close loopholes and tighter supervision by superiors is also important.
6. If subordinates are engaging in glamorous lifestyles and suddenly becoming rich, their superiors should accord them more attention.

The second part of our book examined differing perspectives of social marketing in Asia. Chapter 6 provided key suggestions on the implementation of social marketing in China, Taiwan, Japan and South Korea. This highlighted critical areas, including message framing, source credibility, and media and integration issues. Firstly, using the wrong message in health and social marketing campaigns can have potentially serious consequences: it can turn the audience off the advocated behaviour. Messages can be either loss- or gain-framed. Gain-framed messages focus on the benefits resulting from adopting a specific behaviour, or alternatively ceasing an undesired behaviour. Conversely, a loss-framed message emphasises the potential negative consequences of not ceasing or not engaging in a desired behaviour. Based on Regulatory-Focus Theory (Higgins, 1998), individuals holding collectivist messages have been found to be more responsive to loss-framed messages, while individuals holding individualistic vales are more likely to respond to gain-framed messages

(Uskul, Sherman, & Fitzgibbon, 2009). Consequently, based on the previous discussion, messages are most likely to be effective when they use loss-framed messages.

Secondly, source credibility is an important aspect of social marketing campaigns as they often have to convey relatively complex messages in simple arguments. However, source credibility can vary depending on the cultural and social/historical contexts in which a message is transmitted. Identifying source credibility and messaging strategy issues requires extensive testing. Careful testing may be especially important in contexts where social marketers have experience of adopting a campaign to ethnic minorities in one country – and are trying to transfer these campaigns to the home country.

Third, in terms of media choice, campaigns relied heavily on non-conventional media. Some of the non-conventional media used was driven by availability and access issues, but also cost issues. Consequently, many social marketing campaigns faced the need to be significantly more innovative and explore more imaginative ways of bringing their message across than American social marketing campaigns.

Chapter 7 demonstrated how social marketing was being implemented in practice Singapore, Malaysia and Thailand. Drawing from Andreasen (2006), the chapter explored six criteria that act as a check – each criteria redirects the focus back to the goals of both the programme sponsor and the consumers that the intervention seeks to influence – and a behavioural objective reminds social marketers that their goal is to change behaviour, not just educate or inform. Additionally, audience segmentation requires clear thoughts about who the efforts are aimed towards, while formative research helps ensure an understanding of the consumer and orientation of the social marketing intervention towards the target market. Next, creating an exchange required consideration of what has to be given up by the target audience in order for them to undertake the desired behaviour while the marketing mix pushes social marketers to present holistic solutions that are attractive and valuable, assisting in inducing both trial and repeat behaviour. Finally, consideration of the competition provided social marketers with the awareness that they must consider the competing pressures faced by consumers (many of which are far more appealing than the behaviour that social marketers are attempting to change) when planning to understand how the offering they create will reduce some of those pressures in favour of the behaviour they are trying to influence (Carins & Rundle-Thiele, 2013).

Chapter 8 proposed the implementation of social marketing using the four Ps of marketing (product, price, place and promotion) as a social marketing framework. In terms of product it recommended focusing on high quality and good packaging. Branding was also a critical element. With price, it noted that products distributed free were often perceived by consumers as low in quality. Thus, pricing affordable prices resulted in a higher perceived quality than giving them away for free. With place, it highlighted the importance of *kiranas* (or 'dry grocers'), as these were the local shops where most household shopping was done. The intimate knowledge of *kirana* shopkeepers and friendly social relationships was considered highly important. Finally, with promotion it recommended that about 10 per cent should go to promotions in retail outlets and about 5 per cent go directly to promoting use. The use of mass media and print was highlighted.

Chapter 9 provided an overview of social marketing practice and recommendations in Vietnam, Cambodia, the Philippines and Indonesia. It noted there were a number of key issues that were unique and created challenges for social marketers categorised as follows.

1. sustainable development and the unintended consequences of increasing material well-being on sustainability;
2. poverty and issues associated with alleviating poverty such as the divide between rich and poor and rapid urbanisation of agrarian populations;
3. population health including economic, social, emotional and environmental well-being;
4. access to water and sanitation; and
5. side effects of modernisation and development such as road safety, waste disposal, and water and airborne pollution.

Each country had their own unique challenges when it came to societal change, ranging from educating people to behave in ways that are not traditional to creating public policy frameworks that were inclusive of a myriad of customs and cultures.

It was suggested that social marketing and social change campaigns often focus too heavily on the downstream individuals who are carrying out 'bad' behaviours (Wallack, 1990), rather than influencing government and policymakers to help bring about change. Increasingly, social marketing strategies were going upstream and social marketing was used much more strategically to inform policy formulation and strategy development (Andreasen, 2006). In the case of upstream social marketing, the focus was not so much on the individual or community, but rather on using strong target 'market' insight to inform and develop effective policy and strategy. Part of this was achieved through the effective use of media advocacy. The goal of media advocacy was to influence and lead changes in government policies (Wallack, 1990). This was particularly critical given that government were the gatekeepers of the three important fundamentals of behavioural compliance. Well-designed education and training programmes, combined with effective legislation and proper enforcement, were critical to behavioural compliance in social marketing campaigns, particularly when it comes to those aimed at reducing child or adolescent injury (Harvey, Towner, Peden, Soori, & Bartolomeos, 2009).

The third part of our book covered studies exploring fairness from extant consumer behavioural and psychological theories and research. Important aspects of cultural and social indicators that influence consumers' fairness perceptions were included. This enabled readers to understand the role of fairness and subsequent application towards managing their marketing approaches.

Chapter 10 considered fairness management in China, Taiwan, Japan and South Korea. Here group affiliations and ties were deep-rooted. Thus, when managing information that could potentially be used in fairness judgments, marketers must note the significance of 'in-group' versus 'out-group' comparisons in fairness judgments (Bolton, Keh, & Alba, 2010). Collectivist consumers experienced a greater loss of face when a friend paid a lower price than when a stranger paid a lower price. Similarly, collectivist Chinese consumers experienced a greater loss of face when paying a higher price to a vendor with which they have a long-term relationship than to a newly encountered vendor. As such, if dynamic pricing were to be implemented, marketers must ensure the equal level of prices for all members of each group, although differences between groups may exist.

Whether the equity or the equality rule is utilised to arrive at fairness perceptions depended on several moderators that shaped the situation. When the specifics of the situations were clear, the following conclusion could be made. Those with a task-based goal, in non-personal (or business), short-term, dissimilar and distant relationship circumstances, may prefer the equity rule. Conversely, those with a relational goal, in personal, long-term, similar and close relationship circumstances, may prefer the equality rule. If faced with ambiguous or insufficient information, or limited cognitive resources, it was more likely for equality to over-rule equity (Deutsch, 1985). In Japan and South Korea, the overriding societal goal often emphasised unity and harmony. This suggested that the equality rule may be preferred in general. Reconciling this general tendency and the equity rule often used in the business setting will be a challenge for fairness managers here.

It was impossible to prevent all negative outcomes, whether regarding service failure or product pricing. However, it was feasible to install fair procedures to resolve complaints. It was crucial that interactional fairness was emphasised in this process — to offer a thorough explanation in a polite, sensitive and caring manner of communication. These aspects of interactional fairness contributed to signalling the sincerity of the business in its commitment to be a member of the in-group in a long-term relationship. Although compensation was appreciated by consumers and was influential in determining fairness perceptions, offering compensation was going to backfire if it was given without thorough explanation and without politeness and sincerity. The point was to convey the sincerity of the business in order to encourage customers to feel appreciated and respected, and to assist customers in saving their 'face' especially in public or in front of other customers. Although *guanxi* is cultivated by the exchange of gifts and favours, and a common practice in China and Taiwan (Hwang, Golemon, Chen, Wang, & Hung, 2009), with similarities to *giri* and *con* in Japan and *inmaek* in South Korea (Rowley & Harry, 2011), global marketers must be ethically conscious with such practices in managing fairness. Careful negotiation of the social relationship landscape was necessary, supported by deep understanding of the local consumer psychology.

Chapter 11 presented issues in fairness management in Singapore, Malaysia and Thailand. Here understanding unfairness with regards to customer management may equip managers with a better understanding of such issues so that they can deploy a fairer approach to customer management. In turn, that will help to minimise costly mistakes and support managers to utilise their resources better, so that they can achieve a sustainable competitive advantage.

The consequences of not addressing fairness in efforts to build relationships with customers were seen as a precursor to mistrust (Heath & Heath, 2008). Both fairness and trust were essential building blocks for successful customer management (Payne, Storbacka, & Frow, 2009) and social marketing (Koschate-Fischer, Stefan, & Hoyer, 2012). If customers lose trust, there will be great problems in further developing applications to collect data in order to customise products and services. Regulations may just be one of the threats that could be imposed on unfair use of technological applications. On the one hand, an organisation would want to learn as much as possible about their customers as possible to fulfil their needs and desires, but at the same time this individual treatment could result in discrimination, inequity and unfairness (Nguyen & Simkin, 2013). This was the paradox in customer relationship management (CRM). For managers a warning follows, to emphasise the understanding of fairness and the consequences of how favouring certain customers may stir up a sense of unfairness. Perhaps, if unfair marketing approaches continue, we may very well experience the rise of marketing practitioners who are to be called before members of a Marketing Council. Once the marketing oath is taken, only then will they be able to call themselves marketers.

Chapter 12 provided managerial implications of fairness management in India, Pakistan and Bangladesh. In India, it was suggested that companies that practise conscious marketing embody the ideas of brand fairness and trust, and recognise that long-term survival links profit and prosperity with social justice and environmental stewardship. Eight points to consider were suggested.

1. Firms must identify a higher purpose than simply profit maximisation or shareholder returns; they must realise that it is not about creating and exploiting short term desires, but rather to address important needs of society and individuals.
2. Firms must exist and be managed for the benefit of all stakeholders.
3. Managers must join and align the interests of each stakeholder and develop long-term relationships.
4. Firms must not act opportunistically or engage in exploitation of any kind.
5. Society must be considered as the ultimate stakeholder.
6. Firms must put emphasis on environmental sustainability to improve their goodwill.
7. Firms must seeks to uplift rather than ignore (or exploit) the poorer sections of society.
8. Firms must intrinsically believe that doing the right things ultimately brings improved results.

In Pakistan, the question for managers to consider was to ask what should be done to avoid the potential for such unfairness effect, and to be perceived as a fairer and more trustworthy organisation by customers. Although this was difficult at many levels, there were issues for managers to (re)consider, including those at a personal level. The main focus should be given to minimising the misuse (or overuse) of marketing tools and making management decisions to maintain and enhance relationships for long-term success. Fairer marketing practices help managers in implementing better marketing schemes necessary in today's environment. Three fairness dimensions were developed:

1. awareness and problem diagnosis;
2. managing both targeted and non-targeted customers; and
3. emphasis on positive associations and goodwill.

In Bangladesh, it was the education and re-education of marketing practitioners, highlighting the need to incorporate fairness in order to improve the well-being of firms and society alike, that was emphasised. The chapter advocated a need to resolve these issues of unfair and unethical behaviour by emphasising honesty, impartiality, trustworthiness, uprightness and fairness. Among other things, it suggested that companies need to engage 'hearts and minds', as well as exhibit moral responsibility.

Chapter 13 covered guidelines in fairness management in Vietnam, Cambodia, the Philippines and Indonesia. In Vietnam, to overcome unfairness perceptions, emphasis should be on building ties with the government and on ensuring increased transparency, which subsequently leads to fairness. The important role of incorporating fairness management by the government, highlighting transparency and reducing inequity, was illustrated.

In Cambodia, attention should be given towards perceived exploitation and perceptions of (un)fairness. In this case, the management of fairness could be stirred by using traditional marketing channels, such as a celebrity and events. Ongoing efforts by the government were necessary to ensure fairness in factories, including in areas such as payment of wages, and the length and frequency of overtime. Continuous monitoring and an inspection system were needed for sustainable development. The monitoring process produced a safer working environment and more equitable working conditions, which in turn helped to improve the international credibility of Cambodian factories. The impact of fairness management was significant, as the government was now branding itself as a labour-friendly nation, and the country's expected entry into the World Trade Organization will keep orders and factories in the country.

In the Philippines, it was highlighted that attention should be paid to the devastating effect of negative word-of-mouth, especially due to violations of social norms. It was important to understand how unfairness may arise, when consumers feel exploited and taken advantage of. Firms must avoid being perceived as acting opportunistically — a recurrent theme, which stirs unfairness perceptions, leading to angry customers. If unfairness issues get out of control, firms may face increased control and regulation. It was, therefore, essential that fairness be managed systematically. Successful fairness management often simply involved the inclusion of consumers into the company to build relations, create dual value, develop transparency and develop solutions. These fair practices link well with the concept of CRM.

Indonesia illustrated the close association between discrimination, unfairness and regulation. Fairness management was a complex issue that required an inherent understanding of laws and regulations in order to achieve the desirable outcome of fairness. Table 14.1 summarises the managerial implications arising from our book.

Table 14.1 **Managerial implications**

Chapter	Managerial implications	Countries
2	— Marketers should learn how to integrate ethics into the whole marketing process from product development, setting price schemes, developing advertising and promotion strategies, and choosing places to launch products. — Understanding consumer culture and their perceptions of marketing ethics motivates marketing managers to establish codes of ethics. Marketing strategies should be aligned with consumer culture values and variations in consumers' ethical evaluations of marketing practices for different marketing segments (e.g. children, the elderly, women). — Marketers must understand how local communities evaluate multinational companies' marketing practices to avoid ethical dilemmas.	China, Taiwan, Japan, South Korea
3	— Tourism marketers and policymakers must develop region/country-based systems that are localised and adjust ethical marketing campaigns based on both characteristics of the population and their corresponding views to achieve the best outcomes. — The best way to brand Singapore, Malaysia and Thailand is through physical, human capital, export, culture and heritage, politics, social and ethical. These elements foster positive emotions and are considered key tools to build competitive advantage, focused on ethical considerations. — Identification of across cultural differences in the countries is key to understanding a successful marketing strategy, here concerning status, face and each of the country elements, allowing managers to take actions in order to keep their customers loyal.	Singapore, Malaysia, Thailand
4	— Major ethical marketing issues with regard to customers seem to be sporadic interest of a large number of professionally managed companies even paying lip-service to customer satisfaction, let alone exceeding their expectations. Managing satisfaction indices, in many cases, dominates over managing customer relationships.	India, Pakistan, Bangladesh

(Continued)

Table 14.1 (Continued)

5	— Major ethical marketing issues with regard to the company seem to be internal frauds, fudging of data, leaking company plans and in some cases major frauds. A significant unethical marketing practice impacting on companies which most often does not get noticed is taking a short-cut, short-term orientation and short-changing the company of its long-term potential while showing results and reaping rewards. — For marketers, early education in ethics, fairness and morality may foster greater awareness and improved ethical marketing skills. Ethical decision-making may involve developing professional practice standards that hold that obligations and other standards of moral conduct, determined by the customary practice of the professional community. — Several key duties can be identified that would apply to all marketing professionals: (1) a duty to provide expertise and knowledge within the limits of the marketing function; (2) not to knowingly advance information about a product or service that is untrue; (3) not to use their expertise to knowingly manipulate consumers into purchasing a product or service; and (4) not to use their expertise to target specific groups who are not in a position to make a purchasing decision.	Vietnam, Cambodia, the Philippines, Indonesia
6	— Marketers must identify cultural and other aspects of a social marketing campaign that may need to be adjusted when carrying out campaigns here. — There is a need for more social marketing campaigns to engage local audiences around issues specifically pertinent to countries. — The Framework for Cross-cultural Research in Social Marketing offers an explanatory basis on which to base future research, specifically dividing the external factors and internal factors which are likely to be affected when conducting social marketing campaigns across different countries.	China, Taiwan, Japan, South Korea
7	— Social marketing evaluation is vital for funding bodies and governments to determine whether interventions are successful, and calculations of return on investment are essential to demonstrate the case for continued support of programmes.	Singapore, Malaysia, Thailand

(Continued)

Table 14.1 (**Continued**)

	– Twelve competencies that a practising social marketer should have and presents social marketing using Andreasen's six social marketing benchmark criteria and offers a range of best practice examples of social marketing from Singapore, Thailand and the USA. These six criteria are: behaviour change, audience research, segmentation, exchange, marketing mix and competition. – How a programme is planned, tested and implemented provides a value offering that leads to behaviour change, and this is what differentiates good social marketing efforts from bad social marketing efforts.	
8	– Rather than focusing on selling with product-focused approaches and information-intensive campaigns focus on informing, marketers need to build long-term customer relationships and use a consumer-centred approach, where positive social change is the main objective rather than fiscal targets. The consumer should be an active participant and partner in the whole process of behaviour change. – In order to be effective, campaigns need to be more explicit. The importance of husbands and mothers-in-law in implementing family planning programmes are highlighted. – Media advertising can be effective in creating awareness and understanding of issues, but are limited in their ability to foster behaviour change.	India, Pakistan, Bangladesh
9	– Social marketers can assist governments and non-government organisations to initiate, establish, develop and maintain programmes that will have multi-level impact. – Understanding customer or market needs on their own are insufficient to address the large-scale social problems that exist. – Key issues that face the region when it comes to social marketing can be categorised as: sustainability, poverty, population health, access to water and sanitation and side effects of modernisation, e.g. road safety, waste disposal and airborne pollution.	Vietnam, Cambodia, the Philippines, Indonesia

(*Continued*)

Table 14.1 **(Continued)**

10	— Marketers must note the significance of in-group versus out-group comparisons in fairness judgments. — Management must confirm that organisational and consumer procedures are implemented: (a) consistently, (b) without self-interest, (c) on the basis of accurate information, (d) with opportunities to correct the decision, (e) with the interests of all concerned parties represented and (f) following moral and ethical standards. — Management should be considerate when offering compensation to recover for service failure. Although compensation is appreciated by consumers and is influential in determining fairness perceptions, offering compensation is going to backfire if it is done without thorough explanation and without politeness and sincerity. — Global marketers must be ethically conscious with the *guanxi* practices in managing fairness. Careful treading of the social relationship landscape is necessary, supported by deep understanding of the local consumer psychology.	China, Taiwan, Japan, South Korea
11	— Management must prepare the communications infrastructure and procedures for appropriate data handling in the organisation to create awareness about the consequences of unfairness. — As part of an ongoing effort for fairness, training must be implemented. Depending on the nature of the organisation, a number of training and coaching sessions can be combined with customer service training and fairness. — Marketers must aim to incorporate (and to some extent, partner with) the customers in order to improve the learning relationship, understand the customers' needs better and create 'win-win' situations.	Singapore, Malaysia, Thailand
12	— Management must recognise its role in crafting and articulating a higher purpose for the firm. Fairness management embraces total transparency, and seeks to connect and integrate with customers around long-term mutual value creation.	India, Pakistan, Bangladesh

(*Continued*)

Table 14.1 **(Continued)**

13	– Managers should avoid the potential for an unfairness effect, and aim to be perceived as a fairer and more trustworthy organisation. There are issues for managers to (re)consider, including those at a personal level. The main focus should be given to minimising the misuse (or overuse) of available marketing tools and make management decisions to maintain and enhance relationships for long-term success. – Whichever marketing schemes are being developed, it is imperative that consideration is given to the ways in which a customer develops perceptions of unfairness and negative inferences. – Managers must consider influences and moderators of customers' unfairness perceptions, namely: (1) transaction similarity and choice of comparison party; (2) price comparison; (3) distribution of cost and profit; (4) attributions of responsibility; and (5) buyer–seller relationship stage (trust). – It is important that the non-targeted groups are also managed, to some extent, so that they will avoid spreading negative word-of-mouth or exhibiting other damaging misbehaviour. – Managers must set up appropriate service recovery strategies in any fairness management scheme. In addition, fences and penalties must be established with great care. – Managers must also consider consumer psychology in order to anticipate negative reactions of customers to price differences.	Vietnam, Cambodia, the Philippines, Indonesia

Conclusion

Our book has covered ethical marketing and social marketing and fairness management across diverse economies in Asia. The wealth of insight and cases are useful and relevant for a range of students, academics and practitioners alike. Overall, the cases illustrate that cultural and social indicators greatly influence not only ethical and social marketing but also the way in which perceived fairness is judged, which in turn, influences consumer behaviours. Consumers know what is fair and have clear ideas about what is unfair. Thus, the role of fairness managers is to monitor these and, if possible, influence these to the best of their abilities, in order to induce fairness for all stakeholders.

Fairness management is a complex issue that requires an inherent understanding of laws and regulations in order to achieve fairness. Fairness management in Asia, considered an emerging concept, still warrants much research and we propose more research, such as into the associations between fairness and discrimination and the perceptions towards these. It is especially interesting to understand the point at which one becomes the other. Other issues requiring further research include, to name a few, copyright infringements, labour exploitation, environmental pollution, unethical business practices, fair trade, consumer welfare and government regulation to mitigate unethical issues.

References

Andreasen, A. R. (2006). *Social marketing in the 21st century*. Thousand Oaks, CA: Sage.

Australian Department of Foreign Trade and Affairs. (2014). http://aid.dfat.gov.au/countries/eastasia/vietnam/Pages/other-init3.aspx.

Bolton, L. E., Keh, H. T., & Alba, J. W. (2010). How do price fairness perceptions differ across culture? *Journal of Marketing Research, 47*(3), 564−576.

Carins, J., & Rundle-Thiele, S. R. (2013). Eating for the better: A social marketing review (2000−2012). *Public Health Nutrition 1−2*, (FirstView).

Deutsch, M. (1985). *Distributive justice: A social-psychological perspective*. New Haven, CT and London: Yale University Press.

Enderle, G., & Niu, Q. (2012). Discerning ethical challenges for marketing in China. *Asian Journal of Business Ethics, 1*, 143−162.

Harvey, A., Towner, E., Peden, M., Soori, H., & Bartolomeos, K. (2009). Injury prevention and the attainment of child and adolescent health. *Bulletin of the World Health Organization, 87*, 390−394.

Heath, M. T. P., & Heath, M. (2008). (Mis)trust in marketing: A reflection on consumers' attitudes and perceptions. *Journal of Marketing Management, 24*(9−10), 1025−1039.

Higgins, E. T. (1998). Promotion and prevention: Regulatory focus as a motivational principle. *Advances in Experimental Social Psychology, 30*, 1−46.

Hwang, D. B., Golemon, P. L., Chen, Y., Wang, T., & Hung, W. (2009). Guanxi and business ethics in confucian society today: An empirical case study in Taiwan. *Journal of Business Ethics, 89*, 235−250.

Koschate-Fischer, N., Stefan, I., & Hoyer, W. (2012). Willingness to pay for cause-related marketing: The impact of donation amount and moderating effects. *Journal of Marketing Research, 49*(6), 910−927.

Kotler, P., Keller, K. L., Koshy, A., & Jha, M. (2013). *Marketing management: A South Asian perspective* (14th ed.). New Delhi: Pearson Education.

Nguyen, B., & Simkin, L. (2013). The dark side of CRM: Advantaged and disadvantaged customers. *Journal of Consumer Marketing, 30*(1), 17−30.

Payne, A., Storbacka, K., & Frow, P. (2009). Co-creating brands: Diagnosing and designing the relationship experience. *Journal of Business Research, 62*(3), 379−389.

Rowley, C., & Harry, W. (2011). *Managing people globally: An Asian perspective*. Oxford: Chandos.

Rowley, C., & Wei, Q. (2011). Best practice. In C. Rowley, & K. Jackson (Eds.), *Human resource management: The key concepts* (pp. 6−10). London: Routledge.

Uskul, A. K., Sherman, D. K., & Fitzgibbon, J. (2009). The cultural congruency effect: Culture, regulatory focus, and the effectiveness of gain-vs. loss-framed health messages. *Journal of Experimental Social Psychology, 45*(3), 535–541.

Velasquez, M. (2006). *Business ethics: Concepts and cases* (5th ed.). Upper Saddle River, New Jersey: Prentice Hall.

Wallack, L. (1990). Media advocacy: Promoting health through mass communication. In K. Glanz, F. M. Lewis, & B. K. Rimer (Eds.), *Health behavior and education* (pp. 370–386). San Francisco, CA: Jossey-Bass.

Xia, L., Monroe, K. B., & Cox, J. L. (2004). The price is unfair! A conceptual framework of price fairness perceptions. *Journal of Marketing, 68*(4), 1–15.

Index

Printed in the United States
By Bookmasters